# Month-By-Month

# GARDENING IN NEW JERSEY

Cataloging in Publication Data is available.
ISBN: 1591861101

Published by Cool Springs Press, a Division of Thomas Nelson, Inc.,
P.O. Box 141000, Nashville, Tennessee 37214

First printing 2005

Printed in the United States of America
10 9 8 7 6 5 4 3 2 1

Managing Editor: Ramona D. Wilkes
Horticulture Editor: Ruth Rogers Clausen
Copyeditor: Sally Graham
Production Artist: S.E. Anderson
Illustrator: Bill Kersey, Kersey Graphics
Cover Designer: James Duncan, James Duncan Creative

On the Cover: Dogwood (*Cornus kousa* x *C. florida* 'Stellar Pink'), photo by Pegi Ballister-Howells

Cool Springs Press books may be purchased in bulk for educational, business, fundraising, or
sales promotional use. For information, please email **SpecialMarkets@ThomasNelson.com.**

Visit the Thomas Nelson website at **www.ThomasNelson.com** and the
Cool Springs Press website at **www.coolspringspress.net**

# Month-By-Month
# GARDENING IN NEW JERSEY

PEGI BALLISTER-HOWELLS

COOL SPRINGS PRESS
A Division of Thomas Nelson Publishers
*Since 1798*

## Dedication

To L-Dog, McFly, and The Party to Whom I Am Speaking. For all the
giggles and all the tears. With Love.

## Acknowledgements

It would not be possible to do a fraction of what needs to be done in life without the support of
my husband Tom Costantino. The writing of a book, wedged into the hectic pace of careers,
farm, and family would certainly be overwhelming if Tommy did not back me up on all fronts. He
brings home the pizza, makes pots of coffee (even though he doesn't drink it) and
gets the kids off to school so I can sleep after a late night of writing. My thanks and all
my love . . . forever and a day.

For a chance to pick their brains, I must acknowledge the generosity of several people. I called
Mel Moss of Livingston Park Nursery at all hours of the day and night about nursery stock
varieties and seed starting times. He was always pleasant and full of information. For the chapters
on vegetable and fruits, two farmers were always willing to help. John Rigolizzo and Neil Robson are outstanding farmers and even better friends. The wealth of knowledge they carry
around in their heads is staggering.

Writing a book is very personal; even a "When To" book such as this one. It is wonderful to
be able to work through the details with someone you can trust. It is just as important
to be able to laugh about the ups and downs as you go through the entire process. Ramona Wilkes
started as my editor and turned into a friend. My thanks and appreciation.

It is also important to recognize all those that till the earth. From the farmers that make
New Jersey "The Garden State" to the gardener with pots of tomatoes on the balcony, working
the soil brings together people of all backgrounds and ages. There is a commonality that
overcomes whatever differences may exist. It is a joy and a privilege to work with these people. If
my words can offer a bit of assistance or solve a problem, I am thrilled. More importantly, I am grateful to
work in a field where there is magic in every seed and a kindred spirit in every heart.

Finally, my thanks to Holly. Holly is my faithful companion who just happens to have four feet
and a wagging tail. It is absolutely amazing that she knows when to slip her head under
my hand, and head-off a moment of despair as I sit at my computer writing.
Then she always knows exactly the right thing to say.

# Contents

# Contents

# Introduction

## The Benefits of a Month-By-Month Gardening Schedule

There is *always* a way to play in the garden! Figuring out what to do when is the tricky part. That first warm day in spring, when the sun is shining, motivates you to leave your coat indoors and go dig in the dirt. Unfortunately, by that time, you will have missed much of the planting season.

Plants are triggered as much by the change in day length as they are by temperature. In February and March, it may still be winter on the calendar, but plants are gearing up for spring and so should you. The dormant season is a more peaceful time in the garden, but the more you can tend to early, the less likely you are to be overwhelmed in a rush of spring activity. For some projects, timing is critical.

## TIMING IS EVERYTHING

The planting of container-grown trees, shrubs, and perennials is a bonus for gardeners. They have a tremendous range of possible planting times since there is little to no root disturbance in the process of planting. It is best to allow about six weeks before the ground freezes. That leaves enough time for a bit of root growth before the worst of winter sets in. Other than that, you can plant container-grown material whenever the ground is not frozen. Transplanting, on the other hand, is very particular. The roots are extremely traumatized when you dig up established plants. You want to minimize the impact by doing it at the right time for that plant. That varies from plant to plant. September is ideal for peonies. April is preferred for chrysanthemums. So, for planting new container material, you have tremendous flexibility. Transplanting of established material has a specific window of opportunity. In both cases, you are planting something in a new spot, yet the timing is very different for the two scenarios.

There are certain times of the year when there are many things that need to be done. If you can eliminate those things that can be done earlier, during the slower time of the year, it can help tremendously with getting it all done with a minimum of stress. After all, gardening is supposed to be relaxing and creative. Gardens full of weeds or plants that don't survive add more stress than they take away. A bit of up-front planning to figure out what needs to be done when is enormously helpful.

## PLANNING

Over the winter is a great opportunity to plan what your spring garden projects will be. Make a list of everything you will need. It will probably break down into three categories.

*1* Building supplies

Any type of walkway, trellis, arbor, retaining wall, drainage system, raised bed, or fencing project will probably require a trip to your favorite building supply store.

Get that out of the way on a rainy or snowy day. That way, you will have everything ready to go when the weather chooses to be cooperative. You want to get the construction part of any major garden project out of the way as early in the season as possible. That will enable you to have the planting aspect of the pro-

# Introduction

ject implemented within the planting season of the plants you intend to use in the surrounding landscape. Keep in mind that many of these projects end up taking longer than you expect. It just happens that way. Adjust. Better to plan ahead than to end up planting in 100 degrees on July 4th weekend.

*2* Gardening tools and supplies

Hoses, sprinklers, fertilizer, lime, all sorts of hand tools, mulch, soil amendments, pots, seed starting supplies, plant markers, stakes, gardening gloves, insecticides, fungicides, weed killers, spray equipment, pruning saws, string, and tomato cages should all be purchased before the season actually starts. When the weather is perfect, you do not want to waste the first gorgeous day standing on line at the garden center with everybody else who didn't plan ahead.

It is a really good idea to have your lawn mower maintained and the blades sharpened over the winter. The people who do this for a living are swamped in the spring, and sometimes you have to wait weeks before you get your equipment back. By then you will be living in a jungle. Do the same with your rototiller if you have one. If you intend to rent a tiller, do your research ahead of time

as to where you will rent and what it will cost. Sometimes it is cheaper to rent during the week.

*3* Plant material

## WHERE TO BUY PLANTS

If you will be happy walking into your favorite nursery and picking out this and that when you are ready to plant, you can wait until then to make your purchases. If you have a lot of questions, visit the nursery during the week. A Saturday in April is not the best time to expect a dissertation on the comparative value of an arborvitae versus a juniper. Plant people love to talk about plants, so catch them when they have the flexibility to chat with you without keeping other customers waiting. They will appreciate your consideration, and you will have the opportunity to pick their brains for all the information you require.

If you are seeking specific varieties of shrubbery, expanding your collection of daylilies, or planning a blue garden to go against your white house, you will not want to rely upon only the retail selections. When you refine your desires to the very specific, you will have to do some research to locate what you want. Access to the Internet is an enormous help, but there are

other sources as well. Garden catalogs come in the mail. Some are general and have this and that. These are more like retail stores with a smattering of everything. Some of these same companies have "limited edition" versions of their catalogs where they do feature the more unusual. Both Spring Hill and Park's have done this from time to time. Other catalog companies have a range of items but only carry fabulous varieties.

"Fabulous" usually has a comparable price tag, but sometimes it is worth it to acquire a plant that puts a smile on your face every time you walk by. Wayside Gardens and White Flower Farm both fall into this category.

For collectors, there are catalog companies that specialize in just about anything. You can locate catalog companies that feature ground covers, daylilies, native plant material, wildflowers, peonies, rhododendrons, dwarf evergreens, roses, perennials, shade plants, and just about any other plant category you can imagine. There are also gardening associations that are plant specific as well. That can be a fun way to share and exchange plants. In the absence of a computer, you can often locate these companies by checking the advertisements in the back of a gardening magazine. Sometimes very small ads are placed by very small companies, like classified ads in the newspaper. These small companies sometimes are very specific and may specialize in only one type of plant. If you are interested in what they have, you may have struck gold.

If you know exactly what you want, you can sometimes work with your favorite nursery or garden center to help you get it. They may already know of a wholesale producer that has what you want. You may not be able to make the purchase, but your nursery professional can do it for you. Again, you want to visit on a day in winter when things are slow and the person you need to ask will enjoy the opportunity to help you. That is when they are placing their orders for spring material, so they will be in the best position to order what you need.

All of this plant searching needs to be done well in advance of when you are ready to plant. It is a wonderful activity to get you through the gray days of winter. More importantly, you will be ready for planting when the time is right.

## REDUCING THE WORK

There are other ways of scheduling your projects that spread out the work throughout the year and/or make the work easier by planning in advance. One great idea is to locate your compost pile wherever you intend to make a garden bed in the next year or two. The ground underneath the compost pile becomes rich in organic matter and full of fat, healthy earthworms. When you are ready to plant, spread the compost out evenly and turn the soil over.

Another way to reduce the work in preparing a new bed is to cover the bed with old carpeting in the fall. In most cases, the back is a neutral color, so you can turn the hot pink side down to reduce the impact. The earlier in the fall you can lay the carpet, the more certain you can be that you have effectively killed off all the weeds, even tough perennial weeds, by the time you are ready to turn the soil in the spring. If you hate the idea of old carpeting, you can use black plastic, but it will need to be pinned down. (Old carpeting is generally free and reuses something headed for the landfill. Black plastic is an additional expense and is one more thing to go to the landfill. It is also made from fossil fuel. Is this an ethics vs. aesthetics issue?? You decide!)

The use of lots of organic mulch has many benefits. It moderates fluctuations in soil temperatures, which is equally useful in the heat of summer and the bitter cold winter. It also saves work by reducing weeds and retaining soil moisture. As it decomposes, organic mulch adds organic matter to the soil. Earthworms (excellent garden helpers) pull the organic matter down in to the earth as food and then add the castings (a tidy name for worm poop) to improve the quality of the soil. The worm tunnels aerate the soil and improve drainage. A layer of mulch after the ground freezes in the fall goes a long way in preventing early spring weeds. Piles of mulch around the roses to protect the graft from freezing can be easily spread out throughout the bed in the spring. It is easy enough to plant a few annuals right through the mulch.

Does anyone bag grass clippings anymore? If you do, note my section on composting in the back of this book. You can use them in the compost pile. You can also spread out fresh grass clippings around annual flowers or in the vegetable garden. They are easily tilled into the soil the next time you till as a source of organic matter to improve the soil. Or stop bagging them altogether and let them lie on the grass. If properly mowed, the clippings should be short enough to drop between the remaining blades.

# Introduction

**Don't confuse thatch with grass clippings.** It is a common misconception. Thatch is tough stuff, not the wispy little tender clippings that your mower removes. Clippings decompose in a couple of days. Thatch is dried up old grass plants, more like straw than anything else. Leaving the clippings doesn't make more thatch, so don't worry about that. Maxing out on nitrogen fertilizer will certainly make thatch in a hurry. The faster new grass grows, the faster the old plants accumulate. Consider fertilizing twice in the fall and skipping the spring fertilizer entirely. You will have stronger, deeper roots. The grass will not grow as fast, so it will not need to be mowed as often and there will be less water demand in hot weather. Thatch accumulation will slow way down. Okay . . . there is a down side. You will have to settle for medium green. Without that spring shot of nitrogen you will never achieve deep emerald green. However, instead of mowing, you can spend that time planting flowers or tomatoes, or drinking iced tea in the hammock!

## A Month by Month Overview

The planting of bulbs is an **October** project. Bulbs are a great tool to fight off winter doldrums. The earliest spring bulbs can bloom as early as February, which is just when the weight of the gray days is getting very heavy. It is absolutely amazing that a single small crocus blooming through the snow can make your heart sing! It doesn't matter how many bulbs you plant in the fall. In the spring, you will wish you had planted more. Also make sure you get a few pansies in the garden, somewhere you can see them all winter. A few blooms through a layer of snow are a very welcome sight.

The third week in October is generally considered the time of supreme autumn color in New Jersey. That would be on the early side in the most northern part of the state and a tad later down below the Mason Dixon line. Harvest your pumpkins, pick your apples, and enjoy the beauty the fall season has to offer. Bring in your houseplants early in the month and pot up a few of your summer annuals to enjoy a bit of color indoors.

If you don't get all your bulbs planted in October, you can stretch it to **November.** Harvest your potatoes, Jerusalem artichokes, and horseradish before the end of the month and start up your compost pile. There is always a heavy rain about the third week that brings down the bulk of the leaves. Leaves make great compost. It never makes sense that people bag their leaves in the autumn (a LOT of work) and then buy bags of topsoil or humus in the spring. Then you have to haul it all home (again, a lot of work) and lug it wherever you store it and then lug it again to the garden. With a little forethought, composting is a minimum of work with maximum return. Around the time you are finishing up with the leaf raking, it is time to make pumpkin pie. The best pies are made from cheese pumpkins, although the big hubbard squash makes very good pies as well. Prune your winterberry hollies to use the heavily berried branches for holiday decorations. Store them in a bucket of water in a protected spot out in the yard. You can take the chance there will still be berries closer to the holiday, but if the birds find them first, you are outta luck.

**December** means lots of festivities, including floating the blossoms of Christmas rose in a bowl of water. If you plan to have a Christmas tree with roots, make sure you dig the hole before the holiday, or the ground may be frozen afterwards. Houseplants really struggle with the short days and dry heat. Take down the screens, and you will be amazed at how much additional light comes through. Clean the windows and the room will glow. Outdoors, the trees have shed their leaves, so you can do some limb removal. Remember: only prune what you can reach from the ground by

# Introduction

hand or with a pole pruner. Leave tree climbing to the professionals. Poinsettias are a seasonal favorite. Keep them well watered if you want to keep them gorgeous as long as possible. They are generally grown in a peat mix, which dries out in the blink of an eye.

By **January,** the holiday hustle and bustle are over. Give your tree a few days to acclimate to outdoor temperatures and then get it in the ground. Houseplant fussing in general is a great way to get your hands into the soil again. Clean houseplants can make better use of the limited available light. Believe it or not, there are plenty of catalogs arriving in the mail on a daily basis. It is already time to start some seeds, and more need to be ordered quickly for starting in February.

By **February,** winter is getting old for those of us who need to be puttering about in the garden. Definitely keep your eyes open for that first spring bulb to burst into bloom. Pansies will still be blooming since they are the toughest flowers we can grow. Get busy with all that spring planning and shopping because by next month you will be swamped. Be sure to start all your onion family plants from seed at this time and don't forget to place your order for those crazy varieties of potatoes you want this year. If you wait too long, all the good ones will be gone.

Choose a warm day to prune your fruit trees and follow the sun around the yard to prune back what may be left of last year's perennials. The asparagus should definitely be pruned back as well. Keep an eye on your pussy willows. A warm February will bring out the fuzzy catkins quite early.

Roses get pruned in **March** as do a lot of summer blooming shrubs such as crapemyrtle and the wonderful butterfly bushes. DO NOT prune your spring flowering shrubs unless you don't mind cutting off all the flowers. They set bud last summer and are just waiting for the right time of year to open up. Prune your yew bushes, privet hedges, and burning bushes now, but please: throw away your electric hedge pruners and do some selective pruning to get your shrubs in shape. March 17 is official pea planting day. While you are in the garden, get in your potatoes, onions, and spinach. Annual poppies can be planted from seed. Daffodils will be popping up everywhere along with lots of crocus, miniature iris, and winter aconite. Your fall planted pansies will be spectacular by March, and you can add more by the end of the month.

By **April,** you will be planting up a storm, mowing the grass, spraying the fruit trees, tending tomato seedlings, visiting the garden center daily, and generally spending a lot of time playing in the dirt. From here on in, it is not

deciding what to do, but what to do first. Your cabbage family plants, which includes your cabbage, broccoli, and cauliflower, should go in the ground. If you didn't get your potatoes in the ground, there is still time. Ornamental trees and shrubs should be planted while still dormant, so get to it early in the month. Transplanting from one spot in the garden to another definitely should be done early. April is a great time for a spring application of fertilizer. Daffodils will be overlapping with early tulips blooming in the garden. Be sure to get down pre-emergent weed control to prevent weeds in both your lawn and your garden beds. That really saves on weeding later on. Mulch, mulch, mulch. That is pretty much self-explanatory. Water newly planted material and fertilize what has been in the ground for at least a year.

**May** is more of the same, but it is probably too late to transplant established ornamentals. Plant your chrysanthemums now if you want them to be established enough to become perennial. Watch out for gypsy moths and birch leafminer. Enjoy the late tulips. They are probably the most spectacular. Late tulips will be followed by iris, peonies, and poppies. These are all gorgeous. May is major veggie planting time and annual flowers as well. Summer bulbs such as canna, gladiolus, and tuberous begonias get

# Introduction

planted now. Lots of perennials are available. Find spots to tuck them in here and there or plan a spectacular bed that will give you a blast of color all at once. May is the month of dogwoods and nothing is more beautiful, but a few plants such as the redbud will give it a run for its money. The underappreciated *Aesculus pavia* gets bright red spikes of flowers.

**June** is the month of roses but strawberries are being harvested, so you have to decide if beauty or yumminess dominates the playing field. By later in the month, you will have raspberries and even the neglected mulberry to drop on your morning bowl of cereal. Blueberries just start to appear at the end of the month but then so do the horrible Japanese beetles. Spring lettuce is luscious, and those packets of mixed seeds make having a mesclun salad as easy as snipping your lunch with a pair of scissors. Harvest peas in bunches; they don't like the heat that is just around the corner. After you harvest your cauliflower, pull the plants but leave the broccoli. Smaller heads will continue to develop all summer. Rhododendrons and mountain laurels will bloom this month. Enjoy the roses in the sun, but those shady nooks will be just as gorgeous.

**July** brings daylilies into full color and the first Jersey sweet corn and tomatoes. Nothing is better than a Jersey tomato. Peaches are not far behind, and those blueberries are scrumptious. Summer annuals are coming into their own. The more you remove the dead flowers the better the annuals will hold up. Summer heat really takes a toll on hanging baskets, so water daily—sometimes twice daily. Water deeply when you need to water, but avoid getting water on the foliage. Watering in the early morning is always best. Take cut flowers in the early morning, after they have had the night to recover from heat stress. Continue to pinch the tips of your mums up until the end of the month for bushier plants and more flowers. Succession plantings of many crops can still go in the ground in July from seed. Late planting of zucchini will miss the evil squash vine borer.

**August** brings the bounty from the veggie garden to its peak. You can still plant cabbage family plants for fall harvest. Watch out for the cabbage looper though. They have multiple generations, and there will be many more larvae attacking the foliage in the fall crop than you saw in the spring. Make tomato sauce, freeze peppers, and eat lots of peaches. Sunflowers are blooming. You can leave the seeds for the birds and the squirrels or tie a paper bag over the head and allow the seeds

to mature away from hungry critters. Peegee hydrangeas are getting their fifteen minutes of fame, but garden phlox and giant hibiscus are stiff competition. Continue to remove spent blooms from the butterfly bushes so that they will make more blooms right up to frost.

That brings us back to **September** when lawn care is a major event. That's useful information because so many people want to overhaul their lawns in the spring, and the chances of getting a well established lawn in the spring are way less than in the fall. Besides, there is plenty to do in the spring, so it is great to legitimately be able to push that one project off for a while.

The beginning of this introduction claimed that there was always something to do in the garden. It is absolutely true. Month-by-Month, year-by-year, and even day by day, there is plenty of planting, mulching, watering, pruning, staking, feeding, trimming, and oh yes . . . harvesting, sniffing, looking, admiring, breathing, watching, and in general, thoroughly enjoying your garden all year-round.

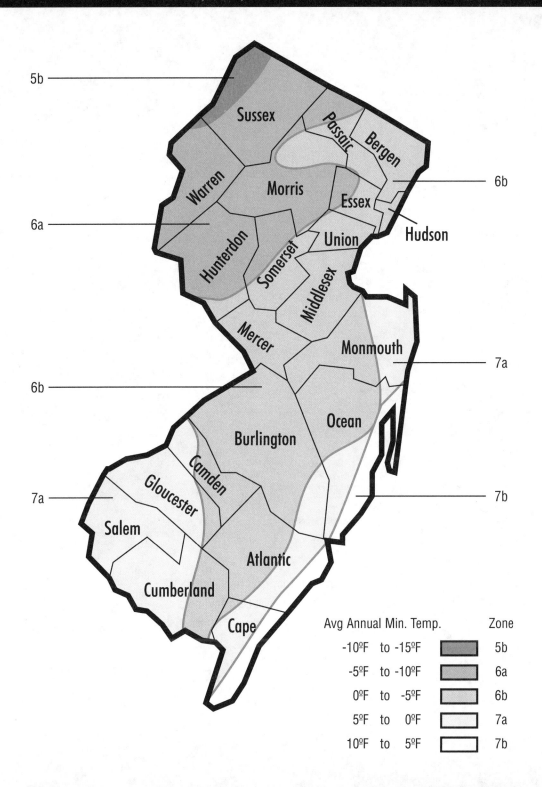

| Avg Annual Min. Temp. | | Zone |
|---|---|---|
| -10ºF | to -15ºF | 5b |
| -5ºF | to -10ºF | 6a |
| 0ºF | to -5ºF | 6b |
| 5ºF | to 0ºF | 7a |
| 10ºF | to 5ºF | 7b |

# CHAPTER ONE

# Annuals

*Annual flowers in the garden are like a red feather boa worn with a simple black dress.*
*They are entirely unnecessary, but at the same time they are the best part!*

By definition, annuals last for one growing season. They are planted in spring, bloom their little hearts out for most of the summer, and quietly fade away in early fall. Most annuals will not tolerate even a light frost, so planting is started after all danger of frost has passed. The **average** last killing frost in the coldest northwest part of New Jersey is May 10, but that is not to say there can't be frost later, sometimes even as late as early June. To avoid disaster with your annuals, hold off planting until Memorial Day weekend and you should be safe.

## PLANTING OPTIONS

**You can plant annuals any of three ways**. The purchase of transplants is the least amount of work and the most likely to give you quick and satisfying results. Growing annuals from **seed** means either starting the seed indoors or direct seeding in the garden. This is more risky but gives you the most options. The number of varieties of annual flowers available as seed is phenomenal. Finally, some annuals can **self-sow,** which means they drop seed

as they bloom throughout the summer, and these seeds then germinate when the weather suits them the following spring. It doesn't get any easier than that, but not many flowers are so cooperative and then you have to be happy with the same flowers in that spot year after year. With every approach, there are advantages and disadvantages. Figuring out what is best for each situation is part of the fun.

It is hard to beat going to your favorite nursery and picking out flat after flat of gorgeous flowers already showing color and just itching to put down roots in your garden. This approach is terrific for seeing how the colors will blend and how the foliage will work with other plants. When **transplanting** young plants already in bloom, it is easier to visualize what the final look will be. The cost can be limiting since the purchase of many flats can get expensive, and your only choices are what someone else decided was worth growing. Still, it is about as close to an instant garden as you can get, and anyone with a love of gardening feels like a kid in a candy shop when surrounded by all those little beauties.

You will need to ascertain mature heights and spreads to help keep everything balanced. Giant **zinnias** can reach 4 feet, but some of the dwarfs stay at 10 to 12 inches. Make sure you purchase the ones that will suit your needs. If you are interested in annuals for cut flowers, they are generally taller and go in the back of a bed, but taller varieties scattered among the shrubs can sometimes brighten up the foundation plantings while providing bouquets for indoors at the same time.

The varieties that **self-sow** have a bit of the garden fairy about them. They spring up here and there with a mind of their own, sometimes almost everywhere. Sometimes they are so thick, they have to be thinned a bit to keep them from crowding each other out. That may be the perfect opportunity to spread them out to other places where they can work their magic.

You may experience an obstacle with weed control among your annuals since pre-emergence weed control cannot be used where you want annuals to self-sow. The material may stop weeds from germinating, but it will prevent your annuals from returning as well.

# Annuals

## Preparing the Soil

You will probably be itching to plant by March or April. Make sure your soil is as ready as you are. As a rule of thumb, take a wad of soil in your hand and squeeze it hard. It should then crumble easily when you manipulate it with your thumb. If it stays wadded up in a lump, it is still too wet to work.

When the soil is ready, rake away the mulch and incorporate organic matter, such as leaf compost, into the soil. If you are doing this by hand, it is an opportunity to yank any perennial weeds that may be about. It will also disturb any weed seeds that are thinking about germinating. New Jersey soils tend to be acidic, so the addition of lime is often recommended. A pH of 6.5 is ideal for most garden annuals. PH test kits are available at most garden centers, or you can have your soil tested by the Rutgers Cooperative Extension Agency. They have an office in most counties.

## Ready to Plant

Growing your annuals from **seed** can be great fun but also a little overwhelming. If you want to get an early start, you will need to grow the seed indoors. But wait! If you don't have really good growing conditions to grow seedlings indoors, you may end up with scraggly transplants that spend most of the summer trying to catch up after a bad start. A greenhouse or greenhouse window is best, but a very bright, unblocked, southern exposure window may do just fine. A grow-light setup may also work.

In general, the use of artificial lights to substitute for sunlight indoors is more trouble than it's worth, but for starting seeds it may be a solution. It is short-term so you will not be making a commitment to an enormous energy bill, and you can adjust the shelves to always provide maximum light to the seedlings. This will ensure the most efficient use of the light and the healthiest young plants.

Under fluorescent lights, keep the light 6 inches above the plants. On a windowsill, turn plants daily.

Using separate containers for each variety is the best way to avoid confusion, but when space is limited that is not always possible. Be sure to mark your rows carefully with a waterproof pen or pencil. Also, take care to plant seeds with like requirements when it is necessary to mix seed in a flat or tray. Requirements that must be taken into consideration include: **amount of light, depth of planting, temperature for germination, time for germination, growing temperature after germination, and time required before planting out.**

All seeds, in any container you may fashion, require drainage in the bottom of the container. Be sure to follow all the requirements as closely as possible for each type of seed. In general, this information is contained on the seed packet. Many mail order seed companies have horticulturists available if you run into trouble. There are also many reference books available with great details on seed requirements, and your County Agricultural Agent will also have most of this information available if you need more than is provided on the packet.

Seedlings will have to be transplanted (relocated) when they show three true leaves. Space them 1 to 2 inches apart. Two inches is better if you have the room. Use a sterile potting soil to keep disease in check. Hold seedlings by their leaves when handling them. If the leaves break off, there is little real damage, but if the main stem bends or breaks, you probably have lost the seedling.

If adequate natural light is unavailable and you can't afford or have no interest in the use of artificial light, many varieties can be direct seeded. In general, seed packets will include planting information that is variety specific. As a general rule, if you do not have specific

# Annuals

instructions, plant seeds twice as deep as the seed is wide.

The date for direct planting in the garden is generally included on the packet.

Sometimes, some varieties take too long to get started and so are unsuitable for direct seeding. If you still have your heart set on a particular flower that has tickled your fancy, don't give up. You may be able to make arrangements for a local greenhouse to grow the seedlings for you. Just make sure you contact them well in advance. Once spring hits, they are very busy.

## Enjoy the Process

An experienced gardener is likely to follow all three approaches: A bed or two of self-sowing annuals where their wild nature doesn't get in the way of a formal planting; flats of red **impatiens** or yellow **marigolds** for mass appeal; and favorite varieties, starting on the windowsill. This involves planning and experience.

The winter months are a great time to wander through the plethora of catalogs that arrive in the mail. Dog-ear the pages of those flowers that seem irresistible and read up on those flowers that are unfamiliar or have given you trouble in the past. **Plan. Draw pictures. Make lists. Be daring.** Get a general feel for the look you are trying to create. The beauty of annuals is that what works well can be recreated. What falls a bit short can be thrown out for something new the following year. If the dramatic look of giant red **zinnias** everywhere proves to be too much, next year tone it down to just a few with a lazy river of white **petunias** surrounding the beds. Let your imagination run away with you! You have little to lose and endless opportunities to work your own garden magic.

## NOTES

_____

_____

_____

_____

_____

_____

_____

_____

_____

_____

_____

_____

_____

_____

_____

_____

_____

# Annuals

## For Sun

| Common Name | Botanical Name |
| --- | --- |
| Hollyhock | *Alcea rosea* |
| Snapdragon | *Antirrhinum majus* |
| Pot Marigold | *Calendula officinalis* |
| Annual Vinca | *Catharanthus roseus* |
| Black-eyed Susan | *Thunbergia alata* |
| Flowering Cabbage/Kale | *Brassica oleracea* varieties |
| Bachelor's Buttons | *Centaurea cyanus* |
| Basket Flower | *C. americana* |
| Cosmos | *Cosmos bipinnatus* |
| Yellow Cosmos | *C. sulphureus* |
| Alyssum | *Lobularia maritima* |
| Mallow | *Malva verticillata* |
| Tree Mallow | *Lavatera arborea* |
| Sunflower | *Helianthus annuus* |
| Strawflower | *Helichrysum bracteum* |
| Globe Amaranth | *Gomphrena globosa* |
| Mexican Sunflower | *Tithonia rotundifolia* |
| Zinnia | *Zinnia elegans* |
| Verbena | *Verbena* x *hybrida* |
| Spider Flower | *Cleome hassleriana* |
| Portulaca | *Portulaca grandiflora* |

## For Sun

| Common Name | Botanical Name |
| --- | --- |
| Annual Poppy | *Papaver rhoeas* |
| Petunia | *Petunia* x *hybrida* |
| Pansy | *Viola* x *wittrockiana* |
| Marigold | *Tagetes* species |
| Garden Geranium | *Pelargonium hortorum* |
| Morning Glory | *Ipomoea purpurea* |
| Four O'Clocks | *Mirabilis jalapa* |
| Hyacinth Bean | *Dollichos lablab* |
| Annual Phlox | *Phlox drummondii* |
| Nasturtium | *Tropaeolum majus* |
| Salvia | *Salvia splendens* |
| Kochia | *Kochia scoparia* |
| Star Scabious | *Scabiosa stellata* |
| Sweet Scabious | *S. atropuprea* |
| African Daisy | *Arctotis stoechadifolia* |
| Stock | *Matthiola incana* |
| Sweet Pea | *Lathyrus odoratus* |
| Love-in-a-Mist | *Nigella damascena* |
| Gazania | *Gazania ringens* |

# Annuals

## For Shade

| Common Name | Botanical Name |
| --- | --- |
| Ageratum (or sun) | Ageratum houstonianum |
| English Daisy (or sun) | Bellis perennis |
| Begonia | Begonia semperflorens |
| Lobelia | Lobelia erinus |
| Forget-me-not | Myosotis sylvatica |
| Silver Dollar Plant | Lunaria annua |
| Impatiens | Impatiens walleriana |
| Balsam | I. balsamina |
| Celosia (or sun) | Celosia cristata |
| Wishbone Flower | Torenia fournieri |
| Foxglove (biennial) | Digitalis purpurea |
| Ornamental Tobacco (or sun) | Nicotiana alata |
| Heliotrope | Heliotropium arborescens |
| Browallia | Browallia speciosa |
| Persian Violet | Exacum affine |
| Fuchsia | Fuchsia x hybrida |

## Annuals Likely to Self-Sow

| Common Name | Botanical Name |
| --- | --- |
| Pot Marigold | Calendula officinalis |
| Cosmos | Cosmos bipinnatus |
| Yellow Cosmos | C. sulphureus |
| Spider Flower | Cleome hassleriana |
| Balsam | Impatiens balsamina |
| Silver Dollar Plant | Lunaria annua |
| Forget-me-not | Myosotis sylvatica |
| Morning Glory | Ipomoea purpurea |
| Ornamental Tobacco | Nicotiana alata |
| Annual Poppy | Papaver rhoeas |
| Bachelor's Buttons | Centaurea cyanus |
| Browallia | Browallia speciosa |
| Love-in-a-Mist | Nigella damascena |

## For Dried Flowers

| Common Name | Botanical Name |
| --- | --- |
| Celosia | Celosia cristata |
| Silver Dollar Plant | Lunaria annua |
| Star Scabious | Scabiosa stellata |
| Strawflower | Helichrysum bracteum |
| Globe Amaranth | Gomphrena globosa |
| Bachelor's Buttons | Centaurea cyanus |

# JANUARY
## Annuals

 PLANNING

Planning is a big part of what goes on in the chilly month of January. The only problem is, the colder the temperature, the more you plan! Sometimes you need to buy the Ponderosa to accommodate what tickles your fancy during the dead of winter.

• One of the best parts of planning is delving into the stacks of seed catalogs that arrive in the mail. **Keeping catalogs in alphabetical order is a big help.** Keeping a pad of sticky notes nearby is also helpful. Marking the pages saves a lot of time when you want to go back later.

• If you have any favorite annuals, **choose a spot** for them right off the bat. Be sure to match sun-loving flowers to sunny garden spots and choose shade tolerant annuals for those darker nooks. Planting annuals in a different spot from last year helps prevent a disease problem.

• When looking around the yard in January, be sure to **consider the deciduous trees**. Once they leaf out, the light patterns will be changed dramatically. Sometimes that can work in your favor. Early **pansies** will tolerate the colder weather and will thrive in the sun. As temperatures warm up, the shade from the leaves will keep pansies cooler and extend their season.

• Flowers for cutting need some special consideration. The plants are generally taller and require full sun. Up against the house they need to go in the back, but in a free-standing bed, they may do better in the middle. You may want to **mix annuals with perennials for cutting**. There are two good reasons to do this: You may not have enough room or energy for two beds, and the annuals will ensure color throughout the season, even when none of the perennials are ready for the spotlight.

The toughest part is probably figuring out what **not** to plant. Decide what you will purchase locally and what you want to grow from seed. **Heirloom varieties, unusual vines,** or a particular color **sweet pea** may require growing the plants yourself. Keep in mind that hybrid seed can be very expensive and you cannot save the seed from hybrid varieties with any hope of producing the same appearance in the offspring. It goes back to the genetics of Mendel with his wrinkled and smooth peas, and can be very disappointing if you are trying to duplicate some magical look from last year. Now **order your seed.**

 PLANTING

It is really too early to actually plant any seeds, but it is the perfect time to **test any seed** you may have to see if it is still viable. Take about a dozen seeds from each seed packet you have held over. Wrap them in a moist, but not soggy, paper towel. Store the wrapped seeds in a plastic bag at room temperature. If the seeds germinate, then the rest of the seed is worth planting. If not, toss them and start with a fresh pack. Give them up to three weeks to show signs of life.

January is also the best time to **gather all the paraphernalia you will need** to start your seeds. What you want to use depends to some degree on where you will be starting your seed.

**Some things to consider:**

You will need **narrow containers for narrow windowsills**. Sideways quart milk cartons fit nicely and can handle rows of seeds, but they will have to be transplanted to larger containers later. Small pots or yogurt cups accommodate several seeds. Later you will thin them to one plant per container. This eliminates the need to transplant, but you will not get many plants for the garden in a tight space.

Make sure you purchase **sterile material for starting seeds**. Vermiculite, sand, or potting soils specific for seed germination will all do the job.

**Grow-light systems with adjustable shelves** can be located almost anywhere. The more adventurous can grow a large number of transplants in a small space with this type of system. Simple electric heat mats are also worth a look. Bottom heat helps with seed germination, especially on a chilly windowsill.

# WATERING

If in doubt about watering needs, always err on the side of too little, especially in January. Cold, soggy soil will allow root rot in the blink of an eye, but the cool temperatures will slow the evaporation process, so dry soil has some fudge room before it causes drought stress.

# FERTILIZING

There is not much to fertilize in January, but be sure to add a water-soluble fertilizer to your list of supplies for starting seed. For annuals held over indoors, make sure you have a water-soluble fertilizer for flowering plants. You will need it shortly.

# PRUNING

Overwintered annuals may be quite leggy at this time. A serious pruning will get them ready to fill in as the days get longer. You may even want to root the cuttings. This is especially advantageous with **geraniums** since they are expensive to replace and younger plants flower with more enthusiasm.

# PESTS

**Container annuals may harbor insects.** In most cases you will just want to toss infested plants, but you will want to do it quickly. These plants can be a source of infestations for other plants. You especially do not want to infest seedlings as that can easily become fatal.

# NOTES

_____
_____
_____
_____
_____
_____
_____
_____
_____
_____
_____
_____
_____
_____
_____
_____
_____
_____

# FEBRUARY

 PLANNING

Planning for your annuals in February is a refining of the process you started in January. Seeds will be arriving in the mail and gathering in piles from visits to your favorite garden centers. For those seeds you intend to start indoors, it is important to work out a planting schedule. The happy **zinnia** only requires about five weeks to be ready to plant in the garden, but the sleepy **begonia** can take up to sixteen weeks. If space is a limiting factor, you may decide to direct seed the zinnias to save room on the windowsill, but direct seeding those slowpokes will waste most of the season getting started.

Some seeds require light for germination. Others require darkness and must be covered. All of this information is generally contained on the seed packet. Most garden annuals are not difficult to germinate, but a few may require soaking for twenty-four hours or refrigeration for a period. It is best to gather all this information early so that you don't realize the day you want to start the **portulaca** seed that you needed to refrigerate it for two weeks.

Annual flowers you may start in February include **bachelor's buttons, begonias, dianthus, dahlia, dusty miller, impa-**tiens, **lobelia, petunia, scabiosa,** and **snapdragon.**

 PLANTING

The temperature for starting most annual flower seeds is between **65 and 70 degrees Fahrenheit.** On a windowsill in February, that may be difficult to achieve. You may want to keep your seed tray in a warmer spot, even one in less light, until the seedlings sprout. For those seeds that require light, an incandescent 40-watt bulb will provide sufficient light for germination. Under fluorescent light, keep the bulbs 2 inches away from the soil surface, but be sure to monitor the temperature. You don't ever want it to go above 80 degrees Fahrenheit, and you don't want the soil surface to dry out.

**Germination is usually ten to fourteen days**, but some will emerge in as few as five days, while others will take up to twenty-one. You will want to be sure of your timing, just in case you get a dud seed.

As seeds emerge, the temperature can be allowed to drop to about 60 degrees Fahrenheit. Too much warmth can cause leggy (tall, skinny, stretched out) plants. Under fluorescent lights, you will continually need to adjust the level of the plants so they stay within about 6 inches of the source of light. If they begin to stretch, they will need to be closer to the light. **Keep the lights on fifteen to eighteen hours each day.** On a windowsill, plants will need to be turned daily. Plants, especially seedlings, will bend toward the light source. They actually grow more rapidly on the shady side of the stem, causing them to lean in the direction of the sun.

 WATERING

Seedlings grow quickly, and they need constant attention at this critical time. Too much water, and they rot. Not enough, and they shrivel up.

Make sure whatever container you use has **drainage.** Then make sure you protect the surface beneath the container from water damage with the use of a waterproof tray. Clay saucers are not waterproof. It also wouldn't hurt to put a layer of plastic wrap on the surface in addition to the tray.

It is best to **water seedling trays from the bottom.** Watering from the top runs the risk of dislodging the seed. Set the trays or containers in the sink or a flat pan of water. Once the surface appears moist, let the tray drain thoroughly. The tray can be placed in a clear plastic bag until the seeds emerge. This will prevent the soil surface from drying out. Remove the bag as soon as the seeds emerge. When the soil gets slightly dry, water using the bottom method described above. This keeps the seedlings dry and reduces your chances of stem rot.

 FERTILIZING

Newly emerged seedlings do not need to be fertilized. They are living off of the stored food that comes in the seed. Fertilizing too early can cause rapid but weak growth. Wait until they are ready to transplant or, if they're in single plant containers, wait until the three-leaf stage to begin regular watering with a dilute ($1/3$ concentration) of water-soluble fertilizer for houseplants.

 PRUNING

Tiny seedlings will not need to be pruned, but they may need to be thinned. **Thinning** is simply removing the unwanted seedlings. In small pots, thin to the healthiest seedling. In rows, plants need to be spaced at least 1 inch apart but 2 inches is better. (Transplanting is relocating seedlings to provide more room, but wait on that until next month.)

 PESTS

The biggest problem with seedlings is **damping off** (when fungus causes rapid wilting or rotting at the base). To avoid this, be sure to sterilize all planting containers and tools prior to use. Follow proper watering instructions. Never use any fertilizer until the plants have three true leaves. Thin overcrowded plantings immediately.

## NOTES

_____

_____

_____

_____

_____

_____

_____

_____

PLANNING

By March, most New Jersey gardeners are itching to get out and do some playing in the dirt. **But don't rush things.** Working the soil too soon damages soil structure. Still, a sunny day in March is a great time to try the plans you made on paper. An evaluation of existing beds will help determine what goes where. Chances are, you will know exactly what you want to put in key locations, but you'll also have some plants that still need a good spot. Some things to consider:

*1* Edging in front of shrubbery beds can soften the look of formal plantings and add color to **evergreens**. Low-growing annuals such as **alyssum**, **petunias**, or **ageratum** work well.

*2* Spring bulbs will benefit from moderate sized annuals to hide maturing foliage. **French marigolds, annual vinca,** or **dwarf snapdragons** will do the job.

Working this out outdoors can help you indoors with organizing your seeds. Six **snail flower vines** may be all you need to grow up a trellis over the front gate. That will leave room on the windowsill for all the giant **zinnias** you need to cover the chain link fence.

If you want new beds:

*1* **Pace them off to get a general idea of size** and then use stakes and string to mark them off.

*2* **Get rid of grass** in what will be the new bed, with old carpeting turned upside down. It is generally heavy enough to stay in place, can be cut to fit whatever shape you want to create, and will smother the grass and weeds. By planning early you can work less, spend less, and achieve the best results.

 PLANTING

It is still too early to plant much outdoors, but one flower is a very exciting exception. Annual **poppies** can be planted from seed in the garden in March. They like to be barely covered with soil, so throwing the seed and then raking them ever so lightly is one method that works. This is not a useful approach for a formal look, but annual poppies can never be accused of being formal. They will self-sow with gay abandon, and the offspring will certainly come up wherever their hearts' desire.

For your more standard annuals, there are many species that get started indoors in March. Early in the month you can still start **bachelor's buttons,** **dianthus, snapdragons,** and maybe **begonias** if you hurry. By mid-month, you definitely want to have your **dahlias, dusty millers, petunias, scabiosa,** and probably your **impatiens** and **lobelias** ready to go. Late March works for **ageratum, alyssum,** taller **marigolds, salvia,** and **verbena.**

See the chapter introduction for details on starting plants indoors.

 WATERING

Continue to water transplanted seedlings, from the bottom if possible.

 FERTILIZING

After transplanting, begin to fertilize seedlings with a diluted ($1/3$ concentration) solution of water-soluble fertilizer for house plants.

For annual flowers that have been kept indoors over the winter, begin to use a water-soluble fertilizer for flowering plants, according to directions.

 PRUNING

Some annuals are pinched when young to encourage bushiness, but not this early. Mature annuals that have overwintered indoors can get very leggy. If you haven't pruned them hard yet, definitely do it now.

##  PESTS

**Damping off** continues to be the biggest problem facing seedlings. (See Pests in February.) Starting with sterile soil, containers, and tools is the best way to avoid the problem. Watering from the bottom and having excellent drainage is also important for healthy seedlings. If any seedlings succumb to the disease, remove them and even take out what may appear to be healthy neighbors. If seedlings are crowded, thin them for better air circulation. Allow the soil to get fairly dry before watering with great care from the bottom.

Insect pests that can show up on overwintered annuals include **scale, white fly, mites,** and **mealy bugs.** It would have to be a very special plant to make it worthwhile to attempt to eradicate these pests and save the plant. New annuals are right around the corner. If you want to try to save infested plants anyway, prune severely and swish the pruned plant in soapy water or spray with insecticidal soap. Isolate it from other plants, especially your seedlings.

## NOTES

## PLANNING

April is when you begin to put your plans into action, but, without fail, some things get shifted around once you are out in the garden. Your spring flowering bulbs will all be up even if not yet all in bloom. You may want to add some annuals to hide ripening foliage of early bulbs.

By this time, the soil should be in good enough condition to work on the beds. Test the soil in your hand as described in the chapter introduction. Allow six weeks for results if you are sending in soil samples to the Extension Agency. Testing in early April should provide enough time to get results before planting annuals out in late May.

Cover prepared beds with a thick layer of organic mulch. It is easy enough to plant through a layer of mulch, and it will keep the weeds down while you are waiting to plant.

## PLANTING

The wonderful, happy, smiling **pansy** brings great joy to the gardener in April. Many fabulous spring bulbs are enjoying their fifteen minutes of fame at that time of year, but it is the pansy that allows gardeners to dust off the trowel and find their favorite pair of gardening gloves.

When properly **hardened off** (allowed to get used to outside temperatures a bit gradually), pansies can be planted wherever the sun shines. They do particularly well under deciduous trees since they will benefit from both the sun shining through leafless trees and the shade later when the weather turns hot. Pansies are an excellent choice for windowboxes and containers. A large pot on the front steps brings a smile with every pass. Plant them at the same depth they were in their trays or cell packs.

If you didn't plant your annual **poppies** from seed outdoors last month, you can still do it (see March for more information). Indoors, you can still plant **ageratum, alyssum, tall marigolds, salvia, statice, strawflowers,** and **verbena** early in the month. Mid-month should see your **asters, balsam, coleus, cosmos, gomphrena, smaller marigolds, nasturtiums,** and **portulaca** in the trays. Late April is reserved for those "jack rabbit" seeds that shoot up quickly. They include **cockscomb, gaillardia, zinnias,** and even **sunflowers,** although they grow so quickly outdoors you don't come out ahead much.

## WATERING

Usually in spring, the ground retains enough moisture that watering is not necessary. However, it is a good idea to water lightly if you have direct seeded **poppies,** and to water in pansies immediately after planting. Poppy seeds are planted close to the surface, so a light watering to keep seeds from drying out is important. Pansies are resilient and require little attention. Cool spring temperatures keep water needs to a minimum, but **if the soil becomes dry, water sufficiently to wet the entire root zone.**

Indoors, newly planted seeds in trays as well as transplanted seedlings should continue to be watered from the bottom. Make sure trays or pots are allowed to drain thoroughly after watering. Watering on the surface can disturb shallow seeds. Placing seeded trays in a clear plastic bag will prevent the soil surface from drying out too quickly. Remove the plastic as soon as the seeds germinate.

## FERTILIZING

For **pansies** planted in the garden, 5-10-5 fertilizer can be mixed into the soil during soil preparation, or newly planted pansies can be watered with a water-soluble fertilizer according to directions.

Seedlings should not be transplanted until they have three true leaves, which happens to be the same time you begin a fertilizer routine. After transplanting seedlings, use a water-soluble fertilizer for houseplants at 1/3 strength every time you water.

# PRUNING

This is tough to accept, but the truth is that the removal of all flowers and buds at the time of planting annuals, including early **pansies,** encourages root development and a more robust plant throughout the season. It is especially important to remove faded blooms on pansies as the dead blossoms mature to seeds rapidly. This takes strength from the plants, causing them to fade earlier in the season as well as to produce fewer flowers along the way.

**Many species benefit from the pinching of young plants to encourage bushiness.** The exact timing of when to do that is species specific and is usually contained on the seed packet. For examples, pinch tall **marigolds** when they

## Helpful Hints

*1* Have several pairs of garden gloves on hand. A rubber-dipped pair is very useful for when the ground is wet. Insulated work gloves make an enormous difference in your comfort level on those first planting days when the weather is still cold. Another pair of very thin gloves, such as those made from goatskin, are best for thinning tiny plants or working with seeds.

*2* A kneeling pad is more comfortable than hard ground and an enormous improvement over wet ground. Some people find that knee pads are too binding and end up being as uncomfortable as hard or wet ground.

*3* As a general rule, if you do not have specific instructions, plant seeds twice as deep as the seed is wide.

reach 6 inches; **torenia**, a shade loving plant, gets pinched at only 3 inches; **cosmos** doesn't get pinched until 18 inches.

# PESTS

Pansies will **rot** at the base if planted too deep. Be sure to plant at the same depth they were in their cell packs to avoid this problem.

**Damping off** continues to be the only major concern for emerging seeds and seedlings. Water only from the bottom and do not fertilize until plants have three true leaves. See March pests for more information.

# NOTES

_____
_____
_____
_____
_____
_____
_____
_____
_____
_____
_____
_____
_____
_____
_____

# MAY
## Annuals

## PLANNING

May is a big month for annual flowers in New Jersey. By mid-month, the first plants can go in the ground, and by the end of the month your garden can be covered in young plants gearing up for a full blast of color.

By following these creative tips, you can create a personal **annual garden.** A theme can be lovely:

*1* An all-white garden is enchanting, almost mystical, but brilliant color is exciting, and soft pastels are very calming.

*2* From a distance, many colors mixed together tend to lose integrity. The eye converts them to a uniform, nondescript shade of dull.

*3* For viewing from a distance, mass planting of a single color will have more impact. Beds viewed as you walk up a path or surrounding the deck can be multicolored, and will be seen close enough to appreciate individually.

*4* Taller plants go in the back of a bed that is being viewed from one side only. The same plants might need to go in the middle if the bed is being viewed all around.

*5* Avoid very straight, uniform rows. Staggered (informal) rows, patches of a particular variety scattered about, and variation in height will make the eye move up and down as well as front to back. The effect will be softer. From a practical point of view, if a few plants don't make it, the gaps will not be noticed in an informal planting. Gaps in straight rows, however, draw the eye.

## PLANTING

April showers bring May flowers, but not if the ground stays wet. Remember, you can plant when a wad of squeezed soil can be crumbled in your hand.

About 2 inches of organic mulch on top of the prepared bed is very useful. It is attractive, retains soil moisture, helps enormously with weed control, and moderates fluctuations in soil temperature. You can **plant your annuals directly through the mulch.** Mulching after planting can also be done, but it requires some finesse not to disturb the young plants.

Soil preparation for direct seeding is identical, except that you won't put mulch down until the seeds come up (or seeds may be smothered). Follow depth of planting directions carefully. For tiny seeds, mixing a bit of sand into the seed packet will give you more control over seed dispersal.

Be sure to **follow spacing directions for transplants**. They will use the same spacing you give to thinned-out, direct planted seedlings (preferably 2 inches apart). If you are careful, you can transplant seedlings to fill in any bare spots. Remember to avoid straight rows. Stick to your plan . . . but don't forget to improvise a little as the spirit moves you!

## WATERING

Water newly planted transplants immediately. If the weather is unseasonably hot or dry, they may need to be watered daily until they get established. Taper off this routine, but **water deeply when you do water.** This will encourage deep rooting rather than a shallow root system that quickly shows drought stress in hot weather.

Water direct seeded beds daily (unless it rains) until seeds emerge. Then taper off to an "as needed" basis as explained above.

# FERTILIZING

If 5-10-5 was incorporated into the soil prior to planting, you may not need to fertilize again until midseason. A water-soluble fertilizer should be used according to directions. **Avoid pushing** emerging seedlings with fertilizer until they show at least three true leaves.

 # PRUNING

Pinching annual plants for bushiness is a plant specific practice. If this is appropriate, it should be indicated on the seed packet. Or when you purchase transplants ask about particular varieties at the nursery. Keep in mind that too much **pinching may reduce flower size in some species.** This can be addressed by removing buds, leaving only a single bud per stem. Then the individual blooms will be much larger. For long-stemmed cut flowers you may not want to pinch, but watch out for floppiness. Taller plants may require staking.

 # PESTS

**Cutworms** are sometimes a problem. They come out at night and sever the stem of young plants at the base. Place a cardboard collar or an empty tuna can around the plant to create a mechanical barrier to the cutworms.

**Aphids** can also show up early in the season. Gently wipe them off (and squish them in the process), preferably while wearing gloves. A mild infestation can be hosed off. If that doesn't do the trick, you may have to resort to the use of insecticide. Insecticidal soap offers some control.

Rarely, **caterpillars** do some damage to young plants. Those that can't be handpicked can be controlled with Bt (*Bacillus thurengiensis*).

**Weeds** are certainly pests. With proper soil preparation, they should not be much of a problem this early. To keep it that way, use a pre-emergent weed preventive material. This works well to prevent weeds from germinating.

The use of an organic mulch is also an important aspect of weed control.

##  PLANNING

**Planning a summer event in the garden?** Centerpieces of annual flowers can be potted up now to be lush in time for the event. Keep in mind color schemes and height. You don't want the centerpiece too tall to see over. One idea is to use smaller pots and cluster them together on the table. Then everyone gets to take one home.

**Leaving for vacation?** Leaving the garden for two weeks can create disaster on your return. Leaky pipe hoses or soaker hoses can take care of things while you're gone. Leaky pipe types are permeable black hoses that ooze water slowly. This type of hose can be stretched along rows or wrapped around clusters of annuals or even large individual plants. Soaker hoses have tiny perforations on one side. Have a friend turn these on while you are away, or set them up with a timer. Give yourself time before you leave to make sure hoses and timer work properly.

**What about containers?** Use water bottles with soaker-type tips to allow water to be drawn into the soil as needed. Some tips can be purchased that fit 2-liter soda bottles, but beautiful decorative versions are available as well. Don't wait until last minute to purchase these. Sometimes, when you want them in a hurry, you can't find them.

##  PLANTING

It is not too late to plant annuals, especially from transplants. Seeds can still be planted, but since they take longer to flower, you should probably stick to those that germinate and mature quickly. **Cockscomb, portulaca, zinnias, cosmos,** and of course, **sunflowers** will still do well from seed. A late planting of annual **poppies** from seed will keep these beauties in bloom until late fall. **Cleome,** also called **spider flower**, does best when planted from seed in early June. It needs temperatures to remain above 40 degrees Fahrenheit.

**Pot your extra transplants** in 4- or 6-inch pots. They will be beautiful on the porch, deck, or front steps. Then, if you lose a few in the garden, you have replacements.

Planting in windowboxes or hanging baskets can be done now. Sometimes it is easier to purchase baskets already in bloom, but **potting them yourself is fun** and an easy way to try different combinations of colors and styles. Always provide containers with drainage and use fresh, sterile potting material.

Any disease organisms in soil will spread rapidly in a container. It is not worth the risk to use recycled soil. Recycled containers should be soaked in a 10 percent bleach solution and then rinsed thoroughly. Be sure to mix plants that have similar requirements. **Impatiens** may cook where **petunias** thrive.

##  WATERING

Anything in a container will need water far more frequently than the same plant in the ground. You do not want newly planted material to get overly dry. Once the root system is established, you will have a bit more flexibility. It is important to water deeply whenever you water to **encourage the development of a deep root system.** In a rainy season, this may not seem important, but during a hot, dry summer, it can make an enormous difference in the well-being of your garden.

Always water your annuals in the early morning. This way, the sun comes out and dries up the leaves. Wet leaves, especially at night, offer an opportunity for leaf diseases to get a foothold. Avoid that whenever possible.

##  FERTILIZING

If you incorporated 5-10-5 fertilizer into the soil during soil preparation, then you don't need to fertilize at this time. If you are using a water-soluble fertilizer, then you need to apply it according to package directions. A side dressing of 5-10-5 fertilizer before the weather gets hot will give flowers a boost for the summer.

# PRUNING

At this time of year, pruning will be more pinching than any serious cutting back.

Many plants, such as **marigolds, zinnias, gomphrenas,** and even **petunias,** will benefit from pinching to encourage branching. Avoid excessive pinching if you are striving for height, such as in the **giant sunflowers**.

Pinch off faded blooms. Some flowers such as **impatiens** self-shed, but that is not the case for most annuals.

Probably your **pansies** will need the most care at this time. They have been in the ground since early spring (or even last fall) and have made many flowers for you to enjoy. Pansies make lots of seeds, so pinch them off every time you walk by. If some of the branches have stretched a bit, prune them back now.

# PESTS

Avoid getting water on the leaves of annuals whenever possible. **Powdery mildew** can be a problem. It is especially

bad on **zinnias** but can show up on a wide range of plants. The first appearance is not usually this early, but keep your eyes open. You'll need to control powdery mildew at the first sign of grayish white spots on the leaves.

**Japanese beetles**, nasty things, first make their appearance in late June. They are very hungry with a diverse appetite. Handpick whenever possible or use an appropriate insecticide. DO NOT use pheromone traps. They work too well. You will draw in far more beetles than you would have had otherwise, and they will be munching all the way to the trap.

Your organic mulch is key to preventing weeds, but that is often not enough. Follow directions on the pre-emergent weed control material you choose for the recommended timing between repeated applications.

## NOTES

_____
_____
_____
_____
_____
_____
_____
_____
_____
_____
_____
_____
_____
_____
_____

# JULY
## Annuals

 PLANNING

Continue to **take lots of notes** on what does well in the garden and what is a total flop. By now, many flowers will be in full bloom. Take photographs to tuck into the pages of your garden journal. A picture is truly worth a gazillion words when trying to visualize the perfect combination of coral **impatiens** with deep purple **petunias.**

It is also a good idea to photograph other people's gardens. Many local garden clubs feature tours of different gardens in the geographic area where they draw members. Not only will you spend an enjoyable day, but you will also meet other gardeners while supporting the club's community service efforts. The last Saturday in July is the Rutgers Gardens Open House off of Ryder's Lane in North Brunswick. The annual garden display is always top notch. **Take pictures everywhere for your journal**, especially of anything particularly lovely or something you don't recognize.

 PLANTING

By July, most planting of your annuals is a done deal. Even so, you may have noticed a few gaps in places where the leaves of your spring bulbs have finally faded. Popping in a few annuals to fill in is fine, but they may need a little extra attention to adapt to the soil under the hot summer sun.

There are only two annuals that get planted to brighten up the fall: **pansies** and **ornamental cabbages**. These two cold-tolerant beauties are started from seed in July. If you have no place to start seed for spring planting, you can enjoy the satisfaction of growing these two from seed in a prepared seedbed outdoors.

 WATERING

Water daily until seeds germinate. In summer heat they will dry out quickly.

As a general rule, you want to water as infrequently as possible but still avoid drought stress. Water deeply to give the entire root system a drink and to encourage a deep root system. **Avoid getting water on the leaves,** and always water in the early morning. How often you will need to water depends on the plants you have chosen, your soils, the amount of sun the plants receive, whether you have mulched, and of course, how much it rains.

In hot weather, water all containers daily. Some that have a high water demand, such as **fuchsia,** may need to be watered twice a day on those few viciously hot days.

 FERTILIZING

Apply water-soluble fertilizer when you water, according to directions on the fertilizer you have chosen. If you are using 5-10-5 fertilizer, a sidedressing in early to mid-July will give plants a boost, but never fertilize if temperatures are above 85 degrees Fahrenheit.

 PRUNING

For larger blooms, you can remove some of the secondary buds farther back on a stem. That way, all the energy goes into maker a few larger flowers.

Always prune dead flowers since they go to seed, look ugly, and weaken the plants. The exception, of course, is later in the season with those varieties you want to self-sow.

Some annuals will get leggy as the season progresses and will need pruning to generate new growth. **Pansies** benefit from regular removal of straggly shoots. They occur more frequently as the weather gets hot. At some point, you may want to yank them. **Petunias** get leggy also. Removal of the longest branches every week will keep the plants generating new shoots and flowers. If they get away from you, prune every other plant in late July. Prune the rest two weeks later, after the first batch has had a bit of time to regenerate.

# PESTS

**Weeds** are pests and need constant control. An organic mulch will help with that, but weeds still pop up. Lightly disturbing the mulch with a rake will take care of very young weeds, but you may still see weeds popping up. Using pre-emergent weed control material on a regular schedule will be your best preventive approach.

**Powdery mildew** may make its first appearance as early as July. Look for gray or white spots on leaf surfaces. Control as soon as you see the problem. **Zinnias** sometimes get the disease severely, but it can show up on many annuals.

**Tobacco budworm** usually does not show up until late July. It has to fly up from the south. After a mild winter, it will show up sooner as it has less dis-

tance to fly. This critter seems to prefer **petunias** and **geraniums,** but watch out for **nicotiana flowers** since they are a close relative of tobacco. Bt (*Bacillus thurengiensis*) may give adequate control, but if the caterpillars are hiding in the buds, they are hard to destroy. Remove affected flower buds and spray repeatedly.

**White fly** is difficult to control but is another pest that has to fly up from the south. This pest can overwinter in greenhouses in New Jersey, but it cannot survive outdoors. The beautiful **fuchsia** is a target for this critter, which has a flexible appetite. Control it with a pyrethrin-based insecticide.

**Japanese beetles** are still hungry and busy laying eggs. Handpick or spray with an appropriate insecticide.

## NOTES

# AUGUST
## Annuals

 ## PLANNING

By this time, all your annuals will be in full bloom, even those that self-sow or any varieties you may have seeded late to extend the season. Remember, from some plants you can even save the seed.

**Morning glories** will self-sow, but over time they tend to revert to classic blue. If you want, you can save the seed from blooms that were particularly lovely. Most **zinnias** will produce seed worth saving, but watch out for hybrids. The next generation will have little resemblance to their parents. The narrow, bean-like pods of **cleome** save readily, and so do **cosmos** seed.

If you have grown hybrids or just don't want to save seed (the plants do get ugly during the process), be sure to make note of the variety and the supplier of any favorites. 'Big Red' is a spectacular hybrid red zinnia that has significantly better-than-average resistance to powdery mildew and produces many large, rich red flowers. It is a Park's seed catalog exclusive, so you have to know where to get it. Write the particulars in a notebook or garden journal, or at least be sure to save the seed packet.

 ## PLANTING

The **pansies** and **ornamental cabbages** you planted in July will need some attention at this time. They will need to be thinned or spread out. If you don't have a lot of space, you can pot them in containers. Don't plant them in the garden until mid-September or even after the first frost. Give them room to grow now so they will provide instant color when their time comes.

 ## WATERING

From a plant's perspective (human, too, actually) the **"dog days of summer"** have come to mean the time when summer is really hot and dusty dry. The weather isn't always like that, but when it is, your annual flowers need deep watering in the cool morning. As a rule, try not to get the leaves wet, but a good hosing to get the dust off the leaves will perk them up. It will also help wash away any insect pests that may be trying to get a foothold. As long as the sun is coming up, the leaves will dry off quickly.

Container plants will certainly need a tremendous amount of water if things heat up. This can be one of those rare times when allowing water to sit in the tray may be the only way to keep hanging baskets from drooping in the afternoon sun.

 ## FERTILIZING

Never fertilize when the temperatures are above 85 degrees Fahrenheit. **Wait for a break in a heat wave** before applying water-soluble fertilizer. If you are using a 5-10-5 fertilizer as a sidedressing, it is even more important to hold off until suitable weather.

 ## PRUNING

By August, some plants will need a serious trim. **Petunias, verbenas, salvias, zinnias, cosmos,** and many others may get out of control without a nip and tuck. In really hot weather, individual blooms don't last very long, so a constant removal of faded blooms (**deadheading**) is necessary to keep plants looking good.

On the other hand, let **giant sunflowers** stretch as far up as they can. **Cleome** makes great cut flowers, but then the side buds produce smaller flowers. This is one plant where the seed pods actually add to the appearance of the plant. The thin wisps are graceful and exotic. Since new flowers continue to be produced at the top, there is no need to deadhead or prune cleome.

Some annuals need a bit of pinching. **Impatiens** are not happy in brutally hot weather. Pinching some of the tallest shoots will encourage them to branch and fill in. **Coleus** flowers are not very exciting. Once in the flower-producing, reproductive mode, they make fewer leaves and so eventually thin out. Pinch off emerging flower spikes and any leggy branches to keep them full.

You will want to pinch your July-planted **pansies** to encourage bushiness if you are growing any from seed. **Do not pinch ornamental cabbages** as they need to form single heads to be as showy as possible.

 PESTS

**Japanese beetles** will be in full force. Handpicking is still best, but a large infestation cannot be controlled by hand. Use an appropriate insecticide and be sure to follow label directions carefully. In hot weather, plants will be more subject to any secondary impacts from the prod-

ucts. **White fly** and **tobacco budworm** continue to fly up from warmer climates. If you find them, they will need to be controlled immediately since both are extremely destructive. Use a pyrethrin for the white fly and Bt (*Bacillus thurengiensis*) for the tobacco budworm.

**Powdery mildew** will continue, or it may be showing up for the first time, depending on weather conditions. Keep leaves dry to minimize the spread. Pinch off leaves showing symptoms (if infected leaves are few). A serious case of powdery mildew will shorten the season of the plants infected. You could replace them with fall **mums**, but if you want to keep the current plants around, it is necessary to spray with an appropriate fungicide.

Weeds will slow down when the weather is hot and dry, but if you water, the weed seeds will take a drink as well. Continue to control weeds by raking the mulch lightly and hand weeding. Follow directions on your pre-emergent material. September's cooler weather will bring a resurgence of weed seed germination.

# SEPTEMBER

## PLANNING

By September, your annual garden is beginning the last hurrah. The only planning left is choosing which plants you need to yank to make way for fall-planted **mums**. Treated as late-season annuals, mums pick up where summer annuals leave off. Mums planted in the fall will probably not return the following spring. If they should return, it's a bonus. Just in case you get a pleasant surprise come spring, plan a location for them where they will not be in the way.

September is a good time to **make decisions about whether or not to save any seed.** Allowing certain flowers to mature into dried seeds will speed up the aging process, but since time is on the downswing for these plants, you will not lose much and you will gain seeds for next year. Those individual plants that were particularly lovely or robust are the plants that will produce the better seed.

## PLANTING

The only planting of annuals you may want to do in September is to pop in a few **ornamental cabbage plants** in places where the summer annuals really need to be yanked. The first frost is not for another month, so you will want to keep your summer flowers going for as long as possible.

Transplanting, however, may be worthwhile. Bring a few summer annuals indoors to brighten up the fall. As a general rule, those annuals that prefer shade outdoors stand the best chance of looking good indoors once summer is over. A plant that thrives in brilliant summer sun does not stand much of a chance indoors over the winter. Pot up **impatiens, begonias,** or **coleus** in a 6- to 10-inch pot. You want the pot full but not cramped. Make sure you have drainage.

Allow at least two weeks for the plant to acclimate to the pot before moving it indoors in late September. Keep the pot outside near the spot it was growing in the ground. That way the shock of being potted up won't be exacerbated by a change in light conditions as well. When you bring it in, choose the sunniest window. The sun coming in from one direction through the glass is fairly close to diffused light all day outside. With luck, you will be able to enjoy a touch of summer all winter long.

## WATERING

Provide your plants with at least one deep soak after the heat breaks. More than one Labor Day weekend has been drowned out at the beach, so perhaps Mother Nature will do the job for you. If not, water deeply in the early morning. Now that temperatures will be dropping, water demand will drop as well. It still may be necessary to irrigate if the sky doesn't open at your request. The **cooler nights encourage leaf diseases,** so it's important to water in the early morning or to use soaker hoses or leaky pipe types of applicators. A deep watering will, however, help the plants with that last push of summer color.

## FERTILIZING

A sidedressing of 5-10-5 fertilizer will give the plants a push to make the most out of the almost ideal September weather. If you are using a water-soluble fertilizer, follow directions carefully.

Continue to fertilize your **pansies** and **ornamental cabbage.** They will get planted out shortly, but they can make good use of the growing time left to them if they have plenty of nutrients available.

# PRUNING

As part of the last blast of color in September's garden, a pruning of the straggly plants can make a big difference. Removal of tall, leggy **zinnia** branches will encourage side shoots to develop. A haircut on **impatiens, ageratum, begonias, salvia, verbena, petunias,** and many others will remove the dried dusty foliage and let the new foliage take over. Don't get carried away with the pruning since you don't have much time for the recovery. Use a light touch. Make sure you tackle this chore early in the month or you will simply run out of time.

Pinch the growing tips of your **pansies** that were started from seed. They will not get planted for another month, but you want them lush to provide color most of the winter.

# PESTS

Waging a major war on pests in September is not really worthwhile. If you have **ornamental cabbages** waiting in the wings, keep a close eye on them. The small white moths you commonly see flitting about in the garden are called **cabbage moths.** They are extremely destructive to edible cabbages and can certainly eat gaping holes in the ornamental varieties as well. Fall cabbages are more susceptible than spring cabbages because the moth has multiple generations in a growing season. The few adults you see in early summer are ubiquitous by September. The larvae are hard to see as they take on the color of the leaves. The large holes or ragged leaves are easy to spot as are the yellow egg masses on the underside of the leaves. Squish the egg masses, remove the larvae by hand, or spray with Bt (*Bacillus thurengiensis*).

# NOTES

_____

_____

_____

_____

_____

_____

_____

## PLANNING

Sometime this month, probably earlier rather than later, you will get your first frost. This is not likely to be a killing frost, but it can still be enough to take the zing out of your garden. You may want to pull out your annuals rather than look at them when they seem so pathetic.

If you have a few plants, possibly close to the house, you can plan to **cover them with a sheet or tarp** when the threat of frost is predicted. By having everything ready when you hear the weather report, you can sometimes extend the season for several weeks. Simply throw the sheet over the top when it gets dark and remove it in the morning. This is also sometimes worth your while in the vegetable garden.

You'll want to have all your replacement plants ready to go into the ground. You cannot expect to have as much of a display in fall as when summer annuals are in full swing, but **pansies** and **ornamental cabbages** should go in key locations where you will be able to enjoy them from the kitchen window or as you walk up the front steps.

 ## PLANTING

Yank frosted, ugly, or dead annuals as soon as possible after they lose their appeal. You want your replacements to have warm enough soil to put down a few roots while there is still time.

How much soil preparation you do is somewhat dependent on how much of the bed you are planting. If you are just planting a few plants for a touch of color, adding organic matter, such as compost, into the planting holes is probably sufficient. If you are filling a bed with **pansies** as part of your plan to deal with the gray days of winter, more serious soil preparation is in order:

- Rake back the mulch

- Spread your organic matter over the area, and till it in, or turn over the bed with a shovel.

- Apply fertilizer (see Fertilizing)

- Reapply a layer of mulch or supplement if much of what was there has decomposed or washed away.

- Plant through the mulch at the same depth the plants were in their containers.

**Pansies or cabbage in pots on the steps will provide color** into December, but as with all containers, these plants will succumb to changes in weather faster than their counterparts in the ground.

If you didn't get to it in September, you can pot up the annuals early in the month that you want to try to overwinter before they are likely to be frosted. You can take cuttings now, but a long winter indoors may encourage legginess. Pot up the plants from the garden, enjoy them for a while, and take the cuttings next month when they have stretched and flowering has slowed down. Candidates for this include **coleus, impatiens,** and **geraniums.**

Access to a greenhouse or greenhouse window will make an enormous difference in your chances for success. Shade lovers will make the best houseplants, but geraniums are high on the list of plants people try to keep over the winter.

 ## WATERING

Water newly planted **pansies** and **cabbage.** You may not need to water again until spring, but always be aware of the absence of rain. It is not as noticeable to humans when the weather is cool, but if the soil gets overly dry, plants will be affected even in cool weather. Container plants will certainly show the effects more quickly.

##  FERTILIZING

Spread a light application of 5-10-5 fertilizer over the area where you intend to plant your fall annuals. Turning the fertilizer into the soil will be beneficial, especially if you haven't been nourishing the soil regularly throughout the summer. **Do not simply toss fertilizer into the planting hole** as it will burn the roots of young transplants.

## PRUNING

Bud removal on **pansies** at the time of planting will give these tough little guys a chance to make some roots before they go full blast into flower production. **Do not prune or pinch your ornamental cabbages.** The look is supposed to be a single stem with a tight head formed with lots of color.

It is a good time to gather seedpods. Snip off the seedpods carefully. In some cases snipping will be difficult. Rather than risk shattering the pods, use a pair of pruners. Make sure the pods have completely dried. The more opportunity the seeds have had to mature on the plant, the greater your chance for seed viability the following year.

## Helpful Hints

*1* Large pots of annuals may be difficult to keep indoors. The sunlight is limited, and large pots take up a lot of room. Cuttings have the advantage of taking up a small space and can fit snug on a windowsill where they get the most light.

*2* Another way to increase light and so extend the life of pretty annuals is to remove the screen from the window where you keep them. It makes an enormous difference in the amount of light they will receive.

At some point the seeds will be released by the plant and by then it is too late to gather them up. Watch the seed maturation process—when some seeds have been released, gather the rest. Store all gathered seed in a sealed container and **refrigerate**.

## PESTS

In the garden, the only pest you need to worry about is the **cabbage worm** on the ornamental cabbages. See September for information regarding control.

If you are bringing any annuals indoors to enjoy while they continue to bloom, or as a source of cuttings to get a head start on next year, keep the plants away from your indoor plants until you are sure they are pest free. It's wise to use an insecticidal soap on any plants before you bring them in.

## NOTES

_____
_____
_____
_____
_____
_____
_____
_____
_____
_____
_____
_____
_____
_____
_____

## PLANNING

November is the perfect time for working with your **overwintering** annuals to get started on your garden for next year. By late in the month, annuals you potted in early October are likely to have dropped quite a few leaves, slowed down on flower production, and stretched towards the sun.

**Gather all the supplies** you will need to do the job correctly. These will include:

*1* Sharp pruners or small knife that has been sterilized

*2* Sterile potting medium, vermiculite, or sand

*3* A source of bottom heat such as a heat mat. (These may be available at your favorite garden center or are readily available through many garden specialty catalogs.)

*4* Large, clear plastic bags

*5* Trays or pots to hold your cuttings. If you are using a sunny windowsill, make sure the containers are the right size to fit on the sill.

*6* Rooting hormone

 ## PLANTING

**Take cuttings** of any potted annuals you may want to propagate. Water prior to taking the cuttings so that they have filled up their cells to capacity with water. That will provide some reserve for that time when they have no roots. Use only a sterile medium. There are many potting mixes available for this purpose, but sterile sand or vermiculite works well, too.

Your cuttings should be about **2 to 3 inches long** but must have several healthy leaves and one very near the bottom of the stem near where it was cut. Remove the bottom leaf. Dip the cut end of the stem into the hormone, but leave just the lightest dusting of the powder on the stem. Too much hormone will cause the stem to rot. Place the stem into the potting medium. If it is a delicate stem you may want to make a hole first with a pencil.

If possible, **supply heat to the bottom of the pot or tray.** The ideal temperature is 65 degrees Fahrenheit at the soil level, but with a cooler air temperature. That way the moisture demand on the leaves is low. There are simple mats available to supply bottom heat. They can be used to encourage seed germination as well.

You can also keep the plants where the air temperature is 65 degrees Fahrenheit. Supplying humidity is important. By placing the container is a clear plastic bag, kept open at the top, you can create a simple greenhouse effect. This is especially true where the leaves are in a warm atmosphere. The higher humidity will reduce the likelihood of wilting. Once the cuttings develop roots, you can pot them up individually or group them together in planters.

 ## WATERING

It is important to **keep moist any cuttings that you are attempting to root,** but don't keep them soggy. They have no roots for water uptake and will show signs of drought stress quickly if they get dry. However, they will rot even faster if left sitting in water.

The parent plants need to be watered, but keep in mind **several variables**. The heat is on, so the air is probably on the dry side, causing the soil to dry out more quickly. However, the plants have been pruned and it is relatively cool compared to summer heat, so water demand is low. After a few weeks of checking every two or three days, you will have a better idea of how often the larger pots need water.

##  FERTILIZING

For your cuttings of annuals, you can begin to fertilize with a very diluted solution of water-soluble fertilizer after the plants have developed roots and have been potted up.

The parent plants will benefit from a diluted solution of fertilizer to give them a boost after they are pruned. Do that once or twice after pruning and then hold off until the days start to get longer and the sun begins to feel strong, probably in mid-February.

##  PRUNING

The tiny rooted cuttings will not need pruning, but keep an eye on them once they start to grow. In the lower light of your home in winter, they will tend to stretch, and constant pinching will encourage bushiness.

The removal of cuttings for propagation should have been a sufficient pruning to trim back any unsightly growth on the parent plants. If you only took a few cuttings, then a more significant pruning would be in order. **Prune to eliminate floppiness or excessive bare stems.** If the plant is floppy, remove the worst at this time and repeat the pruning as the

dormant buds begin to show signs of growth on the pruned shoots.

##  PESTS

There are many insect pests that can show up on rooted cuttings and garden annuals that have been brought indoors. These include **aphids, scale, white fly, mealybugs,** and the tiny **mite.** Outdoors all summer, annuals are exposed to these insects constantly. Once indoors, the environmental conditions are conducive to the reproduction of these pests and not conducive to the use of pesticides for control. Keep plants that were outside over the summer away from houseplants until you are sure they are clean. The use of an insecticidal soap before you bring the plants indoors should go a long way in preventing a major infestation. Keep a close eye on the cuttings and young plants. Hand-picking, spraying with water, alcohol on

a cotton swab, or an alcohol-soaked square cosmetic pad will help contain a minor infestation. If you choose to spray with an insecticide, be sure you find a location with good ventilation and where the plants will not be subject to frost.

## NOTES

_____

_____

_____

_____

_____

_____

_____

_____

_____

_____

# DECEMBER

 ## PLANNING

The annual garden is at rest. By December, even your most cold-hardy summer annuals have given up. **Geraniums** have been known to tolerate temperatures down to 28 degrees Fahrenheit, but even these resilient beauties generally succumb some time this month. Down the shore, you may get a bit of a reprieve as the coast boasts being Zone 7 and the ocean breeze keeps air temperature warmer in the fall. Only your fall-planted **pansies** will put out the occasional bloom in winter.

Still, be sure to combine the holidays with early plans for a spring garden. Leave hints for your own personal Santa or purchase gardening gifts for the gardeners on your list. Here are a few gift ideas:

• Garden gloves for women or men. Look for thin gloves for delicate work, insulated gloves for cold weather, heavy-duty gloves for digging the beds, waterproof gloves for working in wet weather, and long gauntlet types for avoiding rose thorns.

• A kneeling pad. Beautiful ones have made it on the scene in recent years. They are fun, practical, and good for a tight budget.

• A good gardening reference book. The *New Jersey Gardener's Guide* (written by yours truly) is tailored to the climate and environment here in the Garden State.

• A trip to Duke Gardens in Somerset or Longwood Gardens in Kennett Square, Pennsylvania. It will provide inspiration for the spring garden as well as fight back winter blahs.

• A garden planner computer program.

• A garden planner kit. Several versions are available with cutouts and grids to help layout beds, design your yard, and plan your garden. These actually may be more fun than the computerized version as they are more hands-on and gardeners are hands-on people.

• Hose guides. There are gorgeous ones out now made of cast iron. They do the job and look great too.

• A curly hose and wand. This makes watering potted annuals, especially hanging baskets, enormously easier.

 ## PLANTING

If you started any cuttings last month, they may need to be potted into larger pots by now. Flats of rooted cuttings can get all tangled if they're allowed to stay in the trays for too long. Then you damage the young plants as you try to separate them.

Three-inch pots are perfect for the windowsill and provide enough room for your plants to grow. You can pot several rooted cuttings in a larger pot, but make sure you have a spot that gets plenty of sun where a larger pot can fit right in the window. Also, if you are planning to use these as transplants, individual plants will be easier to work with in the garden.

Take care not to locate these young plants near a source of heat. **They still don't have much of a root system,** and the dry air and soil will be an extra strain on a young root system.

 ## WATERING

Think *moist,* not wet. Not too dry either.

Don't overwater. You need to supply a saucer to protect the surface underneath. Make sure it is impervious to water. Clay saucers will seep moisture and can do a lot of damage. Glazed porcelain or plastic saucers do the job. Then make sure that water doesn't sit in the saucer. Delicate young plants will develop root rot quickly.

On the other hand, tiny roots are not yet ready to grab every bit of moisture in dry soil. If soil sits dry, plants will wilt quickly. **The dry atmosphere created by central heat makes this situation more delicate.** Water as soon as the soil dries.

Misting doesn't really help unless you have a misting system that comes on automatically every twenty minutes or so. The occasional mist with a spray bottle does help keep the leaves clean, which is a good thing, but does zilch for compensating for overly dry air.

 FERTILIZING

A diluted solution of fertilizer at the time you pot up rooted cuttings will give young plants a boost. December is home to the shortest day of the year. Plants are doing their best to hang on under limited light conditions. Pushing them at this time is not a good idea. They will produce weak growth that will just need to be pinched back later. Hold off on fertilizer on your other potted annuals until the strength of the sun returns in February.

## Helpful Hints

*1 Woman's Work* is a catalog company that makes serious garden gloves that fit the dimensions of a woman's hand. Work gloves that actually fit a woman are sometimes hard to find locally.

*2* For movie lovers, there's a movie called *Green Card* that is a romantic comedy about a woman (Andie McDowell) horticulturist who marries an illegal immigrant (Gerard Depardieu). By agreeing to marry, he gets a green card and she gets to live in a "married only" building where her apartment includes an enormous conservatory once part of the bygone Golden Era. A great gift for the romantic gardener.

 PRUNING

Anything that is getting leggy will need to be pinched off. Rooted cuttings will benefit from having the centers pinched out to encourage side shoots to develop. Potted annuals will look better if you **snip off the leggiest branches** every time you water. That will keep the plant from needing a major pruning at any time. (A major pruning makes them look really ugly, however, and they take a while to regain their beauty.)

 PESTS

December brings you more of the same insects you may have encountered last month. See November for details.

NOTES

_____
_____
_____
_____
_____
_____
_____
_____
_____
_____
_____
_____
_____
_____
_____
_____

# CHAPTER TWO

# Bulbs

*Let us begin this chapter by dismissing a few general misconceptions regarding bulbs. There are bulbs for all seasons.*

In the minds of many people, bulbs are limited to the spring beauties, **tulips** and **daffodils.** The occasional **hyacinth** may get consideration now and then and even the early spring **crocus**, but the world of bulbs is enormous beyond that ever-present core.

## WHAT YOU MAY NOT KNOW

The world of bulbs allows constant planning, planting, and enjoying. Spring-flowering bulbs must be planned for in the fall. Bulbs that bloom indoors do a good job of holding winter at bay. The scent of a **paper-white narcissus** reminds us of the pleasures of spring even when winter holds us in its grip. You can plant a **fall blooming crocus** in August, even early September, and have flowers in a matter of weeks. And many of the fall crocus species are hardy enough to return year after year.

The hardy **cyclamen** blooms in October. The wondrous **magic lily** shoots up in August. These are just the tip of the iceberg. It is almost as if bulbs were a well-kept secret.

Besides all the hardy bulbs, when you start to investigate the world of tender bulbs, **the variety is phenomenal.** Add in all the things that are not quite bulbs, like tubers and corms, but are generally grouped with bulbs, and the selection becomes staggering. You could plant nothing but bulbs and their friends and have wonderful flowers blooming all year long.

## WHAT BULBS LIKE

You can plant indoor bulbs throughout the winter, but **it's best to start in late fall.** You can even plant outdoor bulbs in containers for indoor bloom. Generally, it just takes a bit of chilling to trigger the bulbs into bloom. Some hardy summer bulbs can be planted in the autumn or early spring, but the tender bulbs that bloom during the summer should be planted in late spring. During the late summer, you plant fall blooming bulbs, and by autumn it is time to start over.

You should know your bulbs' needs before you plant. Most require sun to make a return appearance every year. Even so, they may be flexible.

**Daffodils,** for example, need sun to naturalize and thrive, but because they emerge and bloom so early, they can be planted under deciduous trees. By the time the leaves come out on the tree, the daffodil leaves will have done most of their work replenishing the bulbs for the following year.

Some bulbs will want to stay in place for years without being disturbed. If left alone, they will multiply, spread, and become more beautiful with each passing year. **Winter aconite** is one of these. The sea of yellow flowers that appears in very early spring will take your breath away, especially after a long cold winter.

The **grape hyacinth** is delightful with its deep purple spike of tiny flowers. This is a tenacious plant that will spread over large tracts of land. Grape hyacinth, however, transplants easily and will tolerate a bit of shade—both somewhat uncommon attributes for bulbs. The traditional varieties are easy and joyful to grow, but there are many unusual varieties of grape hyacinth as well. The one that looks like it has a curly perm may be the most fun.

## What to Expect

When planning a garden, follow the same basic rules for bulbs as for most other plants. You want to match the growing requirements of the bulbs with the appropriate environmental conditions in your garden. Virtually all bulbs have no tolerance for wet ground. The better the condition of the soil at the time of planting, the more years you can expect your bulbs to make a comeback.

**If you like the bulb's flowers, then you are going to have to put up with the leaves.** It is the foliage, with its green chlorophyll, that takes sunlight and turns it into plant energy. This process of photosynthesis builds up the bulb to be strong enough to make a flower. Flower production is a drain on the bulb. In commercial production, flower buds are often removed to allow more strength to go to the bulb and so produce a saleable bulb sooner. If the leaves do not receive enough light or are pruned away before fully aging, then not enough energy is transferred into the bulb to bring it back to its former glory.

Some bulbs will only provide a few years of show and then quietly fade away. **Tulips** are like that. **You can expect only three to five years from tulips.** The soldier-straight uniformity can only be expected the first year. Less perfection can sometimes be even more beautiful in year two, but as time goes on you may want to yank them up rather than put up with aging foliage and even smaller blooms (or possibly none!) the following spring.

**Daffodil** leaves emerge earlier than tulip leaves and continue to hang around in the garden until midsummer. **Tulips** deteriorate each season and are worthless after a few years. **Daffodils can naturalize and multiply,** making the most beautiful displays in the spring. The enduring daffodil leaves with all their energy production make the difference. Now if you mow the leaves or, even worse, tie them up in ugly bunches with rubber bands, the leaves are not free to grab the sunlight and process it in their cells.

It is the same with the summer bulbs, but different. The leaves do all the work just the same as in spring bulbs, but different species may have different approaches. **True lilies are spectacular summer flowers.** The plants are tall, sometimes over 6 feet tall, with the flowers appearing on top. So the foliage is working hard for some time both before and after flower production. The **magic lily** produces all its foliage in the spring, which completely disappears by the time the flowers emerge in mid to late summer. You need to understand the life cycle of your bulbs so you don't inadvertently remove the foliage and shortchange yourself as well as the plant.

Unfortunately, bulbs forced indoors, whether hardy or non-hardy species, are rarely worth holding over for a second season. There is just not enough sun indoors for the leaves to work to their maximum potential. It is better to toss bulbs once they flower than to be disappointed with their performance next year. The one exception may be the amaryllis. **Amaryllis leaves have a very long season.** If you move the plant outdoors after danger of frost has passed, you will likely get a healthy fat bulb when it's time to bring it in next fall. Fat bulbs bring spectacular flowers. And after all, that is why we plant bulbs in the first place.

# Bulbs

## For Early Spring

| Common Name | Botanical Name |
| --- | --- |
| Snowdrops | *Galanthus nivalis* |
| Giant Snowdrops | *G. elwesii* |
| Common Crocus (many colors) | *Crocus vernus* |
| Scotch Crocus (many colors, yellow throat) | *C. biflorus* |
| Yellow Crocus | *C. flavus* |
| Lilac Crocus | *C. etruscus* |
| Dogtooth Violet | *Erythronium americanum* |
| Glory of the Snow | *Chionodoxa luciliae* |
| Reticulated Iris | *Iris reticulata* |
| Winter Aconite | *Eranthis hyemalis* |
| Spring Starflower (Zone 6) | *Ipheion uniflorum* |
| Siberian Squill | *Scilla siberica* |
| Grecian Windflower | *Anemone blanda* |
| Spring Snowflake | *Leucojum vernum* |
| Striped Squill | *Puschkinia scilloides* |

## For Mid Spring

| Common Name | Botanical Name |
| --- | --- |
| Daffodils | *Narcissus* species |
| Blue Grape Hyacinth | *Muscari armeniacum* |
| Two-tone Grape Hyacinth | *Muscari latifolium* |

## For Mid Spring (continued)

| Common Name | Botanical Name |
| --- | --- |
| Curly Grape Hyacinth | *M. comosum* 'Plumosum' |
| White Grape Hyacinth | *M. botryoides* 'Album' |
| Double Grape Hyacinth | *M. armeniacum* 'Blue Spike' |
| Hyacinth | *Hyacinthus orientalis* |
| Early Tulips | *Tulipa* species |
| Crown Imperial | *Fritillaria imperialis* |
| Purple Fritillaria | *Fritillaria persica* |
| White Fritillaria | *F. persica* 'Ivory Bells' |

## For Late Spring

| Common Name | Botanical Name |
| --- | --- |
| Late Tulips | *Tulipa* species |
| Wood Hyacinths | *Hyacinthoides hispanica* |
| Foxtail Lilies | *Eremurus* hybrids |
| Voodoo Bulb | *Dracunculus vulgaris* |
| Star of Persia | *Allium albopilosum* |
| Drumstick Allium | *A. sphaerocephalum* |
| Mediterranean Bells | *A. bulgaricum* |
| Giant Allium | *A. giganteum* |
| Yellow Allium | *A. moly* |
| Pink Allium | *A. roseum* |
| Summer Snowflake | *Leucojum aestivum* |

# Bulbs

## For Late Spring (continued)

| Common Name | Botanical Name |
| --- | --- |
| Nodding Star of Bethlehem | *Ornithogalum nutans* |
| Wild Hyacinth | *Camassia leichtlinii* |
| German Bearded Iris | *Iris germanica* hybrids |
| Siberian Iris | *I. sibirica* |

## Early Summer

| Common Name | Botanical Name |
| --- | --- |
| Japanese Iris | *Iris kaempferi* |
| Asiatic Hybrid Lilies | *Lilium x hybrida* |
| Martagon Lilies | *L. martagon* |

## Mid Summer

| Common Name | Botanical Name |
| --- | --- |
| Easter Lily | *L. longiflorum* |
| Aurelian Hybrid Lilies | *L. x hybrida* |
| Tiger Lily | *L. lancifolium* |
| Crocosmia | *Crocosmia x crocosmiiflora* |

## Late Summer

| Common Name | Botanical Name |
| --- | --- |
| Magic Lily | *Lycoris squamigera* |
| Turkscap Lily | *Lilium superbum* |
| Oriental Hybrid Lilies | *L. x hybrida* |
| Autumn Snowflake | *Leucojum autumnale* |
| Autumn Crocus | *Colchicum autumnale* |
| Saffron Crocus (Zone 6) | *Crocus sativus* |
| Longflower Crocus | *C. longiflorus* |
| Zonal Crocus | *C. zonatus* |

## Early Autumn

| Common Name | Botanical Name |
| --- | --- |
| Hardy Cyclamen | *Cyclamen neapolitanum* |

# JANUARY
## Bulbs

 PLANNING

The bulb planning that goes on in January is targeted towards your early and late-spring planted bulbs. Some hardy bulbs like true **lilies** can be planted in the spring. Lilies do require chilling to bloom, but most hardy bulbs sold in the spring are pre-chilled. Where you plant them is very variety dependent. The giant **Aurelian hybrids** bloom in early July and many reach over 6 feet, so obviously they need to go towards the back of the bed. **Tiger lilies** will naturalize, so pick a place where they can hang out undisturbed for a few years. Lilies prefer a bit of shade, especially when the sun is hottest. Shade during midday will prevent premature fading.

When deciding on your bulbs, learn the ultimate height, the long-range life expectancy, the light requirements, and when to expect the bloom to appear. That way, you can plan you bulb garden to fill in any gaps in bloom in the perennial garden or to tie things over between spring bulbs and summer annuals.

Although technically a tuber, and a fussy one at that, **dahlias** make outstanding, long-lived cut flowers. The giant dahlias are up to 10 inches across. These dinner-plate sized varieties can be part of a cutflower garden, grown along a fence, or clustered together as a focal point. You definitely should give some thought to where you put them. Also, they are a bit pricey, so you'll need just the right spot with perfect growing conditions to get maximum effect.

Gather information and plan early, as the more spectacular the bulb, the more likely it will have sold out if you wait until planting time to place your order.

 PLANTING

Hold off on planting anything for outdoors, but don't hesitate to pot up some beauties to enjoy indoors. If you received **amaryllis** bulbs for the holidays, pot them up as soon as possible. Amaryllis kits come with everything you need, so just follow the directions.

Sometimes you can get really lucky and hit a tremendous sale after the holidays. If the occasional barrel of amaryllis bulbs at 50 cents each should cross your path, buy all you can carry. Once they're potted, you can enjoy them yourself, or they make great gifts when visiting friends or going to a dinner party. Amaryllis is not potted deeply like tulips. About $1/3$ of the bulb goes under the soil surface. Use a light soil and give them as much sun as possible.

Paper-white narcissus can be planted every two weeks all winter, starting in late fall. Continue potting up bulbs for a continuous display until spring. Place bulbs in a bulb pot or wide, shallow container. Put a layer of potting soil on the bottom and place bulbs on the surface so they almost touch. Cover with soil. The nose of the bulbs (the top where the leaves emerge) should stick out above the soil. There are some lovely, unusual varieties available. 'Soleil D'Or' is yellow with an orange cup. 'Erlicheer' is a double white. 'Avalanche' and the **Chinese sacred lily** are both white with a yellow cup.

A very strange bulb called a **Voodoo bulb** can be grown on your counter by just sitting there. It will produce an unpleasant smelling but beautiful flower. Once it finishes blooming, you can pot it up. Move it out after danger of frost.

WATERING

Bulbs will not be happy if they sit in water, but if they get overly dry, it is possible for the flowers to dry up. It is up to the gardener to walk the fine line. **Amaryllis** is somewhat less fussy, due to the large water reserve in the bulb. If in doubt, wait a day.

The low, wide containers used to pot bulbs for forcing sometimes do not have drainage holes. Remember that when watering. You do not want to drown your bulbs.

 FERTILIZING

If you have a greenhouse where the foliage will receive strong light, then fertilize with a water-soluble fertilizer after the plants have finished blooming. If you are not planning to keep the bulbs once the flowers are forced indoors, there is really no need to fertilize. Otherwise, **amaryllis** will benefit from regular applications of fertilizer after blooming. They are worth the extra attenton as amaryllis can last for years.

 PRUNING

Prune away flower stalks in potted bulbs to keep the pots looking attractive, especially if other bulbs in the same pot are still likely to bloom. If you want to keep the bulbs, especially amaryllis, cut the flower stalk at the base as soon as the flowers fade. Take care not to cut the foliage.

 PESTS

Bulbs forced indoors are generally pest free. **Insects** harboring on your houseplants will sometimes jump to bulbs. Since most bulbs are somewhat "disposable" after they bloom in a container, it is rarely worth attempting to control an infestation. A spray of water will often contain the problem enough to keep the plants until they finish blooming.

On occasion, **amaryllis** will become infested with **scale** or **mealy bugs**. Wiping the long strap-like leaves with a mildly soapy soft cloth will often solve the problem. The leaves are flat and unconvoluted, making cleaning easy and more effective than with many other plants.

Never bother to spray an insecticide when the bulbs are in bloom. There is always a good chance the flowers will not tolerate the product and you will lose the blooms.

## NOTES

_____

_____

_____

_____

_____

_____

_____

_____

_____

_____

_____

# FEBRUARY
## Bulbs

## PLANNING

February planning for bulbs is much of a continuation of what you did in January with at least one notable exception. By mid-month in a mild winter and certainly by late February in a severe winter, you can expect to see signs of spring. It is the early spring bulbs that are the first to break through winter's icy grip. Begin to check for **crocus, snowdrops,** and **miniature iris** any day the temperature is above freezing and the sun is shining. The first crocus to bloom is like a Louis Armstrong solo. It touches your soul and wakes you up, all at the same time. You don't want to miss it.

February is also a tough month for gardeners. It has been a while since the first frost and cabin fever can be at its worst. You will often find pots of bulbs blooming at the garden center, nursery, or even the supermarket. Do yourself a favor and pick up a pot or two. It will tide you over until your garden comes into bloom.

Check what flower shows are in your area. A new New Jersey flower show called the New Jersey Flower, Garden, and Outdoor Living Show opened in 2003. It is held in Edison at the New Jersey Convention Center late in the month. Very often, the displays of spring bulbs at these events are spectacular.

Exhibitors often use bulbs with enthusiasm. Tricking bulbs to bloom just a bit early may be less difficult than trying to force summer perennials into bloom six months early. It is an excellent opportunity to see named varieties in bloom and the use of different types of garden designs. Taking pictures is certainly helpful when you are trying to duplicate a look or remember the exact color of the 'Angelique' tulip you fell in love with. Keep in mind that weekday attendance is down compared to weekends and so is better for garden photography.

## PLANTING

The planting of bulbs is still restricted to indoors, but that is no reason to slow down on regular plantings of **paper-white narcissus** or even some others such as **calla lilies, amaryllis,** or **clivia** if you can find them.

It is also time to bring out bulbs you may have been chilling for the prerequisite eight to ten weeks. You should move them into strong sunlight and give them a drink. Take care not to waterlog the soil. With just a little attention to their needs, they should begin to pop up in no time.

Give potted bulbs the sunniest location possible. Once the buds are about to open, move the plants into indirect sun to preserve the flowers. Once the flowers fade, move them back to the sun.

## WATERING

Certainly over-watering is the quickest way to kill almost any plant, especially those in pots. Since many bulb pots do not have drainage, the risk is even higher. Bonzai pots almost always have drainage and usually come with matching saucers. They are very adaptable as bulb pots. All bulbs store some water, so if you're uncertain, it's always better to wait a day than risk root rot. Even so, if bulbs get overly dry the flower buds can dry up. **Think moist** and you should be okay.

## FERTILIZING

Spring-flowering bulbs or the tender paper-whites that you force indoors are not worth fertilizing. Once they finish blooming, they generally get added to the compost pile. Potted bulbs that you intend to keep as houseplants or plant in the garden once the weather breaks will do better if fed on a regular basis. A diluted water-soluble fertilizer used every time you water is a good approach, or you can follow the once-a-month application with a more concentrated solution. Be sure to follow the directions on the fertilizer you choose.

# PRUNING

Remove flower stalks at the base when all the flowers have faded so the drying stalks do not detract from any remaining flowers. Be careful not to injure any of the leaves. Once flowering is complete on disposable bulbs, there is not much point in keeping the plants around. The foliage will stay attractive for a while, but when the foliage begins to yellow or get floppy, these plants tend to lose most of their appeal.

If you intend to keep the bulbs, especially if you want to attempt to keep outdoor bulbs that have been forced in pots (such as **tulips, daffodils,** or **crocus**), you need to move the pots into the strongest sun you have indoors immediately after pruning away the flower stalks.

# PESTS

Pests are rarely a problem on forced bulbs since they are indoors such a short time and then become compost fodder.

**Scale** and **mealy bugs** both can show up on **amaryllis,** but wiping off the leaves with a soapy paper towel is usually sufficient to give control. Never spray an insecticide while the plants are in bloom. If you really want to keep a potted bulb plant and washing is not sufficient, isolate the plant and hose it down with a strong spray of water. Once the weather breaks and you can treat the plant outdoors, use an appropriate insecticide according to label directions.

Outside it is still too cold for insect pests on just about anything, so your bulbs are safe for a while yet.

# NOTES

_____

_____

_____

_____

_____

_____

_____

_____

_____

_____

_____

_____

_____

# MARCH
## Bulbs

## PLANNING

By this time, you should have a good idea of what summer bulbs you want. Evaluate what you have in storage. Discard anything soft or moldy. Bulbs or tubers that survived the winter in excellent condition may warrant being divided. Divide those you intend to pot now. Those you intend to use to expand the garden or give away can wait to be divided at planting time. Those that did not fair so well will need to be replaced. Plan to move things around in the garden. You shouldn't plant the same plants in the same spot, year after year. It is asking for a pest problem.

The Philadelphia Flower Show is always in early March. Plan on attending. It is one of the greatest flower shows in the world.

## PLANTING

While it is still too early to plant bulbs outdoors, you certainly can get a head start indoors by potting up many bulbs and their close relatives now. Always use a good quality potting soil with plenty of drainage. These are just a few of the many bulbs that may bring great joy to your garden in the summer, or sooner if you start now:

**Tuberous begonias** get planted now with the hollow side up and the upper surface just above the soil line. If you intend to leave them in the pot, choose a pot where they will be comfortable all summer, about 8 inches in diameter. A smaller pot will do fine if you intend to move them into the garden. Keep at room temperature in a sunny location. Outside they prefer some shade during the summer, but indoors in March they want all the sun they can get.

**Cannas** are related to bananas (hence their enormous leaves). They will produce flowers all summer with a little deadheading. Start them in pots now, but transplant them later into a very large container or right into the ground. Give them lots of sun while they are getting started, and in the garden too.

**Alstroemeria** is probably more easily recognized on the table of your favorite restaurant than in your garden, but this summer bulb is often planted outside with the pots sunk in the garden, and then the pots are stored dry over the winter. If you have some of these, March is the time to bring them back to life. Don't repot until absolutely necessary. They do best when a bit potbound.

**Caladiums** are tuberous plants that are prized for the blast of color the foliage brings to shady nooks. This plant can spend its life in a pot—stored for the winter and sunk in the ground in summer. Tubers can also be potted up and kept at room temperature in a sunny location indoors or in a greenhouse in a bit of protection from strong sun. Humidity is beneficial.

**Calla lilies** will also benefit from an early start, although direct planting later in the season is fine. Use a rich soil and locate in a very sunny location indoors, but blazing sun in greenhouse may be a bit much. You want them a little cooler than room temperature to get them started.

Some summer bulbs have very specific requirements, but planting instructions are usually supplied. If you get them from a friend, be sure to get as much information as possible about planting time, soil and light preferences, and storage requirements.

## WATERING

In general, bulbs need good quality potting soil with good drainage. The soil needs to be moist enough to wake up dormant bulbs. Soggy soil causes root rot rapidly. Sometimes soil that has been stored becomes so dry that it becomes **hydrophobic.** That means it actually repels moisture. You will see little pools of water on the soil surface. It is better to pre-moisten soil when that happens to overcome hydrophobia before planting. Allow hyrdrophobic potted bulbs to sit in a saucer of water until the soil soaks all the water up. Continue to add water to the saucer until water still remains after thirty minutes. Then pour out the excess water.

After initial potting and wetting of the soil, allow the soil to get dry to the touch but never bone dry. Then rewet thoroughly and allow to drain properly.

##  FERTILIZING

Potting soil generally has a kick of fertilizer in it, so it is usually not necessary to fertilize at planting. Once green leaves emerge, begin a regular application of water-soluble fertilizer for flowering plants. While the bulbs are in containers, a diluted solution used every time you water reduces the chance of burning.

Apply 5-10-5 or 5-10-10 fertilizer to foliage of spring-flowering bulbs such as **camassia, tulips, crown imperials, daffodils,** and **hyacinths** as they emerge. A water-soluble fertilizer can also be used.

## PRUNING

Prune any dried up portions of tubers you bring out of storage. Sometimes

## Helpful Hints

*1* Tender bulbs will need to be stored over the winter. It may be easier to plan for this early and plant them in clay pots, large enough for when the plant is in full leaf. These pots can be sunk in the ground. This way all you have to do is pull up the pots in the autumn.

*2* Outside, early bulbs will be in full swing by the end of the month. Be sure to look for **crocus, snowdrops, winter aconite, reticulated iris, spring beauties,** and **glory-of-the-snow.**

what looks like a disaster may still be redeemed with careful pruning. It is essential to retain an **eye** or growing point on every piece you salvage. Some plants, like **cannas,** produce an eye at the end of a bulbous root (really a rhizome), so even a small piece is likely to grow eventually. Some bulbs, such as the **lily,** or corms, such as **gladiolus,** will produce small bulbs or small corms at the base. These can be salvaged even if the mother bulb has deteriorated.

Division of tubers or rhizomes is really much the same, but you get to plant all the pieces.

## PESTS

Be sure to protect the parts you intend to keep by dusting the tubers, bulbs, corms, or rhizomes with bulb dust to prevent rot.

## NOTES

# APRIL
## Bulbs

## PLANNING

The garden is in full swing. Small, early bulbs such as **crocus** or **snowdrops** may still be in bloom, but your **daffodils** should be at the peak of their glory. Early **tulips** will overlap with late daffodils. Take lots of pictures for future reference, especially if you see something you like in other gardens.

Spring bulb catalogs will begin arriving in the mail just as the bulbs are blooming. Find that magical tulip that caught your eye while it is still fresh in your mind.

Check out fall-flowering hardy bulbs such as Autumn Crocus (not really a true crocus but a member of the Colchicum species), fall blooming true crocus, hardy **cyclamen,** and **sternbergia,** (a bright yellow relative of the **amaryllis**). You will want to order these for early August or September planting.

## PLANTING

Now is the time to start your **dahlias** and your **colocasia** indoors. Both need warm temperatures and will do better if eventually transferred directly into the garden. Wait until late May for planting out. Meanwhile, find a warm spot in your home where temperatures stay about 70 degrees Fahrenheit.

**Lily** bulbs can be direct planted in April. Most lilies need a sunny location, but sweet **tiger lilies** can take some light shade. Excellent drainage is a must, so incorporate lots of organic matter during soil preparation. Plant bulbs 6 inches down and 9 to 18 inches apart, depending on the variety.

At the end of April, you can plant **gladiolus** corms and **canna** rhizomes in the garden in all of New Jersey except the coldest mountainous area in the northwest corner. Up there you should wait until early May. Do not transplant sprouted cannas yet if you started them in pots because the foliage will get burned by late season frosts. All danger of frost should be over by the time your direct-planted rhizomes sprout in the garden bed. Plant cannas in moist, well drained soil in lots of sun. Add copious amounts of organic matter. Space about 15 to 18 inches apart and cover with 2 inches of soil. An organic mulch will help maintain soil moisture but is also important to control weeds. Eventually the plants will get so thick that they will shade out most weeds except along the edge of the bed.

Gladious don't mix well with other flowers, so consider a special bed just for them. Definitely choose a sunny location with good drainage. Until the end of July, plan to add corms to the bed every seven to fourteen days to keep a continuous flow of plants in bloom. Improve the soil with lots of compost but avoid manures. Sandy soil is their favorite, but they are not overly fussy. In heavy soils, add compost and sand in a 1:1 ratio. Plant 4 to 6 inches down and 4 to 6 inches apart.

## WATERING

Water everything thoroughly at planting. **Lilies, dahlias,** and **gladiolus** prefer to get slightly dry between waterings, but March planted bulbs and tubers in containers should not be allowed to get completely dry. **Cannas** and **colocasia** both prefer to stay moist but not waterlogged.

If spring is unseasonably dry, a deep watering of bulbs while in bloom will prolong the life of the individual flowers.

## FERTILIZING

In containers of **dahlia** and **colocasia,** use a water-soluble fertilizer in a diluted solution from the time you pot up your roots until they are planted outdoors.

During soil preparation outdoors, you can incorporate 5-10-5 fertilizer into the soil. **Glads** need 5-10-5 fertilizer again when the flowers first show and after bloom. For **cannas,** apply a light side-dressing every two weeks. **Lilies** will benefit from another application of 5-10-5 fertilizer in June.

Plants potted up in March, such as **tuberous begonias, calla lilies, cannas, caladiums,** and **alstroemeria,** will benefit from continued use of a diluted water-soluble fertilizer.

An application of 5-10-5 fertilizer to tall bearded **iris** is appropriate as the new growth emerges. Don't let the fertilizer come in contact with the rhizomes. The same goes for late season **tulips.** Apply fertilizer as soon as the foliage emerges.

## PRUNING

Prune flower stalks of anything that bloomed. Allow the leaves to stay intact for as long as possible. **Crocus** planted in the lawn makes a great display, but try to hold off mowing in that area for as long as possible to avoid pruning the crocus leaves.

Indoors you may want to take a few cuttings from your tuberous **begonias.** It is a good time to root the cuttings to increase your supply.

For trimming and pruning tubers and rhizomes, see the discussion under March.

## PESTS

Control weeds with organic mulch and hand weeding. Some pre-emergent weed prevention materials are safe to use around bulbs. Choose products compatible with both spring- and summer-flowering bulbs. When planting in spring, plant bulbs first, water bulbs in thoroughly, then apply the pre-emergent material.

Scale, mealy bugs, and mites are more likely to be a problem on plants such as **amaryllis** where the bulbs produced flowers indoors over the winter. This month it may be safe to bring the plants outdoors to spray with an appropriate insecticide. Don't leave them out overnight as cold night temperatures may do damage.

Squirrels tend to dig up spring-flowering bulbs. Rabbits and deer will be persistent and generally prefer **tulips** just before they are about to open into full bloom. A fenced in yard with a loose dog will go a long way in keeping away rabbits and deer. Sometimes motion detectors that spray water are helpful. Some deer repellents have moderate success but need to be replaced often.

## NOTES

_____

_____

_____

_____

_____

_____

_____

_____

_____

_____

_____

# MAY
## Bulbs

## PLANNING

May is for planting and enjoying, leaving little time for planning. It's worthwhile to take lots of notes, even just mentally, of things you see that make your heart beat faster. While spring bulbs are peaking, May is the time to plant annuals, many perennials, and your vegetable garden. All those April showers are also making your lawn grow like crazy, so anything you can postpone until after spring will free up a few minutes to take care of something else. While you are sipping iced tea (with mint from the garden) in the heat of July, you can review your notes from the comfort of the hammock.

## PLANTING

Break out a new pair of gardening gloves and clean off the trowel. It is time to get down and dirty!! By the end of May, it's safe to say the danger of frost is past, and you can plant all those tender beauties that will simply burst forth with all their color and beauty.

Very few bulbs will tolerate soggy ground, so top-of-the-line soil preparation is in order. If water tends to stand where you want to plant, consider a raised bed to protect your treasures. The incorporation of copious amount of organic matter such as leaf compost and

some sand (especially in heavy clay soils) will be appreciated. Use an organic mulch on top of the soil after planting.

Many bulbs that you started or purchased in pots can be sunk in the ground as is, making pulling the pots for winter storage a much simpler process. Clay pots work better for this as air and moisture can pass right through the sides of the pots. Plastic pots stay wetter and will not be able to absorb moisture from the soil. Burying the pots works well for your **amaryllis,** which benefits from summer sun. Allow it to get used to stronger sun gradually to avoid burning the leaves. You can also direct plant your amaryllis.

The list of summer bulbs that can be planted now is extensive. A few worth considering are **gladiolus, dahlias, calla lilies, colocasia, caladiums, alstroemeria, lilies, crocosmia, tuberous begonias,** and even the wonderful **magic lily** if you can find dormant bulbs. Less common are **gladiolus**-like **acidanthera,** the fragrant **tuberose,** and the exotic looking **gloriosa climbing lily.** If you come across something so unusual that you have no idea what it is, buy one and try it. Chances are, you can do a little research and find out what you need to know. The excitement will be worth a little risk.

## WATERING

As a general rule, water all bulbs thoroughly at planting. Some will want to stay moist, and many will want to get a little dry between watering, but none will be happy waterlogged. Always water in the morning, and deeply. Many bulbs are planted 6 inches below the soil surface, so they will need more than a light sprinkling to ensure the water reaches the roots.

## FERTILIZING

Apply fertilizer during the soil preparation phase. A balanced fertilizer such as 5-10-5 is a good choice. Bulbs send out roots first, so they will benefit from having adequate nutrients in the soil. As a rule of thumb, a second application of fertilizer can be applied during the vegetative (green only) stage, and then again after bloom.

Another option is to use a water-soluble fertilizer according to the directions. You can still include a pre-planting incorporation of 5-10-5 fertilizer during soil preparation and then use water-soluble fertilizer as an alternative to sidedressing during the season.

# PRUNING

By late May, your **daffodils** and **hyacinths** have probably finished, so it's time to remove all the flower stalks. The use of hand pruners eliminates the risk of pulling the bulbs out, but the stems of daffodils snap easily once you get the hang of it. Early **tulips** will have also faded—remove the naked stalks as soon as possible. Not only are they wicked-ugly but also any seed development takes strength from the bulbs.

In spite of how unattractive fading tulip foliage can be, the longer you allow it to ripen, the more energy it returns to the bulb. It's best if you can wait until foliage is yellow. Cut, never pull, tulip foliage; the bulbs come up all too easily.

# PESTS

There are a few insect problems that can show up, but they are not common.

Wildlife continues to be a problem, especially for your tulips. See April for information.

# Helpful Hints

*1* **Tulips** make outstanding cut flowers, but remember that they continue to grow after being cut. It can make doing an arrangement a bit tricky.

*2* Remember where you planted your **autumn crocus, fall blooming crocus, magic lilies,** and hardy **cyclamen,** or you may accidentally pull them as weeds. These fall bloomers send up foliage in the spring without a hint of bloom.

*3* **Camassia** is somewhat less common than many other spring-flowering bulbs. It blooms with late **daffodils** and early **tulips,** but the flowers are very long lived for bulbs. They can be white, but the more common ones are a lovely blue. They return year after year with few demands.

*4* **Crown imperial** is another May bloomer that is worthy of notice. The crown of flowers looks like up-side-down tulips, but the effect is spectacular *and* nothing will eat them. They smell awful.

Bulb maggots can infest **daffodils.** There is usually one maggot per bulb. Bulb mites eat smaller holes, but a general deterioration of the bulb follows. If you see any stunted growth or misformed foliage, dig up and dispose of the bulbs. Plant their replacements in a different location next fall.

**Tulips** occasionally show signs of **Botrytis** (commonly known as gray mold) but usually only in a wet season. Again dig up the bulbs and discard them, but not on the compost pile. You don't want the disease re-infecting your plants next year. Plant healthy bulbs in a different spot next year.

# NOTES

_____
_____
_____
_____
_____
_____
_____
_____
_____
_____
_____

## PLANNING

Three important groups of bulbs step to center stage at this time: **iris, alliums,** and **Asiatic lilies.** Iris is a tricky group to classify. There are Dutch bulb iris that grow from true bulbs, but the more popular tall bearded iris are grown from rhizomes. They are sometimes grouped with perennials but just as often with bulbs, so we will discuss them here. Asiatic lilies are the first lilies to bloom and are extremely easy to grow. Their colors are often intense.

Alliums are **onions**, but the flowering varieties are very beautiful, easy to grow, live for many years, and yes, sometimes smell like onions. *Allium giganteum* is a 5-inch sphere consisting of hundreds of tiny, star-shaped, purple flowers. They are planted in the fall and are at their peak in June.

Tall bearded iris are sometimes planted in the spring, but it is more common to divide the rhizomes after bloom. **The variety of color is spectacular.** Try as you might to arrange the perfect color combination, a mixed-up mass planting of many varieties may be the most beautiful of all. From a distance, however, all one variety may have greater impact.

Asiatic lilies produce vivid patches of color, and the bulbs spread nicely over time. They are very hardy, easy to grow, and go a long way to filling in the "between spring and summer" garden gap.

While not very common, the magnificent **foxtail lily** (*Eremurus*) should not be forgotten. These are long-lived spikes of flowers that can reach 9 feet. They also bloom during the "gap."

## PLANTING

Lily bulbs can be planted in fall or early spring from dormant bulbs, but if you find **Asiatic lilies** in bloom, you can just pop them in the ground. Follow basic rules regarding good soil preparation and drainage.

You may want to continue planting patches or rows of **gladiolus** (see April for instructions).

It is possible to divide **iris** while in bloom, but it's best if the rhizomes are left undisturbed. Relax, you can cut out a rhizome if your best friend falls in love with one of your irises and you feel the need to send her home with one. These things happen, and irises are more cooperative than many other plants.

Iris need excellent drainage, a sunny location, and are generally planted in mounded beds. Thorough soil preparation with the incorporation of a great deal of organic matter is recommended.

## WATERING

Established iris are very drought tolerant, but if the ground becomes excessively dry, I recommend a soaker hose to avoid getting moisture on the leaves, thus preventing disease.

Do not ignore the foliage of spring bulbs that have finished blooming. **The foliage replenishes the bulbs for next year's flowers.** Try to keep the leaves healthy for as long as possible. Keep an eye on tender bulbs in containers. They tend to dry out quickly.

Overhead watering may miss pots of bulbs sunk in the ground, especially if the foliage is lush. Make sure that water applied actually gets to the pot. **Cannas** and **colocasia** both prefer deep watering with the soil staying constantly moist. Most other summer bulbs have moderate water demands, but don't let them get bone dry.

# FERTILIZING

To help the foliage replenish the bulbs, fertilize your late season spring-flowering bulbs as soon as they finish blooming. Use 5-10-5 or 5-10-10 fertilizer or a water-soluble fertilizer according to directions.

# PRUNING

Be sure to remove flower stalks from all spring-flowering bulbs after the flowers fade. **Daffodil** leaves can be snapped off as they yellow. **Don't trim them or tie them with rubber bands.** If the leaves can't photosynthesize light into energy then they cannot replenish the bulbs to make next year's flowers. Wait to prune **tulip** leaves when they are mostly yellow. Or at least wait as long as possible. In general, wait as long as you can to remove leaves on bulbs. Use hand pruners for less risk of pulling the bulb with the stem.

**Lilies** are more likely to set seed than other bulbs. Prune away the cluster of faded flowers just below where the flower stems branch out. The tall center stalk with the many short sword-like leaves will live for some time. This is not a problem if mixed with other plants as the foliage is rather attractive.

## Helpful Hints

*1* For cut flowers, choose an **iris** stem with several buds and the first flower open. The individual flowers are not long lived, but the buds will open over several days in a vase.

*2* You may not want **alliums** as cut flowers unless you know the ones you have won't make your house smell like onions. However, alliums are attractive as dried flowers, too. After they have dried on the plant, you can remove them carefully for indoor use. By then they will have lost their onion scent.

# PESTS

I recommend dipping iris divisions in a **10 percent solution of chlorine bleach** to prevent disease. Allow the rhizome to dry for several hours, out of sunlight, before planting.

**Alliums** are mostly pest free. **Lilies** have few problems, but gray mold, Botrytis, will sometimes affect young shoots. If the shoots die back, remove them. It is possible that the bulbs will recover the following year, but you may want to spray preventively with an appropriate fungicide as soon as new growth emerges.

The biggest problem you may have to face this month is iris borer. **Larvae hatch from April to June** and burrow into the leaves first and the rhizomes later. The leaves with holes and oozing can be removed, but once the borers get into the rhizome it is necessary to resort to more serious insecticides. Check with your County Cooperative Extension office for current recommendations. The borer leads to a bacterial rot, which is even more destructive and smells terrible. Rotted portions of the rhizome need to be removed and the healthy part treated to control the disease.

# NOTES

_____

_____

_____

_____

_____

_____

_____

_____

_____

# JULY
## Bulbs

## PLANNING

By July you need to be in full swing planning for fall planting of spring bulbs. You also need to plan space for fall-blooming bulbs.

If you are really interested in doing a mass planting of a single anything (for example, a formal bed of 200 red **tulips**) or if there is a stunning new variety out, order early. You may be able to put in an order through your local nursery if it will be carrying what you need. Many bulb catalog companies put a July 31 deadline to early buying discounts.

Fall-flowering bulbs get planted in August or early September, so do not delay in planning and purchasing. Finding a spot may be tricky once the garden is full of summer annuals. One suggestion: Pull your **pansies** as summer heat takes its toll, and save these spots for planting autumn-flowering bulbs.

By this time, most of the leaves from spring bulbs will be ready to remove. Note: If you intend to divide or add bulbs in the fall, you will need to know where it is safe to dig. Before the last leaves get yanked in July, come up with a plan. If you have many bulbs and only intend to add a few, mark the areas where there are no bulbs.

## PLANTING

One approach to propagating **iris** is to make your divisions immediately after bloom. For many varieties, that would be early July. For an older planting, you will want to dig up the entire clump. Divide healthy rhizomes that have either a single (a straight rhizome) or double fan of leaves (a Y-shaped rhizome). Trim the fans to about 4 inches. Dispose of older, woody rhizomes and anything soft or damaged. The smaller the division, the longer the planting will take to rebloom. Larger divisions have to be divided again that much sooner. Find the balance that works for you. See June for planting techniques.

Another bulb that can be planted in July is the wonderful **Magic Lily**, *Lycoris squamigera*. In July, the bulbs are completely dormant. This relative of the amaryllis will not bloom until August or September, but its behavior is nothing short of magical. Stalks will appear with a total absence of leaves, then a cluster of tubular, deep pink flowers will burst out like a pink explosion. Magic lily likes sun but will tolerate some shade. Choose a permanent spot—they do not like to be moved. Space 5 to 8 inches apart and 5 inches down.

Make sure you get the last of your **gladiolus** in the ground by the end of the month. The middle of the month is better, but glads can be flexible . . . to a point.

Check April for planting directions.

## WATERING

By July, temperatures can be soaring and rain nonexistent. If that is the case, you will need to water deeply at least once a week. **Iris** are drought tolerant, but **cannas** and **colocasia** will not perform to expectation without adequate moisture. Taller **Aurelian hybrid lilies** will bloom this month. They will need an occasional deep watering, but try not to use overhead sprinklers as lilies are somewhat prone to gray mold.

Anything in containers will require more attention to watering. Planters crammed with plants for a lush tropical look may need to be watered daily. Check soil moisture often, and water deeply at the first sign of drooping.

## FERTILIZING

As a general rule, do not apply fertilizer when temperatures are above 85 degrees Fahrenheit. You can fertilize with a dilute solution of water-soluble fertilizer if you get a break in the weather. Side-dressing with granular fertilizer is too risky in the heat. It may still be sitting there, ready to burn your roots, when the temperature goes up again.

# PRUNING

Remove flower stalks as the flowers fade. Bulbils can be removed from the stalks of **Asiatic lilies** as they appear and can be replanted to increase your lily supply. This process will give exact genetic duplicates of the plant from which they came. Not all lilies provide this service, but when they do, it makes propagation a cinch.

Smaller **dahlias** will be in bloom by now. Remove fading flowers. Pinch or lightly prune for shaping. Tuberous **begonias** may also benefit from the occasional pinching, especially if grown in lower light. Cuttings root easily.

# PESTS

Continue to monitor iris for iris borer and its follower, bacterial rot. See June for information.

By July, Japanese beetles are out. They particularly like **canna** leaves but will eat a wide range of plants. Handpick whenever possible. Severe infestations may require an insecticide. Check with the Cooperative Extension Office for current insecticide recommendations.

Powdery Mildew may be making its first appearance this month. It, too, can appear on a wide variety of leaves. Of the summer bulbs, **dahlias** may be the most susceptible to this. A strong brew of chamomile tea is said to have some effect in controlling powdery mildew. Try 3 to 4 bags per pint of water. Cool and apply with a hand sprayer. Repeat daily for a serious infection and once week for continued prevention. If the problem persists, you may need a fungicide. Contact your Cooperative Extension Office for current recommendations.

## Helpful Hints

*1* Cut flowers will last longer if you gather your flowers in the early morning. Better yet, water deeply early one morning and cut your flowers early the next day.

*2* The tall Aurelian hybrid lilies that bloom in July often need staking. The flowers are so heavy that they can weigh down the stalks, especially after a rain.

*3* You can use inexpensive tomato cages to mark where space for bulbs is available. Cut the straight wires on a conical cage so you end up with three circles with three "legs" each. Trim the legs to about 4 inches. Place the circles in areas where you intend to plant. You can cover them with mulch so they are not unattractive. If you only have a few bulbs in an area and intend to add many, use the same wire circle over existing clusters of bulbs, exposing the rest of the ground for planting.

*4* Plan on purchasing some of your bulbs locally. It is important to support local growers because they are the true plant lovers that will be there when you need them.

## NOTES

_____

_____

_____

_____

_____

_____

_____

_____

_____

_____

_____

_____

_____

# AUGUST
## Bulbs

## PLANNING

By this time, you should have a good idea of the performance of your summer-flowering bulbs. Make notes of those hardy summer bulbs that will benefit from division. Separating the bulbs gives the individuals room to reach blooming size once again. Most of these get divided in the fall along with spring-flowering bulbs. Hardy summer bulbs that would fall into this category include **lilies, crocosmia, and iris** (if they haven't been divided by then). Even those that don't require division can often be divided in the fall if you just want to increase your supply. Remember, a picture is extremely helpful when planning the layout for next year.

## PLANTING

There are a number of bulbs that can get planted in August. One is the pretty, petite, Dog-toothed **violet,** *Erythronium americanum.* It prefers not to be divided, but if you must, do it now and replant immediately. Plant purchased bulbs immediately, as they dry out quickly. Choose a moist, woodsy soil where it won't get overly dry. Dog-toothed violet prefers light to moderate shade.

Two species of **snowflake** can be planted in August: *Leujocum vernum* (spring snowflake) and *L. autumnale* (autumn snowflake). The autumn-blooming species may not bloom this year. To be sure of fall bloom, it is better to plant in the spring. The spring snowflake will tolerate light shade. The autumn version prefers sun. Plant 2 to 3 inches deep. **Autumn crocus** (*Colchicum*) and **fall-blooming crocus** (*Crocus*) can both be planted in August for blooms in September or October.

Wear gloves when handling **colchicum** since the toxic drug colchicine is derived from the plants. Plant 3 to 4 inches deep in well-drained soil in light shade. Flowers appear in September to October, foliage in spring.

There are several species of hardy fall-blooming crocus for New Jersey Gardens. Those hardy throughout the state, even to Zone 5 in the cold northwest, include *C. cancellatus* (white or lilac), *C. zonatus* (rose-lilac), *C. longiflorus* (bright lilac), *C. ochroleucus* (cream and orange), and *C. speciosus* (light blue). The famous **saffron crocus,** grown for the stigma which is the expensive spice, is hardy to Zone 6 and so can be grown in most of the state. Plant about 4 inches down in full sun.

Hardy **cyclamen,** *C. neapolitanum,* is best planted early in the month, in light shade. Space the tubers 6 to 8 inches apart and about 2 inches down. Use soil with significant amounts of compost. The delicate pink blooms appear in October, and the heart-shaped foliage, streaked with silver, unfolds in spring.

## WATERING

Water bulbs deeply after planting. Warm soil with adequate moisture encourages rapid growth of flowers on the fall-blooming varieties as well as root growth on those planted or transplanted for spring bloom.

Apply an occasional deep watering to summer bulbs with foliage if the weather is hot and dry. Late-planted **gladiolus** will need moisture to grow and bloom before frost. **Dahlia** blooms will last significantly longer if properly watered. Avoid overhead sprinklers.

If it doesn't rain, moisture-loving bulbs such as **cannas** and **colocasia** depend on weekly deep watering to look their best.

Containerized bulb plants that have grown all summer are probably jammed in their pots by now. Hot August days will see them wilting rapidly. Water thoroughly, making sure the entire pot receives a drink. Overly dry soil will repel moisture, so if the soil became excessively dry, allow the pot to sit in water until it drinks its fill. Then dump the excess.

##  FERTILIZING

It may be beneficial to use water-soluble fertilizer according to directions. Non-hardy plants, such as **begonias** and **dahlias,** that continue to put out flowers all summer may need the boost as soil nutrients are drained. Hardy bulbs that have finished their bloom, such as **crocosmia** and many **lilies,** need the nutrients for the foliage to replenish the roots for next year. Even summer bulbs that have finished, such as **calla lilies** or **Peruvian daffodils,** will benefit from an application of water-soluble fertilizer as long as the heat is not excessive.

##  PRUNING

Some plants, such as **lilies,** make seed pods readily. Prune the dead flowers unless you intend to propagate your bulbs from seed.

Some early summer bulbs may go dormant by later this month. The early **Asiatic lilies** may have died back by now. Remove the stalks with a hand pruner to avoid yanking out the bulbs. Bulbs can be replanted immediately if that happens, but it is a nuisance easily avoided.

**Cannas** will produce flowers all summer, up until frost. Even the spherical seed pods are interesting, but they get ugly as

# Helpful Hints

*1* **Gladiolus** do not have to stay in the ground until frost. They require six weeks of regeneration time after bloom. The first plantings of corms that bloomed in early July can be removed in late August. This may make room for early **mums** or other September-planted flowers.

*2* Giant **dahlias** often do not come into bloom until late July or early August. The large flowers require large plants to support the massive blooms. Once flowers begin to open, the plants may require staking.

they dry. Remove them very carefully with hand pruners. The next flower stalk is often hidden beneath the sheath of the faded flower.

**Caladium** leaves suffer in summer heat. Remove those that are unattractive.

##  PESTS

Cooler temperatures and moisture on the leaves encourage the production of powdery mildew. Handpick or spray Japanese beetles with an appropriate insecticide. Check with your County Cooperative Extension Office for current control recommendations.

In a wet summer, slugs are a problem, especially in a shady garden. To handpick them, wear gloves and look for them at night with a flashlight. **Caladiums** are probably the most likely to suffer, but with lots of mulch and lots of rain, slugs can be found at the base of many plants. Pull back the mulch

away from plants. Fill a 1-pound coffee can ⅓ full with beer and sink the can up to rim. Replace the lid after cutting a 1-inch-square hole in the center. Remove slugs when they drown. (At least they drown happy!)

## NOTES

_____

_____

_____

_____

_____

_____

_____

_____

_____

_____

_____

# SEPTEMBER
## Bulbs

 ## PLANNING

By September, you need to have all your **tulips** in a row (in your mind at least). Nurseries and garden centers will have enormous displays of bulbs for sale. In many cases, the displays are open cartons, and you can sort through and pick individual bulbs. Look for firm, undamaged bulbs without any nicks, soft spots, or mold. **Daffodils** are sometimes sold with "double-noses." Those are good choices since you will get one flower per nose. Shop early as handling sometimes causes the noses to break off.

Always plant a number of spring bulbs together. You will need to plant a lot of smaller bulbs such as **crocus** or **windflowers** together to have impact. Eventually, they will spread and create a sea of color, but that takes time. Two or three alone will likely get lost in the shuffle. For larger-flowered species such as tulips or daffodils, plant small clusters in odd numbers. It has a more balanced appearance. If you're planting more than about nine though, it doesn't really matter if it's even or odd.

Avoid straight rows. Soldier-straight rows of tulips look fine unless the third and eighth ones are missing. Then your eye is drawn to the gaps rather than the flowers. Staggered rows reduce the risk of disappointment.

Daffodils for naturalizing can be ordered at bargain prices by the case or bushel. Planted in a field or in and about the edge of a deciduous wood, they can spread and be happy without much fuss. Closer to the house in a more formal look, feature some of the doubles or even collect the pink-cupped varieties as a treat for yourself and your friends.

Remember that critters favor tulips and dislike daffodils. Spring bulbs that escape munching include the spring (*Leucojum vernum*) **snowflake, fritillarias, hyacinths, grape hyacinths,** and **alliums.**

 ## PLANTING

Plant very early any fall-blooming bulbs that you didn't get planted in August. See last month for a list. It is not too late, but don't waste any time if you want to enjoy the flowers this year.

As a rule, the earlier in the spring your bulbs are supposed to bloom, the earlier in the fall you should plant them. *Galanthus* sp. (**snowdrop**), *Crocus* spp., *Eranthis* (**winter aconite**), and the tiny *Iris reticulata* are the first to bloom and so should be the first in the ground.

Your **summer snowflake,** *L. aestivum*, should also be planted in September, although it is a summer bloomer. Plant 4 to 5 inches down and 4 inches apart. It will tolerate light shade.

Planting depths vary from species to species. **Snowdrops** should be 3 inches down and 3 inches apart. **Crocus** is better 4 inches deep and 4 inches apart. *Iris reticulata* is 4 inches apart and 3 inches down. Winter aconite should only be 2 inches deep and no more than 3 inches apart.

September is also another excellent time to divide your tall bearded **iris**. The choices are immediately after bloom, approximately six weeks after bloom, or in September. See June for planting information.

## WATERING

Stop watering your **amaryllis** now. The bulbs require a rest to have the best chance of blooming again. Those planted directly in the ground will get rain, but pots sunk into the ground can be pulled up and put under shelter.

**Winter aconite** tubers will benefit from an overnight soaking in warm water prior to planting. Water all bulbs after planting to make sure the bulbs are firmly set in the ground. After the heat of summer, the ground is often very dry; however, ground-drenching rains often occur in early September. Once that happens, it is usually not necessary to water again unless it is an unusually dry autumn. If the ground stays dry or dries out again, water deeply to encourage a deep root system on your bulbs. Roots grow in the fall, and you want a well-established root system for the plants to endure long term.

 FERTILIZING

Stop fertilizing all tender bulbs, as they need to begin to rest for winter storage.

Incorporate compost, bone meal, and fertilizer into the soil during preparation for bulbs being planted now. The use of 5-10-5 fertilizer is fine to give bulbs a good start. Bone meal applied beneath the bulbs acts as a long-term fertilizer. It releases nutrients for the bulbs to use as the bone meal decomposes. **Acid soils will benefit from an application of lime,** but a soil test is required for precise rates.

 PRUNING

Continue to prune away developing seeds on **cannas.** Take care not to cut the stalk below the next emerging flower spike. New flowers, somewhat hidden from view, form beneath the sheath of the previous bloom.

Prune away all faded blooms, browning foliage, and developing seeds. Some pruning of leggy branches may be in order on **dahlias** or tuberous **begonias** just to keep them looking tidy. Prune judiciously as you do not want to encourage a great deal of new growth on these plants that will be going dormant next month.

 PESTS

Any pests on plants you intend to bring indoors, such as tuberous **begonias** or **caladiums,** need to be controlled outdoors to prevent them from jumping over to your houseplants. Pest control indoors, especially in the winter, is a messy, unpleasant business and best avoided. Mites, mealy bugs, scale, and possibly white fly can all make an appearance. The use of insecticidal soap, even as a precaution, is one approach. If any of these pests occur in large numbers, you may need to resort

**Helpful Hints**

*1* Choose a location for very early blooming springs bulbs where you can appreciate the show from a window or as you walk to your car.

*2* For a special treat, fill your lawn with **crocus** bulbs, giving your yard an entirely different look. Just make sure you delay mowing until the foliage has had a chance to replenish the bulbs. Usually by the time the lawn needs mowing, the leaves are fully or almost fully matured.

to something stronger. Be certain the material you choose is labeled for **both the insect and the plant in question.** Spraying a single leaf as a test is also a good idea.

NOTES

_____

_____

_____

_____

_____

_____

_____

_____

_____

_____

_____

# OCTOBER
## Bulbs

## PLANNING

October is the month to take your plans and put them into action. Local plant suppliers start out with an enormous selection of bulbs at the beginning of the month, but this will dwindle. Make your purchases early.

You may want to do some planning for indoor winter blooms. Hardy bulbs will require a cold treatment. Allow ten to twelve weeks of chilling for early varieties and sixteen weeks for late-season varieties. Temperatures of 50 degrees Fahrenheit for the first three or four weeks will allow for the best development of roots. The rest of the chilling time should be at about 35 degrees Fahrenheit.

## PLANTING

Most hardy, spring-flowering bulbs need a sunny location. The earliest varieties, such as **snowdrops, crocus, winter aconite,** and early **daffodils,** can be planted under deciduous trees as their foliage does most of its growing and food production before the leaves come out on the trees.

Soil preparation is critical for extending their life, as bulbs need excellent drainage and often do not want to

be disturbed for many years. Double digging of new beds is especially important in heavy soils. The addition of a great deal of organic matter will open air spaces in heavy soils as well as hold onto soil moisture (without the ground staying soggy).

Depth and spacing is variety dependent, so follow each variety's planting instructions. The earliest bulbs are generally smaller and planted about 3 inches deep. These would include **glory-of-the-snow, crocus, snowdrops, reticulated Iris** (*Iris reticulata*), and **winter aconite.** Spacing can vary slightly, but 3 inches is a good rule of thumb.

Later blooming bulbs are often larger and planted deeper. These would include **crown imperials, hyacinth, camassia,** and **lilies.** Smaller **narcissus** are planted only 3 to 4 inches deep while the larger flowered varieties go as deep as 5 to 6 inches. A helpful rule is to plant narcissus bulbs 3 times as deep as the bulb is wide. **Tulips** are generally planted 5 to 6 inches deep, but those planted as deep as 10 inches have a better chance of producing larger flowers for more years. Deep planting also allows for easier planting of annuals over the bulbs, thus hiding maturing foliage. Large lily bulbs can be spaced as much as 18 inches apart.

In gardens where squirrels dig up bulbs, consider covering the planting with

large-gage chicken wire. The leaves will come up right through the fencing. Cover the wire with an organic mulch to keep it from looking ugly.

Hardy bulbs in containers require a loose, high quality potting soil. Wide, shallow bulb pots with drainage are generally the best and reduce tipping. You can plant several different kinds of bulbs in a single wide pot, almost touching. One half-inch between is sufficient. **The bulbs should fill the pot,** since an excess of soil around the bulbs will encourage rotting. Small crocus corms can be planted above the larger tulips and daffodils, creating an extended period of bloom. Provide cool temperatures (50 degrees Fahrenheit) for three to four weeks for root development, and chill at 35 degrees Fahrenheit for another six to twelve weeks, depending on varieties.

## WATERING

Water all bulbs immediately after planting, even those in containers, to make sure they become well seated in the soil as well as to ensure that they begin root development. It is usually not necessary to water again unless the autumn weather is exceptionally dry. Properly stored bulbs in pots do not need to be watered again until taken out to begin growth.

##  FERTILIZING

Because of the energy stored in bulbs, bulbs in containers do not need fertilizer. Generally, forced bulbs are not worth fertilizing or keeping as they are unlikely to produce flowers again.

Soil preparation for hardy bulb planting includes incorporation of 5-10-5 fertilizer at a rate of 2 pounds per 100 square feet. The incorporation of bone meal during soil preparation provides nutrients over an extended period of time as the bone decomposes.

##  PRUNING

There should be no need to prune anything on newly planted material.

**Callas, cannas,** and **dahlias** should be cut to the ground as soon as they have been touched with a light frost. Dig up whole clumps of tubers. Shake off excess earth but do not separate or wash. Allow them to dry for several days out of the sun and store in dry peat moss or perlite. Store them at 35 to 50 degrees Fahrenheit in a fairly dry location. Callas need slightly warmer storage temperatures of 40 to 50 degrees Fahrenheit.

**Gladiolus** need six weeks after bloom to develop the next year's corm. Dig up the corms and remove foliage flush with the corm. Allow to dry in a warm, dry location, out of the sun, for about two weeks. Put dried corms in old pantyhose and hang them up for good air circulation at 40 to 50 degrees Fahrenheit.

**Caladiums** and **colocasia** should both be dug up after the first light frost. Shake off the excess earth and allow them to dry out of the sun for about a week. Store in dry peat moss over the winter at 55 to 60 degrees Fahrenheit.

Remove all yellowed **amaryllis** (*Hippeastrum* hybrids) foliage. Store in the dark at about 40 to 50 degrees Fahrenheit.

## PESTS

Discard any spring bulbs with mold or soft spots. Rotate your beds when planting fresh bulbs (i.e. tulips should not follow tulips in the same bed). This helps to minimize disease buildup in the soil.

## Helpful Hints

*1* If you are in the warmer parts of the state or have a sunny protected nook, you may be able to leave some **cannas** in the ground over the winter. Dig up enough, with a few extra just in case, to replant your bed the following spring. Mulch the rest heavily. If they come up the following year, you may have eliminated the chore of digging and storing the tubers in the future. If they do not return, replant and start over.

*2* **Calla lilies** can be planted as winter blooming plants at this time. They will need a summer dormancy and can be started again next fall.

You will have more success with your bulb storage if you **dust the corms, bulbs, and tubers** with a combination fungicide and insecticide.

## NOTES

_____

_____

_____

_____

_____

_____

_____

_____

_____

_____

PLANNING

November planning revolves around getting all your remaining bulbs in the ground. You really can stretch things out until the end of the month, but the longer you wait, the less chance the bulbs will have to develop a sturdy root system before the ground freezes. Late-planted bulbs sometimes only produce leaves the first year. However, they are not worth holding over until spring. You are better off potting up bulbs for indoor forcing than holding them over for spring planting.

It is also a good time to strategize for indoor blooms. Your **amaryllis** bulbs (really *Hippeastrum* hybrids) can be started up again after sixty days of rest. It takes approximately one month from the time they begin to break dormancy until they bloom. If you start a bulb up every two weeks, you can have flowers for most of the winter.

**Paper-white narcissus** also takes about one month to bloom from the time you pot it up. Start the first week in November and pot up a few every two weeks.

 PLANTING

See October planting information for common spring-flowering bulbs. Again, try to get them in the ground as soon as possible within the month. A less common bulb (really a tuber) and one that deserves more attention in New Jersey gardens is the **desert candle** or **foxtail lily.** The genus is *Eremurus*, and there are several species and hybrids that are readily available. They produce flowers in June or July, the tallest of which is *E. robustus*. This one can reach 10 feet, but they are of questionable hardiness in Zone 5. The Shelford hybrids are among the most readily available, and these are hardy throughout the state.

Foxtail lilies don't mind being planted a bit later than other bulbs. Choose a very sunny location but out of the wind. The flower spikes shoot way up, but the foliage stays about 1 foot tall. Foxtail lilies don't like to be moved, so choose your location carefully. Plant 6 inches down but 2 feet apart. Mulch heavily over the winter. Once established with proper winter protection, they will produce flowers for many years.

When starting up your **amaryllis,** hose out some of the old soil and replace with fresh soil. If the bulb has divided, now is the time to separate the bulbs into individual pots. The pot should be 2 to 4 inches wider than the bulb. This allows up to 2 inches of soil between the bulb and the sides of the pot. If you are not dividing, it is usually not necessary to repot. **Amaryllis prefer to be potbound.** Water thoroughly to help it wake up, but wait until growth begins before adding more water. Then place in a very sunny window and keep the soil moist, but never soggy.

**Paper-whites** can be planted in a pot with just pebbles. Space 1 inch apart. Make sure the bottom of the bulb is always above the water line and the developing roots are always in the water. Paper-whites can also be planted in soil. Make sure the nose is above the soil.

 WATERING

For all bulbs being forced indoors, it is best to water thoroughly and then wait until new growth emerges. After that, keep them moist.

Outside, water newly planted bulbs immediately after planting. Bulbs in the garden rarely need water after this. However, be aware of winter drought conditions. In that case, you may need to water, but that is rare.

##  FERTILIZING

Forced spring bulbs, **paper-whites,** and other tender **Narcissus** are not worth fertilizing because they are not worth keeping after they bloom. Bulbs planted outdoors this month should be fertilized during soil preparation with 5-10-5 fertilizer and bone meal.

**Amaryllis** bulbs can be fertilized with a diluted water-soluble fertilizer when watering. **Calla lilies** being grown indoors should receive the same type solution when watering.

## Helpful Hints

*1* By the end of the month, spring bulbs may be available locally for significantly discounted prices. As long as they are firm, they may be worth purchasing for forcing or even planting outdoors if you can get them in the ground quickly.

*2 Ornithogalum caudatum* is the **false sea onion** or **pregnant onion**. It is a tropical relative of hardy *Ornithogalum pyrenaicum* **Star-of-Bethlehem.** The pregnant onion grows almost entirely above the soil. Very long, straplike leaves grow from the bulb and papery onion-like layers peel away from the bulb. Beneath the layers, small bulbs develop and appear as the papery layers slough off. These "babies" can be used to propagate the plant. Starting in the early fall and progressing throughout the winter, the plant produces long stems topped with a long spike of tiny, star-like flowers. The spike continues to produce new blossoms at the tip for months. The ultimate length can be 5 feet long or even more. It's an excellent houseplant for winter flowers.

##  PRUNING

Fall-planted bulbs are still dormant, and those being forced in containers are just getting started. They require no pruning at this time.

If you have enjoyed a tuberous **begonia** indoors for a while, it may be starting to look a little stretched out due to indoor growing conditions. You may want to prune back the branches and root the cuttings. Then cut back on watering the plant to force dormancy.

##  PESTS

Neither bulbs in the ground nor those potted up for forcing indoors should be having any pest problems at this time. Keep an eye on potted material you may have brought indoors. Mealy bugs, mites, white fly, and scale may all show up. The biggest problem will occur if they spread to your other houseplants. At this time of year, the simplest thing may be to remove the foliage and force dormancy. If you are lucky enough to have a warm day, it may be possible to take the plant outside and spray with an appropriate insecticide. Be sure the label lists **both the plant in question and the targeted pest.**

## NOTES

# DECEMBER

 ## PLANNING

Continue to plan for winter flowers indoors. If you have cold storage space, you have the opportunity to continue to pot up spring bulbs for forcing in containers. Without much cold storage, you are limited to the tender *Narcissus* varieties, **amaryllis** (*Hippeastrum* hybrids), **calla lilies, clivia,** or try **freesia** or **alstroemeria** if you want to get daring.

Both **gloxinia** and **cyclamen** are available as houseplants over the winter. Florists' cyclamen have very showy blooms and are full of cheer for dull winter days. The bright red varieties are an excellent alternative or enhancement to the beautiful red **poinsettia,** a holiday favorite. Cyclamen can flower for several months indoors if kept cool, 60 to 65 degrees Fahrenheit, and not overwatered or allowed to dry out. Gloxinia is another tuberous plant that will continue to flower indoors for several weeks. While both are difficult to bring into bloom, they are worth having for the winter color and joy they provide. Consider either of these for your own home or as gifts when visiting during the holidays.

While you are planning, there are other holiday gifts that bulb gardeners will appreciate. Consider the following:

- A bulb planter makes a good gift. This is a device that removes a core of soil in the garden bed for easy placement of the bulbs. There is another device with a similar use that attaches to a power drill and augers out a core of soil. One could say this is for "power planting."

- Pots specific for forcing bulbs tend to be wider than traditional pots but shallower. Decorative bulb pots for the bulb gardener would be appreciated, especially since forced bulbs are often put on display.

- Include decorative stones or those pretty, flat-on-one-side glass marbles for forcing **paper-whites.**

- Most catalog companies offer gift certificates for bulbs.

- Consider a bulb reference book. There are many good ones from which to choose.

 ## PLANTING

**Amaryllis** is a common gardener-gift for most any holiday. It often arrives in a box with pot, soil, bulb, and directions included. Pot these up immediately. Chances are the storage conditions were not ideal through the marketing process, so you do not want to add to the plant's

stress any more than necessary. Sometimes the pots included are not very attractive. You may want to supplement with a decorative pot that enhances the beauty of the plant.

As a general rule, flowers appear about a month after starting up the bulb. Sometimes leaves emerge first and then the flower stalk. Sometimes no leaves appear until the flower is about to bloom. If the leaves fully elongate without any sign of a flower, you probably will not get one. Keep the bulb anyway. With strong sun during its growing season, it should produce a flower for you next year.

Plant another pot or two of lovely **narcissus. Chinese sacred lilies** or the yellow **'Soleil d'or'** are both lovely. **Clivia** are grown much like amaryllis but have more of a sputnik of smaller flowers than the gigantic trumpets of the amaryllis. They are just as spectacular though and so are worth a try.

 ## WATERING

**Amaryllis** need a soil drenching to get them started, but do not water again until you see signs of life. **Tender narcissus** are watered the same way if potted in soil. If in stones or marbles, keep the water level up to, but not touching, the base of the bulbs.

Take care not to over-water the pretty **cyclamen** and **gloxinia** you have for indoor color. They both have tuber-like corms that rot quickly if sitting in water.

## FERTILIZING

Use a diluted water-soluble fertilizer when you water **amaryllis, clivia, gloxinia, cyclamen, calla lilies,** or any tender bulbs you intend to put out once the danger of frost is over. **Tender narcissus** and forced hardy **spring-flowering bulbs** are not worth fertilizing as they will get tossed once they finish blooming.

## PRUNING

Prune away faded blooms on your **cyclamen, gloxinia, clivia,** or any other bulb you have forced, even **paper-whites** and close relatives. When you have several bulbs in a pot, some may bloom later than others, and you do not want dead blooms detracting from those at the peak of loveliness. This is especially true if you have potted different varieties or species in the same pot.

 PESTS

One pest that you need to watch out for is the cyclamen mite. This extremely tiny creature appears beneath the bud scales of developing buds. Both foliage and flowers emerge distorted. The location of the insect offers protection from pesticides making control extremely difficult. Infested plants are best discarded. Once the mite makes an appearance on a **cyclamen,** it can spread to other plants and does notorious damage to **African violets.** This is another reason to get rid of the source of the infestation early. Don't let this scare you away from purchasing a cyclamen, however. These pests are rarely encountered in thriving plants purchased from reputable growers.

## NOTES

_____

_____

_____

_____

_____

_____

_____

_____

_____

_____

_____

_____

_____

_____

# CHAPTER THREE

# Fruits

*Growing fruit is an adventure, but it requires serious commitment to be successful. And yet, one can never underestimate the power of a pie made from homegrown blueberries.*

## A WORLD OF CHOICES

Fruits offer many choices for many tastes. There are tree fruits, which include **peaches, nectarines, pears, plums, apples,** and a few oddballs such as **mulberries, persimmons, pawpaws,** and even **figs.** Brambles include your **raspberries** and **blackberries.** Blueberries grow on bushes as do **gooseberries** and **currants,** but gooseberry plants have thorns like brambles. **Grapes** grow on vines, and so do **hardy kiwis. Strawberry** plants have some vine-like characteristics but fall into a classification all their own. They grow as herbaceous plants that produce runners. The runners have baby plants on the tips that root to the ground.

In most cases, all of the above fruits get planted in the early spring. **Strawberries** are the first to bear fruit followed by **raspberries,** which overlap with **mulberries.** (They taste great all together covered in heavy cream.) **Blueberries** first start to bear in late June and continue through most of August if you have early, mid-season, and late varieties. **Wild cherries** and cultivated cherries bear in late June along with early blueberries. **Gooseberries** and **currants** also bear anywhere from late June until mid-July. Both are long lasting on the vine and will hold ripened on the vine for a week or more in good condition.

**Peaches** and **nectarines** begin in early July, and different varieties continue to bear into September. **Hardy kiwis** have a long growing season since they bear fruit on new growth. Ripe fruits either fall to the ground in September or pluck easily from the vine.

Summer **apples** are early, appearing by late July, and are generally used for pies. An old favorite is the **Starr** apple. These early apples are generally green. In late August, the **Macintosh** begin to be harvested. They tend to be on the soft side but are still enjoyed fresh for baking as well. Macs are followed by **Galas** and **Red Delicious.** The tart, firm, later-season apples like **Winesap** and **Stamen** get harvested in mid- to late October in time for Thanksgiving pie. Newer varieties are even later and require cold weather to initiate ripening and increased sugars. These include **Suncrisp** and **Autumn crisp** as well as a few others.

**Pears** are a later-season fruit with the earliest varieties beginning in late August. Later varieties last until late September. **Persimmons** are not harvested until after a frost, or they are unbearably tart. **Pawpaws** are harvested about the same time.

**Figs** are not really hardy in New Jersey, yet many people make the effort to cultivate them anyway. The traditions of wrapping your fig tree are sometimes handed down from generation to generation.

Figs have two sets of fruit buds. Those that survive the winter, either in the warmer parts of the state or on those plants adequately wrapped, will bear fruit in late August. The second set of buds ripens later and run a neck-and-neck race to finish ripening before the first frost.

**Grapes** are increasing in popularity at an incredible rate. The New Jersey wine industry is making its mark and seems to be particularly successful with its many fruit wines. Grapes can even be used for shade over an arbor. Those that are the hardiest in New Jersey are derived from the native species *Vitis labrusca*.

The **Concord grape,** which is one of the most popular backyard grapes, originated in Concord, Massachusetts around 1840. It is a cross between *V. labrusca* and *V. vinifera*, the **European grape** commonly grown in California. Some vinifera types can be grown in the east, but choose your varieties carefully. All grapes ripen later in the season. The earliest are harvested in late August, but the classic Concord bears in late September.

Production of fruit for the home gardener requires specific attention to the demands of each type. Weather can play an enormous role in your success. Cold springs can kill off flower buds on **peaches, nectarines,** and **plums.** Don't even bother attempting to grow **apricots.** Late frosts will kill off the flower buds more years than not. Weed control in **strawberries** can be a bear, but the fruits picked really ripe out of your garden will probably be among the best you have ever tasted.

Fall-bearing **raspberries** are easier to cultivate since they can be mowed rather than pruned in the early spring. Thornless **blackberries** are worth looking for since blackberries with thorns are brutal. **Gooseberry** thorns aren't any fun either, but you are highly unlikely to experience gooseberries unless you grow them yourself.

## PLANNING, PREPARING, BUYING

As soon as the compost pile thaws, **turn over the pile to expose finished compost at the bottom** of the pile. Having compost as a source of organic matter is the best way to prepare the soil for planting. Prepare the ground thoroughly, adding copious amounts of organic matter to either sandy or heavier soils. In heavy clay, you may want to add some sand as well, but always add organic matter and sand in a 2:1 ratio.

Most fruits like a pH of about 5.5 to 6.5. It may be necessary to add lime during soil preparation in areas where soil pH tends to be low, but **never add lime for blueberries.** They require an acid soil no higher than 5 but will tolerate acidity as low as 3.5. The ideal is 4.5. The only way to really know what is required is to have a soil test.

When you get ready to buy, **there are some pollination facts to remember. Peaches** are self-pollinating, but **apples** will require more than one variety for fruit set. **Pears** are sometimes self-pollinating, but you get better fruit set with more than one variety. Sweet **cherries** generally require cross-pollination, but the tart cherries, generally used for baking, are self-pollinating. Do not underestimate the quality of the fruit for eating fresh just because they are called "tart." Unfortunately, not all sweet cherries are compatible, so be sure the two you purchase are a good match. Some newer varieties are self-fruitful, and these make good pollinators for other varieties. 'Stark Gold' is a universal pollinator that is not self-fruitful, but this variety has the distinct advantage of being neglected by birds.

**Japanese plums** require a pollinator, but since there are compatibility issues

# Fruits

with these, also, choose wisely. **European plums** do not absolutely require a pollinator, but you will get better fruit set if you have more than one variety. The **American plums** are more shrub-like, and probably the best known of these is the **Beach plum.** These are hardy and self-pollinating but very rarely available commercially.

## PLANTING

**Late March or early April is generally the ideal planting time for many things, including fruit trees, blueberries, and raspberries.** You should make sure you will have everything on hand you will need to plant your fruits when the weather breaks. A large bucket, 5 gallons or a little larger, is used to soak the bare-root, dormant trees prior to planting. A pair of sharp hand pruners is used to prune any damaged roots and the branches of newly planted trees. Contact your County Extension Office for space requirements for all the fruits you intend to plant. Familiarize yourself with all the insects and diseases you need to watch out for as well as the appropriate time and materials to control these pests. Timing is everything. Specific planting instructions can be found in this book in the month that action is needed.

## WATERING

If at all possible, keep water off developing fruit. If overhead watering is the only option, be sure to water in the early morning so the fruit dries quickly when the sun comes out.

Water all newly planted fruits deeply if the soil begins to dry. **Figs** will do best with constant moisture as will **kiwi** vines. Young **grapes** need water to get established, but hold off adding water to mature vines until the first hint of wilting. Established fruit trees generally do not require irrigation unless the weather approaches drought-like conditions. Then be sure to water deeply rather than using frequent shallow watering. This is especially true during the month preceding harvest on all fruit trees.

## PRUNING

Thinning of **peaches, nectarines,** and **apples** is often necessary to produce a quality crop of reasonably sized fruit. Peaches and nectarines produce fruit on the underside of the branches. You need to lift the branches to see all the small fruits that are hidden among the foliage. If most of the blossoms set fruit, the result will be an enormous number of golfball-sized fruits that are almost all pit and very disappointing.

Time your thinning of peaches and nectarines to when the fruits are about the size of your thumb. Press your nail into the fruit to see if the pits are hard. Once the pits begin to harden, they will pull away from the limbs more easily. Remove all those fruits that are distinctly smaller or larger than the rest.

**Apples** produce fruits only on the outermost part of the branches. This is why apples are pruned with a central leader and many shorter branches from the trunk. This allows for easy access to the mature fruit.

More pruning information can be found in this chapter, month to month.

## PESTS

Most tree fruits require regular spraying with all-purpose home orchard spray if you want a good harvest. **Apples** that aren't perfect can still make outstanding applesauce. New varieties of tree fruits are being developed with more insect and disease resistance, but the ultimate in varieties that make perfect fruits on their own is still a ways off. All-purpose **grape** sprays are available for home vineyards. Even stuffed grape leaves are pretty wonderful, so you may not care about the fruit quality. Be sure to contact your County Extension Office for a spray schedule.

# Fruits

**Cherries** are prone to root rot. This is one disease that must be controlled from before bloom until harvest with a regular spray program. Damp, rainy, foggy, spring mornings are conducive to the disease getting established.

## OTHER CONTROLS

• Remove all damaged fallen fruits to reduce disease the following year.

• Pull back mulch a bit to minimize slug hiding spots.

• Set out 1-pound coffee cans filled halfway with beer to catch slugs. (A tablespoon of sugar in the beer makes it more appealing to slugs. Apparently they have a sweet tooth, too.) Sink the cans, up to the rim, into the ground. Put the lid back on with a 1-inch square hole cut in the center. Check for and remove drowned slugs daily.

• To discourage birds, dangle aluminum pie tins on strings from stakes. New, metallic streamers are also available that are prettier in the garden, with much the same effect.

Apple maggots begin laying eggs on developing fruits by late June in the southern part of the state. All-purpose home orchard sprays will provide control as part of your spray program, but the use of traps offers helps. Traps of sticky, red apple-like spheres catch the adults and hold them fast. Apparently the adults prefer the red fake apples to tiny green ones. Hang them 4 to 6 feet apart in the tree.

## THEY'RE WORTH IT

Fruits are not the easiest of plants to grow in the backyard, but they are very much appreciated at harvest time. Growing fruit is an adventure, but it requires serious commitment to be successful. And yet, one can never underestimate the power of a pie made from homegrown blueberries.

## Helpful Hints

### When Is a Fruit a Fruit?

*1* Fruits bring to mind the warm, lazy days of summer. A tree-ripened **peach,** all juicy and fuzzy, is a perfect way to slow time as you take a big bite and let the juice run down your chin. Technically, lots of things are fruits that we might not expect.

*2* Fruits can be defined both as a botanical term and for use in food preparation. The "fruit" of a plant is the part that bears the seed, so by definition **tomatoes** and **eggplants** are fruits. However, the household definition suggests it is a vegetable if it is eaten with the principal part of the meal.

## NOTES

_____

_____

_____

_____

_____

_____

_____

_____

_____

_____

_____

_____

_____

# Fruits

## APPLES

Make sure you plant two apples for pollination. The varieties must be compatible. Check with your supplier to get the right combination.

| Early varieties | Mid season | Late |
|---|---|---|
| Paulared | Macoun | Jonagold |
| Royal Gala | Starkspur Ultramac | Mutsu |
| Jonamac | Empire | Suncrisp |

## BLACKBERRIES

Darrow

**Thornless**

| Dirksen | Chester | Black Satin |
|---|---|---|
| Navahoe | Hull | Arapaho |

## BLUEBERRIES

Two varieties required for cross-pollination

| Early | Mid season | Late |
|---|---|---|
| Earliblue | Bluecrop | Jersey |
| | | Coville |
| | | Elizabeth |
| | | Herbert |
| | | Darrow |
| | | Wareham |

## CHERRIES

Requires 2 varieties for pollination

| Sweet, dark | Sweet, white, yellow, or pink |
|---|---|
| Viva | Emperor Francis |
| Summit | Gold |
| Royalton | |
| Blackgold | |
| Hedelfingen | |

**Self fruitful**
**Tart**

| Montmorency | Balaton | Galaxy |
|---|---|---|
| Surefire | Meteor | North Star |

## CURRANTS

| Red | White |
|---|---|
| Red Lake | White Imperial |
| Minnesota | |

## ELDERBERRY

| Adams | Nova | York |
|---|---|---|

## GOOSEBERRIES

| Red | White |
|---|---|
| Poorman | Downing |

## FIGS

| Brown Turkey | Celeste |
|---|---|

## GRAPES

**Table**

| Blue | Red | White |
|---|---|---|
| Glenora | Reliance | Lakemont |
| Venus | Finset | Himrod |
| | Vanessa | |

| Red wine | White wine |
|---|---|
| Baco Noir (FA) | Cayuga White (FA) |
| Concord (A) | Niagra (A) |
| Steuben (A) | Delaware (A) |
| | Catawba (A) |

**FA = French American**
**A = American**

## KIWI

Plant male and female for pollination

Ananasnaja
Dumbarton Oaks
Meader

**Self-fertile**

Issai

## MULBERRY

Requires female to produce fruit. There are generally enough wild mulberries that an additional male is not necessary.

Weeping Mulberry
Illinois Everbearing
Contorted Mulberry

# Fruits

## NECTARINES

| Yellow fleshed | White fleshed | |
|---|---|---|
| Harflame | Crimson Snow | Redgold |
| Rose Princess | Fantasia | |

## PAWPAWS

**Plant two for pollination**

| | | |
|---|---|---|
| Mango | Mary Foos Johnson | Davis |
| Mitchell | Overlease | Prolific |
| Rebecca's Gold | Sunflower | Sweet Alice |
| Taylor | | |

## PEACHES

| Yellow fleshed | White fleshed |
|---|---|
| Flamin Fury PF #5B (E) | Scarlet Pearl (E) |
| Harrow Diamond (E) | Southern Pearl (E-Mid) |
| Redhaven (Mid) | Raritan Rose (Mid) |
| Early Loring (Mid) | Carolina Belle (Mid) |
| Harrow Beauty (Mid) | Blushing Star (Mid-late) |
| Loring (Mid-late) | |
| Redkist (Mid-late) | |
| Madison (Mid-late) | |
| Encore (Late) | |

## PEARS

**Plant two for pollination-but Bartlett and Seckle are not compatible**

| | |
|---|---|
| Bartlett | Anjou |
| Bosc | Aurora |
| Spartlett | Seckle |

## PERSIMMON

**Plant two for pollination**

| | |
|---|---|
| John Rick | Meader |
| Garretson | Early Golden |

## PLUMS, EUROPEAN

**Better pollination is achieved with 2 varieties**

| | |
|---|---|
| Blufre | Stanley |
| President | |

## PLUMS, JAPANESE

**Plant two for pollination**

| | |
|---|---|
| Santa Rosa | Ebony |
| Shiro | Ozark Premier |

## RASBERRIES, RED

| June bearing | Everbearing |
|---|---|
| Reveille | Heritage |
| Titan | Caroline |
| Lauren | Josephine |
| Latham | |
| (Gold) | |
| Goldie | |
| Kiwigold | |
| Anne | |

## RASPBERRIES, BLACK

| | |
|---|---|
| Allen | Bristol |
| Dundee | Lowden |
| Jewel | |

## RASBERRIES, PURPLE

| | |
|---|---|
| Royalty | Brandywine |
| Clyde | |

## STRAWBERRIES

| Early | Mid-season | Late |
|---|---|---|
| Earliglow | Lester | Sparkle |
| | Raritan | Lateglow |
| | Guardian | |

# JANUARY
## Fruits

 PLANNING

In January, the world is too cold to be doing much outdoors. It is a good time to plan and prepare for the tasks ahead.

**Be sure to have your pruning tools in order.** A sharp pruning saw, hand pruners, and long-handled loppers are what you need. They should be sharp and well oiled. Have on hand a pair of insulated work gloves. Pruning on a not-too-cold sunny day is a great way to shake off winter blahs, but even in the sun, hands can get cold quickly.

**Start placing orders.** Fruit trees are generally shipped bare root at the right time for planting, but you will want to place your orders early to be sure to get the varieties you need. Our feathered friends prefer the red **cherries**. The red color is a lot of the appeal even to humans, but if you love cherries and hate battling with the birds for your share of the crop, yellow fruits may be a viable alternative.

Many fruit trees are listed in the chapter introduction, but three less common tree fruits are **persimmon, mulberry,** and **pawpaw.** Persimmons are a North American native with Asian counterparts. The Oriental varieties are not as hardy and not great choices for New Jersey. The North American species, *Diospyros virginiana,* can be found growing wild in New Jersey. In addition to its fruit, persimmons are prized for the dense, dark wood. You will probably need a male and female persimmon to produce fruit, although seedless, self-pollinating varieties exist.

Mulberries are extremely common as wild trees but are rarely if ever found under cultivation. The **red mulberry,** *Morus rubra,* is a North American native. The black, *M. nigra*, and the white, *M. alba*, hail from Asia. All can be found naturalized, although the black is probably the least hardy and so the least common in New Jersey. There are male and females, but many are self-pollinating. A female **weeping mulberry** may be an excellent choice for a small yard as it fills several niches with one tree. Named varieties of mulberry are available for sale, or you can just let one or two wild ones grow. If you enjoy the fruits, **mulberries are a low maintenance fruit tree**—a gift in itself.

**Pawpaws** (*Asimina triloba),* are also North American natives with a very tropical look. You will need two for pollination, but be sure to stick to named varieties for good quality fruits. There is a range in flavors, so fruits from seedlings may be disappointing. Its ripe fruit has an almost custard-like quality with large, brown, bean-like seeds.

 PLANTING

There is no outdoor planting in January, and fruits are not generally grown from seed. Just for fun, though, you may want to start some citrus seeds. The winter fruits are readily available and delicious, so you can start seeds from those you eat. You can encourage germination by soaking the seed for several days (change the water daily), although some sources claim it is best to plant the seeds immediately. Use standard potting soil and plant 1/4 inch deep. Germination may be as fast as seven days or may take up to a month. It can take years, but a healthy citrus plant is capable of bearing fruit in a container. They self-pollinate with the help of bees, so you only need one for a crop.

 WATERING

Water containerized fruit trees when they get moderately dry. This will not be frequent if they are kept cool and dormant, but do not entirely ignore them as they can suffer from "winter drought" if the soil gets bone dry and sits that way for any period of time.

Keep germinating citrus seeds moist.

##  FERTILIZING

No fertilizer is required for fruit trees at this time. Do not even fertilize your containerized citrus in the winter.

##  PRUNING

**Apple** and **pear** trees are both pruned to maintain a central leader, like a Christmas tree. Annual pruning is advised for several reasons. The removal of dead or damaged branches is helpful in preventing disease. Pruning away branches with poor crotch angles minimizes the risk of breakage when limbs are laden with fruit, and removal of suckers balances fruit production.

First remove all dead wood. Then remove one of a pair of crossing limbs as they will damage each other. Limbs pointing straight down should all be removed. Upright branches growing near the trunk should also be removed. Of the young branches growing up, thin where they are too thick. If the leader becomes too tall or bends over, cut to a side limb at the desired height.

*1* It may be worthwhile to put some of the limbs removed from your **apples** and **pears** in a bucket and force early bloom. Use cool water and locate out of direct sun in a cool location. Allow the branches to warm up slowly. As soon as you see color on the buds, arrange them in a vase. Keep a close eye on the water level as these branches will use a lot of water as they wake up.

*2* While growing citrus from seed is fun, seeds from hybrid fruits may result in offspring with a lesser quality fruit. If this is a more serious interest than "just for fun," purchase named variety plants already potted. Fruit production will be sooner and, in all likelihood, better.

## PESTS

Pests are not much of a problem in the winter. Keep an eye on potted citrus as mealy bugs feast on citrus leaves. Wipe leaves with a wet, soft cloth, spray with an insecticidal soap, or check with your Cooperative Extension Office for current pesticide recommendations.

## NOTES

# FEBRUARY

 PLANNING

February is the month to plan for your **small fruits.** Consider **blueberries** for the home garden. They are shrub-like in size and so are easily managed for pruning and harvesting. The flowers are lovely and abundant in spring, and the plants make an excellent hedge.

**Strawberries** easily adapt to a tight spot. Strawberries are shipped bare root and are best planted in early to mid-April. Plan on a spot where there is plenty of sun and excellent drainage. Plant early, mid, and late season varieties to spread out the harvest. Everbearing or "day neutral" strawberries are generally not as successful as the June bearers.

**Kiwi** vines will need a place with strong support. The self-pollinating varieties are less aggressive and will bear fruit sooner but the flavor is not as good. For the other varieties you will need one male for every three females. Kiwis have ornamental value and may be the perfect plant for covering an ugly fence.

**Grapes** are on the rise in popularity as new vineyards seem to be springing up everywhere. The vines require full sun, excellent drainage, and something upon which to climb. When grown up an arbor, they provide shade from summer sun, but the need for long vines will reduce fruit production and quality. When grown primarily for fruit production, vines are trellised on two horizontal wires. Most varieties suitable for growing in this area will not require cross-pollination, but check the variety you select to be certain. Plan on 8 feet between plants in a row.

**Brambles** include **raspberries** and **blackberries.** Brambles need lots of sun and excellent drainage. June-bearing raspberries are delicious but bear on old growth. They require careful pruning in the spring. Everbearers produce some fruits in June, but the bulk of the crop starts in August. Everbearers can be mowed in spring, sacrificing the June fruits but eliminating tedious pruning. Blackberries are not as sweet but are loved for jams, jellies, and baking. Stick with the thornless varieties. They are much easier to manage.

 PLANTING

There still isn't any outdoor planting going on in February. Things pick up in the pruning department, so there is plenty to keep you busy.

 WATERING

Continue to keep container plants moist.

 FERTILIZING

Everything is still sleeping. Let it rest.

PRUNING

Prune **peaches, plums,** and **cherries** when temperatures are above freezing. Cherries do better with a central leader, more like apples. See January for information on pruning apples. Peaches and plums should be pruned to an "open bowl" with three major limbs selected with an open center. This keeps the trees lower for easier management and allows better air circulation and light penetration.

Remove branches that attach to the main trunk with a crotch angle of less than 45 degrees. Choose your **three primary branches** to have an open habit. Once the framework of the tree is established, maintain at a height of 7 to 8 feet. Remove all dead wood, one branch from each pair of crossing branches, all vigorous suckers growing straight up through the center of the trees, and branches that have been pulled down due to the weight of earlier crops. Thin excess suckers. You may also want to cut back on fertilizer to reduce suckering in future years.

When **grapes** are grown up a trellis for summer shade, **you need to leave longer canes,** which will reduce the quantity of fruit. Volumes have been written on the culture of grapes and the production of wine. For options, seek out one of the many dedicated reference books.

Everbearing **raspberries** are easy to prune. Just mow them with the mower set on high. You will lose the June berries, but it is worth the sacrifice for the reduction of work. For June bearers—and if you want the June crop on everbearers—prune out old canes that bore fruit at ground level. Also **remove all diseased, injured, and weak-looking canes.** Prune the rest to 24 to 36 inches. If the patch is overly thick, you may need to thin a bit as well. Aim for 4 to 5 canes per running foot of row.

**Gooseberries** and **currants** can be pruned now. Remove the oldest and weakest wood at ground level. Aim for a total of about 15 healthy canes on a mature plant.

**Blueberries** need to be pruned annually to maintain vigor. Prune one or two of the oldest branches at the base. Then remove all dead or weak smaller branches. Always remove crossing branches and branches growing towards the center. Remove some of the twiggy. fruit-bearing shoots that are 3 inches or shorter.

**Kiwis** should be pruned severely while dormant, on a day when temperatures are above freezing. Fruit is produced on the current season's growth, but that growth must occur on one-year-old wood. Kiwis require a sturdy trellis and are trained much like **grapes,** so a number of trellis systems and plant forms will be acceptable. Establishing a trunk and structure early in the plant's life goes a long way to having fruit in years to come.

**Pawpaws** require little pruning, but you may want to remove dead or damaged branches and any branches growing toward the center, crossing, or otherwise in an uncooperative direction.

## PESTS

Watch for insect infestations on potted citrus. Make sure you have your insect and disease control materials on hand for when the season begins. Spray schedules are available for all home garden fruit crops from your **Cooperative Extension Office.** Request them now so you have them on hand.

## NOTES

_____

_____

_____

_____

_____

_____

_____

PLANNING

By March, your ordering should be complete, and you should be thinking about planting. Late March or early April is generally the ideal planting time for many things, including **fruit trees, blueberries,** and **raspberries.** All require lots of sun and excellent drainage. For disease control purposes, make sure your raspberries are not going in the same ground where you have just raised any of the solanaceous crops such as tomatoes, peppers, eggplants, or potatoes.

If trees or beds are being planted in places that currently are planted in grass or a mixture of grass and wild things, then you are better off killing off the grass prior to planting. Use a glyphosphate total vegetation killer (such as Roundup®) on unwanted sod. **This should be applied when the unwanted sod is actively growing, and two weeks prior to planting your fruit trees.** This type of weedkiller travels through the leaves to the roots and kills the entire plant. You do need adequate lead time for it to be effective.

If the herbicide route doesn't appeal to you, you can smother the sod with old carpeting or heavy black plastic. This is most effective if you start in the fall, but if you start in early March, it will probably have killed off the growth sufficiently by mid-April, which is still in time to plant. Make sure the plants are completely dead and not just yellowed, or they will return from the roots.

 PLANTING

Unwrap trees and bushes as soon as you receive them. Keep roots moist and store at a cool temperature, but above freezing, until you are ready to plant. If you need to keep the plants longer than a few days, you should "heel-in" the plants in moist soil in the shade. That means to cover the roots in loose soil, such as a compost pile, to protect them from drying out. When the planting site is ready and you are ready to roll up your sleeves, soak bare-root trees, bushes, and canes in water for an hour. They can stay in the water up to overnight, but not longer than that. Prune off roots that are dead or damaged. On trees, shorten roots that are excessively long to 15 inches.

Prepare a large planting hole with room for the roots to be spread out in their natural shape. The bud union of grafted trees should be above the soil level. Plant **blueberries** with the lower roots not more than 5 inches below ground; the upper roots need to be covered with about an inch of soil. Plant **raspberries** 2 inches deeper than in the nursery. You can decipher this by looking for the dark line on the canes. Space raspberries 3 feet apart in the row with 10 feet between rows.

Tamp down soil firmly after planting, taking care not to damage any roots.

 WATERING

Water thoroughly after planting.

FERTILIZING

Do not fertilize any of these fruits at planting. Fertilize newly planted trees with 10-10-10 fertilizer after the leaves sprout. For established fruit trees, apply 10-10-10 fertilizer while they're still dormant.

Begin to fertilize **blueberries** eight weeks after planting. Use a 10-10-10 fertilizer, but take care not to over-fertilize as it will burn the roots. Established blueberries are fertilized in late March with 10-10-10 fertilizer at a rate of $1/4$ pound per plant.

For **raspberries,** apply 1 pound of 10-10-10 fertilizer per 100 feet of row, ten days and forty days after planting. Established rasberries receive 2 to 3 pounds of 10-10-10 fertilizer per 100 feet of row, before new growth appears.

One- to two-year-old **grapes** receive ½ pound of 10-10-10 fertilizer in March. Established grapes receive 1 pound in March and the same in May. Apply by hand around the base of the vine, taking care not to apply it too close to the trunk.

Late March is a good time to fertilize hardy **kiwi** vines. Use a 10-10-10 fertilizer. Use only ⅛ of a pound on second-year trees, but each year increase that slightly until the vines receive ½ a pound of fertilizer each spring starting at about five years old.

**Pawpaws** are heavy feeders. An application of 10-10-10 fertilizer once a month from late March through June will encourage healthy growth and heavy fruit production.

## PRUNING

One-year-old **apple** and **pear** trees are pruned to a height of about 36 inches. They don't usually have many side shoots. Two-year-old trees are pruned to ensure a central leader, and side shoots are pruned in half. Remove all side shoots from the trunk that form an angle less than 45 degrees, and remove all branches less than 24 inches from the ground.

## Helpful Hints

*1* Spacing of fruit trees is dependent on the variety and degree of dwarfing provided by the different rootstocks. Know the ultimate height and width of the trees you purchase so you can provide enough space.

*2* **Cherry** trees are often quite large, which makes harvesting the crop difficult. Some New Jersey farmers train them into an open bowl shape to make the fruits more accessible.

*3* **Fig trees** are considered to be deer resistant.

*4* Unwrap fig trees on a warm, cloudy day in late March. Let the tree get used to light gradually. Make sure no bitter cold weather is predicted; otherwise, you can delay unwrapping. However, the sooner you unwrap safely, the better the chance you will have of harvesting a crop.

Prune **peaches, nectarines, plums,** and even some **cherries** to 24 to 30 inches from the ground. Then prune side branches to 2 to 3 buds. On **blueberries,** remove the top ⅓ of growth to help establish a sturdier root system. New **raspberry** canes should be cut back to 6 inches before planting. See February for pruning established raspberries.

March is the right time to prune your **blackberries** since they are a little more susceptible to cold damage than raspberries. Shorten canes to 4 to 6 feet. Prune dead canes off at ground level. Blackberries require a two-wire-type trellis. Attach canes to the trellis in a fan-like configuration.

## PESTS

Be prepared to spray dormant oil on fruits trees early in the month, controlling insect infestations before they start.

## NOTES

_____

_____

_____

_____

_____

_____

_____

# APRIL
## Fruits

## PLANNING

If the ground was not ready to be worked in March or if weekend weather was unsuitable for weekend gardeners to get it all done, early April is still acceptable for planting most fruits.

Keep a close eye on fruit trees as the flowers are beautiful. In general, **peaches, nectarines, plums,** and **cherries** will bloom the first week in April. **Apples** and **pears** follow in about two weeks. This may be slightly later in the colder parts of the state and will, of course, vary somewhat from season to season.

## PLANTING

**Strawberries** are generally planted in the first two weeks of April. Avoid locations where tomatoes, peppers, eggplants, or potatoes were recently planted. Strawberries require plenty of sunshine and excellent drainage. An ideal spot is on the top of a hill or on a gentle slope. Strawberry blossoms are vulnerable to late spring frosts. The function of the hill or slope is to allow the coldest temperatures to settle below the strawberry beds, providing an element of protection from cold damage.

**Strawberry** plants are spaced 24 inches apart in the row; allow 3 to 4 feet between the rows. When planning your beds, keep in mind you will need to be able to reach the center of the beds to pick berries. An easy reach will also make any hand weeding easier. Beds that you can access from both sides allow more flexibility.

Prepare the soil at least 8 inches deep, but hard clay would benefit from double-digging. Add organic matter, from the compost pile if you have one, and some sand if the soil is high in clay. When sand is added, **always mix in organic matter and sand in a 2:1 ratio.** Place the plants so the roots are slightly spread out but go downwards without curling or bending. Check carefully to be certain you are placing the plants at the correct depth. The center bud needs sun, but the roots need to be covered in soil.

**Grapes** can sometimes be planted in March, but you are better off waiting until early April in most years. The ideal plant is a good quality one-year-old vine. Grapes, like **strawberries,** prefer a gentle slope to minimize frost damage. Choose a high spot in your yard that receives full sun to locate your grapes. Heavy clay soil needs a great deal of amending to ensure adequate drainage. Sandy loam soils are best. Add lots of organic matter and some sand to lighten up heavy soil.

**Keep grape roots moist, even during planting.** Wet burlap placed over the roots will protect them until they get in the ground. Prune away injured roots. Dig a hole in the prepared ground that is deep enough to accommodate the roots. The roots should be gently spread and not cramped. Plant the vine 1 inch deeper than it was in the nursery. Tamp down the soil gently as you fill the hole. Put a stake in the ground to support new shoots as they grow. Space vines 8 feet apart. If you have enough to plant more than one row, space rows 10 feet apart.

## WATERING

April is the rainy season, so no watering should be needed. However, always water-in newly planted material to help the soil fill in the air pockets and to get roots established.

## FERTILIZING

**Strawberries** will not need fertilizer until June. Do not fertilize newly planted **grapes.**

# PRUNING

Prune away all the flower blossoms on your newly planted **strawberries.** This will direct plant energy towards developing a robust root system and more strawberries in years to come.

Newly planted **grapes** that are one-year-old plants should be pruned to 6 buds on a single cane. Remove all other canes. One of the remaining buds will become the main trunk of the vine. Prune two-year-old vines to 6 to 10 buds.

 # PESTS

Controlling weeds in **strawberries** is critical to a producing a worthwhile crop. Hoe and weed by hand while weeds are tiny. This is less work and significantly more effective than waiting until weeds get sizable. Black plastic is very effective as a weed barrier. It also warms the soil early, which results in earlier berries. Organic mulch is effective but may harbor insects. In addition, organic mulch may have to be moved to accommodate the rooting of runners. Be sure to use the newer designs of plastic mulch which allow for water penetration. Again, rooting of runners may be problematic.

## Helpful Hints

*1* **Strawberry** beds generally produce for three years. In April of the third year, start a new bed. That way your last year of harvest overlaps with the "establishment year" when the new bed does not yet bear fruit, and you don't skip a year of production.

*2* **Grape** vines can be used for a variety of crafts. The vines remain flexible for some time after pruning. They can be shaped into wreaths or baskets, woven through pergolas to be attractive and increase shade, or draped around entranceways to soften hard lines. Try not to disturb the vines after they have been molded the way you want them. They will dry slowly, become woody, and will last for years if not handled too roughly.

The biggest problem on **grapes** is black rot. To prevent this disease, you will need to begin spraying early in the season, at the time the buds first swell.

The first pesticides to control insects and diseases on tree fruit are generally sprayed just prior to the buds opening. No insecticides are sprayed during bloom since that would injure bees and prevent pollination, but on some trees fungicides are recommended. After the petals fall off, it is time to begin the routine of regular spraying. Follow the directions on the spray schedules provided by your County Cooperative Extension Office and the label directions on the control materials you purchase.

## NOTES

# MAY

## PLANNING

By May, you should be planning how to enjoy eating all the luscious fruits you are going to be harvesting. By the end of the month, you can expect to be picking your first **strawberries.** It takes about thirty days from the first bloom to the first picking. Pick every other day, but only take fully ripened berries. Berries with white patches are not fully ripened. Strawberries will not continue to ripen after harvest. Pick with the stem attached. Avoid picking when the plants are wet, and always remove any fruits you come upon that have been damaged by birds or insects. Refrigerate the fruits as soon as possible after harvest.

## PLANTING

**Fig trees** in containers can be planted out now. Figs are not really hardy in most of New Jersey, but the urge to plant, grow, and eat figs is very powerful. It must have something to do with figs being referred to as "food of the gods" somewhere along the line. Choose a sheltered location in full sun. Locating your fig near the foundation of the house on the south side, protected from the west wind, may be the best spot. In the right microclimate, you may get away without even wrapping, but a cold winter

will kill the plant to the ground even if the roots survive. Since it is the overwintering fruit buds that are likely to give you a crop, you may want to wrap it in the fall even if it is in a protected location. **Wrapping is essential in an exposed location,** especially in the colder parts of the state. Figs may not even be worth trying in Zone 5.

**Figs** prefer a pH of 5.5 to 6.5, so the addition of lime may be necessary. However, when planting up against the foundation of your home, lime can leach from the walls and raise the pH in the immediate area. Have a pH test performed on the soil right where you intend to plant so you can adjust appropriately. A heavier soil is ideal for figs, but it should still drain well. The addition of organic matter during soil preparation may be beneficial, but for this plant you should not need to add sand.

## WATERING

Water your **fig** thoroughly after planting. Figs are generally drought tolerant but will benefit from a deep watering if the ground becomes excessively dry.

On occasion, May weather can become very hot and dry. If that should be the case, **water all newly planted fruit plants before the ground gets overly dry.** Newly planted material does not have enough of a root system established to compensate for dry ground. For strawberries, you will need to apply 1 inch of water per week during the fruiting season if Mother Nature doesn't do it for you. Water in the early morning so the plants dry quickly as the day warms up. Watering at night when temperatures are cooler can encourage disease.

**Blueberries** also need 1 inch of water per week during the growing season.

**Raspberries** have a high water demand. June bearers will need 1 to 2 inches of water per week in May if the weather turns hot and dry. Everbearing varieties can do with a little less since they will not be setting fruit for several months.

## FERTILIZING

The time to first fertilize your **blueberry** bushes is during bloom. Apply $1/8$ pound of 10-10-10 fertilizer around the base of each plant, taking care not to get the fertilizer too close to the trunk.

## PRUNING

Prune away all the flowers on newly planted **blueberries**. This will encourage a stronger root system for crop production in future years.

Continue to remove flowers on newly planted **strawberry** plants.

Keep an eye on **kiwi** vines. They require occasional pruning throughout the season. You will want to remove any "watersprouts" as they develop. These are vigorously growing shoots that develop from older wood, especially the trunk. Also, untangle or prune branches that become entwined as they grow.

## PESTS

The use of organic mulch around the base of trees, shrubs, vines, brambles, and strawberries will help to moderate soil temperatures, reduce water evaporation, and control weeds. Weed control is especially important and difficult in **strawberries.** Managing weeds is critical around newly planted vines such as **grapes** and **kiwis** but becomes less critical as the plants become established. The thick foliage on the vines shade out the weeds to some degree, and the foliage is above the weeds so it's not competing for light and air.

It's especially difficult to produce a crop of tree fruits without closely following an insect and disease spray schedule. New varieties are being developed all the time with natural resistance to these problems being bred into the plants. Great strides are being made, but there are no guarantees of resistance as of this time. **Never spray insecticides during bloom,** but regular spraying throughout the season is necessary to produce quality fruit.

## NOTES

_____

_____

_____

_____

_____

_____

_____

# JUNE
## Fruits

 PLANNING

With a little luck, June brings an overlap of **strawberries, raspberries, mulberries,** and early **blueberries.** Serve them all smothered with heavy cream or whipped cream in a big bowl. Pretty as a picture and tastes even better!

**Sweet cherries** and **tart cherries** also bear in June. Sweet cherries are first, followed by the tart varieties. Each cherry tree has a short harvest season, usually only about five days. Cherries also have a short shelf life in the refrigerator, only about a week. They freeze well, but you should pit them first. Have a cherry pitter on hand.

**Raspberries** need to be picked daily. Strawberries will probably do just fine if harvested every other day. Blueberries are about the same. Mulberries can be picked every day, but they have no shelf life so just pick what you can eat that day or the next.

 PLANTING

A sucker removed from a **fig** tree, especially if it has a piece of root attached, has been known to take with surprising ease at this time. Stick it in the ground with a little shade from strong sun and keep it moist. Look for signs of life as tiny green leaves emerge at ground level.

**Strawberries** are sending out runners in June. You need to move organic mulches out of the way and place runners where you want them. When growing strawberries on plastic, you will need to cut holes in the mulch to create a place for the roots of the runners to come in contact with soil.

 WATERING

Continue to keep **strawberries, blueberries,** and bearing **raspberries** well watered. Strawberries and blueberries require 1 inch of water per week. Raspberries need up to 2 inches per week.

 FERTILIZING

Fertilize **strawberries** in early June with 2 pounds of 10-10-10 fertilizer per 100 square feet. This is when the runners are rooting in and need the boost.

This month, your **blueberry** bushes will get their second application. Apply $1/8$ pound of 10-10-10 fertilizer around the base of each plant, taking care not to get the fertilizer too close to the trunk.

 PRUNING

Thin **peaches** to have enough space for 4 fingers between each fruit. That will allow sufficient room for the fruits to grow. **Nectarines** require more room, so allow the width of 6 fingers between fruits. Thin apples to 5 or 6 fingers between fruits. **Never look down** at the pile of fruits on the ground while you're thinning. It is more important to pay attention to the fruits left on the branches.

In some years, late frosts will damage so many buds that there will be very little thinning necessary. In other years, you may end up with twice the number of tiny fruits on the ground as left on the tree. As a rule of thumb, a mature seven- or eight-year-old peach tree can carry approximately 800 peaches to a good size and flavor. (See chapter introduction for more on pruning.)

 PESTS

**Cherries** are prone to brown rot. At this time, cherries can absorb water through the skin of the maturing fruits so **avoid overhead watering.** Fruits will swell and split. Brown rot sets in almost immediately.

As soon as cherries begin to show color, especially red varieties, it may be necessary to cover the trees with netting. This is usually available at most garden centers. Without netting, you will be sharing a large portion (if not all) of your cherries with your neighborhood bird friends. **Blueberry** bushes may need to be netted this month as well.

Slugs can be unpleasant as well as destructive in the **strawberry** patch. They are worse in a wet season. Birds also do their fair share of damage.

Apple maggots begin laying eggs on developing fruits by late June in the southern part of the state. All-purpose home orchard sprays or the use of traps will provide control. (See chapter introduction for more on controlling pests.)

## Helpful Hints

*1* You can turn powdered lemonade into something wonderful by taking a small amount of prepared lemonade and pouring it into the blender. Add 2 or 3 fat **strawberries** and blend. Pour it back into the rest of the lemonade and stir. You will have pretty pink lemonade, with bits of fresh strawberries. This is a real summer treat!

*2* **Mulberries** are one of Mother Nature's gifts. The fruits are very sweet when fully ripe but have no shelf life, so pick and eat them. They are produced in abundance on wild, or occasionally on planted, trees with very little attention from the gardener on hand. The biggest drawback is the tiny green stems. They will not pull out without damaging the fruit. Your best bet is to pinch them off with your fingers or snip them off with a sharp pair of scissors.

*3* Cherry pitters are not the most common of kitchen implements, so don't wait until you are ready to harvest to shop for one. If you can not find one locally, a computer search will turn up a wide array of styles and prices.

*4* Clean, pitted **cherries** can be packed and frozen in syrup ($1/2$ water, $1/2$ sugar) for serving uncooked, or add $3/4$ cup of sugar to 1 quart of cherries. Mix until the sugar dissolves, cover the container, and freeze for use cooked in pies and other recipes.

## NOTES

# JULY
## Fruits

 ## PLANNING

By July you have to say goodbye to **strawberries** for another year. **Cherries** have finished up, too. However, you can start dreaming of **blueberries** and **gooseberries.** Blueberries are just getting started. With the right selection of varieties, you can continue to have berries through August. Gooseberries and **currants** are generally in full swing the first half of July. If you are not harvesting your own gooseberries, you will probably not get to eat them. They rarely, if ever, show up at the market.

July brings the first **peaches**, and the earliest **apples** show up by the end of the month. These early apples are often green and are generally considered cooking apples. Most are used for pies.

If you planted **Japanese plums** you could get these by the end of the month. However, they are far more common in California than here. The early bloom is subject to late season frosts and so, like **apricots,** often do not produce a crop.

 ## PLANTING

July is definitely not planting season, but you do want to keep an eye on your **strawberry** runners. The runners set by early July are the ones that will bear fruit for you next year. Narrow your strawberry rows to about 12 inches with all the new runners. Remove the oldest plants and mow the bed with your mower set on high to clip back the leaves. This will rejuvenate the bed for next year.

 ## WATERING

All plants bearing or about to bear fruit will need to be deeply watered on occasion if the summer turns hot and dry. Trees will need deep watering with a hose at a trickle at the base of the tree. Move it around so the entire root zone gets a good drink.

**Grapes** will tolerate dry soils better than other fruit-producing plants, but water deeply at the first hint of wilting leaves. **Blueberries** continue to require 1 inch of water per week, applied all at once, to saturate the root system. Everbearing **raspberries** begin to bear later this month and will benefit from generous watering. They prefer 1 to 2 inches of water each week. The use of soaker hoses (those with holes on one side or the weepy types that resemble rubber cork) will saturate the ground without ever getting water on the leaves or fruits.

 ## FERTILIZING

Fertilizing anything in hot summer weather is a dangerous proposition. Any time it's above 85 degrees Fahrenheit, just hold off until things cool off. There is too great a risk of burning the roots.

The renovated **strawberry** patch will need some fertilizer to help get re-established for next year. Apply 2 pounds of 10-10-10 fertilizer for every 100 square feet.

 ## PRUNING

As soon as June-bearing **raspberries** finish fruit production, you need to do some pruning. June-bearing types are biennials. In alternating years they produce vegetative canes (only canes and leaves) one year, and the next year these same canes return and produce flowers and yummy raspberries. Then they die. Fruited canes need to be removed at ground level to control disease, allow for air flow, and generally keep the patch healthy.

**Kiwis** are vigorous growers. Prune long shoots back to 4 or 5 buds about once a month during the summer. This keeps the growth more compact and able to produce an abundant number of fruits.

**Peaches** and **nectarines** are sometimes summer pruned. If excessive suckering has occurred in the center of the tree, this will take energy from developing fruit as well as shade the fruits. Shade inhibits coloration. Hand prune upright shoots in the center of the "bowl" created by the three primary branches. This will open the canopy to allow sun to hit the fruits from the inside as well as the outside.

**Apples** tend to develop "watersprouts," suckers forming at the base of the tree, which should be removed as necessary.

## PESTS

Continue to follow your spray schedules for all fruits. Apple scab, which shows up as early as June but is not really obvious until now, results in orange spots on leaves and fruits. Once it shows up, there is little to do to control the disease. Cedar-apple rust is a disease that often spends part of its life on the native **red cedar** (*Juniperous virginiana),* but can appear on any **juniper.** This, too, must be controlled during the incubation period in very early spring. Infected fruits are blemished but still edible, especially for pies or applesauce. However, they have very little shelf life. A bigger problem is premature leaf drop, which weakens the trees, especially when it is repeated for several years. Some resistant varieties of apples are available, but many popular **apples** are extremely susceptible. Adhering to the spray schedules provided by Rutgers Cooperative Extension is your best chance for avoiding these problems.

Weed germination slows in hot weather, but remove weeds since they compete with your fruits for moisture and nutrients. This is especially necessary for newly planted material and smaller plants such as **strawberries** and **raspberries**.

## NOTES

_____

_____

_____

_____

_____

_____

_____

_____

_____

_____

_____

_____

# AUGUST

##  PLANNING

In August you should be planning what to do with all the fruit you will be harvesting.

In the southern part of the state, **figs** may begin to ripen towards the end of the month. Figs must be soft and almost ready to drop on their own before picking. They should pluck easily from the branch. If they resist, leave them for a few more days.

The late season varieties of **raspberries** begin bearing in August. They are sometimes called "everbearing" because they will produce a small percentage of their crop on last year's growth just like the rest of the June bearers. The bulk of the crop, however, is produced on the **current season's growth** later in the season. They are also sometimes referred to as "fall bearing." If you mow them in spring, they produce no June crop and so are strictly late summer and fall bearing, but even if you do not mow, most of the crop arrives later in the season.

By now almost all of the **peach trees** bearing fruit are producing "free stone" peaches. Within these fruits, the pit or "stone" is very loosely attached to the flesh. It removes easily, which makes canning or freezing much easier.

**Plums** continue to ripen throughout the month. Later Japanese varieties overlap with early European varieties. European types continue into September, which overlaps with hardy American plums like the **beach plum** that grows wild along the Jersey shore. Allow plums to ripen on the tree. Only pick them when they pull away with a very gentle tug. They should taste very sweet. **"Lip puckering" tartness** means they are not yet ripe enough. **Japanese plums** will continue to ripen after being picked. **European plums** will not. Leave the stem attached to avoid damaging the skin. They will keep longer. Handle with care; plums are somewhat fragile fruit.

**Grapes** will begin to be harvested late in the month and through September.

##  PLANTING

August is still not planting season. Spring-planted fruits should have produced some roots by now, but hot, dry August weather can still overcome young plants. Be sure to continue to give them the TLC they need to get through their first season.

##  WATERING

**Raspberries** need lots of water, up to 2 inches per week, to produce an abundant crop. It is still better to keep the water on the ground rather than overhead. The use of soaker hoses or weepy type hoses can make a big difference in keeping fruit dry so they will have a longer life both on the vine and on the shelf. June bearers do not need as much water at this time since they are not producing fruit.

**Figs** are developing and also need lots of water. Water trees deeply if the soil should become dry.

Continue to water all spring-planted fruits if it doesn't rain. This is their first summer, and they will succumb to drought stress rapidly if the roots get overly dry.

##  FERTILIZING

Fertilize **strawberries** again in mid-August but switch to 10-6-4 fertilizer at a rate of 3 pounds per 100 square feet. This is the time the buds set, and the extra nitrogen is a big help to the plants.

##  PRUNING

Continue to prune **kiwi** vines back to 4 or 5 buds since vigorous new shoots grow with great enthusiasm.

##  PESTS

Continue to follow up on your spray programs. Black rot is a serious problem on **grapes** and affects both the leaves and the fruits. The problem tends to get worse over time. Young plantings may produce a crop without spraying, but once the disease becomes a problem you can expect to see it every year. The wetter the growing season, the worse the problem can be.

## Helpful Hints

*1* **Peaches** freeze easily. Skin peaches according to directions provided in July. Sprinkle with citric acid (also known as Vitamin C and sometimes sold under different marketing labels) to prevent browning of the fruit. Follow label directions. They can be frozen in freezer bags or plastic containers with or without sugar. They also can be packed in syrup ($1/2$ water, $1/2$ sugar) and frozen in containers.

*2* **Blueberries** are great snacks for kids, terrific on cereal, fabulous in pancakes, yummy on top of ice cream, and absolutely delicious just about any way you can think to eat them. They are also extremely high in antioxidants, important components in the battle to prevent cancer.

Black knot is a disease that can affect **cherries** but is far more common on plums. If you have followed a **plum** spray schedule, this should have been controlled with everything else. However, it can be recognized by swellings on the branches. At first they appear greenish but are more recognizable in later stages when they turn black, hard, and crusty. If you see it develop over the summer, plan on pruning out the infected areas in the fall or early spring, and definitely plan on implementing a spray program for the following year.

## NOTES

_____

_____

_____

_____

_____

_____

_____

_____

_____

_____

_____

# SEPTEMBER

## PLANNING

It is possible to plant **strawberries** in September in a specialized system called "plasticulture" (see planting). You need to purchase small strawberry plants known as "plugs." These are young plants that have been grown in a greenhouse and arrive as transplants rather than the dormant plants you receive in the spring. Since they are never available locally in the fall, you will have to order plugs to arrive by mail.

September is a big month for harvesting **grapes,** late **peaches** (which are among the best for flavor), **raspberries, European plums, American plums, apples, pears,** and **figs** if you are very lucky. Apples that ripen in September include **Galas, Jonathan, McIntosh, Cortland, Liberty,** and both **Golden** and **Red Delicious** late in the month.

**Seckel pears** are about the first pears of the season. **Anjou** and **Bartlett** follow, and late in month you can expect **Bosc** and **Red Bartlett.** Look for **Kiefers** after the Anjou and Bartlett but before the Bosc. Kiefer pears are light green, and the flesh is grainy but they have great flavor. Wait until you see the yellow jackets hovering around the fruits before you harvest. Most pears can be picked a little green since they will ripen nicely indoors. The Kiefers will not.

The everbearing **raspberries** are at their best in early September. Pick daily to make sure you don't waste any of those luscious berries. If you decide to venture into wine making, raspberries and **grapes** are a great combination.

Hardy **kiwis** are ready for harvest. They should come off the vine with a gentle twist. **Issai,** the self-fertile variety, does not ripen all at once, so check every day or every other day to get all the fruit.

## PLANTING

**Strawberries** are generally grown in raised beds. Prepare the soil deeply (see below for fertilizer needs). Add organic matter to sandy soil and both organic matter and sand in a 2:1 ratio to heavy clay soils. Adjust soil pH to between 5.5 and 6.5.

Create a bed 5 feet wide, and cover it in plastic that is stretched fairly tight and secured around the outside edge with a covering of soil. Cut holes in the plastic and space plants 18 to 24 inches apart with 4 feet between the rows. Use overhead watering to cool plants down if you are planting on a hot day. **The use of floating row covers is critical with this system.** These are lightweight materials that protect the plants but still allow light to pass through. Secure the cover around the edge of the beds with piping, bricks, sandbags, or something else suitable. Make sure the wind will not get up under the row cover and tear it off during the winter. Row covers must be removed at the first sign of bloom in the spring. If not damaged, they can be reused the following year. By using this system in September, you will harvest strawberries in June.

## WATERING

Dropping temperatures and drenching rains around Labor Day eliminate heat stress on developing fruits. **Raspberries** are bearing heavily, and they continue to have a heavy water demand. Just in case it doesn't rain, remember to irrigate without getting the fruits wet, if that is possible. The use of soaker hoses or weepy type hoses makes it easier.

Make sure you thoroughly water in your newly planted **strawberries,** but do not over-water.

## FERTILIZING

Add 10-10-10 fertilizer at a rate of 2 pounds per 100 square feet when preparing the ground for plasticulture **strawberries.**

Fertilizer applications in the fall can trigger new growth and delay dormancy. If an early cold snap should occur, plants can be damaged. It is best to wait until early spring to apply fertilizer in most cases.

# PRUNING

Pruning on fruits is also best delayed until late winter or early spring.

# PESTS

Practice good sanitation. Removal of dropped fruits and infected leaves is an important step in preventing reinfection next spring. These materials can be added to the compost pile, but they should be buried under soil or partially decomposed compost. This will contain the spores and prevent starting the cycle over again come spring. Bag the leaves and fruits if they can't be buried in some way.

Control the **peach tree** borer, which can actually affect all stone fruits including **nectarines, plums,** and **cherries.** You can identify an infestation by the red-

dish-brown, gummy, sticky ooze found at the base of the trunk. At this point, your only option is to **dig the critters out.** Inserting a stiff wire into the opening and working it up into the cavity created by the borer until you hear the borer "pop" is a slightly unpleasant but effective approach. You can also use a sharp knife and slit the trunk with a vertical cut until you see the borer, but you have to be careful—**don't do excessive damage to the wood.** Stay in touch with the Cooperative Extension Office in case new control materials become available.

## Helpful Hints

*1* **Peaches** and **apples** can be frozen now for use in pies later. Peel, remove seeds, slice, and lay in a pie plate on top of plastic wrap. Place in the freezer. When frozen, remove from the pie plate, wrap in the plastic wrap so it is well protected, and place back in the freezer. When you want a pie, roll out your crust, drop in your frozen fruit, and you are ready to go.

*2* Less than perfect apples can make great applesauce. Try cooking some **pears** in with the apples for a delicious twist to an old favorite.

*3* Homemade wine can be a fun project. In simple terms, the fruit is selected, the stems removed, and then the fruit is crushed. Crushed **grapes** are fermented and pressed for red wines or pressed and fermented for white wines. Many books are written on the subject, and information is also available through the Cooperative Extension Office. Do your research in advance and have all your equipment on hand. When the grapes mature on the vine, you will be very busy.

## NOTES

_____
_____
_____
_____
_____
_____
_____
_____
_____
_____
_____
_____

# OCTOBER
## Fruits

 PLANNING

**Apples** are still in abundance and will still need harvesting, especially in the colder part of the state. **Rome Beauty** (a good apple for baking) will be picked this month. **Winesap** and **Fuji** are both in season and so is **Arkansas Black,** which is an excellent storage apple.

Late season **figs** are running a neck-and-neck race with the first frost to ripen before they are done in by cold. In a mild fall, you can get lucky, but all too often the frost wins by a nose.

You will know the **pawpaws** are ripe when their skins turn yellow. Sometimes they drop from the tree at just the right time for picking. They should have a custard-like texture (remove the large, brown, bean-like seeds and eat with a spoon).

**Persimmons** are a late-season fruit that should not be harvested until after a frost. Persimmons turn color early, so a bright red fruit is not an indication of being ripe. The American varieties all must turn soft, and some must even get all wrinkled after several frosts to develop sweetness. Experience will teach you what to look for on the varieties you have. Some unripe Oriental varieties are not as powerfully tart as the American varieties picked too early, but some are.

Some Oriental persimmons are still firm when ripe, while others get soft.

 PLANTING

It is still possible to plant **raspberries** or **blackberries.** This should be done after the other plants have lost their leaves.

**Gooseberries** and **currants** may actually do better with fall planting as they get started growing very early in the spring.

**Grapes** can be planted in October in most of the state. In the colder northern counties, it would be better to wait until spring.

Fruit trees can also be planted in October. Consider staking them to make sure they don't blow over during winter winds.

For all of the above, see specific planting directions in March and April.

 WATERING

By this time of year, watering should be at a minimum. It is important, however, not to let plants go into the winter dry. If the long, hot summer was never corrected by Mother Nature, you do want to give all your fruit-bearing plants a deep watering before the weather gets cold.

 FERTILIZING

Applications of fertilizer this late in the season is not a good idea. It encourages a new flush of growth when plants really need to be preparing for winter dormancy.

 PRUNING

There is very little to prune on fruit trees and plants in the fall. Allowing all the year's growth to remain on the plant helps the plants get through the winter. Hold off until the worst of winter is over to do any pruning. A warm day in February is a good time to start thinking about pruning again.

 PESTS

The most important aspect of pest control at this time of year is to clean up the garden. Dropped fruits and leaves allow insects and diseases to re-infect or re-infest your plants again next year. **Some years, wasps are drawn to apples** on the ground, which can be a serious problem for small children.

Anything you rake up should go in the compost pile, but not on the surface. It needs to be buried to prevent spores from floating around and get back to places where you don't want them. If this is not possible, you will be better off bagging the material and sending it away with the trash than leaving it in an open pile. Sometimes fruits deteriorate on the tree without dropping. They shrivel and turn brown. These "mummified" fruits are somewhat unpleasant and should be removed. Just bag them and throw them away.

Trim grass and weeds away from the trunk. **Do not use a string trimmer** as it will damage the bark. Tall weeds and grass become a haven for small creatures that may decide to nibble away at the bark for a winter meal. Pull back organic mulch for the same reason.

## Helpful Hints

*1* Peeling **apples** can wear on you if you have a lot to do. Apple peeling devices are available that core and peel apples by turning a crank. These seem to work distinctly better on hard, crispy apples. Softer varieties tend to turn to mush.

*2* If you are making applesauce, you can skip peeling up front in favor of mashing after cooking. This has the advantage of imparting a bit of color from the skins to the mashed apples, which is very attractive. Use a potato ricer to separate the skins from the sauce.

*3* If you make the mistake of harvesting Oriental varieties of **persimmons** a bit early, they can be ripened in a brown paper bag with an apple. The apple emits natural ethylene, which encourages ripening. However, it doesn't work on the American types of persimmons.

*4* You may want to consider painting the bottom $1/3$ of the trunks of fruit trees with diluted white latex paint may have a benefit for preventing pests. The white paint reflects the sunlight, which prevents warming and subsequent cracking. Without the paint, the sun can warm the bark on the trunks of fruit trees on very cold sunny days. The warmth causes the bark to expand. The wood of the trunk does not warm and does not expand. When this happens, the bark can actually "crack" almost as loud as a firecracker. The splits in the bark become entry points for disease and insects.

## NOTES

# NOVEMBER
## Fruits

 PLANNING

November is a big month for holiday cooking, and your **homegrown** fruits can provide what you need to make great tasting recipes (and earn some extra bragging rights). **Granny Smith apples** get harvested in early November. They are excellent keepers and the firm apples peel easily. Use them for terrific apple pies. Many apples store for a while, so you should have plenty of apples for late fall and early winter.

**Apples** and **cranberries** together make a great pie combination. Be sure to buy several bags of cranberries to store in your freezer so you will have them all year for cooking.

Later in the month, you will want to mulch around the base of your fruit trees. An organic mulch such as bark nuggets, shredded bark, wood chips, partially composted leaves, or even shredded leaves can be used to protect the soil and roots.

 PLANTING

November just is not the time for planting much of anything. The ground is cold, if not yet freezing, so roots will not

 Helpful Hints

*1* The fruit of Kousa **dogwoods** is considered edible. It has a somewhat grainy texture but an interesting flavor. It is attractive in appearance, and the birds love it.

*2* Dried **blueberries** are now available and absolutely delicious. They make great snacks, or toss a few into your pancake batter.

have a chance to get established. Once soil temperatures drop below 45 degrees Fahrenheit, roots do not grow.

 WATERING

Only water if the ground is really dry, but then water deeply. Don't let plants go into the winter dry. Once completely wet, the soil will not dry out too quickly in colder temperatures.

 FERTILIZING

You don't want to fertilize anything now.

PRUNING

There may be a bit of pruning to do. You should remove any broken branches and also any branches that may be crossing. Branches rubbing together over the win-

ter could be damaged. Better to remove one now than lose both later.

PESTS

Make time to paint the bottom part of the trunks of your fruit trees with white latex paint (see October Helpful Hints). Buy the cheapest paint you can find and then dilute it a bit. Three parts paint to 1 part water should be a good mix.

When you mulch your fruit trees, **do not pile the mulch up against the trunk.** Mulch can be up to 6 inches deep, but think "donut." Leave a little space between the mulch and the trunk so you don't create cover for small furry creatures such as mice, chipmunks, and voles. They can do a tremendous amount of damage to your fruit trees by eating the bark and girdling the tree.

# DECEMBER

## PLANNING

The garden is at rest, and it is good to put aside your work gloves and hand pruners in favor of cookie cutters and curling ribbon.

Spend some time stringing **cranberries** with lots of popcorn, drying **apple** rings on strings over the wood burning stove, and eating Clementine **oranges** one after another.

**Strawberries** are mulched later in the month. Make a note to remove the branches from your Christmas tree at the end of the holidays or from a neighbor's tree when it's put it out by the curb. These branches make great mulch for strawberries. Lay the branches on top. The natural curve of the branches will hold them up a bit above the plants. That way they will not smother the strawberries.

## PLANTING

There's not much you can plant right now, but for fun, you can try planting an **avocado** pit. (It's a fruit too!) It is not likely you will ever see an avocado appear, but the tree makes a spectacular tropical looking houseplant.

## Helpful Hints

Here are a few holiday gift ideas for the fruit gardeners on your list.

• A great old book for children is *Mr. Apple's Family* by Jean McDevitt. This was copyrighted in 1950. Mr. Apple names his five children apple names, such as McIntosh, Jonathan, and Snow. Then they move into a crookedy house in the country, right in the middle of an apple orchard. (This book is a personal favorite from childhood. I hunted it down to share with my own children.)

• A great book on canning and preserving is *Putting Food By* by Janet Greene, Ruth Hertzberg, and Beatrice Vaughn.

• A Johnny Appleseed Tree, grown from softwood cuttings taken from the last known, living apple tree that was planted by Johnny Appleseed makes a great gift. Contact the American Forests Historic Trees Nursery at www.historictrees.org.

Place the teardrop-shaped pit in water with the point up. Hold it in place, so it is half submerged in water, with toothpicks. When a root begins to emerge from the bottom, pot it in fresh potting soil. It needs a sunny window to grow into an attractive plant, and never let it get overly dry.

## WATERING

Don't water anything outside unless the ground is exceptionally dry. If necessary, water on a day when temperatures are above freezing.

## FERTILIZING

Don't fertilize anything this month.

## PRUNING

Don't prune anything either.

## PESTS

See November Pests for a review of pest control when mulching.

# CHAPTER FOUR

# Ground Covers & Vines

*There are ground covers for shade, which is great since you can't coax grass to grow in deep shade even if you make sacrifices to the grass gods.*

The most widely used ground cover of all time is grass. However, there are a lot of yards where conditions are not conducive to grass. Shade is the biggest obstacle, but wet ground is a serious impediment as well. So if you are stuck with bare ground, enthusiastic weeds, or are just bored to tears with grass, it is time to investigate the world of ground covers.

Ground covers are grouped with vines because many ground covers *are* vines. They grow along the ground until they have something to grow up on, then they head for the sky. The "Big Three" ground covers are **pachysandra, English ivy** and **myrtle** (also known as **periwinkle** or **vinca**). English ivy puts the "Ivy" in "Ivy League." That is where higher learning and foliage-covered buildings are inseparable. Myrtle has the claim to fame that it gets pretty "periwinkle blue" flowers in the spring. It creeps along the ground sending out roots. It is considered a vine, but it doesn't climb or twist or cling. It may make it a few feet up the trunk of a tree if it can put a root or two into the fissures of the bark, but it never gets very far.

These are workhorses in the world of ground covers, while being only a hair less boring than grass. Maybe two hairs.

## Many Choices

If you are going to go through all the trouble of planting ground covers, let's spice things up a bit. **Creeping phlox** blooms for months in the spring. **Lily-of-the-valley** can spread thickly in the shade and intoxicate you with the scent. The pale pink variety is even more special. Sensitive **fern** spreads beautifully in deep shade, and the bizarre sporulating fronds add winter interest. The delicate white flowers of **sweet woodruff** are also sweetly fragrant, but the foliage is lovely on its own. **Ajuga** comes in lots of varieties, each with its own interesting foliage, but the flowers are pretty, too, and sometimes considered the main attraction.

There are ground covers for shade, which is great since you can't coax grass to grow in deep shade even if you make sacrifices to the grass gods.

In the sun, you can have grass, but you may want to try something different. *Lamium* and *lamiastrum* will both do well in shade, but *lamiastrum* is less likely to become invasive. The pretty **foamflower** is the genus *Tiarella*. Its airy spikes of white flowers appear in the spring above very attractive foliage that adds interest all season and even bronzes nicely in the winter.

## Designing

The use of areas planted with ground covers can delineate outside "rooms." In the sun, a swath of thick **sundrops** will give brilliant flowers and direct visitors where you want them to go. At the very least you will have less grass to mow. The **chameleon plant** (*Houttuynia cordata*) can be aggressive in wet areas but slows down in drier ground. The leaves are quite colorful. You may not want this in blazing sun, but in a fairly sunny to light-shade location this ground cover will provide lots of bright contrast.

When you are thinking of making garden rooms with ground covers, you need a bit of space in which to play. Not necessarily rolling acres, but enough space to compartmentalize a bit. In an urban space, even a tiny garden is a welcome respite from concrete and blacktop. When space is limited, think vertical. That is where vines can come in very handy. They can cling, attach with tendrils, or entwine. **Climbing hydrangea** clings with root-like attachments. **Clematis** has delicate tendrils that grasp finer supports like wire trellises or ugly chain link fence. Then there are the spiraling types like **wisteria** that encircle the support. This can be both beautiful and dangerous because its strength is phenomenal. Wisteria entwined on your Victorian porch can eventually cause the supports to come crashing to the ground. Wisteria can even strangle a living tree.

Vines on arbors can be used for making shade. On a concrete wall, they turn ugly into lovely. In a tiny backyard, they can create your own private secret garden. On a large property they can create drama. And certainly, on the walls of a university, they raise the tuition.

## Did You Know?

### Planting on a Very Steep Slope

Regardless of artistic interpretation, if the slope is greater than 20 degrees, you will need to consider building some type of terracing. This can be done with wood or stone. Depending on your spirit of adventure, you can use tires or cinder blocks. While cinder blocks are ugly by themselves, used on end in a symmetrical pattern they have an interesting look. With many ground covers, they are eventually hidden from view for the most part anyway.

A final possibility is to leave whatever is growing on the slope at the onset in place. Then plant your ground covers at the closest possible spacing in small areas on the slope. This will prevent a complete mudslide, and the ground cover will fill in quickly in the starter areas. Repeat every year until you have finished the job. In the meantime, the established pockets will spread.

## PREPARING THE SOIL

If you are planning to plant ground cover in soil that has been bare for some time, the ground may be very hard and compact. Make sure you have lots of organic matter on hand to incorporate into the soil and help loosen it up. Leaves placed in the fall season before planting improve the soil conditions as leaves decompose. Then you just till them under when you turn over the soil.

In bare spots under trees, you are often competing with roots, so **digging can be difficult.** You may want to build up the soil 2 or 3 inches by adding very mature compost to the surface. Then turn it under the best you can. You may not be able to turn the full depth of a shovel blade, but hoe in the compost with whatever soil you are able to cultivate. **Don't build up the soil deeply around the trunks of trees.** This can damage the bark over time. On young trees, it creates

# Ground Covers & Vines

JANUARY · FEBRUARY · MARCH · APRIL · MAY · JUNE · JULY · AUGUST · SEPTEMBER · OCTOBER · NOVEMBER · DECEMBER

opportunity for small rodents to tunnel and then chew on the bark.

Changing the grade in the general area 6 inches up or down can compromise the root system of established trees, so do not dump a load of topsoil and think that will solve the problem. This will cause the roots of shallow rooted trees to eventually rise to the surface, so try to work within the confines of what you have. Once the ground covers get established, they are quite adept at weaving their roots between the roots of the trees, so give them a good start and they should be fine.

## Planting

Make sure your supports for any vines are in the ground prior to planting. Installation at a later date risks damaging the root system of the vine you're working with. **Plant ground cover or vine container plants at the same depth they were in their containers.** When planting ground covers from divisions, bury the roots up to where there is a definitive line or change in color that indicates the transition from root to stem. If you look closely, it will become fairly obvious. Planting ground covers on a slope requires some forethought. **Plant in staggered rows** to reduce runoff and erosion. On slightly steeper

slopes, it may be necessary to build up the soil around each plant, creating a level area to catch water and retain soil. For planting on a steep slope see Helpful Hints.

## Watering

How much water you need to apply is extremely dependent on the weather, the soil type, and the immediate environment. Recently planted vines and ground covers will need water sooner than well established plantings. The use of a deep, organic mulch will retain more moisture in the soil and keep the roots cooler. Cooler roots will have less water demand. Ground covers in shade usually need to be watered less frequently. Once the soil dries out, you need to water deeply. Sandy soil will definitely dry out more rapidly than soils high in organic matter. Organic matter will hold moisture while sandy soil allows it to run right through. It is best to incorporate lots of organic matter into the soil at planting, but you can still improve the soil's water-holding capability by using organic mulch. As it decomposes, worms will bring it down into the soil, improving the soil in the process.

# Ground Covers & Vines

## Vines for the Sun

| | |
|---|---|
| Chinese Wisteria | *Wisteria sinensis* |
| Japanese Wisteria | *W. floribunda* |
| Bower Actinidia | *Actinidia arguta* |
| Kolomikta Actinidia | *A. kolomikta* 'Artic Beauty' |
| Silver Fleece Vine | *Polygonum aubertii* |
| Crimson Glory Vine | *Vitis coignetiae* |
| Porcelain Vine | *Ampelopsis brevipedunculata* |
| Trumpet Creeper | *Campsis radicans* |
| Honeysuckle | *Lonicera* sp. |
| Clematis (roots in shade) | *Clematis* spp. |
| Morning Glory (annual) | *Ipomoea* x *multifida* |
| Black Eyed Susan (annual) | *Thunbergia alata* |
| Hyacinth Bean (annual) | *Dolichos lablab* |
| Scarlet Runner Bean (annual) | *Phaseolus coccineus* |
| Mandevilla Vine (tender) | *Mandevilla* varieties |
| Perennial Sweet Pea | *Lathyrus latifolius* |
| Sweet Pea (annual) | *L. odoratus* |
| Snail Vine | *Vigna caracalla* |

## Vines for the Shade

| | |
|---|---|
| Climbing Hydrangea | *Hydrangea anomala petiolaris* |
| Virginia Creeper (or sun) | *Parthenocissus quinquefolia* |
| Boston Ivy | *P. tricuspidata* |
| English Ivy | *Hedera helix* |
| Akebia | *Akebia quinata* |
| Dutchman's Pipe (or sun) | *Aristolochia durior* |
| Bittersweet (or sun) | *Celastrus scandens* |
| Oriental Bittersweet (or sun) | *C. orbiculatus* |
| Climbing Fumitory | *Adlumia fungosa* |
| Moonseed | *Menispermum canadense* |
| Canary Bird Vine (annual) | *Tropaeolum peregrinum* |

## Ground Covers for the Sun

| | |
|---|---|
| Moss Pink | *Phlox subulata* |
| Lamb's Ears | *Stachys byzantina* |
| Creeping Juniper | *Juniperus horizontalis* |
| Dwarf Japanese Juniper | *J. procumbens* 'Nana' |
| Evening Primrose | *Oenothera* spp. |
| Chameleon Plant | *Houttuynia cordata* |
| Creeping Cotoneaster | *Cotoneaster adpressus* |
| Stonecrop | *Sedum kamtschaticum* |
| Two-row Stonecrop | *S. spurium* |
| Shortleaf Stonecrop | *S. cauticola* |
| Bearberry, Kinnikinnick | *Arctostaphylos uva-ursi* |
| Creeping Thyme | *Thymus serpyllum* |
| Woolly Thyme | *T. pseudolanuginosus* |
| Daylily | *Hemerocallis* hybrids |
| Creeping Baby's Breath | *Gypsophila repens* |

## Ground Covers for the Shade

| | |
|---|---|
| Hosta | *Hosta* spp. |
| Sarcococca | *Sarcococca hookeriana* var. *humilis* |
| Wintergreen | *Gaultheria procumbens* |
| Sweet Woodruff | *Galium odoratum* |
| Periwinkle (also sun) | *Vinca minor* |
| Pachysandra | *Pachysandra terminalis* |
| Bugleweed (also sun) | *Ajuga reptans* |
| Goutweed Variegated | *Aegopodium podagraria* 'Variegatum' |
| Spotted Dead Nettle | *Lamium maculatum* |
| Winter Creeper (vine) | *Euonymus fortunei* |
| English Ivy (vine, also sun) | *Hedera helix* |
| Yellow Archangel | *Lamiastrum galeobdolon* |
| Moneywort | *Lysimachia nummularia* |
| Lily of the Valley | *Convallaria majalis* |
| Blood-red Geranium | *Geranium sanguineum* |

PLANNING

January is the time to do a great deal of garden planning. In this book, each plant type is addressed in its own chapter, but in truth you really plant all of them at the same time. This is to make sure everything works together. No one has all their shade trees in one spot and all their ground covers in another. It is all a giant puzzle where all the pieces have to fit. But unlike a jigsaw puzzle, the garden pieces can change as they grow over time. So plan for things to work together.

If you intend to plant on trellises, you can get going with building them now. If you are not the do-it-yourself type, then start shopping around. Use the gardening catalogs arriving in the mail and check out the spring supplies in garden centers. If it is at all possible, **you want to have the trellis installed prior to planting,** even if the plant may not actually need any support immediately. That way, there is no damage to the roots as you install the support system.

With both ground covers and vines, you need to plan the look you are trying to achieve. If you are simply trying to cover bare ground under trees, you choose something that will cover the ground. You may want to think evergreen, and you definitely need to think about shade tolerant plants. Watch out for ground covers that will climb because eventually they may damage the tree. You can either be prepared to keep them under control or choose ground covers that keep their feet on the ground.

If you just want space covered, spreading **junipers** can be effective. This may not excite you. It doesn't excite me. But different varieties of junipers and a few big rocks and scattered **daffodils** can get the job done.

When planning for vines, you must consider what they will be climbing and include it in your plans. Maybe you want to hide something wickedly ugly. You will need the "sticky fingers" type to climb on wood or cinder block or brick. These are either root-like appendages or tiny suckers that have the most amazing ability to hold fast. These, like the common **English ivy,** will do little or no harm to the surface of anything stone-like, but the higher moisture needed to maintain a wall covered in foliage may encourage more rapid deterioration of anything made out of wood. A vine-covered wood structure will be better off with a trellis to support the vine. If you are trying to hide an old shed, perhaps it doesn't matter. Install the trellis with a few inches between the trellis and the wooden wall for some air circulation.

For spiraling vines, make sure you supply something that cannot easily be pulled down. Heavy metal pipes are less crushable than wood and stand up to **wisteria**. Yes, metal pipes are much uglier, but wisteria is so robust you won't have to look at the pipes for long. Lovely, gentle **clematis** on the porch is a better choice. Wrought iron trellising is usually fine enough for the delicate tendrils, but chains hung from the eaves can also be very effective.

 PLANTING

January is not the time to be planting anything.

 WATERING

Unless you are in the middle of a winter drought, you shouldn't have to water anything outside. If you have a **mandevilla vine** indoors, give it plenty of sun and water it when slightly dry. Don't overwater.

 FERTILIZING

Do not fertilize anything now.

 PRUNING

If you have a few vines in containers,

you can prune any shoots that are looking scraggly. Save a major pruning until next month when the plants will be ready to respond to the longer days and stronger sun.

 # PESTS

Mealy bugs and mites are both problems on **English ivy** grown in containers. Mites are probably somewhat more destructive as they are rarely spotted until the plant is in serious stress. If it is a small plant, spray in the sink or shower with a fairly fierce stream of water. Then cover the soil in aluminum foil and swish the foliage in soapy water.

Mealy bugs are easier to see but are less likely to be washed away in a stream of water. However it won't hurt to try. Spraying with 50 percent rubbing alcohol and water will give some control. So will the use of insecticidal soap. Treat repeatedly, every five days, to control emerging adults before they have a chance to lay more eggs. If the problem persists, you may have to resort to insecticides. Check with the Cooperative Extension Office for current recommendations.

## Helpful Hints

*1* Remember that ground covers on slopes have the distinct advantage of not needing to be mowed.

*2* Many of the fancier **English ivy** varieties are not hardy outdoors. You may want to enjoy them on the porch as hanging baskets, but they probably will not survive our winters.

*3* The term "Ivy League" was coined in 1937 by Caswell Adams, a sportswriter at the *New York Herald Tribune.* He had been assigned the Columbia-Pennsylvania football game for the following afternoon. Disappointed in his assignment, he asked his editor "Whyinhell do I have to watch the ivy grow every Saturday afternoon?" Stanley Woodward, another sportswriter at the same paper, overheard the remark. Finding humor in the reference, he coined the term Ivy League in a column a few days later. The eight competitive schools had long resisted any formal formation of a league or conference, so the choice of words was a bit tongue in cheek. Eventually, a conference was formed, and they called it the Ivy League.

## NOTES

_____

_____

_____

_____

_____

_____

_____

_____

_____

# FEBRUARY
## Ground Covers & Vines

 ## PLANNING

February is still planning mode. Towards the end of the month, if the weather is spring-like, you may be able to do a little pruning, but for the most part, stay indoors.

It is the time to get your orders in for those ground covers you discovered in catalogs. Certainly the "big three" will be available locally. **Ajuga** is not hard to come by either, but there are many varieties. If you want one in particular, you should probably order it. It also depends on the quantity you want. **Sweet woodruff** is also around, but most garden centers don't carry enough to cover large areas.

Vines are not quite the same. It is not likely you will want thirty **wisteria** vines or twenty-five **clematis.** This would require an enormous amount of trellising. Unless you want a particular variety, there is a good chance you will be able to find what you seek at your friendly neighborhood nursery.

The dependable **blue rug juniper** or the more delicate *J. procumbens* 'Nana' are readily available. More than about five or six of these plants may warrant an advanced order.

Make sure you get to a few flower shows. They always feature arbors and trellises for dramatic effect. You may get inspired. A new New Jersey Garden show (started in 2003) is held this month in Edison at the New Jersey Convention Center. It is a smaller show, but so far has had top-notch exhibits. It is generally held in late February.

 ## PLANTING

It is still definitely not time to plant, but make sure you get all your trellising prepared and even "planted" if the ground is not frozen.

 ## WATERING

There should be no watering needs now, unless the weather has been overly dry.

 ## FERTILIZING

It is still a bit too early to fertilize outdoors. Any vines you have in containers indoors can be fertilized starting that first day you are standing in a sunny window and you notice the heat is back in the sun. It usually happens about the third week in February. If you can feel the heat, your plants can too.

 ## PRUNING

Before you apply your first spring "wake-up" dose of fertilizer, you may want to prune your indoor vines. They will respond to the stronger sunlight and burst of nutrients rather quickly. You will want to make sure this new growth appears where you want it. A healthy new shoot at the end of a long scraggly vine is rather wasted. No matter how robust it may be, it will look ugly dangling off of a bare stem.

Prune the longest, ugliest vines back towards the pot. Make sure you leave 1 or 2 leaf nodes for the dormant buds to develop. Allow shorter vines to continue to grow even if they are a bit bare.

**Never wrap long bare stems around the pot.** Eventually you will end up with 6 miles of bare stem and a few pathetic leaves at the tip.

 ## PESTS

Mites and mealy bugs continue to be the biggest problem on indoor vines. The **Hoya vines**, also called **wax flower**, are particularly prone to mealy bugs. These pests can be washed off with some success on the regular flat-leaved varieties. However, the contorted 'Hindu Rope

Plant' has such twisted leaves that the mealy bugs hide in the crevices and are almost impossible to eradicate. "Swishing" in soapy water is probably the only way to penetrate all the grooves. Do your best to manage the problem in this manner. When the weather breaks, you may want to resort to insecticides to end the plague.

## Helpful Hints

*1* For a creative Valentine's gift, give your plant-loving lover a **string of hearts** (*Ceropegia woodii*). This is a delicate vine with very pretty, succulent, heart-shaped leaves. It usually stays compact in a small pot but can hang down several feet. Occasionally it will produce small pink flowers.

*2* Consider building trellises out of extruded, recycled plastic lumber. This will never rot and is actually more dense than wood. It is definitely sturdier than the hollow "resin" trellises that appear flimsy and even a little tacky. The white extruded plastic can be indistinguishable from painted wood unless you look very closely.

The larger pieces of plastic lumber are very solid, but if you cut thin strips you can easily bend it to form archways or fans. It will never rot, rust, or need painting. It can be cut with traditional tools, hammered with nails, or screwed. Whatever color you are able to get, the extruded lumber will be the same color all the way through. It may be more expensive than wood, but you will make up the difference quickly with the dramatically reduced maintenance.

## NOTES

# MARCH

 ## PLANNING

Later in the month, it will be time to move into action mode, but when March comes in like a lion, you have to stick with planning and dreaming about the onset of spring. Luckily, the Philadelphia Flower Show is the great dispenser of the winter blahs. It is held early in the month at the Philadelphia Convention Center. If you are unsure how to create the perfect trellised nook or secret garden or romantic bower, you can pretty much guarantee that you will come away from the flower show with more ideas than can be implemented in a lifetime.

It is also time to take advantage of the occasional warm day to go out and mark out your spots for ground cover, especially where grass has struggled. Consider cutting up old carpeting into the shape you want the bed to take. Place the carpeting upside down where you want to grass to die. Cut the carpet a few inches bigger than you actually want the bed so the grass will won't grow out from the edges.

The use of a total vegetation killer, like Roundup®, will be effective, but you may want to try the carpeting, or even black plastic, before resorting to herbicides.

 ## PLANTING

In order to be able to plant in March, you need to be sure the soil is in the right condition to be worked. The soil should not be so wet that it stays wadded up in a solid lump when you squeeze a handful tightly. Open your hand and press the wad with your thumb. If it crumbles easily, you can start digging. If it rolls around like a sausage, go back to reading *War and Peace* for a while.

By the end of the month, you may be able to plant many things, but April is generally a more dependable time.

 ## WATERING

March is usually a fairly wet month. It is not necessary to water anything outdoors under those conditions. Water vines in containers as needed.

If you plant any vines or ground covers late in the month, **make sure you water them in thoroughly.**

 ## FERTILIZING

Late March is a good time to apply fertilizer as long as the ground is not frozen. If your ground covers are grown primarily for foliage, you can apply a light sprinkling 10-10-10 granular fertilizer. You should hose it off the foliage so it doesn't burn. If you are working with a ground cover where the flowers are of more significance, you may want to use a lower amount of nitrogen. Too much nitrogen can inhibit flower formation. In this case, a light sprinkling of 5-10-5 fertilizer will be more beneficial.

In general, more vines are grown for flowers than are ground covers. Again, use 10-10-10 for foliage types and 5-10-5 for those that you expect to bloom.

 ## PRUNING

If the weather is cooperative, pruning can be done late in the month but always on a day when temperatures are above freezing. Dead vines can be removed at any time, but **be sure you can distinguish dead vines from dormant ones.** Dormant **clematis** looks pretty dead. Some clematis bloom on old wood in the spring. You do not want to remove living shoots from spring flowering vines since you will be taking the flower buds. Other varieties bloom on new growth in the summer. A few bloom on both. You need to know how your flowering vine produces flowers to know when to prune. Spring bloomers are pruned right after bloom.

Ground covers can be pruned back along the edges to keep them in bounds. If herbaceous ground covers are showing signs of winter damage, you can mow them with the mower set on the highest setting. This will remove the burnt foliage and encourage dormant buds to fill in rapidly. This treatment should correspond with a spring application of fertilizer to speed up the "filling in" process.

Shrub-type ground covers also get pruned now or early next month before the burst of spring growth. In that way, the new growth will fill in any bare spots and cover any naked-looking stubs left from pruning cuts. Remove dead branches or brown tips. Prune branches that are too long or too tall, cutting to a side shoot or the main trunk. **Junipers** will fill in better if cut to a side shoot showing green foliage.

## PESTS

Pests are not usually a problem at this time of year.

## Helpful Hints

*1* Ground covers should eventually fill in sufficiently to become their own weed barrier, but until that happens, you should use an organic mulch. Mulch also has the benefit of decomposing and so adding organic matter to the soil over time. Since ground covers are often in their spot a very long time, this is one way to help keep them thriving.

*2* If soggy leaves have accumulated over the winter on the surface of your ground cover, you want to be sure to rake that off as soon as possible. Left for a significant period of time, it can smother the plants.

## NOTES

# APRIL

## PLANNING

Planning definitely begins to shift over to action mode at this time. Planning helps planting in that you will need to know how many plants it will take to fill in a certain area. You then need to balance how many plants you need (and can afford) with how long you are willing to wait for them to fill in a space. Using fewer plants means they will take longer to fill in the area and you will have to keep weeding in the meantime.

Each type of ground cover has a range of planting spaces. Most shrub-type ground covers, such as **creeping junipers,** are placed on 3-foot centers. However the beautiful **dwarf Japanese juniper** (*J. procumbens* 'Nana') grows more slowly than the other common varieties but may have a larger spread at maturity. So it is important to understand the specifics of whatever you have chosen.

**Sweet woodruff** planted on 7-inch centers with good soil preparation and appropriate summer watering will fill in by autumn. **Ajuga** has a spreading range of 6 to 12 inches. Obviously, planted on 6-inch centers, Ajuga will fill in more quickly. **Ivy** has its own characteristics to factor into the picture. It is usually spaced on 12-inch centers. Planting ivy closer won't change that. (There is an old saying "The first year it sleeps, the second year it creeps, the third year it leaps.") **Myrtle** has a range of 6- to 12-inch centers.

Climbing vines grow differently. They usually require a minimum of about 5 feet between plants, but there is an enormous difference in both the rate of growth and the ultimate size of a **clematis** and a **wisteria.** The clematis stays rather polite and demure compared to the wildly aggressive and enormous wisteria. Again, know the details of what to expect from the plants you have chosen and plan accordingly.

## PLANTING

Good soil preparation is crucial for vines and ground covers if you expect them to stay in their allotted space for years to come. Make sure you are planting sun-loving plants in the sun and have chosen shade-tolerant ground covers for shady areas.

See the chapter introduction for planting information.

## WATERING

Water all newly planted vines and ground covers thoroughly. Established plantings rarely need supplemental water in April.

## FERTILIZING

If you didn't fertilize established vines and ground covers last month, you can still apply fertilizer in April. Weather permitting, earlier in the month is better than later. See last month for more specifics.

For newly planted vines and ground covers, fertilizer can be mixed into the soil during initial preparation, or a water-soluble fertilizer can be applied after planting. The use of 10-10-10 fertlizer would be for ground covers and vines that are primarily planted for their foliage, but use 5-10-5 fertilizer for plants whose bloom is of greater significance.

## PRUNING

While dead vines, branches, or shoots can be removed at any time from just about any type of plant, do not prune spring-blooming vines until after the flowers fade. See last month for more information on spring pruning of vines and ground covers.

## PESTS

**Pachysandra** gets a disease called canker. It manifests itself with a circle of flattened plants with collapsed stems. If left untreated, the entire patch will eventually be taken down. It needs to be sprayed at budbreak, seven to ten days later, and again in another seven to ten days for a total of 3 sprays. Check with your Cooperative Extension Office for current recommended materials.

**Winter creeper** is a popular ground cover in the genus *Euonymus*. It is unfortunately subject to the unpleasant *Euonymus* scale, which can also sometimes be spotted on our other friend, **pachysandra.** This is best controlled with a dormant oil in April. However, you will be happy to know that the Philip Alampi Beneficial Insect Laboratory has successfully released beneficial insects that specifically control this destructive nuisance so it is less of a problem than it used to be.

## Helpful Hints

### Dividing

April is a great time to divide many of your ground covers. Dig them out carefully. Some have distinct crowns that separate easily. Others have tuberous roots with "eyes" or growing points that can be replanted. Some, like **English ivy,** can be removed with a stem and root attached. If you need to cover additional ground, you may be able to do it more economically by dividing what you or a gardening friend already has in the garden.

## NOTES

# MAY

## PLANNING

Later in May, you will find the spring-blooming **clematis** in outrageous display mode. The flowers can be 8 inches across and in abundance. Luckily, there are also summer bloomers for later in the season. **Fiveleaf akebia** is an aggressive plant that needs a firm hand or a cold winter to keep it in bounds. The foliage is quite attractive, however, with five leaflets arranged palmate, like an umbrella. In mid-May you may see the small purple flowers in the same cluster as larger pale pinkish ones. The dark ones are male, and the pink are female. The fleshy purple fruits are edible but rarely appear under cultivation.

The red varieties of **trumpet honey-suckle** will bloom in late May. The vines are on the scraggly side, but they attract hummingbirds. 'Sulphurea' has attractive yellow blooms but no scent and probably no hummingbirds. (These fast flying tiny dynamos are attracted to red first and foremost.)

In the world of ground covers, the delightful and brilliantly colored *Phlox subulata* is a show stopper for most of the month. Known as **creeping phlox, moss pinks, mountain pinks,** or just **pinks,** this thick ground cover is never invasive and always welcome. **Lily-of-the-valley** also blooms in May. The sweet scent is so enticing that it is often used in powders and perfumes. **Ajuga,** or **bugleweed,** will bloom toward the middle of May, although the attractive foliage is the main event. **Sweet woodruff** is similar, with May blooms but lovely foliage as the primary reason for planting. With sweet woodruff, however, you also have the lovely scent.

## PLANTING

Planting ground covers and vines is not much different from planting most other things. The ideal planting time is late March or April, depending on the weather. By May, most plants are out of dormancy, but early in the month the risk is minimal.

Container plants can really be planted any time since there is little to no stress to the root system by simply popping it into the ground. Some ground covers are sold by the flat and have to be pulled apart for planting. That may not be as risk free. Earlier in the month is always better than later, to avoid high temperatures and dry ground.

May is the perfect time to plant annual vines, after danger of frost has past. These would include the hyacinth-scented **snail vines,** sunny yellow **thunbergia, morning glories,** purple foliaged **sweet potato vine, hyacinth bean,** and **scarlet runner bean.** It is also time to move your **mandevilla vine** outdoors if you kept it over the winter.

Understand the spacing needs for whatever you plant. Refer to the chapter introduction for more planting information.

## WATERING

Always water in newly planted vines and ground covers just as you would anything else. This initial watering has as much to do with helping the soil to fill in around the roots as it does providing water.

Use a bit of common sense. Since the month can be quite warm and the soil dry, you may have to water. Since ground covers are commonly planted in the shade as an alternative to grass or to create a woodland atmosphere, it is less likely these areas will become dry enough to require watering, but it can happen.

# FERTILIZING

If you applied a granular fertilizer in April, you do not need to apply fertilizer in May. If you used a water-soluble fertilizer in April, you may want to fertilize again in May, depending on the recommendations of the fertilizer you use.

Whatever type of fertilizer you use, remember that vines and ground covers grown primarily for the foliage, such as **actinidia vine** and **pachysandra,** will do better with a higher nitrogen fertilizer such as 10-10-10. Too much nitrogen will inhibit flower formation, so for flowering vines such as **clematis** and ground covers such as **pinks** you should stick to less nitrogen such as 5-10-5 fertilizers.

# PRUNING

**Japanese honeysuckle** is extremely aggressive, but the exotic flowers and sweet scent persuade gardeners to keep it despite the drawbacks. Prune it hard early in the month to keep the vines under control. It flowers on new growth, so you will still have blooms from June to September.

**Silver fleece vine** (*Polygonum aubertii*) will also bloom later in the season. It, too, can be aggressive, so a significant pruning now will keep it in bounds.

**Wisteria** will finish blooming by the middle of the month. It can be quite aggressive, so prune the side shoots to form more of a trunk and train the remaining shoots to head in the direction you desire.

**Virginia creeper** can show up everywhere. While it can be very useful for shade or privacy, it is also murderous on other plants. On the bright side, it gets beautiful, red, fall color.

 # PESTS

Take care when pulling out weedy vines that you are not inadvertently exposed to **poison ivy** in the process. Poison ivy has three leaflets while **Virginia creeper** has five.

The leaves emerge reddish and quite shiny in early May. They lose the shine and turn medium green as they mature. All plant parts contain the oil that causes an allergic reation, even when they're dead.

## NOTES

_____

_____

_____

_____

_____

_____

_____

_____

_____

_____

_____

_____

_____

_____

_____

# JUNE
## Ground Covers & Vines

## PLANNING

Some of your **clematis** varieties will still be blooming in June. Your **trumpet honeysuckles** may still have a few flowers early in the month but by the end of the month you should be able to see the white and yellow blooms of the **Japanese honeysuckle.** (Watch out for that one. It can become a nuisance if left unattended for a year or two.) The incredibly lovely **climbing hydrangea** blooms in late June and continues into the following month. This one is slow to get established but is well worth the wait. Climbing hydrangea is deciduous but adds a bit of winter interest with its exfoliating bark.

Certainly you can expect an enormous display of flowers on your **climbing roses** this month. Technically, climbing roses are not vines, even though they climb (sort of). They do not spiral, cling by rootlets or suction cups, or have twining tendrils. To create the lovely bower of roses you imagine from the perfect Victorian garden, you must weave or tie your rose canes to the support. For more information about how to care for climbing roses, see the Roses chapter.

## PLANTING

Any of your annual vines that didn't get planted in May can still be planted early this month. Any containerized nursery stock such as **creeping junipers, cotoneasters,** or even spreading **ornamental grasses** that you may use as ground covers can be planted now. At this late date, however, you want to pay extra attention to soil preparation, mulching, and appropriate watering to make sure the plants don't immediately go into stress during the first heat wave.

Containerized perennial-type ground covers such as **daylilies, ferns, evening primrose,** or **sweet woodruff** can also be planted now. It is not, however, a great time to divide these same plants. The root systems tend to get damaged in the process. While dormant, they can handle it, but in the middle of the growing season it is not worth the risk.

## WATERING

Water all spring-planted vines and ground covers when the ground gets slightly dry. Recently planted material will not yet be able to thrive in truly dry ground, so if you are experiencing a lack of spring rain, water thoroughly in the early morning. The use of an organic mulch around newly planted ground covers will help retain soil moisture.

## FERTILIZING

For annuals vines, most of which are flower producing, you should mix in a 5-10-5 fertilizer during soil preparation or water in thoroughly with a water-soluble fertilizer for flowering plants.

If you choose a water-soluble fertilizer, continue to feed annuals and other vines and ground covers according to label directions. Remember that plants grown primarily for foliage do better with a higher level of nitrogen. Different types of water-soluble fertilizers are available for the different plant types. Choose the one that is most appropriate for what you have in your garden.

## PRUNING

When your **creeping phlox** or **pinks** have finished blooming, you may want to mow them with the mower set on the highest possible setting. This will remove any possible seed heads and encourage bushier new growth. The ultimate result is even more flowers the following year.

**Climbing roses** are pruned right after they finish blooming. See the chapter on Roses for more details.

Spring blooming **clematis** can be pruned after it blooms as well. Clematis are fairly tidy, however, and rarely need much pruning except to remove the dead vines. Prune those clematis that bloom on both old and new wood very lightly or else you may eliminate the summer display.

**'Arctic Beauty'** is perhaps the most popular of the *Actinida* vines. They can be quite aggressive and may need the occasional pruning throughout the season to keep them in line.

## PESTS

Euonymus scale can show up at any time on **winter creeper,** *E. fortunei,* and even on **pachysandra.** Check with your Cooperative Extension Office for current control recommendations.

Weed control is important in newly planted beds where the ground cover has not yet covered the ground. The use of organic mulch will help.

Japanese beetles hatch out later this month. They don't usually feed heavily on many vines and ground covers, but they can be devastating on **climbing roses.** Populations are generally light in

June and can be handpicked. Do not use pheromone type traps. They catch many beetles but not before they eat everything on the way to the trap and lay copious numbers of eggs in your lawn.

Slugs will feed voraciously on **hostas,** especially if it has been a wet season. Pulling back the organic mulch makes the environment somewhat less attractive to slugs. The use of traps is effective in this case. One-pound coffee cans, filled halfway with beer and a dollop of molasses, will draw in slugs like bees to honey. Sink the can into the ground up to the rim. Cut a 1-inch hole in the center of the lid and place it on the can. Collect dead slugs daily (wear gloves).

## NOTES

# JULY
## Ground Covers & Vines

## PLANNING

Your **climbing hydrangea** may still be blooming early in the month, and your **Japanese honeysuckle** will be getting started. Many of the honeysuckle varieties are less aggressive than the species. 'Harlequin' has pink flowers, variegated foliage, a great scent, and fall color. Best of all, it stays about 8 to 10 feet long. Lathyrus, the perennial **sweet pea,** will be blooming now, and **silver fleece vine** may be getting started by the end of the month. **Clematis** that blooms on new growth will also be in flower. Campsis, the bright orange-red flowered **trumpetcreeper,** will first show color sometime this month as well. **Dutchman's pipe** (*Aristolochia durior)* is grown for the abundant foliage that tends to stay flat against a house or trellis. It is used for quick but attractive cover. The funny little brownish flowers that look like a pipe will show up at this time of year.

## PLANTING

July heat is not a great environment to plant much of anything. If you find something irresistible in a container, plant it on a cloudy day or in the evening. This will give it a chance to settle in and take up some water. If the plant is in blazing sun, you may want to provide a shade cloth for a few days.

Early September, after the weather breaks, is a good time to plant many things. Perhaps you want to hold onto your special find until planting conditions are more favorable. Choose a bright spot with some protection from mid-day sun. Keep the container well watered.

## WATERING

Recently planted vines and groundcovers will need water sooner than well-established plantings. Cooler roots in shade will have less water demand and usually need to be watered less frequently. If watering is necessary, water deeply. See the chapter introduction for more watering considerations.

## FERTILIZING

It is rare that you will want to fertilize anything in July, but if you do, be very careful not to burn the roots. Above 85 degrees Fahrenheit, any fertilizer may cause damage. If you are using a water-soluble fertilizer, you may want to use a half concentration as a safeguard.

## PRUNING

Some vines grow quickly and need an occasional nip or tuck throughout the season. While you are at it, you may want to take some cuttings for propagation. Many vines can be propagated by semi-hardwood cuttings. To take some cuttings:

- Choose shoots that are about 6 inches long with a minimum of three leaf nodes. It is always better to prune these the day after a good rain or a deep watering. This way the cutting will have less chance of going into water stress.

- Take the cuttings in the early morning after the plants have had all night to replenish their reserves.

- Remove the bottom leaves and dip them into a rooting hormone. This requires light dusting of the powder, not a coating like when you are breading chicken.

- Plant using a sterile potting material.

- Provide some humidity by covering with a cloche or wrapping plastic around some stakes or other support.

• Keep cuttings out of direct sun. Once roots have formed you can gradually remove the "greenhouse" material.

 PESTS

**Powdery mildew** can show up on a variety of plants. **Aphids** can be a problem on **honeysuckle.** Check with the Cooperative Extension Office for current control measures.

## Helpful Hints

*1* The magnificent but fast growing **silver fleece vine** can be pruned hard in the winter to contain it, but in the right spot it is quite dramatic if left to grow with enthusiasm. You may, however, want to choose its location with some care. Flies often hover about the clusters of flowers.

*2* The pink and red blooming varieties of **honeysuckle** are a great attraction to hummingbirds.

*3* On the ground, look for **daylilies** to be blooming. They are addressed under perennials, but if planted thick enough, they can be effective as groundcovers. This is especially true for the more compact varieties with a long bloom such as 'Stella D'oro' or 'Butterscotch Ruffles'.

*4* Long **wisteria** vines can be used to make wreaths or baskets. When you prune your wisteria after it finishes blooming, you can save the vines. They will weave most easily when they are still somewhat green and flexible. If you hold them too long, they will break when you want them to bend.

## NOTES

# AUGUST

##  PLANNING

By August, you can certainly begin planning for next year. There are probably lots of vines and groundcovers you have spotted along the way that you have placed on your "absolutely can't live without" list. Some of these may do fine with fall planting, so keep that in mind for September. Fall garden catalogs are already torturing your mail carrier as they are coming in abundance. Place your orders now.

It is also a good idea to visit your local nurseries on a regular basis throughout the year. They often feature plants at the time they are in bloom, so you can see what you're getting. If you are looking for something to spice things up in August when there is a dearth of woody things blooming, take a cruise by your "Little Nursery around the Corner" and see what's hot in a pot.

You may find some of the late-blooming clematis showing off. *C. tangutica* has the common name **lemon peel clematis,** which isn't very appealing in my opinion, but also goes by **golden clematis.** The petals are thicker than most in a lovely shade of golden yellow. They are not very "clematis-like" in that they resemble hanging bells rather than the classic flat open bloom that comes to mind when one thinks of clematis flowers. They also produce very interesting seedpods, which look like the "Cousin It" of the flower world. **Autumn clematis** (*C. paniculata*) produces a plethora of fragrant white flowers, starting in late August. There are a number of hybrids that bloom in late summer as well. 'Lady Betty Balfour' is dark purple with an abundance of contrasting pale yellow stamens. 'Ramona' (hereby dedicated to my editor, Ramona Wilkes) is a large-flowered variety, with blooms up to 8 inches across. It produces an abundance of flat, open blooms from late summer through early fall.

The ground cover **rock rose** *(Helianthemum nummularium)* can produce a second round of blooms in late summer or early fall if pruned back after the initial flowering. Several of the sedums bloom in late summer. 'Dragon's Blood' is a deep-red flowered variety of *S. spurium. S. cauticola* also blooms in late summer. **Bearberry,** a groundcover suitable for down the shore in the sun and sand, has small, pink flowers in the spring followed by bright red berries in late summer.

##  PLANTING

August is still too hot and dry to do much planting. If you come across some containerized vines in bloom, you can plant them if you promise yourself you will give them the extra attention they need. If the ground is very dry, you may even want to water the ground deeply the day before you dig.

A little shade provided by a shade cloth will make summer heat a bit easier on the plants. Make sure they have been well watered before planting, and water in immediately after planting. Plant after the sun goes down so they have some time to settle in and take up some water before having to cope with High Noon.

When planting enough groundcovers to cover any significant area, you may need a large number of plants. Before you invest that kind of time and money, minimize your risk and wait until the weather breaks next month. If you are just popping a potted plant into a nook in your rock garden, then go for it, but follow the above suggestions.

## WATERING

Water anything you intend to plant before you plant it, and also immediately after planting. Always water deeply when you water. It is best to water in the early morning so the foliage has a chance to dry off as soon as the sun comes out. Watering at night, while it is cooler, allows the foliage to remain damp through the night, encouraging diseases.

# FERTILIZING

If you are fertilizing your garden with a diluted water-soluble fertilizer, you should cut the concentration in half during the hot months. Annual vines, such as *Thunbergia*, **snail flower, scarlet runner bean,** or even **morning glory,** may benefit from a light application of fertilizer. However, woody vines will be going dormant soon and late applications of fertilizer may encourage new growth that will be tender come frost.

 # PRUNING

Removal of developing seedpods from flowering vines may be beneficial. **Wisteria** pods are very interesting velvety long "beans." They twist to open and disperse their seeds. You really do not want wisteria seedlings popping up everywhere. Some **clematis** seed pods are very attractive and actually part of the appeal of the plant, but as they brown and get ugly they, too, should be removed.

**Kiwi** vines may be bearing fruit now, but they also send out some very aggressive shoots. **Wisteria** does also. Prune the wayward branches on an as-needed basis.

 # PESTS

Powdery mildew is even more likely to make an appearance in August as cooler nights are more conducive to the disease. Flies may be drawn to the scent of the **silver fleece vine.** While you may not want to eat under a bower covered with fleece vine, the flies do no harm to the plant. Some weeping forms of **Norway spruce** are ground-hugging, so if you have chosen one of these, you may want to keep a close eye on it for mites. In many cases, a fierce spray of water from the hose will wash away a large percentage of mites.

This pest can also show up on **creeping phlox** and **English ivy,** so if they look a little pale, this could be a symptom of infestation.

# NOTES

# SEPTEMBER

 ## PLANNING

September is another action month. The weather is cooling down and you get to clean up from the summer as well as start preparing for next spring. Those ground covers that did really well for you may warrant division. Vine plants may need a little guidance to grow where you want them. All vines are hard to move once they get going. Twining vines spiral around things and those with sticky fingers are attached with amazing strength. You may be able to yank them off, but they leave a mess. On the side of your house, you may want to do some pruning and redirecting of this year's growth to avoid future ripping and tearing.

There are vines that have seasonal interest at this time of year. The annual vine **thunbergia** produces flowers all summer, but in September it is often spectacular. The **autumn clematis** and **golden clematis** produce flowers in late summer and early fall, but the seedpods on both are very interesting as the flowers fade. *Ampelopsis brevipedunculata* (who names these things?) is, thankfully, also known as **porcelain vine.** The flowers are nondescript in summer, but the berries which follow are in shades of green, turquoise, bright blue, and violet.

 ## PLANTING

Vines can be planted now, if you come across them at your local nursery or even if you want to transplant some of your own. Vines that do some running along the ground may have already produced some roots, making propagation easy. **Climbing hydrangea** and **ivy** are both very cooperative this way. **Myrtle** is more ground cover than a major climber, but it does enough creeping that you should be able to find rooted shoots that you can move. **Winter creeper** (*Euonymus fortunei*) climbs a bit more but is still used more as a groundcover than a climbing vine. It roots readily at almost any time of year, but if you can find a few shoots with roots, your job will be easy.

Do not move seedlings of **wisteria**, no matter how much you are tempted. Seedlings often disappoint in their ability to produce flowers. If you have a wisteria that takes your breath away, you are better off trying to layer it now and transplant it once it makes a few roots in spring. Layering is the simple method of propagating by pinning a shoot to the ground (see June's "Helpful Hints" for more information).

Spring blooming ground covers can be divided now. **Pinks, mountain pinks, moss pinks,** or **creeping phlox** (all common names for *Phlox subulata*) do very

well with division in the early fall. Sometimes the center of an older patch may die out. Dig out the clump, discard the dead ugly part, and replace with younger **growth from the outer edge.**

**Sweet woodruff** will also divide easily now, but if you don't get to it, it can wait until spring. **Ferns,** on the other hand, should wait until spring to be divided. **Lily-of-the-valley** is another ground-cover that does best with spring division.

 ## WATERING

Usually early September brings an abundance of rain, but not every year. If the ground remains dry from summer heat and drought, you will need to continue the occasional deep watering. Once the weather breaks and soil moisture levels improve, you can discontinue deep watering on established plantings unless the weather turns exceedingly dry.

**Any patches of ground covers you intend to divide should be watered deeply the day before** you are ready to do the work. That way they can replenish water reserves before their roots are ripped.

Water newly planted vines and ground covers immediately. If the weather turns hot, transplanted divisions may need a bit of daily watering until either the weather cools off or they put out a few roots. In most years, September weather is perfect for transplanting, but the occasional return to summer heat early in the month can stress newly divided plants.

 FERTILIZING

Ground cover will benefit from an application of fertilizer in early spring, but it is not necessary right now.

 PRUNING

Pruning now is more for tidying up the plants. There are lots of flower stalks and shriveled leaves that would benefit from a snip. Ground covers that have overstepped their bounds may warrant a trim, but don't get carried away.

 PESTS

The population of slugs can be quite impressive at this time of year, especially if it has been a wet summer. They reproduce with great enthusiasm. As slugs are hermaphrodites, they all lay eggs, lots of eggs, in the cool, moist mulch around your shade-loving plants. If you come across the eggs, you should destroy them. Eggs look like clusters of translucent spheres, about the size of okra seeds.

## Helpful Hints

*1* September is the ideal time for all major lawn work. Grass is the most popular ground cover of all time. See the chapter on lawns for what you should be doing at this time.

*2* It is time to begin the transition of bringing non-hardy vine indoors for the winter. Some of the more exotic **English ivies** and the tropical beauty, the **mandevilla vine,** will do well indoors over the winter, as long as you keep them in a sunny window. Move them into lower light outdoors for a week or two before bringing them into the house.

*3* You may be able to see slugs when they're mating. At dusk, look in areas where they hang out. They tend to climb up the sides of the house, up branches, and up tree trunks. The mating pair dangles down on a rope of slime. They gyrate at the base of the rope, and when they are done, one drops to the ground and the other climbs back up, consuming the rope as he/she travels.

## NOTES

_____

_____

_____

_____

_____

_____

_____

_____

_____

_____

_____

# OCTOBER
## Ground Covers & Vines

 PLANNING

The big event in any garden in October is fall color. One of the first plants to color up is **poison ivy.** You may not want to cultivate it, but it is a beautiful shade of red. **Virginia creeper** and its cousin **Boston ivy** both turn scarlet in the fall. **Porcelain vine** foliage is a very rich gold, but it is even more attractive because of the contrast against the blue, green, and violet berries. **Honeysuckle** rarely shows autumn color, but it does get lots of berries. Some are blue or black, but far more are either bright red or bright yellow. Birds love them.

**Hardy kiwi vines** (*Actinidia arguta*), turn a nice yellow. So do the **bittersweet vines,** both the Oriental (on many invasive lists, however) as well as the native **American bittersweet.** Of even more importance are the fruits which open to reveal bright red seeds. The fruiting vines are sought after for indoor decoration. They make particularly lovely wreaths. **Crimson glory vine** is a close relative of the grape, but the fruits are **inedible.** The fall foliage is crimson (are you surprised?).

**Wintergreen** ground cover turns a dark reddish purple. **Rock cotoneaster** is a shrub-type ground cover. The foliage turns orange-red in autumn. The cultivar 'Little Gem' has spectacular fall color.

 PLANTING

You need at least six weeks before the ground freezes for newly planted vines and ground covers to get sufficiently established to be able to endure winter. In the warmer parts of the state, Zone 7, that may give you most of the month to get a few more plants in the ground, but earlier is definitely better than later. In most of the state, limit yourself to the first two weeks. In the cold northwest corner, confine any new planting to the first few days.

 WATERING

Water newly planted material as soon as you put it in the ground. If the ground is dry, you may want to water any recently planted material as well. One more deep watering should hold things until spring.

No ground covers or vines should go into the winter dry. If the ground freezes throughout the entire root zone of a plant, it cannot take up any water. If a plant goes into winter dry, frozen ground provides no way to compensate, and winter drought will take its toll. If it is plump and full of water, it can live in the cold using stored water for a long time.

 FERTILIZING

No fertilizer is needed now. Wait until spring.

 PRUNING

Plants are doing a fair amount of self-pruning. Leaves are beginning to fall. It won't make much difference to most vines, but ground covers smothered in matted leaves will definitely suffer the consequences. Rake the leaves up and throw them onto the compost pile.

 PESTS

Pests are not as common a problem on vines and ground covers as on other things. Most of these plants are fairly resilient. Euonymus scale gets on a few things, including **winter creeper** (*E. fortunei*) and **pachysandra.** Spider Mites can infest **English ivy** and even **moss pinks,** but as the weather cools mites become less active. A serious scale infestation warrants control, but the most important spray will be the dormant oil spray next April. Make a note of anything infested with scale this season so you'll be prepared to stop it early with the smothering action of the oil.

## Helpful Hints

*1* The **Oriental bittersweet** is far more aggressive than the native **American bittersweet** and can reach 30 feet. The American is not as aggressive (although both can smother plants they are entwined upon) and can only reach 20 feet. The Oriental has more rounded leaves, but an easier method to distinguish the two is that the fruits of the Oriental are in small lateral clusters. On the American, they are in terminal clusters.

*2* The fruits of the **hardy kiwi** often ripen in early October. They are delicious and very high in vitamin C.

*3* **Mums** bloom in September and October, but those robust potted mums that you pop into the garden don't really look like groundcovers. You may be surprised, however, to see how groundcover-like established mums can behave. If you plant small **chrysanthemums** in the spring and allow them to get established by the fall, the following spring they can be a thick mat of green. Keep the tips pinched all summer, and they will stay much more compact, producing many flowers on shorter stems.

# NOVEMBER
## Ground Covers & Vines

 ## PLANNING

Things slow down in November. Certainly it is time to reflect on what was wonderful and what was not. Early in the month, you may still enjoy the brilliant colors of fall foliage. The vivid reds that appear on **poison ivy** and **Virginia creeper** begin so early that they also finish early. One good nor'easter and most of the colorful foliage disappears from all the deciduous plants, not just the vines.

The only real problem with this is that the leaves land on the ground covers and that can be deadly. A thick mat of soggy leaves will smother ground covers in short order. A bamboo rake will come in handy. When the leaves are dry and fluffy, a leaf blower will do the job.

As an alternative to the leafblower, I have to say that a little leaf raking is good for the soul. It is a time to reflect; it is good exercise; and a pile of leaves in the middle of the yard simply screams to be jumped into. On the other hand, raking a big yard with lots of trees sort of loses its charm quickly. At what point one turns in the *feng shui* of a rake for the roar of a leaf blower is clearly a personal decision. Maybe you need to meditate on it until they all blow away. No! No! You must get them off the ground cover . . . then meditate.

 ## Helpful Hints
### Helping Feathered Friends

Thick vines are wonderful shelters for birds in the winter. **Bittersweet, Virginia creeper, Boston ivy,** and any of the ornamental grapes (or even the edible grapes if you don't eat them) provide food along with the shelter. If you have vines with no fruit, hang seed balls, pine cones filled with peanut butter, or bags of suet under the vines to feed your feathered friends while they are staying out of the wind.

 ## PLANTING

November is not the time to be planting anything. You need at least six weeks for the roots to get established enough to withstand the upcoming winter. The ground could freeze by the end of the month. Even if it doesn't actually freeze, roots stop growing when soil temperatures hit 45 degrees Fahrenheit. If you have something in a container, sink the entire pot into the ground in some protected nook and pile mulch up around it. You can pull it out for planting in early spring.

 ## WATERING

If you planted anything in September or October and it hasn't rained, you should continue to give it an occasional deep watering. On the off-chance that the ground is still dry from summer drought, one more deep watering of everything will minimize the chance of damage from winter drought. In most years, however, this is not necessary.

 ## FERTILIZING

No fertilizing is needed until spring.

 ## PRUNING

**Bittersweet vines** with their brilliant red seeds bursting out of their yellow-orange pods can be collected early in the month for use indoors.

You can also remove the last seedpods and eye-poking vines that just can't be where they want to be. When you are done, hang up your pruners until spring.

## PESTS

The pests are taking it easy. So should you.

# DECEMBER
## Ground Covers & Vines

 PLANNING

By December, things have definitely shifted gears from gardening to gift shopping. You may need to finish raking or blowing off a few leaves from your ground covers. Now may also be a good time to think "trellises."

For large gardens, you can build an arbor with vines planted up the posts. You will still need some type of support to get the vines to climb the posts. Lattice can be purchased, cut and nailed to the posts, or you can purchase simple wooden trellises to place at each post.

These same wooden trellises can be placed up against the house. **Clematis** will need something fairly delicate as the tiny tendrils cannot cling to lattice. Wrought iron trellises are often beautiful and delicate enough for clematis to attach. So are those made from copper tubing. Make sure you match the height of your vine with the size of the trellis.

The "obelisk" is somewhat "tower-like." It can be made of copper tubing or wrought iron or sometimes wood. They are available in various heights and can be placed almost anywhere, making them suitable for annual vines such as **thunbergia** or **morning glory.**

## Helpful Hints

In keeping with my movies-with-plants theme, any of the Tarzan movies probably has a vine in play somewhere along the line. Also, Meg Ryan and Kevin Kline's predicament in the romantic *French Kiss* revolves around starting a vineyard.

Trellises can be large or small, ornate or quite plain. For a **wisteria** vine, the best trellis is probably made from heavy pipe. In a few years it will be completely covered, but the vine won't be able to pull it down. An airy vine like clematis or even one of the annuals might do well on a very ornate trellis. This way you see the beauty of the trellis itself in winter, rather than just the bare vines.

Don't forget about gates and trellises. They can make a charming entrance to the yard or garden. They, too, are available in wood, wrought iron, or (dare we even mention it?) plastic. This plastic is usually called "resin" (a practice something akin to the marketing effort to change the name of prunes to dried plums). Some plastic "lumber" is indistinguishable from painted wood unless you examine it quite closely. The hollow-tube type is not as elegant.

 PLANTING

It is not time to plant. It is time to shop, bake, eat, and in general, make merry.

 WATERING

Water indoor vines as needed. Outdoors, things can take care of themselves.

 FERTILIZING

No fertilizer is needed now.

PRUNING

There is really nothing to prune in December unless there is a bit of something you want for decoration.

PESTS

Children peeking in secret places to find presents would fall into this category. However, take the natural balance approach. A small amount of peeking can be tolerated without causing serious harm. The other (gardening) pests are not a problem now.

# CHAPTER FIVE

# Houseplants

*Plants in pots that live in your house are called houseplants. This makes sense to everyone, except perhaps the plants.*

If plants had a say in the matter, they would probably prefer to be putting down roots in some tropical island, where the sun is warm and temperatures hover at a steady 80 degrees Fahrenheit. For that matter, wouldn't we all?

In truth, it is that tropical aura that drives us to put plants in pots that fill our homes with life and color and beauty. In the gardening season, houseplants often take a back seat to **roses, peonies,** and **tomatoes.** For those who are apartment bound though, houseplants play an even greater role. Without a patch of earth, many apartment dwellers pot annual flowers in windowboxes and have a tomato or two in 5-gallon buckets.

**The bond between humankind and plants is a strong one.** There is something about cultivating the earth, even if it is a cluster of clay pots or baskets hanging on the deck, that touches a place very deep. A blooming **African violet,** a cheerful **begonia,** or a lush **spathiphyllum** can really help during the long gray days of winter. There is also something calming about fussing with houseplants, especially after a less than perfect day. Watering, turning, plucking, and snipping your plants all help to make the transition from the busy routine of the day to the equally busy domestic routine of the evening. Or perhaps it is a way to wind down after the kids are in bed.

A healthy houseplant is a thing of joy. A wickedly ugly, straggly plant is not. When the plant stops giving you joy, compost it. But with the right plant in the right spot, and just a smidge of genuine TLC, your plants will thrive and your house will be their happy home.

The plants that make the best houseplants are those that thrive in a bit of shade when in their native environment. Sun-loving tropicals, such as the fantastically colored **crotons,** just don't hold up long as houseplants. They need the strong sun to continue to produce the vivid colors and compact growth. In most living rooms, the plants turn predominantly green, the leaves get smaller, and the gaps between the leaves get larger.

**Ferns,** on the other hand, are often woodland plants, used to being shaded by the forest around them. These are much more tolerant of the light conditions in your New Jersey living room.

## SHOULD THEY BE OUTSIDE OR IN?

Interpretation of lighting requirements is also a tricky subject. **Ferns** that prefer filtered light in the woods may require the sunniest spot in your home. Sun coming in a window is coming only from one direction. Outside, the light hits the plant from all directions. In New Jersey, the day is much shorter in the winter, whereas in tropical areas the day length does not fluctuate so dramatically from season to season.

In many cases, the sunlight coming into your home is filtered by a screen, which can **reduce the incoming light by as much as 20 percent.** If you have a screened window next to an unscreened window the difference is obvious. Also, do I dare say it?!! Your windows are probably not that clean. Even when you clean them till they sparkle, they just don't stay sparkling for long. Add a sheer curtain or drapes, and you have reduced the available light that much more.

If the leaves of your plant are smaller than when you purchased it, the variegation is lessened, the **cactus** looks skinny and floppy, or the branches have lots of stem but not a lot of leaves then your plants are growing with less than adequate light.

Some houseplant-lovers choose to move their plants outdoors for the summer. This is a way to help the plants make up for the less than ideal growing conditions they must endure from October through May. You need to approach this plan with caution. **Moving plants outdoors must be done gradually.** The sudden change to strong sun can turn leaves into crispy critters. In most cases, the plants will recover fairly quickly since they are now growing under such improved conditions. They will need more water (unless they get rained on) and will benefit from a regular application of fertilizer. They are also much more exposed to infestation from a variety of insect pests. Controlling insect pests outside is annoying. If the infestation comes back indoors for the winter, it becomes a nightmare.

Returning plants to their winter spots also requires a thoughtful approach. The change to indoor light intensity will certainly not scorch anything, but the prolonged yellowing and dropping of foliage is a sorry state of affairs. Allowing plants to acclimate to lower light conditions slowly, over about two weeks time, will make the adjustment easier for your plants and you, too!

Choosing the right plants for the growing conditions of your home is **the best way to have happy plants** and improve your home environment. If you have plants that are thriving in their indoor home, there is no need to move them out for the summer. Maximize the light available, locate plants as close to the source of light as possible, avoid heat and drafts, and water properly. If you do all that, you and your plants will co-exist to your mutual satisfaction.

## THE IMPORTANT POT

The wrong container can spell disaster. Pots must have drainage. If not, sooner or later the root system will end up sitting in water and that will be the beginning of the end. Clay pots are infinitely better than plastic or even glazed porcelain. Clay allows the passage of air and water through the sides of the pot. This helps moderate excess soil moisture and keeps the roots aerated.

**Pots with drainage need saucers.** With regard to clay, what is advantageous for the pot can be disastrous for your windowsill, table surface, or carpeting. Clay saucers should not be used, but if you prefer the look of clay, use another saucer underneath. Water oozes through a clay saucer, staining or warping whatever is underneath. Plastic or glazed porcelain is best.

Pot size needs to be just right. If in doubt, it's **better to be a bit potbound than to be in an oversized pot.** Excess soil acts as a sponge, creating a waterlogging effect even in the presence of what appears to be adequate drainage holes. Being slightly potbound can encourage bloom. When transplanting to a larger pot, always go up only one pot size at a time, even if the plant is very squeezed in the smaller pot. Let the roots work their way into the new soil a bit before upgrading a second time.

# Houseplants

## Where Do I Put Them?

### PLANTS FOR AN UNBLOCKED SOUTHERN EXPOSURE

| Common Name | Botanical Name |
| --- | --- |
| Burro's Tail | Sedum morganianum |
| Cactus | Opuntia spp. Mammillaria spp. Notocactus spp. |
| Century Plant | Agave spp. |
| Citrus Plants | Citrus spp. |
| Coleus | Coleus blumei |
| Croton | Codiaeum spp. |
| Crown of Thorns | Euphorbia splendens |
| English Ivy | Hedera helix |
| Flowering Maple | Abutilon striatum |
| Gardenia | Gardenia jasminoides |
| Jade Plant | Crassula argentea |
| Living Stones | Lithops spp. |
| Ming Aralia | Polyscias fruticosa |
| Moses in the Cradle | Rhoeo spathacea |
| Panda Plant | Kalanchoe tomentosa |
| Pregnant Onion | Ornithogalum caudatum |
| Purple Heart | Setcreasea purpurea |
| Purple Passion | Gynura 'sarmentosa' |
| Roses, Miniature | Rosa hybrid |
| Sensitive Plant | Mimosa pudica |
| Shamrock plant | Oxalis sp. |
| Wax Plant | Hoya carnosa |
| Zebra Plant | Aphelandra squarrosa |

### PLANTS FOR AN UNBLOCKED EASTERN OR WESTERN EXPOSURE

| Common Name | Botanical Name |
| --- | --- |
| African Violet | Saintpaulia ionantha |
| Aloe | Aloe vera |
| Aluminum Plant | Pilea cadierei |
| Areca Palm | Chrysalidocarpus lutescens |
| Artillery Plant | Pilea microphylla |
| Bear's Foot Fern | Polypodium aureum |
| Begonia | Begonia spp. and hybrids |
| Benjamin Fig | Ficus benjamina |
| Birdsnest Fern | Asplenium nidus |
| Bleeding Heart Vine | Clerodendron thomsoniae |
| Boston Fern | Nephrolepis exaltata |
| Bottle Palm | Beaucarnea recurvata |
| Button Fern | Pellaea rotundifolia |
| Chenille Plant | Acalypha hispida |
| Christmas Cactus | Zygocactus hybrids |
| Corn Plant | Dracaena fragrans 'massangeana' |
| Dumb Cane | Dieffenbachia seguine |
| Emerald Ripple | Peperomia caperata |
| False Aralia | Dizygotheca elegantissima |
| Fish Tail Palm | Caryota mitis |
| Flame Violet | Episcia cupreata |
| Gasteria Oxtongue | Gasteria x hybrida |
| Gold Dust Dracaena | Dracaena godseffiana |
| Gold Fish Plant | Columnea spp. |

# Houseplants

## PLANTS FOR AN UNBLOCKED EASTERN OR WESTERN EXPOSURE

| Common Name | Botanical Name |
| --- | --- |
| Haworthia | *Haworthia papillosa* |
| Holly Fern | *Cyrtomium falcatum* |
| Japanese Aralia | *Fatsia japonica* |
| Lady Palm | *Rhapis excelsa* |
| Madagascar Dragon Tree | *Dracaena marginata* |
| Monkey Puzzle Tree | *Araucaria araucana* |
| Nephtytis | *Syngonium podophyllum* |
| Orchids | |
|   Moth Orchids | *Phalaenopsis* spp. |
|   Royal Orchids | *Cattleya* spp. |
|   Spray Orchids | *Dendrobium* spp. |
| Peacock Plant | *Calathea makoyana* |
| Philodendrons | |
|   Elephant Ear Philodendron | *Philodendron domesticum* |
|   Heartleaf Philodendron | *P. oxycardium* |
|   Red Bristle Philodendron | *P. squamiferum* |
|   Tree Philodendron | *P. selloum* |
|   Velvet leaf Philodendron | *P. verrucosum* |
| Orchid Cactus | *Epiphyllum* hybrids |
| Piggy-back Plant | *Tolmiea menziesii* |
| Pothos | *Scindapsus aureus* |
| Prayer Plant | *Maranta leuconeura* |
| Rabbit's Foot Fern | *Davalia fejeensis* |
| Rubber Plant | *Ficus elastica* |
| Sago Palm | *Cycas revoluta* |
| Schefflera | *Brassaia actinophylla* |
| Sea Onion | *Bowiea volubilis* |

## PLANTS FOR AN UNBLOCKED EASTERN OR WESTERN EXPOSURE

| Common Name | Botanical Name |
| --- | --- |
| Silver Squill | *Scilla violacea* |
| Silver Vase Bromeliad | *Aechmea fasciata* |
| Spider Plant | *Chlorophytum comosum* |
| Split leaf Philodendron | *Monstera deliciosa* |
| Staghorn Fern | *Platycerium bifurcatum* |
| Star Flower | *Stapelia nobilis* |
| String of Hearts | *Ceropegia woodii* |
| Variegated Aloe | *Aloe variegata* |
| Variegated Peperomia | *Peperomia obtusifolia* 'Variegata' |
| Watermelon Peperomia | *Peperomia sandersii* |

## PLANTS FOR AN UNBLOCKED NORTHERN EXPOSURE

| Common Name | Botanical Name |
| --- | --- |
| Anthurium | *Anthurium clarinervium* |
| Bromeliad | *Nidularium innocentii* |
| Cast Iron Plant | *Aspidistra elatior* |
| Chinese Evergreen | *Aglaonema commutatum* |
| East India Holly Fern | *Polystichum aristatum* |
| Peace Lily | *Spathiphyllum* sp. |
| Snake Plants | *Sanseveria* species |
|   Birdsnest Snake | *S. trifasciata* 'Hahnii' |
|   Mother-in-laws Tongue | *S. trifasciata* |
|   Pencil Snake | *S. cylindrica* |
| Table Fern | *Pteris ensiformis* |

# JANUARY

## Houseplants

## PLANNING

The holidays are over, the days are short, and the weather is cold. This is the perfect time to turn your attention to your houseplants. They will appreciate the attention, and you will get a bit of "zen" relaxation from the experience.

You will need to include cleaning your plants in your maintenance plans. Dust gets on the foliage and clogs things up. A dirty leaf just can't utilize available light as well as a clean leaf. Light, being at a premium throughout New Jersey in January, must be used to every possible advantage.

A fairly strong spray of water will get the bulk of the dirt off, but a soft cloth will make many leaves shine. Old tee-shirts are great for this. Large smooth leaves will benefit the most from polishing. These include the leaves of the **rubber plant, the cast iron plant,** or even the heart-shaped **philodendron leaves.**

While you are at it, wash all the saucers and wipe around the plants. Sometimes insects leave sticky residue that gets very dirty. If you come across the sticky residue, then look around for the source. You will want to control the insect, or at least isolate the plant since many insects will spread throughout your plant population.

## PLANTING

Since plants are not growing with gusto during the shortest days of the year, transplanting may not be wisest thing to do. Those plants that are extremely pot-bound can be potted up one pot size. Use a sterile potting soil in a clean pot with drainage.

Some plants will begin to get stretched out due to the lower light conditions. Taking the occasional cutting will help keep them compact while providing material to start new plants. Be sure to take the cutting the day after a thorough watering and use a light dab of rooting hormone to help get things started. Place the cutting, with a leaf node at the base of the cutting, into sterile potting material such as perlite or vermiculite. Avoid excessive heat or strong light as the cuttings will not be able to take up much water until they generate some roots. When the cutting has generated roots 1 to 2 inches long, they can be potted up into a sterile potting soil in an appropriately small pot.

## WATERING

Watering needs for houseplants are based on their water usage and the environmental conditions rather than a schedule. Heat dries the air. The closer the plants are to the source of heat, the quicker they will dry out. The soil may dry out quickly even if the plants are growing slowly. Stick your finger in the soil. If it feels dry as far as you can feel, it needs to be watered. If in doubt, wait another day.

Some plants wilt when thirsty. **Coleus** and **spathiphyllum** both do this. Other plants give no notice but simply shed leaves with gusto. The holiday **poinsettia** is famous for this, but so are **Boston ferns** and even the **weeping** or **Benjamin fig.** Keep an eye on the soil so you don't end up with naked plants.

## FERTILIZING

There is no need to fertilize houseplants at this time of year.

## PRUNING

January is a bit early for pruning. If, however, you have a few plants that have gotten overly leggy or had a nervous breakdown and dropped all their leaves, you should prune now. Consider adding spent **poinsettias** to the compost pile. Without proper watering they can get ugly fast. If you want to nurse them back to health, they will need a serious pruning. That way, the dormant buds further back on the stems will sprout and begin to make a more compact and full plant.

A major pruning before the spring burst of new growth can prevent stretching, but the occasional floppy branch or naked stem should be removed when noticed. **Begonias** fall into this category, as do **coleus,** some succulents such as **burro's tail,** and even the many varieties of the great houseplants **philodendron** and **pothos.**

 ## PESTS

Insect pests proliferate indoors with the benefits of central heat. Mites are probably the most hazardous simply because they are so difficult to see. By the time the damage is obvious, they are likely to number in the thousands.

Mites are related to spiders and make very unsophisticated webs. You can sometimes see the webbing in the crotches of the leaves or stems. The insects can be seen on the upper surface of the leaves but are generally more abundant on the underside. If you **wipe you finger on the underside** of the leaf and it comes out all dusty, chances are that dust is really mites.

Mites suck the chlorophyll out of the leaf leaving a tiny yellow dot. These dots cluster together and create a yellow cast to the leaf. If you examine a yellow leaf with a magnifying glass and see yellow polka dots, that's a clue you have a mite problem.

Mites reproduce rapidly and can spread to a wide variety of plants. Isolate an infested plant and deal with the problem immediately. Washing the plant with a very strong stream of water will wash many insects away. Spray the underside of the leaves thoroughly. Repeat this every three to five days for at least 3 treatments. If a more serious approach is necessary, the use of insecticidal soap or 50 percent rubbing alcohol and water will help. Spray a small portion of the plant first and determine if it can tolerate the treatment before spraying completely. Check with your Cooperative Extension Office for current pesticide recommendations if the problem is more serious. Spray the plant outside on a warm day, following label directions carefully.

## NOTES

_____

_____

_____

_____

_____

_____

_____

_____

_____

_____

PLANNING

Roll up your sleeves and get ready to dig in! Soak clay pots in a 10 percent bleach solution to kill any residual organisms, and scrape off any salt deposits. Find saucers to go with the pots. Plastic or porcelain is best.

Have a collection of trivets around. They can be used to raise the saucers off of surfaces. The air space prevents any moisture seal that can damage whatever table or floor the plant sits upon.

Make sure your decorative pots have drainage, or you can plan to use the **"pot within a pot"** approach. A clay pot placed inside a decorative pot uses the decorative pot as an oversized saucer. Putting a couple of inches of stone in the bottom can create a space for overflow. Remember, roots sitting in water are almost instant death.

Have a supply of good quality potting soil. Garden soil doesn't work as well in pots. You should maximize growing conditions so the plants can be happy in spite of being in a pot, so starting with the best potting soil is a step in the right direction.

 PLANTING

Do a lot of transplanting at one time to avoid repeated mess and cleanup.

Remember to repot by going up only one pot size at a time. Cover the hole in the bottom with a clay shard so the soil doesn't fall out. For plastic pots that have more than one hole or even in clay pots, you can cover the bottom with a square of paper towel. That holds the soil in place but still allows the water to drain out.

Put soil in the bottom and place the plant in the pot so that $1/2$ to 1 inch of the pot is still above the soil line. Do not place the plant deeper in the new pot unless the roots are still exposed at the surface. Then just barely cover the roots. Planting too deep will cause the stem or trunk to rot.

In some cases, you may want to divide the plants. **Ferns, asparagus ferns, spider plants,** and sometimes even **spathiphyllum** (to name a few) will be so thick with roots that the only way to divide them is to saw the rootball in half, vertically. Remove any unattached root pieces or shoots that end up with no roots left. The remaining pieces get potted up with about 1 inch of fresh soil around the division.

Press the soil down firmly around the plants but not so hard that you squeeze out all the air spaces. In some cases, the plant may need a bit of support. Cactus or snakes plants have small roots systems and may need help staying upright until they get established. **For tiny plants, plastic forks make convenient stakes.** Place three forks around the plant, with the tines in the soil. Chop sticks, thin wooden dowels, or wire hangers can all be serviceable. You can even purchase special stakes with a wire circle at the top to hold the plant just for this purpose. Once the plant is established, you can remove the support.

 WATERING

Water newly potted plants thoroughly. That helps the soil to settle in around the roots and fills in any air spaces. **Make sure the plants can drain thoroughly.** Let them sit in your dish drainer in the kitchen, on the deck outside, in a milk crate, or even just in the grass to give them plenty of time for the excess water to drain. Then put them in a clean saucer in their permanent spot. Of course you can't leave them outside to drain if the weather is too cold. Check the weather and look for a warm day.

# FERTILIZING

That first day you detect the strength of the sun is back is the day you start to fertilize your houseplants again. A water-soluble fertilizer for houseplants used in a dilute solution every time you water is the safest approach. It doesn't take much excess fertilizer to do damage in the confined environment of a pot. Use the most diluted solution recommended on the fertilizer you choose, but use it regularly to provide a **constant supply of nutrients.**

It should not be necessary to fertilize newly repotted plants if you used a quality potting soil. In most cases, potting soil comes with a kick of fertilizer to help plants get a healthy start.

 # PRUNING

Major pruning can be done in late February or early March. See the discussion of pruning in next month's entry if you want to get an early start.

1 Inexpensive plant trivets can be made from ceramic tiles. Tiles leftover from a home improvement project can be used if they are 4 inches or larger. You can sometimes pick them up at a garage sale for almost nothing, but even new they are not expensive. Small rubber feet that self-stick are available by the sheet. You can also use felt or cork circles that are also self-stick. Put these on the corners of the tiles to create an air space as well as to protect the table surface from scratches, then place the tiles under your plants.

2 A laboratory wash bottle has a small stream of water that is easily directed into the smallest of pots. This is a huge improvement over getting the inevitable overflow from a watering can.

## PESTS

When handling your plants, you may come across a very sticky residue from scale insects. Use a mild soap on a wet soft rag to wipe the residue from the leaves and the surrounding area. After a thorough wiping, **spray soapy water into the nooks and crannies** that are impossible to reach with a rag. Isolate the plant to prevent further infestations and keep a close eye for a return appearance. Scale is difficult to control without an insecticide. Even so, the soap and water should contain it sufficiently to keep the plant alive until the weather permits spraying outside. Insecticidal soap will give some control, but check with your Cooperative Extension Office for current control recommendations.

## NOTES

_____
_____
_____
_____
_____
_____
_____
_____
_____
_____
_____
_____
_____

# MARCH
## Houseplants

 PLANNING

Any repotting that you didn't finish up in February can certainly be done in early March. It is way too early to put any of your plants outside. By late March there are a great many outside projects that need to be tackled, so it is best to finish up with your houseplants before you need to direct your efforts elsewhere.

 PLANTING

It's not too early to bring in lots of cuttings to force into bloom. **Pussy willows** will often get into full fuzz sometime during the month of March. Bring in the branches to chase away the last vestiges of winter. If put in water, the fuzzies will continue to open, turn yellow as the anthers matures, and then fall off. If you want to keep pussy willows indefinitely, put them in a dry vase. Other branches that force easily are winter-blooming **jasmine, forsythia,** and even the pruned branches from your **peach** and **cherry trees.**

 WATERING

Continue watering as needed. Less heat and higher humidity from late-season rains means the soil will dry out more slowly from evaporation, but the increased rate of growth and stronger sun may have the plants using more water. If you repotted into larger pots, the extra soil will hold a supply of water longer, so take care not keep the soil waterlogged. The soil should feel dry to the touch when you stick in your finger but not so dry that soil pulls away from the sides of the pot. **Cactus** and **succulents** can be allowed to get bone dry, but do not let them stay like that or even they will deteriorate.

Your plants may go into a bit of shock after transplanting and may not use as much water until they adjust to their new environment. The water needs of each plant will shift slightly with the changes in its environment.

 FERTILIZING

Use a very diluted water soluble-fertilizer whenever your water. If you have houseplants that flower, make sure you are using a fertilizer specific for flowering houseplants. This type of fertilizer is lower in nitrogen. Foliage has a high demand for nitrogen, so with a high nitrogen fertilizer you will get an abundance of leaves, but you may not see blooms.

A few plants that can give you blooms include **African violets, Streptocarpus species** and their tiny cousins the **Sinningias, Epicias,** the many **begonias** that are grown as houseplants, **oxalis, orchids, crown-of-thorns, spathiphyllum,** the **goldfish plant,** and even the finicky **gardenia.** Some of these are tricky. Keeping consistent levels of fertilizer and soil moisture can go a long way to helping them bloom.

 PRUNING

Pruning your houseplants now eliminates leggy growth from less than ideal light conditions. It is also a way to take cuttings for additional plants.

Some plants that have woody trunks, such as **yucca,** many **dracaenas,** and the **rubber plant,** get so tall they either scrape the ceiling or get a palm tree look with lots of leaves near the top but a mostly bare stem. In many cases you have to bite the bullet and cut it off a bit below the actual desired height, otherwise it will be too tall as soon as it starts to grow again. **Do not cut your Norfolk Island pine if it gets palm-tree-like.** It will not resprout, although you can root the top and start all over. Most others will send out a side shoot or several side shoots over time. For something like a rubber plant, you can cut the tallest of several trunks way back and cut the second after the first has sprouted. Continue this until all the overly tall trunks have been brought down to size.

Plants that have many shoots provide the luxury of pruning the worst offenders and allowing the rest to continue to grow. Vine-like plants such as the **wandering Jews, philodendrons,** and **pothos** fall into this category. This is more aesthetically pleasing than cutting the single trunk of **yucca. Do not wind the stems around the pots.** You can end up with miles of bare stem with a few scrawny leaves at the tip. Cut half the shoots, those that are the longest, way back towards the pot. Only leave one or two leaf nodes left on the stem. This is where the new shoots will emerge. After these get a few leaves, cut any other shoots that are more bare stem than foliage.

**Cactus** and **succulents** grow so slowly they don't usually need a lot of pruning. They tend to drop many leaves or segments when they are handled. Then the bare stems should be removed. The succulent leaves and cactus pieces will often root when placed on the soil surface. Pushing them into the soil causes them to rot, so let them do their own thing.

**Benjamin fig, gardenias, crown of thorns, tibouchina,** and other woody

shrub-like plants get pruned like bushes. Keep overall shape in mind, but remove dead branches first, one of a pair of crossing branches, branches that grow towards the center, and anything that just doesn't look healthy.

## PESTS

Watch out for the mealy bug. They can be particularly bad on citrus, and if they get into the crevices of any of the contorted **hoyas,** they are all but impossible to eliminate. These critters look like miniature white armadillos. They leave white sticky residue in the leaf crotches and suck out the juices from the plants. They are easy to kill with a damp rag, but they are persistent. Rubbing alcohol on a cotton swab can be effective, but their ability to return is uncanny. Check with your Cooperative Extension Office for current control recommendations.

## NOTES

_____

_____

_____

_____

_____

_____

_____

_____

_____

_____

_____

_____

# APRIL
## Houseplants

 PLANNING

By April, your houseplants should be overhauled and ready to make the most of the spring season. If they're not ready however, most repotting, division, and pruning can be done throughout the growing season. Some plants will put out such a growth spurt that they outgrow their pots quickly. It is a good idea to always have on hand a selection of pots for the occasional upgrade or division. Small pots are handy for rooted cuttings.

Avoid any major changes to plants while they are in bloom, as they are less flexible during this time. Transplanting while in bloom may cause all the buds to fall off.

 PLANTING

Any cuttings that have rooted should be potted up when the roots reach 1 to 2 inches in length. Be sure to use a sterile potting soil and only pots with drainage.

The use of rooted cuttings can be a fun way to start a dish garden. A dish garden is in a pot that's usually wider than it is high, planted with a variety of plants. One of the most important considerations for this type of planting is to choose plants with similar growing requirements. For example, a dish garden of all **succulents** would work well together, or try grouping **snake plants** with **philodendron** and a gold dust **dracaena. African violets, streptocarpus,** and a few **spider plants** might make a nice combo as well. You can certainly get creative, but an African violet with a cactus would eventually be deadly to one or the other or both.

 WATERING

Rooted cuttings have very little flexibility regarding watering. During the first few months, they will need special attention to keeping the soil moist but never soggy.

Continue watering when the soil gets dry. If you find that certain plants are beginning to wilt or drop leaves before you get to your regular watering, that may be a clue that they need a bigger pot. In this case, make certain that root crowding is the issue rather than drowning. If a plant is growing poorly because the soil is kept too moist and then you put it in a bigger pot, you will kill it for sure.

If plants are wilting, **one trick is to lift up the pot.** If it is unexpectedly light, it is overly dry and needs to be watered more often, given more water when you do water, or planted in a bigger pot that can hold more water. If the wilted planted is heavy when you pick it up, the soil may be completely saturated and the plant is drowning. Let it dry out thoroughly, prune the top a bit to compensate for any root damage, and water very carefully until it recovers.

 FERTILIZING

Houseplants are growing strongly at this time of year. The days are much longer, the sun is stronger, and the heat is off. If April showers are doing their thing, then the humidity is up as well, making a perfect environment for your houseplants to thrive. That means all of your houseplants will benefit from regular applications of diluted solutions of water-soluble fertilizer. Follow the label directions for the most diluted suggested strength and then use that to water your plants whenever the soil gets dry.

Granular fertilizer, encapsulated fertilizer which dissolves slowly over time, or fertilizer spikes can also be used. There is more risk of burning the roots with these more concentrated products, but if you follow label directions to the letter you should be fine. For blooming plants, make sure you use a product specific for flowering houseplants.

# PRUNING

Pruning of houseplants at this point is on an as-needed basis. Some plants require continual pruning to keep them tidy. **Begonias** are that type of plant and so are many of the vine plants. **Vines** can get quite long with all the attractive foliage near the tips. Remember, if you wrap the vines around the pots, you end up with a tremendous amount of bare stem. A better approach is to prune the longest vines back to the pot every now and then. Leave about 2 inches of stem with 1 or 2 leaf nodes to resprout. If you do it throughout the growing season, you never are stuck with having to prune the entire plant hard. It is the best way to

avoid an ugly, naked plant that takes months to recover.

 # PESTS

Mites, mealy bugs, and scale are the three insect pests that tend to plague houseplants the most. See January, February, and March for descriptions and controls. The most important aspect of controlling these pests is to be able to identify them before the problem becomes severe. A heavy infestation can kill a plant, make it so ugly you don't want it anymore, or, worse, spread to your other plants.

# NOTES

_____
_____
_____
_____
_____
_____
_____
_____
_____
_____

PLANNING

It's very important in May to plan what you are going to do with your houseplants once danger of frost has past. If you intend to put them outdoors, you need to do it gradually. Even sun-loving plants will burn if moved from shadowy indoors to blazing full sun. You will need to make sure you can water them easily, they will not be subjected to overly strong wind, and they will have the light exposure they need to be happy.

Think carefully about this decision. Moving plants outdoors exposes them to insects. They often go into shock with the dramatic change in environment, even when moved out gradually. **They must have drainage!** Indoors you can water judiciously, but if it rains heavily, the pot without drainage will become waterlogged after a heavy downpour.

Plants that go into shock with the transition will recover relatively quickly since they are now growing with high humidity and lots of sun. Unfortunately, when the same plants make the return trip indoors, they are also subject to going into shock, and they will not recover as quickly in the darker autumn lighting of your home. You may have to go through the entire winter looking at them sparse and scraggly. If your houseplants are growing to your satisfaction under their current indoor conditions, you may want to leave them right where they are and avoid the polar fluctuations in their environment.

 PLANTING

If you want to plant some of your houseplants in the ground in their pots, you can do that. This only makes good sense if the plants are in clay pots, but the advantage is the **roots will stay cooler and the soil will not dry out as quickly.** This may be a good approach if you are going on vacation. You may still have to have someone water them while you are away, or perhaps you need some type of slow watering system, but it will give you some cushion of protection that is better than leaving potted plants exposed to summer sun.

 WATERING

High humidity cuts down on evaporation and transpiration, but hot weather can dry out potted plants daily. Plants are growing at a peak rate at this time of year. Heat stress is not a threat yet, so the air conditioning is not blowing cold air while plants are left to sit in a really hot sunny window.

As the plants get larger, the water demand will increase. You must know your plants. Even if you have a schedule that works fairly well, there may be one or two that just can't wait as long as the others. In hot weather, those that tend to droop may droop that much sooner. Sometimes you can help potential droopers by putting them in a pot one size larger.

 FERTILIZING

Fertilizing continues the same as last month. If you use monthly doses of a concentrated fertilizer, **continue to do the same** but take care not to over-fertilize, especially as the weather gets hot. If you are using a diluted water-soluble fertilizer, continue with that practice until Thanksgiving.

 PRUNING

If plants are growing with gusto, you may need to prune the occasional plant hard. This is more of a problem when plants reach a certain size that they can't easily be moved into a larger pot or they begin to reach the ceiling. Plus, if you don't have enough window space for a larger plant then you have to keep the ones you have down to size.

Woody houseplants with multiple trunks should be pruned one trunk at a time. Let the first one resprout before moving onto the second. Some plants are better off if you start over. **Spider plants** get ugly, with lots of bare soil and no easy way to prune the grassy foliage back to fill in the pot. The "babies" are small plants that appear at the tips of wiry arching stems. They can be pruned away and planted in another pot, used to fill in the same pot, or put in water to develop a few more roots before repotting.

Another plant, the **strawberry begonia** (not a begonia at all but *Saxifraga stolonifera*), grows the same way. Some plants, like the true **begonias,** grow very rapidly and begin to flop over. They need regular trimming to keep them in bounds. They root easily so you can always start more. The classic **aloe vera**

can get so heavy at the ends of the branches that they just snap off. You can prune this back to almost nothing and it will come back, but it is better to prune off the occasional branch that is hanging heavy. Aloe pieces can sit for weeks and still root when you pot them up.

# PESTS

Outdoors you need to check plants for insects every time you water. Inside, be careful if you should need to bring in any plants. Insects are very active now and will spread quickly. Check under January, February, and March for descriptions of the three primary pests of houseplants: mites, mealy bugs, and scale.

# NOTES

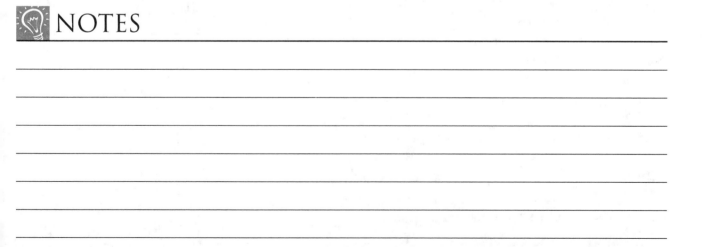

# JUNE
## Houseplants

 PLANNING

Houseplants in June often take a back-seat to **roses, alliums, peonies, poppies,** and assorted goings on in the vegetable garden.

Take some time to get your houseplants' window space sparkling clean. You can run saucers through the dishwasher after you rinse off any nasty stuff. Sometimes insects hide in nooks and crannies in windows, like crevices around the screen or in the molding. Getting everything thoroughly clean at least once a year really makes a difference in how your plants look and how the house feels around them. When the leaves are clean and bug-free they do a much better job of using the indoor light.

At this time of year, plants that grow with enthusiasm will fill in new pots quickly. The **asparagus ferns, rabbit's foot fern, coleus, purple passion,** the many *Tradescantia* (**wandering Jews**), **Swedish** and **grape ivies,** and lots more will all fill in a bigger pot quickly. You will need to decide just how big you want to go before pruning and dividing.

 PLANTING

You may discover that the occasional plant is growing roots out the bottom of its pot. Some plants like to be a bit pot-bound and are best left in cramped quarters until they fall over or the pot splits. **Snake plants** *Sansevieria* sp. can sometimes stay in the same pot for ten years or more. One day, out of the blue, they may surprise you with a spike of flowers. The tiny blooms are very sweet smelling and are the most fragrant in the evening. When they have a lot of loose soil around them, they almost never flower. **Aspidistra,** or the **cast iron plant,** is a slow grower that also rarely needs a larger pot.

**Scilla** grows out and over the sides of a pot. You can pluck off individual bulb-like shoots to start new pots or move the whole patch into a pot wide enough for it to spread out.

 WATERING

Now is a good time to consider giving your plants a cleaning with your garden hose. Getting rid of all that winter dust makes plants look vibrant and healthy. In some cases, it sprays away bugs, and the occasional saturation of the soil can reduce salt build-up from the regular use of fertilizer. **Allow the pots to get fairly dry first.** You don't want to saturate a plant in a pot that was recently watered thoroughly.

Adjust the spray nozzle to get the force you need. While hosing down the foliage, the soil should be watered until the water runs through with some gusto. If these plants are not used to sun, find a bright spot out of direct light so the leaves don't burn while draining and drying.

Leave the plants on the grass or a deck until you are certain they have drained, then return to the watering schedule that worked before. If you repotted any, those individuals may not need to be watered quite as frequently. If some of the soil washed away in the cleaning process, use fresh potting soil to top off the pots after the soil has finished draining.

Drying the leaves with a soft cloth can raise a nice shine. It also helps get rid of any bugs that may be trying to get started.

 FERTILIZING

Continue your current fertilizer program. Take care not to over-fertilize if you are switching programs. For example, if you are using a water-soluble fertilizer every time you water, you may want to skip a few waterings with fertilizer before switching over to a granular or spike. If you have used a granular or encapsulated slow-release fertilizer, allow plenty of time for it to dissipate before starting a water-soluble program.

##  PRUNING

Continue pruning as needed. When plants get too big for their pots, they either need to be pruned or potted up. The size of the pots you use will be based on available space in adequate light and your ability to lift and manipulate an enormous plant. Remember, **you may have to move that 20-inch pot** outside to fight bugs or just to clean your carpets.

##  PESTS

Continue to monitor for the big three: mealy bugs, mites, and scale. Another pest, fungus gnats, fly up in a cloud of tiny brown critters. These adults do no damage but are very annoying. The problem is more with the larvae. They feed on decaying roots and so are more likely show up if the soil is overly moist.

To fight fungus gnats, allow the soil to dry out significantly more than usual. Then mix dish detergent (**not dishwasher detergent**) at a rate of 2 tablespoons per quart of water, and saturate the soil. Let the soil get very dry a second time and repeat the process. After the soil dries thoroughly, rinse the soil with a steady stream of clean water. After all of this, the larvae should be gone, and you can go back to a more normal watering schedule, but keep the plant a bit drier than before to discourage the gnats' return.

## Helpful Hints

*1* If lines of salt appear on the outside of your clay pots, it may indicate you are not watering thoroughly when you water. The fertilizer-enriched water only reaches so far down and then stops, creating a layer of fertilizer at that point. Water so that water runs out the drainage hole. That way you can be sure the entire root ball got a drink and you have not created a salt concentration along the way.

*2* Garage sales are a great place to get saucers to use under your plants. Clay saucers can allow seepage, which is a good trait in pots but destructive in saucers. Odds and ends such as real china saucers, dessert plates, or sandwich plates can be perfect for the job and quite inexpensive. Sometimes you get lucky and find them with a pretty flower border that shows around the edge of the pot.

## NOTES

_____
_____
_____
_____
_____
_____
_____
_____
_____

# JULY
## Houseplants

 ## PLANNING

You may need to plan for someone to take care of your houseplants while you are away on summer vacation. If you will be away for a week, you can probably make do; for two weeks, you may want someone to visit once or twice.

If you keep your house air conditioned while away, the plants will lose water more slowly. If you move your plants out of the sun, this will also slow down water loss. Plants will not suffer excessively from the lower light indoors, but they may suffer severely if they get overly dry. **It is better to risk lower light and move them inside.** Putting each plant in a clear plastic bag will increase the humidity around them as though you were putting them in a miniature greenhouse. If you water them thoroughly before you go, they may last seven to ten days.

Watering devices exist that water slowly over time. Drip irrigation systems are available for a small investment. These can be reused for many years with proper maintenance. There are also attachments for 2-liter bottles. The bottles are filled with water, the attachment inserted, and the bottles inverted. Water seeps out slowly, keeping the soil moist without allowing it to become saturated. Decorative but more expensive versions of this technique are also available.

 ## PLANTING

Any plants that you know will dry out before you return or before someone can come to check on them, may warrant being put in one pot size larger. The larger pots will hold water longer, but judge carefully as you don't want to expose them to over-watering.

Any other planting will continue to be done on an as-needed basis. Always keep a supply of quality potting soil and a selection of clean clay pots. Accidents can happen, especially when kids and pets share the same house with plants. You need to be prepared with back-up potting materials when your favorite **begonia** takes a tumble.

 ## WATERING

Watering in hot July weather takes on a whole new meaning. Heat may actually slow down the growth of some plants, but with strong summer sun and adequate water many houseplants will continue to grow at an amazing rate. **Cactus** that sat looking like plastic plants all winter may surprise you in the summer. While cactus like it on the dry side, the occasional deep watering will help them grow to be all they think they can be.

Avoid getting water on the foliage of any plants when they are in full sun. Drops of water can sometimes act as a magnifying glass for the sun and cause burn spots on the leaves.

If Mother Nature decides to be overly generous with rain, you should empty the saucers of excess water. Most years this is not a problem, but the summer of 2003 was wet enough to drown your plants if you were not being careful.

 ## FERTILIZING

Continue with fertilizer applications of very diluted water-soluble fertilizer. High temperatures are not conducive to the use of granular fertilizer. **It is just too easy to burn the roots** when it is above 85 degrees Fahrenheit.

You may want to eliminate the use of fertilizer if you are going on vacation. If you have moved the plants out of direct sun, they will be slowing down their rate of growth anyway so they won't miss it for a couple of weeks. It isn't worth the risk of someone else being overly generous and burning the roots. If you feel they need it, you can apply a slightly more concentrated dosage when you return.

# PRUNING

One way of cutting back on water needs while you are away is to give a bit of a pruning to those plants that can handle it. You may not want to cut back the single stalk of your **dracaena**. **Tradescantia, philodendron, coleus, begonias, ivy,** and many others can handle a slight haircut to help them through the time you are away.

Otherwise, prune you plants whenever they need it. Always try to do selective pruning that removes the longest stems or branches while maintaining a natural shape. When you clip branches close to the pot, be sure to leave at least one or two leaf nodes to resprout.

 # PESTS

Mites, mealy bugs, and scale can show up at any time. (See pests in January, February, and March.) On occasion, the grubs of Japanese beetles have been found to feed on the roots of houseplants. They usually lay eggs in the grass but can also lay them on the surface of the soil of the potted soil. The earliest deposited eggs begin to hatch in late July. While this is not a likely problem, if you plants are failing for no obvious reason, it may be worth checking the soil.

## Helpful Hints

### Layering

While your plants are outside you may want to try propagating a few by a layering technique.

*1* Fill a pot with good-quality potting soil right next to the plant you want to propagate.

*2* Lay a branch or shoot on top of the soil in the new pot.

*3* About 12 inches from the tip, near a node, wound the branch by cutting the stem at an angle so the cut is about 2 inches long and goes into the stem about halfway.

*4* Take a piece of coated wire (coated is better so it won't cut the stem) and bend it into a "hairpin" shape. Use the wire to pin the shoot to the soil surface.

*5* Insert a thin dowel or stick into the soil. Tie the end of the shoot to the stick so that, once the plant develops a root system, the top of the plant will be growing upright.

*6* Take care to make sure the wound stays open while you are pinning and staking. Then cover the wounded area with soil.

*7* It can take awhile to grow, so be patient. Don't go peeking every few days, either, or you may disturb the developing roots.

# NOTES

## PLANNING

By the middle of the month, you will begin to notice that the nights are cooler. The summer season is winding down, and you need to give some thought to exactly how you are going to move all those houseplants back inside. They may be significantly larger than they were at the onset of the season, and a different arrangement may be warranted. During the winter, the sun is lower in the sky, so more of the length of the window, from top to bottom, is flooded with light. The strength of the sun is not as intense, so placing plants directly in the sun makes a difference in the benefit they get.

Hanging plants so you can take advantage of light higher up is a way of **capturing the light and creating a graceful look** at the same time. Some pots you want to hang could be very heavy, especially those in clay pots. When using brackets to hold hangers, you must take into consideration a very secure way of attaching them to the wall. Finding the stud is best, but there are mollys and butterfly bolts that will help significantly. If you are unsure of the best way to do this, talk to a carpenter or even the helpful person at your favorite hardware or building supply store.

Plant poles use springs to hold them between floor and ceiling. Sometimes you can use coat racks to do the same job, but you must be very careful to place the plants on the coat rack in a way that is balanced. That way they can't tip over.

However you choose to arrange you plants, give yourself some time to get it all together. You really don't want to pull your plants in last minute to avoid a frost and have them scattered on the floor and the dining room table while you figure out what to do with them. They won't be happy and neither will you.

## PLANTING

While evaluating who is going to live where, you may need to divide some of the bigger plants so you can bring a more diminutive plant back into your home. It's better if you **make this call early in the month.** That way, the plants will have some time to get used to their new situation while benefiting from the ideal growing conditions of the summer. It may be more than they can handle to have their roots chopped up, be shoved into a smaller pot, and have to adapt to indoor light and central heat all in one shot.

Plants that don't divide easily might be among those you should attempt to layer. See last month's "Helpful Hints" for how to do this.

## WATERING

Watering continues on an as-needed basis, but try not to let the soil ever get overly dry. On really hot days, the plants cannot tolerate bone dry soil for very long.

Take care not to get water on the leaves in the cool of the evening. Cooler nights encourage the disease called powdery mildew. Not all houseplants are subject to it, but it is an adaptable disease that is significantly encouraged by wet leaves during cool nights.

## FERTILIZING

As long as your plants are thriving as expected, continue with regular use of diluted water-soluble fertilizer. Avoid granular fertilizer as long as daytime temperatures stay 85 degrees Fahrenheit or above.

## PRUNING

Sometimes a hard pruning will be all that is needed to fit robust plants back into their winter digs. If you know that to be the case, this pruning should be done in mid-August. As with dividing, you want the plants to be able to compensate for the change while still under ideal growing conditions. Pruning hard will leave the plants looking a little rough around the edges for a while. **Let the buds break** and begin to give the plant a lush, albeit more compact, look before it's time to bring them inside in mid-September.

 ## PESTS

Powdery mildew is a leaf disease that often begins to show up in early August, but it can appear earlier in a wet season and later in a dry one. It is definitely more likely to show up on plants that live outside during the summer. Look for it on **begonias** and **African violets** as well as many other plants.

White flies are nasty critters. They must fly up from a warmer climate to infest your plants and therefore may not show up until August. Once they get here, white flies are quite a nuisance. You can easily recognize them by the white cloud that swarms around the plants when they are disturbed. You definitely want to get them under control before you bring the plants back in the house. While they cannot survive our winters outdoors, they will do just fine in your living room. Check with your County Extension Office to find out current control measures.

# Helpful Hints

### Air Layering

If you would like to attempt air-layering, about 12 inches from the top, slice a wound into the stem much like you would with layering into the soil.

*1* Dab on a bit of rooting hormone and shove a wad of damp sphagnum moss into the wood to keep it open.

*2* Wrap a large wad of moss all around the area and dampen it with a spritz from a water bottle.

*3* Wrap plastic wrap around the whole mess, then secure the plastic to the stem above and below the moss with string or tape.

*4* Keep the stems warm, at room temperature at least, and keep the moss moist. They should root in about a month.

*5* Cut the stem with the roots and pot it up.

For those more woody plants that need to be sized down to fit in your home, you may want to consider air layering. This could work for those plants that aren't conducive to laying on the soil surface (see "Helpful Hints" above). Examples of plants you may want to air layer would be the **rubber plant, crotons, dracaena,** and **dieffenbachia.**

## NOTES

_____

_____

_____

_____

_____

_____

_____

_____

_____

_____

PLANNING

September is a beautiful month. The cooler temperatures and the increase in rainfall make flowers bloom and colors radiant. While it is a time to enjoy the beauty of everything and to slow down just a bit as the rush of summer winds down, it is also time to start planning for autumn.

Plants that are outside need to move indoors. If you started planning last month where everything will go, then by now preparing may be as simple as cleaning the windowsill and moving a few small tables under the window.

**Right after Labor Day,** you should start moving your outside plants into lower light conditions. The more gradual you can make the transition from summer sun to living room indirect light, the easier the plants will make the adjustment. Don't rush everything indoors because you heard there may be an early frost. If you are only working with three or four small plants, it may be possible to bring them in for the night if temperatures are predicted to drop lower than normal and then move them out again in the morning. However, when you start dragging the 7-foot **weeping fig** around, you are not going to want to bring it through the door more than once. Once the threat of cold damage is out there, you should have your plants acclimated to lower light enough so you can bring them in and leave them there. Moving them in three increments, over about a week each, should do the trick.

 PLANTING

To houseplants being brought inside, the change in environment to poorer growing conditions is extremely stressful. The trauma of being repotted may make matters worse. Of course, if you are moving plants into a greenhouse, then you have minimum change in light and can feel free to repot anything that you think needs it. In the colder part of New Jersey, if you want to make houseplants out of some of your annuals, you need to pot them up very early in September.

If plants that have stayed indoors all summer are in serious need of a bigger pot, then give it to them. Keep in mind, however, they will be slowing down their rate of growth. **If they are borderline, it may make sense to leave them where they are** and repot just before the spring growth spurt in February or March.

 WATERING

The transition from outdoors to indoors is another tricky time for watering. If your plants have a bad reaction to the change, they will not be growing as strongly and the water demand will drop. Air temperatures are down and days are beginning to shorten, so the sun isn't drying out the soil as rapidly. Also, it rains a lot more in September than it does in July and August (most years), so be careful not to drown the poor things.

You should definitely stop watering your **amaryllis.** It needs about eight weeks of dormancy to ensure next year's bloom.

Once they are indoors, water plants when they get fairly dry to the touch. **Cactus** and **succulents** can handle getting bone dry if not left like that for too long. When you do water, make sure the entire root system gets a drink.

 FERTILIZING

If you have been using a very diluted concentration when feeding your houseplants, then keep that up. If you stopped the use of fertilizer because the temperature was above 85 degrees Fahrenheit, you can pick up again with water-soluble fertilizer, or you can use a granular or encapsulated type according to the directions on the package.

# PRUNING

You may need to do some pruning to allow plants to fit in your home.

If you didn't get to it in August (the better time), prune what you must to get the plants to fit, but try to keep it to a minimum. The plants don't need the extra hassle of adjusting to yet another change within a short period of time.

# PESTS

Check every plant carefully before you move it indoors. While you are providing the opportunity for plants to adjust to lower light conditions, you should be lifting leaves, peeking at them through a magnifying glass, and peering at every nook and cranny. The last thing you want to do is bring an infested plant into your home. Even if you don't see anything, you may want to hose everything down, and spray with an insecticidal soap. If you have **any doubt** that your plants are clean as a whistle, keep them isolated from other plants until you are certain.

## Helpful Hints

*1* When moving plants indoors, you may be able to take advantage of an enclosed, unheated porch. It will not work for the entire winter, but it will be a good transition area and may stay warm enough to hold plants into early December. Keep a close eye on temperatures. You don't want plants out there if it gets below 45 degrees Fahrenheit at night.

*2* Deciduous trees may block south-facing windows. However, generally the leaves fall off by Thanksgiving, so even if those window sills are not the best location now, you could move things around as the seasons change to maximize the light you have.

*3* Often skinny window sills are not wide enough to accommodate a plant of any significant size. If you want a project, **you can remove old, skinny windowsills and replace them with deeper ones.** Window sills that are shaped to fit the slot are available from a lumber yard. Removing the old ones can be tricky if you want to do it without destroying the wall. Ask the staff at the lumber yard, the windows manufacturer, or a competent carpenter for the right trick, according to the windows your have. Once you have done the installation, give the sills a few extra coats of paint or polyurethane to protect the wood. To be extra careful, you can cut a piece of plexiglass to fit the sill and set the plants on it instead of directly on the wood.

# NOTES

_____

_____

_____

_____

_____

_____

_____

_____

_____

# OCTOBER

## Houseplants

 PLANNING

If the early fall is mild, you may be able to leave many of your houseplants out into early October. There are a few notable exceptions, however.

The **Christmas cactus** really needs to be left outdoors or in an unheated environment at least until the end of the month. If the temperature is going to drop below freezing, you will need to bring it in. The plant requires cold nights in order to set flower bud. Some varieties bloom more easily than others, but as a general rule, in night temperatures at 65 degrees Fahrenheit or higher the plant cannot set flower bud. If temperatures are between 55 and 65 degrees Fahrenheit at night, Christmas cactus will require long nights to set flower bud. That consists of thirteen hours or so of uninterrupted darkness each night. If temperatures are between 45 and 55 degrees Fahrenheit at night, it will set flower bud regardless of night length.

You can leave **geraniums** out longer than a lot of things. They can tolerate a light frost as long as temperatures never dip lower than about 30 degrees Fahrenheit. They are sun-loving plants, so leave them out to capture as much sun as possible. The longer they must endure indoor lighting conditions, the less likely they are to make it to the following spring.

Your **poinsettias** need to come indoors early in the month, in a place where they will receive **only natural light.** That includes no artificial light at night from street lamps, your garage flood lights, or any other source. As long as they receive light only during sunlight hours, they will be able to bloom. If artificial light is added, even just flicked on and off, it can reverse the nightly buildup of plant hormones required for bloom.

If you don't have such a spot in your home, you can put it in a closet for thirteen hours every night. Start this in the beginning of October and continue for sixty days. Poinsettias still need strong sun during the day.

 PLANTING

Annuals being made into houseplants need to be potted up very early in the month. Plants that thrive in shade outdoors in the summer make the best houseplants in the winter. You can pot up **coleus, wax begonias,** and **impatiens.** Try to disturb the roots as little as possible when you dig them up.

You may want to take cuttings rather than dig up the plants themselves. Use a dab of rooting hormone to get faster root development and use a sterile potting medium. Small pots of shade-loving annuals can fit nicely on a narrow windowsill and bloom all winter long. I have four pots of **wax begonias** on a narrow north-facing, but unblocked, windowsill in the kitchen. They have bloomed non-stop for about six years.

 WATERING

Continue to water on an as-needed basis. Monitor your plants closely; there are a lot of changes to their environment this month, and their water demands may change. Usually we start turning the heat on this month. While it is best to locate plants away from sources of direct heat, sometimes the heat ducts happen to be under the sunniest windows. It might be worthwhile to turn off or close these ducts if possible.

You can sometimes purchase sleeves or hoods to direct the warm air in the most advantageous direction. On cooler autumn days with ever decreasing sunlight, if the plants are forced to be in a sunny spot near the blowing heat, the soil may dry out very rapidly, possibly more than you would expect. Compensate by watering accordingly.

FERTILIZING

Continue to fertilize thriving house-plants according to the fertilizer program you were using throughout the growing season.

If plants are struggling with shock as they adjust to changes in their environment, you may want to hold off on fertilizer applications until you are certain they have acclimated successfully.

 PRUNING

Your **amaryllis** plant has probably yellowed by now if you stopped watering it in September. Once the leaves have turned yellow, they can be pruned off. Store the dormant bulb in a cool (not cold) location for eight weeks.

Deadhead spent blooms on all your houseplants as needed.

 PESTS

Continue to monitor for any signs of insects. This is especially true for those plants that spent the summer outdoors. While all insect pests are problematic,

mites seem to thrive in the dry atmosphere of your heated home. Isolate all infested plants as soon as the problem is identified. Some control options include swishing the plant in a bucket of soapy water, hosing the plant with a fairly fierce spray of water, wiping the plant with a soft soapy cloth then dabbing the bugs with rubbing alcohol, and spraying the entire plant with 50 percent rubbing alcohol and water or using an insecticidal soap.

If the infestation is caught early and the above treatments applied vigorously, that may be enough. If not, check with your Cooperative Extension Office for specific control recommendations for the pest and the infested plant.

NOTES

## Houseplants

## PLANNING

Although winter is not official for another month, there are almost always a few cold days that tell of what's ahead. Usually around the third week or so of November, a heavy downpour strips trees of their beautiful fall foliage. It is a bit sad to see them bare their branches for the long sleep, but in many cases it allows more light into your home.

The unheated porch may be getting too chilly now (below 40 degrees Fahrenheit). **Move plants to those suddenly-sunny, south-facing windows.**

If you can take down the screens to your windows, you can increase your available light by as much as 20 percent. (If the screens were yucked up with dust and accumulated spider webs, it can be even more.) There's less chance of letting in bugs now anyway, if you want to open a window.

The heat is on most of the time, and that means dry air. **Grouping plants together actually increases humidity** in a general area with water transpiring from the foliage as well as evaporating form the soil. However it's not usually enough to compensate for very dry air. Pebble trays are effective and a simple answer for adding moisture. Trays are filled with pebbles and then filled halfway with water. Put your plants on top. The trays should be at least as wide as the widest part of the plant. As the water evaporates, it adds to the moisture in the immediate area. Take care never to over-fill the trays. If you do, the pots will be sitting in water and the plants' roots may rot. The use of saucers can prevent that, but remember clay saucers will soak up water and eventually transfer it to the roots.

## PLANTING

There isn't a lot of planting going on now, with the exception of fixing pot-bound plants or planting cuttings that have developed roots. You may find that some plants are drying out too rapidly if they are near a source of heat. A bit of extra soil and a larger pot may offer protection, but don't go more than one pot-size larger.

## WATERING

This is a time to be very tuned-in to your plants' needs. They're not growing nearly as much as during the sunnier months, so the water demand is generally down. However, dry heated air can increase water demands. If you find your plants are drying out too quickly, you can water more often, move your plants to a cooler spot, or put the plant in a slightly bigger pot. It's okay if your **cactus** gets a bit drier than in the summer since the lower light really slows these sun-loving plants. If you allow them to go dormant, you can reduce the leggy, stretched out growth that can occur in the winter. A few drops of water now and then may be sufficient to get them through the darkest part of the winter.

## FERTILIZING

Continue with your regular fertilizer program until Thanksgiving. After that, do not fertilize again until February or March. Many fertilizer labels will encourage continued use of their product throughout the winter. In warmer climates, further south, the temperatures and slightly longer days may warrant year-round fertilization, but **winter in New Jersey is a sleepy time for plants,** and you are better off not force-feeding them.

## PRUNING

If you need to prune, do it judiciously. You may find that certain plants have a bad reaction to the shorter days and the overall onset of winter. For example,

**Benjamin** or **weeping fig** will drop many of its leaves at the drop of a hat. It is not uncommon to find yourself with a mostly naked tree, especially if you brought it in from outside. A light touch of selective pruning will help maintain an attractive shape, encouraging it to fill in more in the center rather than just at the tips of the branches. Excessive pruning will only add to the plant's shock.

Any summer annuals you brought in to brighten your home may be stretching. Regular nipping of the tallest shoots helps keep them tidy and attractive a bit longer.

## PESTS

Insect pests continue to need constant monitoring. If you haven't yet discovered any insects on the plants you brought in from outdoors, you may be in the clear. Even so, check any yellowing leaves carefully. See last month for additional suggestions.

## Helpful Hints

*1* Keep an eye on **poinsettias** you are trying to force into bloom. Once they start to color up, they will continue the process and will no longer need careful monitoring.

*2* **Christmas cactus** also may show signs of budset by late in the month. **Thanksgiving cactus** is really the same plant selected for earlier bloom and may bloom in time for the holiday. Take care to keep growing conditions and watering as uniform as possible. While Christmas cactus and its cousins are easy to grow, they get finicky when about to bloom. Buds drop easily if environmental conditions fluctuate. Avoid sources of heat and drafts, and don't allow the soil to get too dry or sit wetter than usual.

*3* Evergreen trees are good to plant on the north side of your home in order to cut back on winter wind and heat loss. At the same time, deciduous trees on the south provide shade in summer and allow the sun's warmth to penetrate the barrier in winter. That may warrant a rethinking of where you have located your plants.

## NOTES

# DECEMBER
## Houseplants

 PLANNING

December is a busy time of year, but not necessarily with your houseplants. The short days, warm dry air, and slow growth of most of your houseplants almost puts them on automatic pilot. You want to try to keep all the environmental conditions as consistent as possible. A humidifier will be helpful, or even a pot of water on your wood burning stove will help compensate for the dry atmosphere created by burning wood. If you can keep your plants in decent shape in December and January, the two darkest months, they should be fine.

Of course many households will have the addition of the festive **poinsettia.** Don't be afraid to try something a little different. There are red with splashes of white or pink, red that look like rosettes, red that are all crinkled, burgundy, pink, pink with white splashes, white, and white with pink splashes.

Here are a **few Tips for getting the most enjoyment out of your poinsettias:**

*1* **Choose plants that have little yellow "beads"** in the center of the colorful bracts (bracts are modified leaves that turn bright colors). The yellow beads are the true flowers. They indicate the plant has been well cared for and has a potential for a long life. Once the true flowers fall off, the plant starts to age or revert to all-green vegetative growth.

*2* **Remove the plant from its protective sleeve immediately.** If you purchase it as a gift for a later day, replace the sleeve when you are ready to bring it back out to the car.

*3* **Avoid extremes in temperatures.** Do not leave your poinsettia in the car, near a heater, or near a door that opens and closes (creating drafts).

*4* **Keep it well watered.** Poinsettias are generally potted in a very lightweight potting mix. This minimizes the chances for diseases to cause root problems, but it also means they can dry out quickly. Unfortunately poinsettias give no notice when they are thirsty. They go from wilting to dropping leaves before the wilting has become particularly noticeable.

*5* **Use a porcelain or plastic saucer under your poinsettia.** The pretty foil paper may hold water for a while, but it is much too easy for water to leak through even the tiniest hole.

If you should decide to use some of your other houseplants as places to hang holiday ornaments, take care to use very lightweight ones. Paper birds, small origami sculptures, and the paper chains we all made in grade school are good choices. The **Norfolk Island pine** is a favorite houseplant for dressing up. Use tiny lights and lightweight ornaments. These pines seem to put up with the decorations better if they don't weigh down the branches.

Of course, the granddaddy of all houseplants this month is a balled-and-burlapped **Christmas tree.** Large steel tubs work well to hold the tree. Put some rocks on the bottom to provide drainage—even Christmas trees don't want to be sitting in water. Put something under the tub, such as an old shower curtain, to prevent water damage, and even an old blanket to prevent scraping the floor. Around the edge of the tree, stuff newspapers soaked in water to prevent surface roots from drying out. Keep the temperature in the tree's room as cool as possible. Look for more information about choosing a Christmas tree under December in the Trees chapter of this book.

##  PLANTING

Your houseplants should be holding their own with the right amount of water and minimal impact of indoor environmental conditions. Remember to maximize light, make an effort to keep some moisture in the air, and avoid heat sources and cold drafts. Don't repot. The last thing you need to do is add repotting to the stress your plants are under.

If you want to have some indoor color and pot up a few things, look under December in the chapter on bulbs. Indoor forcing of tender **narcissus,** such as the delicate **paper-whites,** or the dramatic **amaryllis** will let you play in the dirt a bit. If these bulbs are started in December, they will bloom after the holidays during the grayest part of winter. You will really enjoy the cheer they bring while in bloom.

##  WATERING

Water on an as-needed basis. Plants located near sources of heat will definitely dry out quickly. **Poinsettias** may need to be watered as often as every other day. Remember to use a porcelain or plastic saucer. The material they are potted in is generally very heavy in peat

moss. When that gets dry, water runs right through it as if it were in a colander. Make sure you let the plant soak up what it needs. Then make equally sure it doesn't sit in water any longer than it needs to become thoroughly wet.

##  FERTILIZING

No fertilizer is needed at this time.

##  PRUNING

You shouldn't need to prune anything at this time. If the occasional long shoot gets properly trimmed that is fine, but it is better to wait to do significant pruning right before the flush of new spring growth, generally **late February or March.**

## PESTS

The three big pests to look for are mites, mealy bugs, and scale. These pests and controls are discussed individually in January, February, and March chapters. The use of insecticides in your home is not recommended, but you may be able to spray outdoors on a warm day if the weather is cooperative.

## NOTES

_____

_____

_____

_____

_____

_____

_____

# CHAPTER SIX

# Lawns

*Rolling lawns are an American institution. Lovely to look at and delightful to wiggle your toes in on a hot day, they can also be a lot of work. It's important to pick a lawn that suits your lifestyle.*

## PLANNING YOUR LAWN

There are those homeowners who strive for an emerald green carpet look with a perfect pattern of diagonal mowing stripes and not a dandelion to be seen. Then there is the "pebble lawn" look, common down the shore, where not even a blade of grass is visible. Since grass is so much easier on feet than those ubiquitous round rocks, the pebble thing doesn't seem to make much sense where everyone runs around barefoot most of the time.

**Planning for your lawn requires learning a little about your grass choices.** It also requires an understanding of how you intend to use your grass. A lawn just for appearance may require a different approach than a lawn needed to accommodate toddlers in the back yard or family football games. **Clover** is a sweet little plant that isn't poisonous, doesn't get overly tall, and has no thorns. However, if you have many clover flowers and babies playing in the grass, the flowers draw bees in large numbers. That may not be a good combination.

For rough and tumble areas such as play areas for kids or where dogs romp, **tall fescue** is a resilient option. It is often used in playgrounds and park areas. While many lawn grasses can and should be blended together to get the best possible lawn, tall fescue is coarser than other lawn grasses. The patches are very obvious when mixed in, so you are better off having a pure stand. When mowed, it looks attractive, especially the newer, less coarse varieties. Without the finer grasses for comparison, few people will know it is being grown for its sturdiness rather than beauty.

**It's important to pick a lawn that suits your lifestyle.** It makes walking barefoot through the grass that much more satisfying. Exactly how green does your lawn need to be to make you happy? You fertilize in the spring to get the lawn to "green up," which it does. It's the nitrogen in the fertilizer that makes it green. It also makes it grow quickly. That means it will have to be mowed more often, which generates more clippings. It will also generate more thatch.

Once you have decided how much of what kind of grass you want and where, decide what other elements are going into the same areas. Major lawn renovation is best done in September, but plan ahead for installing spring plants along with decks, pools, swing sets, and fences. Significant planting or building projects will take a toll on your lawn, so get as much of these things out of the way before you attempt to roll out the perfect green carpet.

## GROWING OPTIONS

Rutgers University has one of the finest grass breeding programs in the world. New Jersey residents are lucky to have many high quality grass varieties in their own backyard (so to speak), selected and bred to suit their environmental needs exactly.

Below are three primary types of grass from which to choose. They are all **cool-season grasses** that do best in spring to early summer and perk up again in late summer throughout the fall. They are dormant at the hottest time of summer and the coldest part of winter. Buy only certified seed. You always want to have several varieties of the different types of grass in the mix, not just one **bluegrass**, one **fescue**, and one **rye.** It's easier for some ugly disease to come in and kill off one kind of grass. Different varieties show enormous differences in their susceptibility to different diseases. Two or even three varieties of each species is best.

## Seeds

*1* **Kentucky Bluegrass:** This is the number-one most important grass species for New Jersey. Bluegrass is the foundation of most lawns but does not do well in the shade. The more shade you have the higher the percentage of **fine fescue** you need in your seed mix (see fescue below). Bluegrass requires full sun and moist soil conditions, but the soil must still drain well. You have to be careful not to mow it too short because it doesn't like that, either. When you choose your seed, you want several different varieties of

bluegrass to minimize susceptibility to disease. In the sun, you want about 60 percent of your lawn to be bluegrass and about 20 percent each of fine fescue and turf-quality **ryegrass.** In a sunny area, you want to use 2 to 3 pounds of very high quality grass seed per 1000 square feet of lawn.

*2* **Fine Fescue:** This group includes the hard **fescues** and the **red fescues** which include both the **chewings** and **creeping fescues.** Fescues are the best for shade, but even these will not grow in deep shade. Fine fescues are a good choice for poorer soils and drier conditions. Stay far away from soggy ground, don't be overly generous with fertilizer, and don't mow it too short. The red fescues spread a little from rhizomes. Hard fescue doesn't spread at all. When using this group, don't hold out too much hope they will fill in any bare spots since spreading is not really their strength. For a shady lawn, you want 60 percent fine fescue and 20 percent each **bluegrass** and **perennial**

**rye.** You will need 3 to 4 pounds per 1000 square feet of lawn. This is because fescue has only 600,000 seeds per pound and bluegrass has 2,200,000 seeds per pound. To get enough seeds to create a thick lawn, you need more pounds of fescue than bluegrass to get the same number of seeds.

*3* **Perennial Ryegrass:** Perennial ryegrass is more tolerant of shade than bluegrass but less than fescue. One of its most important characteristics is that it germinates rapidly, usually in less than ten days and sometimes as quickly as five. This provides cover to prevent erosion and to keep down weeds while waiting for the **bluegrass** to come up. They are not as fussy about soil types as bluegrass, but they are also not as compact, so the lawn may need frequent mowing to stay picture perfect.

# Lawns

## SOD

As an option to seed, you can put down sod. Information on planting sod can be found in April's section of this chapter. Sod is mature grass that has been harvested with a really interesting machine that skims away the grass from the field, creating strips that are 1 to 1½ feet wide and 4 to 6 feet long. The pieces come with enough soil and roots to hold the pieces together like an area rug.

Buy only certified sod. There are a great many excellent sod farms in central and southern New Jersey that glisten emerald green perfection as you drive by. If you plan to use sod, keep in mind it must be installed within hours of being delivered. Make sure it will arrive **after you have completed your soil preparation.** The ability to water will be critical, so any water restrictions should also be considered.

Many people think that because they put down high quality sod, they are set for life. There is no doubt that when you get sod established, it is thick enough to keep out weeds. However, if you are having trouble with soggy ground, overly acidic soil, or too much shade, sod will deteriorate rapidly unless you correct these problems.

Shady areas have to be seeded to have any chance of establishing a shade-tol-erant lawn. Keep in mind that sod requires a high percentage of **blue-grass** to stay intact during harvesting and installation. It is the spreading root system that allows grass to be cut for sod; however, bluegrass doesn't grow in shade and shade-friendly fescue does not spread the same way, so it doesn't make good sod.

## ALTERNATIVES FOR SHADE

By July, you may find that, because the trees are in full leaf, the shade from the larger trees causes the grass some difficulties. To avoid this struggle, in deep shade you should just forget about grass. Instead, consider a shade-loving ground cover. **Moss** also grows in the shade, especially if it is moist. Moss is green and quite pretty but slippery to walk on, so it may not be acceptable under some circumstances. Different ground covers do well under different circumstances, so be sure you choose something that will do the job. The added interest of ground covers will add detail to your landscape without a lot of additional work.

## GRASS CLIPPINGS

If you are pushing for the ultimate lawn, you need to address the issue of the grass clippings early on. Raking grass clippings gets old real fast. You need to consider the purchase of a bagging lawnmower. Then you have to decide what to do with your clippings. Composted by themselves, they turn into the stinkiest mess this side of a stack of dirty diapers. They decompose quickly and mat into a solid mass, depleting the pile of oxygen. Then the anaerobic stink-making microbes take over, and you have a mess. Mixing them in with leaves or partially decomposed compost will eliminate much of this problem.

Fresh grass clippings actually make good mulch in the flower or vegetable garden, providing you haven't used any weed killer this season. Clippings have to be used immediately after mowing since they become a mess in a matter of hours. Using a mulching lawn mower is another alternative. That sends the clippings up into the blades of the mower for another pass at getting chopped up. When the clippings are small enough to filter down between the blades, they can be left on the lawn. As they decompose, they actually release nitrogen back into the soil. If you mow frequently enough, you don't even need a mulching mower, but if the grass gets so long the clippings form a mat on the surface of the lawn, it will smother the grass underneath.

# Lawns

## THATCH

Contrary to popular belief, thatch has nothing to do with grass clippings. Those tender clippings that grow at the tips of the grass plants decompose in a matter of days. Thatch is dead grass that is the result of new grass growing on one end of the grass plant while the older end becomes tan and straw-like as it ages. Forcing grass to grow quickly causes more thatch to be generated.

Thatch can become quite thick. It can be advantageous in that it creates a bit of a cushion, which is helpful on athletic fields and where children play. What is not so good is that seed, water, fertilizer, and any pesticides you may need to apply get caught in the thatch layer and never make it down into the soil where they need to be.

## Helpful Hints

*1* Many home gardeners are enthralled with power tools. They can be a real time saver. However, they are very loud, require a fair amount of maintenance, and use energy in one form or another. If you have a small, fairly level yard, consider the new push mowers. That is **push,** as in push powered. They are inexpensive, lightweight, and far easier to push than the original versions. (Those felt like they were made of cast iron.) They are great for condos, townhouses, and urban houses with small front and back yards. **(We have one at the beach, and the kids, ages eight and nine at the time of purchase, would fight over who got to mow the patch of grass . . . it is that easy!)**

*2* If you are a cat owner, you may want to plant some oats, which are actually a grass. This is especially true if your cat likes to nibble on your houseplants. Many houseplants are poisonous. Some cats know instinctively which plants to avoid, or it's probable that what tastes best to them is not poisonous. Other cats make more dangerous choices. Having a pot of oats growing on a windowsill can help with that problem. You should probably have two: one for nibbling and one for growing to replace the nibbled one when it gets down to nubs. Use regular potting soil, get seed from a farm store or a catalog, and place in a very sunny window.

*3* If you are very lucky, **crocus** and **snowdrops** planted in the lawn will begin to poke their noses up. If the weather has been mild, you may be in for an early spring treat.

## WATERING

When you water your lawn, you need to put down 1 inch of water, in the early morning, all at once. Sprinkler systems all too often are set to water two or three times a week. If a lot of homes in your neighborhood have sprinkler systems and many are operating at the same time, your water pressure may drop considerably. That means it will take longer to put down the 1-inch requirement. If this is not taken into consideration, you will end up watering less than 1 inch, several times a week. In response to getting less water, grass roots will rise to access the water near the soil surface. That exposes the roots to warmer soil temperatures and more rapid dehydration, reducing the lawn's tolerance to heat and drought. So if you miss an application of water or watering restrictions come into effect, your lawn has no flexibility and will succumb to the additional stress rapidly. Deep watering once a week in the early morning will encourage deeper roots and more drought tolerance.

A watering plan for your lawn is very important. **Once you commit to doing it, you really need to stick with it for the duration.** When planning a watering schedule, consider having zones, where each zone is watered once a week. Attempting to water large areas can sometimes reduce water pressure so not enough water is being applied, especially if everyone in the neighborhood has the same idea.

# Lawns

**Cool season grasses** would much prefer to go dormant in hot weather. If allowed, they turn brown, stop growing, don't need to be mowed, and then recover when weather conditions become milder. Watering during periods when cool season grasses want to rest is a bit of shoveling against the tide. If you choose to water, it too requires 1 inch of water per week put down **all at once,** in the early morning. If you can't do this, your lawn will be trying to rest while being forced to grow without enough water to accomplish the task. Plus, if you water in hot weather, you will have to mow more frequently. If you can think of other things to do with your time in 90-degree weather, consider letting the grass do what it really wants to do anyway . . . go to sleep.

## AERATING

If you have removed a layer of thatch before planting, you may need to aerate the soil. **Aerating relieves serious soil compaction and allows more air, water, and nutrients to enter the soil.** Solid tine aeration equipment makes holes by compressing the soil sideways. Core aeration actually removes a core of soil, which can be left on the soil surface. The small cylinders of soil will disappear after the first good rain or irrigation. Core aeration makes spaces without adding to an existing compaction problem. Solid tines compress both sideways and down. The holes may look the same from both processes, but core aeration is an improvement where solid tines make the problem worse in the long run.

## IMPROVING THE SOIL

Nitrogen is the substance that greens up a lawn. It is the first number of the three numbers that appear on a fertilizer bag. A good spring fertilizer is 10-6-4. Nitrogen not only gets used up quickly but it is also not retained in the soil for long. Phosphorus and potassium last much longer. Once adequate levels of these two nutrients are reached, they are easier to maintain. Phosphorus and potassium are more critical to root growth and so are sometimes applied in higher doses in the fall such as with a 5-10-10 fertilizer. New Jersey soils tend to be acidic, so lime is added to bring the pH up to the proper level. Lime also supplies calcium.

The only way to know for sure the nutritional level and pH of your soil is to **have your soil tested.** Your County Extension Office can do this for you and will also provide instructions for collecting your soil samples. Information on the nutritional level of your soil will be sent back to you with instructions for making adjustments.

While you're following planting instructions in this book, the use of a soil amendment is often suggested. Sometimes heavy soils are lacking sand in addition to organic matter. Topdressing is an application of ¼ inch of **topsoil** or **organic matter** on top of existing grass. Some "topsoil" is simply the uppermost layer of earth removed from some other location. When you are purchasing topsoil, even the best topsoil, some part of what you are paying for is material that you already have in excess. Topdressing with ¼ inch of compost may be more beneficial. Compost is organic matter and will be pulled down into the soil through the action of worms and the freezing and thawing of the ground over the winter.

If you choose topsoil, make sure it's certified. Certified topsoil has to meet some standard of clay, loam, organic matter, sand, and gravel and should have a neutral, or close to neutral, pH. Rutgers University has a published standard of percentages for these components, but other similar standards exist.

## INSECTS AND DISEASES

So you have a beautiful, dark green lawn that is growing like gangbusters and pretty as a picture. Then, the lawn diseases get hold of it. That dark green growth is very fine and tender, and organisms that thrive on high nitrogen simply drool over it. Once diseases are advanced enough for them to be identified, there is rarely much that can be done.

**Lawn diseases are significantly dependent on environmental conditions.** As the cool, wet spring changes to the hot, dry summer, the diseases that creep up are completely different. Once you have had a lawn disease, you may want to plan for preventive treatments the following season. A medium-green lawn is tougher, grows more slowly, generates less thatch, and is more resistant to disease. That is not to say "never fertilize." You just want to find a happy medium.

The Japanese beetle is a lawn pest that you will read much about. Nematodes and milky spore disease can both be effective in controlling Japanese beetle grubs. Milky spore can take up to three years to become effective but will then suppress the grubs over the long term. Unfortunately, these controls have no effect on other white grubs that are similar in both the appearance and damage to Japanese beetles. More insects and diseases are discussed each month in this book.

## Helpful Hints

Consider these options when deciding the kind of lawn you want to have and how hard you want to work at it:

- Will you be using seed or sod?
- Can you tolerate medium-green grass?
- Do you want an abundance of shade trees?
- Will you be collecting those clippings or leaving them?
- Do you expect weeds or "wildflowers" to speckle your lawn?
- Will there be small children and a family dog playing on the lawn? Or teenagers playing touch football?

## WEEDS

Another problem is, of course, weeds. A weed is simply a plant growing where you don't want it. Almost everyone agrees **dandelions** are weeds, unless you are a south Jersey farmer famous for his dandelion wine or a five-year-old picking a bouquet for Mommy (or the mommy receiving it). On the other hand, no one thinks of the mighty **oak** as a weed. If, however, you have 376 oak seedlings coming up in your front yard, your opinion may change. A few dandelions, a bit of **clover,** pretty spring **violets,** even **grape hyacinths** can pop up through the grass. If you decide you like them, they can become wildflowers.

A perfect lawn runs completely counter to society's movement towards things more natural. You cannot have a weed-free lawn with no bare spots and no crabgrass unless you wage a constant war to keep the undesirables from getting a foothold. Sometimes you can handweed the offenders, but things like wild onions, thistle, creeping Charlie (also called ground ivy), and dandelions will return from the tiniest speck of root left behind. If they make you crazy, break out the weed killer.

If you need help with any pest problem, you can always check with your Cooperative Extension Office for the current controls and recommended pesticide. Always follow label directions to the letter.

# Lawns

## Which Grass Is for You?

**Common Name**
(*Botanical Name*)

**Recommended Varieties**

### Hard Fescue
*Festuca longifolia*

Discovery, SR3100, Reliant II, Warwick, Ecostar, Brigade, Nordic, Spartan, Aurora, Aurora II, Oxford

| Shade Tolerated | Tolerates Wet Sites | When to Mow | Mow To | Spreads | Fertilizer Needs | Texture | Drought Tolerance |
|---|---|---|---|---|---|---|---|
| Moderate | No | 4 inches | 2 inches | No | Light | Fine | Slight |

### Kentucky Bluegrass
*Poa pratensis*

Midnight, America, Princeton 105, Blacksburg, SR2000, Eclipse, Unique, Shamrock, Washington, Preakness, Suffolk, Ram I, Adelphi, Livingston, Glade, Cheri, Lofts 1757, Julia, Liberty, Challenger, Moonlight, Bedazzled, Sonoma, Cabernet, Jefferson, Liberator, Totlal Eclipse, Award, Moonshadow, Langara, and Lakeshore

| Shade Tolerated | Tolerates Wet Sites | When to Mow | Mow To | Spreads | Fertilizer Needs | Texture | Drought Tolerance |
|---|---|---|---|---|---|---|---|
| None | No | 4 inches | 2 inches | Yes | High | Fine | Slight |

### Perennial Ryegrass
*Lolium perenne*

Brightstar II, Palmer III, Premier II, Calypso II, Panther, Monterey, Secretariat, Catalina, Prelude III, Repell III, Divine, Laredo, Citation III, Manhattan III, Prizm, Elf, Accent, Top Hat, Omega III, Manhattan IV, Pinnacle II, Amazing, Applaud, Jet, Elfkin, and Citation Fore

| Shade Tolerated | Tolerates Wet Sites | When to Mow | Mow To | Spreads | Fertilizer Needs | Texture | Drought Tolerance |
|---|---|---|---|---|---|---|---|
| Light | Slight | 4 inches | 2 inches | No | Low | Fine | Slight |

### Red Fescue
*Festuca rubra*

**Chewing Red Fescue:** Shadow II, Magic, Victory II, SR5100, Brittany, Tiffany, Brideport, Treazure, Jamestown II, Banner II, Ambassador, Intrigue
**Creeping Red Fescue:** Jasper, Flyer II, Shademaster II, Jasper II, Cindy Lou, Aberdeen, Navigator and Salem

| Shade Tolerated | Tolerates Wet Sites | When to Mow | Mow To | Spreads | Fertilizer Needs | Texture | Drought Tolerance |
|---|---|---|---|---|---|---|---|
| Moderate | No | 4 inches | 2 inches | Slight | Low | Fine | Slight |

### Tall Fescue
*Festuca arundinacea*

Crossfire II, Houndog V, Falcon II, Jaguar III, Coyote, Coronado, Southern Choice, Genesis, Pixie, Tomahawk, Barlexas, Lancer, Marksman, Fine Lawn Petite, Virtue, Tulsa, Safari, Rebel Junior, Duster, Cochise, Apache II, Falcon III, Rembrandt, Millenium, Plantation, Olympic Gold, Silver Star, Tarheel, Wolfpack and Prospect

| Shade Tolerated | Tolerates Wet Sites | When to Mow | Mow To | Spreads | Fertilizer Needs | Texture | Drought Tolerance |
|---|---|---|---|---|---|---|---|
| Moderate | No | 4 inches | 2 inches | Very Slight | Low | Medium Coarse | Moderate |

### Zoysiagrass
*Zoysia japonica*

Meyer

| Shade Tolerated | Tolerates Wet Sites | When to Mow | Mow To | Spreads | Fertilizer Needs | Texture | Drought Tolerance |
|---|---|---|---|---|---|---|---|
| None | No | 2 inches | 1 inches | Yes | Low | Medium | High |

# JANUARY
## Lawns

 PLANNING

You should give some thought to how you will, or won't, water your lawn next summer. It is important to address the real situation that water is not always available. When water reserves are low, lawns become a lower priority than some industrial uses, agricultural applications, and supplying the ever-increasing number of homes in the state. A lawn that is developed with regular irrigation will suffer if restrictions prevent continued watering midsummer. A lawn maintained without irrigation will never know the difference. Factor that in as you plan.

**Cool season grasses, grown throughout the state for the most part, have the ability to go dormant during hot weather.** These grasses actually are happier if allowed to do that. When the weather returns to more amiable growing conditions (remember they are "cool" season grasses), they will wake up and pick up where they left off.

If you are interested in having a sprinkler system installed, do your research now. You will want it installed early so the lawn can recover from the construction before the weather gets hot.

 PLANTING

Of course, no planting of lawn grasses is being done in January. However, you should have a soil test now if you think you might invest time, money, and effort into putting down sod or overseeding later (see April).

 WATERING

Not having to water the lawn is one advantage to winter.

 FERTILIZING

No fertilizer is necessary this month. Lawns use higher amounts of nitrogen in the spring since nitrogen is more critical to leaf growth. If you can have your soil tested now, you will have the results in time for spring applications of lime and fertilizer.

 MOWING

There is not really much to do for your lawn at this time of year.

 PESTS

There are two diseases that can appear from November through February. They are both called snow mold. One is pink and the other gray. They are most likely to occur when there is a long period of snow cover over ground that is not frozen. When the snow melts, you will see patches of either light yellow that turn grayish white or light brown that turn dirty white or slightly pink. Prevention includes maintaining a proper pH of 6.5 to 7, applying **no high nitrogen fertilizers in the late fall,** and mowing the grass as long as it is growing. Grass matted down under the snow is the ideal environment for this disease. As environmental conditions change, the disease will stop spreading. Wait for spring to overseed bare patches.

NOTES

_____
_____
_____
_____
_____
_____
_____

## PLANNING

This is a good time to prepare your equipment and purchase all your supplies. Lawnmower blades need to be sharp to do the job correctly. Sharp blades make a clean cut. Dull mower blades leave a ragged tip on the individual grass blades, which becomes an opportunity for disease to creep in. **It is best to have two sets of blades sharpened now.** When it is time to re-sharpen the first pair, you will have the second pair waiting in the wings. That eliminates the waiting time, and some very long grass that can develop while the blades are in the shop.

Take the time to get your mower serviced, or break out the service manual if you are a do-it-yourselfer. (Use caution when handling your mower, especially near sharp blades. If you don't feel confident, take it to a professional.) Key things to do include:

*1* Change the oil

*2* Change spark plugs

*3* Turn the mower over (if practical) while it's empty of oil and scrape the underside of the deck.

*4* Paint the underside of the deck with a rust-protection type of paint

*5* Inspect belts on the power wheels. Replace them if dry or cracked

*6* Grease "zerk fittings" with a grease gun

*7* Oil moving parts

*8* Make sure the opening for "pull starts" is free of debris

**Do not wait until the last minute to bring in equipment to be serviced.** As the season gets closer, professional service providers get busier and busier. If you want to have your equipment ready to mow when the grass is ready to be cut, bring it in this month!

Other items you may want to purchase early to have on hand include:

• 10-6-4 50 percent slow-release fertilizer. This is sometimes called "organic," but that term is being used less and less. Once a standard for lawns, it is getting hard to find.

• Granular limestone. Pulverized is absorbed into the soil more rapidly, so if you have a serious pH problem you may want to put up with the slight messiness of pulverized limestone for the quicker action.

• Grass seed for overseeding bare spots or frost seeding. Grass seed that has been stored in a shed may not be reliable. Excessively hot or cold temperatures will cause seed to deteriorate. Be sure to purchase quality seed.

• Pre-emergent crabgrass preventer. These types of materials prevent crabgrass seed from germinating. If you don't want crabgrass, this is a much better approach than trying to kill crabgrass after it emerges. Most pre-emergent materials are not compatible with putting down grass seed.

• Broad-leaf weedkiller. This type of product can be purchased by itself or as part of a "weed and feed" combination product. If you don't mind the violets, clover, and dandelions but detest the wild onions and thistle, you are better off spot treating with weedkiller. If you are striving for emerald green perfection, the combination material applied throughout your lawn area will be more effective.

## PLANTING

There is an approach to seeding your lawn called **"frost seeding."** This is a somewhat non-scientific approach to seeding your lawn. It is best done in the early part of the month to take advantage of the freezing and thawing of the ground as temperatures fluctuate. Ideally, you want the ground to freeze and thaw two or three times after seeding. This enables the seed to drop into the tiny spaces in the soil created by the freezing and thawing process.

**Successful frost seeding requires good seed-to-soil contact.** Open bare patches or places where the grass has become thin are places it is worth trying. Since frost seeding requires no soil preparation, it is very easy, but it is not a great approach for overseeding your entire lawn.

If you have bare patches that you know need attention, you have nothing to lose by frost seeding except the cost of a little seed. If it works, you are ahead of the game. If not, you can still till, amend, plant, water, and keep your fingers crossed the next time.

 MOWING

Not time for this either!

 PESTS

Snow molds can still show up now if the snow cover is melting. There's not much you can do about them now, but see January Pests for preventive measures that can protect your lawn against them next year.

 WATERING

No water yet!

 FERTILIZING

It's almost that time!

NOTES

_____

_____

_____

_____

_____

_____

# MARCH
## Lawns

 PLANNING

Between the middle of March and the middle of April is the best time to do spring seeding of lawns. There are three primary types of grass from which to choose. All three are cool-season grasses that grow best in spring to early summer and start up again in late summer, continuing growth throughout the fall. These grasses are dormant at the hottest time of summer and the coldest part of winter. Each grass is described in more detail in the chapter introduction. Depending on the growing conditions of your yard, you will use a mix of these seeds, as outlined in the introduction:

*1* **Kentucky Bluegrass:** requires full sun and moist soil conditions, but the soil must still drain well. It will not grow in shade

*2* **Fescues:** are the best for shade but not deep shade. They grow well in poorer soils and drier conditions, making them less fussy than bluegrass.

*3* **Perennial ryegrass:** protects soil against erosion and keeps down weeds while waiting for the bluegrass to come up.

 PLANTING

Major lawn renovation projects should be reserved for September.

Think about it. If you were a cool-season grass seed, would you want to germinate in cold, soggy, spring ground? And then have to grow in cold wind? And then, just as you start to think you are going to be a real grass plant, experience soaring temperatures while your infantile root system goes into major heat stress? Or, would you rather germinate in soil warmed by summer sun, emerge just as air temperatures cool down, and have a couple of "cool" months to settle in before winter takes hold?

Spring is for **overseeding** thin areas, filling in bare spots, and fixing ruts and damage from winter weather and construction projects. **When overseeding, the seed needs to be in contact with soil to germinate.** Where there are bare batches and where you can see soil between the grass, go ahead and overseed.

Take a hard rake to the soil surface to stir things up. Grass seed does best if it is ever so slightly covered with soil . . . less than 1/4 inch. Sprinkle with water 2 to 3 times daily after planting, keeping the new lawn moist, until grass germinates. As it becomes established, you will water deeply and less frequently. Remember,

**bluegrass** can take up to thirty days to germinate. **Fescue** comes up in seven to fourteen days, and speedy **ryegrass** arrives in only five to ten days.

Places where there is so much thatch that you cannot see soil may not be suitable for spring seeding. The thatch will have to be removed, and that wreaks havoc on the grass you want to keep. Save that project for September.

 WATERING

As stated above, seed requires a daily sprinkling of water until the seed germinates, then taper off until the grass is on its own. Established lawns rarely need water. At this time, spring seeded lawns don't have robust roots the first summer. When weather gets hot, be sure to follow the correct watering procedures of 1 inch of water put down all at once, in the early morning.

 FERTILIZING

Apply lime and fertilizer according to a soil test (see chapter introduction).

Ten pounds of 10-6-4 fertilizer per 1000 square feet is a good standard feeding. Once your pH has been brought up to neutral, a maintenance application of **20 pounds per 1000 square feet** of pulverized or granular limestone once per year is sufficient to keep it there. If you don't know your pH, apply the 20 pounds and get a soil test for next year. If you applied fertilizer late in the fall, around Thanksgiving, you may be able to delay or skip a spring application of fertilizer.

Lime and fertilizer can be applied at the same time as seed. That is not the case, though, with weedkillers, some insecticides, and most pre-emergent materials.

 MOWING

Mow as soon as the grass needs it. Once it starts growing, it will grow like gangbusters. Try not to let the grass get taller than 4 inches, and mow to a height of 2 inches. Even with a mulching lawnmower, the first thick cut often has to be bagged since it is so heavy, thick, and wet.

 PESTS

Two diseases make their appearance just as the grass begins to green up in the spring. Both diseases start out as tiny purple to black spots on the leaves. Leaf spot turns into tan spots with darker brown edges. Melting out disease (yes, that's it's name) works its way down the blade into the crown and roots. Generally, two applications of fungicide are necessary at seven-day intervals. Check with your Cooperative Extension Office for current fungicide recommendations. These diseases are considered **"high nitrogen" diseases**, and switching to a primarily fall fertilization program may help to cut down on the problem in the future. Your other option is to ignore it since it will stop spreading when the weather changes. You may be left with some bare spots that will require patching.

Young **dandelion** plants will be easier to kill when they first start to grow in the spring than when they are in bloom. Spot treat with a broadleaf weedkiller.

## NOTES

_____

_____

_____

_____

_____

# APRIL
## Lawns

## PLANNING

By April, most of your gardening chores are in full swing. If there are areas of thin grass that you want to overseed or a few bare spots left over from disease or dog pee, then you can do that now, but be sure to get your seed down by the middle of the month. Don't even think about it after May 1.

Sod is more costly than seed but is less work to get established. It can be put down almost anytime the ground can be properly prepared (although you are better off avoiding the heat of summer) and eliminates the issues around seedling failures.

## PLANTING

Planting sod requires the same type of soil preparation as if you were starting from scratch with seed. Make sure you get all this done **before you order your sod to be delivered** but not so much in advance that your yard can become a mud hole.

To prepare for Sod:

*1* **Strip away all existing grass and weeds to bare soil.** You can use a total vegetation killer such as glyphosate (Round-up® for example), cover the area with old carpeting or black plastic until it is dead, or rototill it. Some weeds may return if they are simply rototilled, but the thickness of the sod will help prevent that.

*2* **Incorporate organic matter, such as compost,** to improve both sandy and heavy clay soils. Straight organic matter is better than topsoil unless you working with a subsoil and planning to add 4 to 6 inches of topsoil. If that is the case, make sure you get certified topsoil and not something that came from "the top" of somewhere.

*3* **If you missed getting a soil test back in January, spread pulverized or granular limestone.** Spread 75 to 100 pounds of pulverized or granular limestone per 1000 square feet, and 20 to 25 pound of 10-6-4, 50 percent slow-release fertilizer per 1000 square feet.

*4* **Till all this in** to a depth of at least 6 inches; 8 inches is better. Smooth it all out so there are no ruts or low spots. Also, make sure there is a gentle slope away from buildings.

*5* **Roll lightly** to provide a firm bed.

*6* **Water the bed lightly.** If your prepared soil gets powder dry.

When Sod arrives:

*1* **Install your sod immediately** after it arrives. The hotter the temperature, the less time it will keep if piled up in a heap.

*2* **Lay your sod strips so they fit tightly together** but do not overlay or have gaps. Start at the bottom of the slope and place the strips horizontally across the slope. Stagger seams so it is like laying bricks.

*3* **Roll after placement** so the roots snuggle into the soil.

*4* **Water thoroughly.** You may need to water part of the area before you finish laying the sod if you are planting a large area.

## WATERING

Seeded or newly sodded lawns will need frequent watering until established. Established lawns should not need water right now.

## FERTILIZING

If you fertilized established lawns in March, they will not need to be fertilized again. If you didn't fertilize, see last month for instructions. Properly planted, your new sod should have adequate nutrients to get through the spring and summer.

# MOWING

Mow as soon as necessary. Do not let grass get higher than 4 inches. Mow to a height of 2 inches. If you can mow when it's 3 inches to a height of 2 inches, that is even better.

# PESTS

Spot-treat weeds with a broadleaf weed-killer, or if you have a heavy weed load, you can apply weedkiller to your entire lawn **unless** you have overseeded.

When the **forsythia** is in bloom, apply pre-emergent weedkiller to prevent crab-grass. This is an old husband's tale that is correct, according to Dr. John Meade, weed specialist at Rutgers University. So forget the calculations and follow the forsythia. Dr. Meade says it's usually about the first week in April, but the very latest is April 23.

Sod webworms begin feeding in the spring. They burrow through the soil and nibble on grass blades at night. They will be fully grown by June. Check with your Cooperative Extension Office for current control recommendations.

## Helpful Hints

• If you develop an appreciation for dandelion flowers, you don't have to use as much weedkiller. Save it for really nasty things like poison ivy and sticky thistles.

• Grass clippings can be used as a mulch around flowers and shrubs if used fresh, or it will get stinky fast.

# NOTES

# MAY
## Lawns

## PLANNING

By this time of year, mowing should be in full swing. Whatever spring lawn renovations you had planned should have already been carried out. Keep an eye on areas where you applied seed. The different grasses have different germination rates. **Kentucky bluegrass** will be up in fourteen to thirty days. **Fescues** are a bit quicker, so you will see them poke up in seven to fourteen days. **Ryegrass** is the speedy one, and you should see signs of life in only five to ten days. These time ranges are based on temperatures between 68 and 75 degrees Fahrenheit. If you are having a cool spring, expect to wait the longer amount of time.

Unfortunately, if they don't come up, there really isn't much you can do. In bad areas, you can lay a bit of sod. See April for just how to do that.

What you should be doing now is planning to head down the shore for Memorial Day weekend. Down there, where all that sandy soil gets between your toes, grass is not as popular, and the **"pebble lawn"** is utilized. If you are not crazy about rocks, maybe you should consider **zoysia grass.** In general, people either love it or hate it. If it is invading your finer lawn grasses, you may consider it a weed. It is not a great choice for most homes since it does not green up until mid-May and turns brown again in mid-October. Down the shore, however, it may be the perfect alternative to painful rocks.

**Zoysia grass** is drought tolerant in hot weather, can be mowed close (from $1/2$ to $1^1/4$ inches), and tolerates heat stress and wear and tear. It does, however, require full sun. When it gets well established, it becomes quite thick and is effective in keeping out summer weeds. You almost never have to water it. Since its season matches the summer season at the beach, it may be a match made in heaven . . . or at least at the shore and that is pretty close to heaven.

## PLANTING

After May 1, it's too late to do any seeding. However, now is the right time to plant **zoysia grass.** Zoysia is generally planted from plugs (2-inch squares) from mid-May through June. Zoysia seed is available but is generally not successful in New Jersey.

To plant **zoysia** plugs the soil needs to be properly and thoroughly prepared just as if you were planting your cool-season grass seed or sod. (See April for soil preparation.) Thatch must be removed prior to planting and the removal repeated sometime in mid-May through June, every year after it is established. The plugs should be spaced at 8- to 12-inch intervals. Press plugs into the hole to ensure good soil contact. Do not cover the plugs with soil.

## WATERING

Keep newly planted plugs of **zoysia grass** moist during the first two to three weeks after planting. Established zoysia rarely needs water, but if it starts to turn grayish during periods of drought stress, apply 1 inch of water slowly but all at one time.

Continue to water newly planted sod until it is firmly knitted with the soil. Then taper off. Continue to water seeded areas daily until germination, then taper off gradually.

## FERTILIZING

If you have not yet fertilized your cool-season grasses, apply 10 pounds per 1000 square feet of 10-6-4, 50 percent slow-release fertilizer.

Immediately after planting your **zoysia** plugs, apply 10 pounds of 10-6-4 fertilizer per 1000 square feet of lawn. Repeat in two weeks.

If you don't like **zoysia grass,** only fertilize in the fall to discourage spring green up of the zoysia that may be mixed with your other grasses.

 ## MOWING

**Zoysia grass** is best kept short ($1/2$ to $1 1/4$ inches). This is especially true if you favor the zoysia in a lawn of mixed grasses. During the cool spring, zoysia grows slowly, so the need to mow is infrequent. Hot weather brings on a growth spurt of zoysia, so expect to mow once a week when heat hits.

Cool-season grasses are growing rapidly and need to be mowed weekly or even more often if you intend to let the clippings stay on the lawn. Remember, never mow more than half the height. When the grass reaches 4 inches in height, mow to 2 inches.

If you don't like **zoysia,** then let the cool-season grasses get tall, never cutting below 3 inches.

 ## PESTS

Grubs may be feeding voraciously. They are in the last stages of development before maturing into adult beetles. No chemical control is effective in killing them in these advanced stages. Wait until mid-July through August for effective treatment.

Chinch bugs may appear anytime as they overwinter as adults and begin laying eggs in the early spring. Eggs hatch rapidly, mature in thirty to forty days and lay another generation before returning to hibernation for the winter. It is possible to find all stages of development at any given time in your infested lawn. Adults are black, about $1/5$-inch long, and appear whitish when their wings are folded over their backs. Damaged areas of the grass are brown and get larger as the bugs eat their way to the outside of the area. Control in late May or early June. Check with your Cooperative Extension Office for current control recommendations.

## NOTES

_____

_____

_____

_____

_____

_____

_____

_____

_____

_____

_____

_____

_____

_____

# JUNE
## Lawns

 PLANNING

If your lawn is a mess, don't spend a lot of time worrying about it. You can kill it all off in August and start over in September. There is so much else going on in the gardening world right now that you can budget your time and energy elsewhere with better results.

Occasionally, sod shrinks and you end up with gaps between the strips. **Kentucky bluegrass,** the primary component of sod, may fill in the space. If not, you can plan on overseeding in the fall.

 PLANTING

**Zoysia grass** can be planted throughout the month of June. If you still need to do this, see May for planting information.

If you really want to plant cool-season grasses now, you can plant sod. But I recommend that you prune the roses and leave the lawn overhaul until the early fall.

 WATERING

June is when watering may become an issue, especially later in the month. Those lawns that were spring seeded or sodded may not have quite the tolerance for summer heat that fall planted or well-established lawns will have.

Late April seedlings of **Kentucky bluegrass** will have germinated in late May. Those baby grass plants will need some serious TLC if June weather turns super hot earlier than normal. Taper off from daily sprinklings of the seeds to deeper water applications every other day. Eventually, you will be putting down 1 inch of water per week, all at once, in the early morning.

Roots do the lion's share of growing in the fall. If your lawn is fall-seeded it should be able to withstand the hot weather. Remember, even with established lawns, put down 1 inch of water per week, early in the morning **or do not water at all!** Shallow watering doesn't reach the entire root system and thus encourages the roots to grow towards the surface. This, in turn, brings the roots into the warmer, drier parts of the soil, making it more vulnerable during drought conditions. It's better to let the grass go into summer dormancy than to water it too little.

 FERTILIZING

If you are planting **zoysia** now, apply 10 pounds of 10-6-4 fertilizer per 1000 square feet of lawn immediately after installing the plugs. Repeat in two weeks.

If you planted **zoysia** in May, it is time for the second application of 10-6-4 fertilizer at a rate of 10 pounds per 1000 square feet.

If you have not yet fertilized your cool-season grasses, June is your last chance. You never want to apply fertilizer when the temperature is above 85 degrees Fahrenheit; this will do more harm than good.

 MOWING

Continue to mow on an as-needed basis. Try not to mow if the grass is wet. It is harder on equipment and encourages the spread of disease. Cool season grasses get mowed at a height of 4 inches down to 2 inches. **Zoysia** needs to be kept shorter; when it reaches 2 inches, mow to one inch.

 PESTS

Japanese beetle grubs, which feed on roots of your lawn, will be hatching out as adults later this month. If you had serious damage to your lawn, you need to consider whether you want to control the grubs for the upcoming cycle. The window for control is mid-July through August. Whatever you decide to do, **don't hang those pheromone-type bag traps.** They draw in beetles from everywhere in a glassy-eyed sexual frenzy. You may think you have done a terrific job because you have a large bag of dead beetles, but they laid thousands of eggs on your grass before they landed in the bag.

Sod webworms emerge as lawn moths in June. They are sometimes called "cigarette moths" because of the way they look when they land on the grass and close their wings. The moths do no damage but lay eggs while flying or at rest. The eggs hatch in about one week and begin feeding again. It is possible to check for the webworms by breaking apart a clump of soil. Check with your

Cooperative Extension Office for current control recommendations.

Wild onion, also known as wild garlic, is a weed that will be very obvious at this time. It is not a true grass even though it looks more like a grass than a broadleaf weed. It is not poisonous and has no

stickers, but it does grow more rapidly than your desirable grass. It can sometimes be handweeded, but the bulbous roots resprout readily if you don't get the whole thing. Repeated spot treatments of a broadleaf weedkiller will be more effective.

## NOTES

_____

_____

_____

_____

_____

_____

_____

# JULY

## Lawns

## PLANNING

July is a time for minimal lawn maintenance. You mow when it gets too tall, and you spend as much time as possible wiggling your toes in the cool green blades and drinking lemonade with fresh strawberries. It is a good time to make some observations, and note which grasses works best and which did not perform as expected.

Now that the trees are in full leaf, the shade from the larger trees may be causing the grass some difficulties. As your trees mature, the grass will deteriorate. The closer to the trunk of your trees, the deeper the shade and the poorer the grass. If you are fighting moss in the same area, this indicates a moisture problem along with the shade. You will be shoveling against the tide if you insist on attempting to establish grass in a location such as this. On occasion, the removal of some tree limbs will let in more light, but that is a temporary fix and not necessarily enough of a fix to get healthy grass. The tree roots also take up a great deal of the available moisture, so the grass is competing for water as well as light.

Ground covers may be a better option than grass. Some are quite attractive and provide a woodland quality. A mixture of **ferns** and **sweet woodruff** is a lovely combination. Even the planting of shade-loving shrubs such as **azaleas** and **mountain laurel** can be an attractive alternative to grass under the trees. If space is limited and you can't afford to fill up that area, then maybe you just want to remove the grass in a circle around the trunk and cover the space with an organic mulch.

If you plan this out now, when you are ready to do major lawn renovation in the fall you will know where not to plant grass. Planting only in those areas where conditions are conducive to a healthy lawn will make lawn maintenance significantly easier. The added interest of the ground covers will add detail to your landscape without a lot of additional work.

## PLANTING

Sod is the only type of grass you can plant now, and only if you have no other choice about when to plant. **Sod in piles will not hold up long in summer heat.** It must be installed within hours of being delivered. See the month of April for planting details. Before planning to install sod, consider that water application is that much more critical while the sod is knitting, and even after that if the weather gets brutally hot. If any water restrictions are in place now, skip the whole idea. It is too much of an investment in time, money, and hard work to risk not being able to water it sufficiently.

## WATERING

Remember, if you water established grass in hot weather, you will have to mow more frequently. Consider letting it go dormant and finding more fun things to do with your time.

If you choose to water, you have to do the job correctly or you will end up doing a lot of damage. See the chapter introduction for an overview of proper watering.

Established **zoysia grass** is very tolerant of heat and drought. Only water if it begins to turn gray. Then apply 1 inch of water all at once.

## FERTILIZING

You definitely do not want to fertilize in July. It is just too hot.

## MOWING

Follow standard mowing procedures. You mow cool-season grasses when they reach 4 inches and cut them back to

2 inches. You mow **zoysia grass** when it reaches 2 inches and cut it back to 1 inch.

 PESTS

Don't apply weedkillers this month, as the high temperatures will greatly increase the chances of your grasses sustaining damage.

The first Japanese beetle eggs that were laid begin to hatch in mid-July. It is when these grubs are newly hatched that they are the most easily controlled. **You are not likely to observe damage to the sod when the grubs are newly emerged,** so apply the appropriate material now if you have had a problem in the past. If you want to check, you can lift a square of sod with a square bladed shovel. If you find 6 to 8 grubs just below the surface,

you should consider treatment. Less than that, the lawn can probably tolerate the infestation. More than that means serious trouble. Check often if you have any reason to think you may have a problem. Lifting a piece of sod to check is really no big deal. Just lay it back down carefully and water it thoroughly to help it re-knit.

Fusarium blight, Pythium blight, and rust are all lawn diseases that first show up about this time. Fusarium starts out as light green areas but turns to tan in thirty-six to forty-eight hours. Pythium is most noticeable in the early morning as a spots or group of spots about 2 inches in diameter edged in blackened grass blades. Rust looks like rust-colored powdery spots on the individual blades. **Preventive control is the only thing that is really effective.** As the environmental conditions shift, the diseases will fade away. If the problem becomes serious, you can spray preventively next year.

 NOTES

_____

_____

_____

_____

_____

_____

_____

# AUGUST
## Lawns

# PLANNING

By August, it is time to start planning for major lawn renovation projects in September. If you have at least 30 percent of desirable grass left in your lawn, you may want to try to save what is there and seed on top. This still requires major preparation of the lawn area. If you have less than 30 percent desirable grasses, the use of glyphosate (as in Roundup®) will kill off everything. Apply this approximately two weeks prior to seeding. This method can also be used for difficult growing areas where you prefer to try ground cover.

**Have a soil test** done to determine your lime and fertilizer needs. Do this as early in the month as possible to allow time to get the results prior to seeding. Make a note to apply a broadleaf weedkiller at least two weeks before seeding, but not until the temperature drops below 85 degrees Fahrenheit. **Follow directions to the letter.**

Check for low spots and depressions. These will need to be filled level with the surrounding ground.

Once you have taken the above preparatory steps, you will need to remove any thatch that has built up and anything you have killed off. Doing this by hand is quite a chore, so investigate where you can rent, borrow, or purchase the equipment you will need. Dethatching machines will remove thatch from exisiting turf, but a sod cutter may be more effective to remove the top layer if you are starting from scratch.

# PLANTING

Don't plant seed grass in August. You can, however, plant sod any time the soil can be properly prepared. It's best to plant later in the month since the air temperature cools rapidly as August becomes September, putting less stress on the newly planted grass. Planting information for sod can be found in April.

# WATERING

If you are watering your established cool-season grass, continue to apply 1 inch of water per week, applied all at one time, in the early morning.

If you chose to plant sod, it will need to be watered daily until the roots knit with the soil. Then taper off until you are watering once a week, in the early morning. As the weather shifts to cool autumn weather, you can probably stop watering altogether.

# FERTILIZING

You will not need to fertilize until next month; however, go ahead and do a soil test early this month. Fertilizer applications are most effective when applied in accordance with soil test results. (See the chapter introduction for more on soil testing.)

# MOWING

Mowing continues in the same way you've been doing it so far. Mow cool-season grasses when they reach 4 inches in height and cut to 2 inches. **Zoysia grass** gets cut at 2 inches back to 1 inch.

# PESTS

Watch out for Japanese beetle grubs in the lawn, especially if you have had a problem in the past or have observed the adults feeding in the area. See July for instructions on checking your sod for grubs. If you wait until the damage is obvious before you take action, the grubs will be bigger, stronger, hungrier, and harder to control.

If you choose to apply an insecticide, it is necessary to mow the grass shorter than usual, remove the thatch, and water the grass deeply. Apply the control material according to directions, and water in to make sure the insecticide gets down into the root zone where the grubs are doing their damage.

Powdery mildew is a lawn disease that usually first appears in August. Look for a grayish-whitish coating on the leaves. Powdery mildew does better with higher amounts of nitrogen, so **you may want to delay an early fall application of fertilizer or use only fertilizer that is low in nitrogen.** Next year, you may want to lighten up on your nitrogen application in late spring. Also, more sun and better air circulation will help prevent the disease; therefore, it's good to collect the clippings when you mow.

## Helpful Hints

### Have You Tried These?

• If you don't want the herbicide approach to grass removal, you can consider covering areas with old carpeting (turned upside down) or black plastic. You would want to do this early in the month to provide enough time to completely kill off, down to the roots, whatever was growing in the lawn.

• If you have a large lawn and would rather do something else than mow all the time, consider allowing a part of it to become a meadow. Even lawn grasses are quite lovely "ornamental grass" when allowed to get tall and set seed. Fill the area with **crocus** and **daffodil** bulbs and let them naturalize. Add a few purple **coneflowers** and seed with annual **poppies** and **cosmos** for summer color. You will need to remove nasty weeds like **poison ivy** and **thistle,** but you might find the softness of a wild meadow a pleasant balance to the more formal areas of the lawn.

• Nematodes and the milky spore disease can both be effective in controlling Japanese beetle grubs but have no effect on other white grubs that are similar in both appearance and the damage they do. Milky spore can take up to three years to become effective, but then the Japanese beetle grub suppression will be long term. If other insect pests should become a problem, it is possible that the insecticides necessary for control may reduce the effectiveness of your biological controls.

## NOTES

##  PLANNING

September is **the action month** for lawn care. You can revitalize an existing lawn or totally start over. Overseeding areas that have been damaged by summer diseases should also be done at this time.

Luckily, you don't usually have to do all of these things at once. You should have your August soil test results by now. Base your lime and fertilizer purchases on the soil test results and the size of your lawn area. Go out and purchase all your supplies if you haven't already. See the chapter introduction for an overview of grass seed choices.

## PLANTING

Remember, if you want to revitalize an existing lawn, you need to have 30 percent or more of desirable grass. See the chapter introduction for more information on any of these important steps:

*1* **Eliminate weeds:** Two weeks prior to seeding, apply broadleaf weed killer to reduce the weed population.

*2* **Thatch removal:** Seed must be in direct contact with soil to germinate. There are special machines designed for this. While small areas can be done by hand, it is very hard work.

*3* **Aerate** (If necessary.): If the soil is hard and compact, aeration allows air, water, and seed to penetrate into the root zone of the grass. **Only use a core aerator.**

*4* **Apply topdressing:** First, mow the grass more closely than is otherwise recommended. Set the mower to ³/₄ to 1 inch and mow carefully. Topdressing is an application of ¹/₄ inch of topsoil or organic matter on top of existing grass. If you choose topsoil, make sure you get certified topsoil. Using compost as a topdressing may be more beneficial to your soil.

*5* **Apply seed:** For sunny areas, use primarily **Kentucky bluegrass,** and for shady areas you will want primarily **fine fescue.** Add a bit of perennial rye in either case. See March for planting instructions.

*6* **Water immediately.**

If you have less than 30 percent desirable grass, you need to eradicate everything you have and start over:

*1* **Eliminate all growth:** Kill with a total vegetation killer at least 2 weeks in advance, or cover with old carpeting one month in advance of seeding. A sod cutter is useful to strip away all the dead material, or you can rototill the material into the soil.

*2* **Prepare the soil:** Incorporate lime, fertilizer, and organic matter into the soil to a depth of at least 6 inches. Eight inches is even better. If the organic matter or topsoil is left on the surface, the roots will stay mostly in the layer of quality material, and they will be more vulnerable to temperature fluctuations.

*3* **Fertilize:** If you didn't do a soil test in August, apply 75 to 100 pounds of pulverized or granular limestone for each 1000 square feet of lawn. For fertilizer, apply 30 to 40 pounds of 5-10-10 fertilizer per 1000 square feet.

*4* **Add organic matter:** Organic matter, such as leaf compost, should be spread at a rate of 1 to 2 cubic yards per 1000 square feet and rototilled into your soil. Rake it smooth and level before applying seed. Roll lightly if you are installing sod over the prepared soil.

*5* **Apply grass seed:** Use a drop or cyclone spreader. Then rake lightly and roll with a weighted roller.

*6* **Water immediately:** Install a layer of clean straw or salt hay to keep the seed moist and prevent erosion. The grass will grow up through the light mulch, so the straw or salt hay can be left in place.

See April for details regarding the installation of sod.

 WATERING

Water newly seeded lawns 2 or 3 times a day until the seed germinates. This is just a light sprinkling, not a deep watering (that creates mud). Your seed will not all come up at the same time. **Bluegrass** can take up to thirty days to germinate. **Fescue** comes up in seven to fourteen days, and speedy **ryegrass** arrives in only five to ten days.

If you choose sod instead of seed, see April for installation information. Water your sod immediately after installing it. This should be within the first hour if it is a hot day. If you are installing large areas of sod, you may have to work in sections, watering one section before you have finished installing another section. Beyond installation, new sod will need thorough watering once daily. **Note: This is a deeper watering than recommended for dampening new seed.** Repeat this water application until the roots have thoroughly knitted with the soil. Adequate rooting generally takes between two and three weeks. Then taper off by watering every other day, then every third day, and so forth, until cooler weather and higher soil moisture in general makes watering unnecessary.

# Helpful Hints

*1* For areas of deep shade, September is a great time to plant ground covers. It's best to do this before seeding or sodding so you don't have to walk on the lawn area while things are getting established.

*2* Topdressing is helpful in filling minor depressions under sod. Major depressions, however, need to have the sod lifted, topsoil or organic matter placed beneath the sod, and the sod returned to its spot. Too much topdressing above ground will smother underlying grass.

 FERTILIZING

With proper soil preparation (see Planting) there should be no need to apply additional fertilizer to newly seeded or sodded lawns.

**For established lawns, apply both lime and fertilizer** based on the results of August's soil test. As a general rule, you can apply 10 pounds of 10-6-4 fertilizer at a rate of 10 pounds per 1000 square feet. If you want to encourage root growth, you can use 10 to 15 pounds of 5-10-10 fertilizer per 1000 square feet.

An annual application of 20 to 25 pounds per 1000 square feet of granular limestone will maintain a proper pH if it's already at a proper level.

 MOWING

Continue to mow as usual on an as-needed basis. Dormant lawns will pick up their rate of growth and may need more frequent mowing now that the weather has cooled off.

 PESTS

If grubs are a problem, an application of grub control material is still recommended. However, the ideal window is mid-July through August, so the sooner the control material is applied, the more effective it will be.

Many of the summer diseases will continue to show up early in the month but disappear as the weather changes. Powdery mildew will continue with the cooler nights. See August for more information.

Slime molds can appear any time but are much more likely to show up under moist conditions. Luckily, they dry up and disappear in a few days. When they occur on organic mulch, you can rake the mulch to speed up the drying process.

# OCTOBER

 ## PLANNING

Depending on how late in the month you put down your seed, you should see something green early this month. If all the work was done over Labor Day weekend, you should have a nice stand of grass by now. If you finished up at the tail-end of the month, your perennial rye will come up first, followed by the **fescue.** You may have to wait a while for the **bluegrass.** It should all be green before Halloween.

If you didn't sharpen you mower blades all season, they are probably as dull as loaf of stale bread by now. Change the blades and get the dull set sharpened before storing them.

By the middle of October, your **zoysia grass** will have turned brown. Down the shore, zoysia turns brown just about the end of the season, so no one cares that it gets ugly. For year-round living, the early brown is a major disadvantage. It is possible to dye it green. One application of dye can last all winter, but it does look a little strange. (If it could be dyed purple it might be fun, but this green does not look natural.)

 ## PLANTING

Refer to seed planting instructions in September. If you just didn't get it all done in time, you can still plant grass seed in early October, but be sure to finish up by the end of the first week (even earlier in that cold northwest corner). After that, your grass just won't have time to make an adequate root system to get through winter.

Sod is, of course, still an option. See April for more information. Don't skimp on soil preparation even for sod. It is a costly proposition, so you want to make sure you do it right.

 ## WATERING

Seed will continue to need daily sprinkling until all the seed germinates. Air temperature drops in October, and the intensity of the sun begins to wane. Taper off watering gradually after germination. Go from light watering daily to somewhat deeper applications every other day, to every third day, and so forth, until you are down to once weekly. By that time, Mother Nature should have taken over. If not, remember to apply 1 inch of water, in the early morning, applied all at one time.

 ## FERTILIZING

If you followed all the directions for newly seeded or sodded lawns, no fertilizer should be needed at this time. If you did not get around to applying fertilizer to your established lawn, you can still do that in October. It is definitely better early in the month rather than later. If you don't have a soil test to go by, apply 10 pounds of 10-6-4 fertilizer per 1000 square feet of lawn, and 20 to 25 pounds of pulverized or granular limestone per 1000 square feet.

 ## MOWING

Continue mowing whenever it becomes necessary. Mow your **zoysia** as long as it is growing. Once it turns brown, you don't have to worry about it until it greens up again in the spring.

 ## PESTS

By this time, you have missed the window to control your Japanese beetle grubs. In the middle of the month, grubs move further down into the soil to overwinter 3 to 6 inches below the soil surface. In spring, usually mid-April, they move back up to begin feeding again. You will just have to live with them until next summer when the window for control opens again.

An application of broadleaf weedkiller in October is a good control for many perennial weeds, especially dandelions. Dandelion seed germinates over the summer and early fall. The plants are still tender and relatively susceptible to chemical control. Apply on a day when the temperature is above 70 degrees Fahrenheit but below 85 degrees Fahrenheit. Do not mow the day before or the day after.

## Helpful Hints

*1* If you have discovered you have bumps in your lawn, it may be moles. Moles live to dig, and they eat along the way. They are probably eating your grubs. There are a few controls for moles, including dropping chewing gum or smoke bombs into their runs, but as long as you have grubs, other moles will come to take their place. If you control the grubs and so eliminate the food source, the moles will go away.

*2* October is the month to plant bulbs. Filling your lawn with **crocus** bulbs is a wonderful way later to get out from under winter's grip come late winter and early spring. The mighty blooms battle winter and always win.

A liquid broadleaf weedkiller that contains two or three active ingredients is best. Don't spray on a windy day, as your ornamentals can be harmed by even very little exposure. Granular materials are a little easier to use and should be applied in the early morning while the grass is wet from dew. Weeds need to be actively growing for chemical control to be effective. **Do not use if you have just seeded.** Instead, wait at least eight weeks after all the seedlings have emerged.

## NOTES

_____

_____

_____

_____

_____

_____

_____

_____

_____

_____

# NOVEMBER
## Lawns

 ## PLANNING

Planning your Thanksgiving dinner is more important than planning for your lawn at this time of year. Anything newly planted this fall should be established by now, or at least thriving. Work on that new recipe for pumpkin cheesecake and let the lawn take care of itself.

 ## PLANTING

You can still plant sod if you are desperate for a green lawn. You will get instant results, and a bit of the pressure is off regarding the immediate need to plant once the sod arrives. You have a larger window in cooler weather, but you should still plan to plant the same day the sod is delivered, or the day after that. See April for planting specifics.

 ## WATERING

Water new sod if you plant it, but by now the rest of the lawn should be on its own. Of course, anything newly planted may need a drink if the weather is unseasonably dry. If needed, apply 1 inch of water, all at once, in the early morning. It takes 1 inch to penetrate the entire root zone.

## Helpful Hints

*1* If you mix your grass clippings in with your leaf pile, you will speed up the decomposition of the leaves significantly. Leaves are high in carbon and low in nitrogen and water. Grass is low in carbon and high in nitrogen and water. Together they make a perfect recipe for compost.

*2* If the pile gets stinky, it means it ran out of oxygen. Grass does not have much room for air, and the microorganisms use up what oxygen there is very quickly. Adding leaves will make more air spaces. You can also turn the pile more frequently to keep the oxygen level higher.

 ## FERTILIZING

Apply 5-10-10 fertilizer for root development. This lower nitrogen fertilizer reduces the chance of snow mold disease. If you use 10-6-4 fertilizer, make sure it is 50 percent slow release. Apply either type at a rate of 10 pounds per 1000 square feet.

 ## MOWING

Continue mowing as necessary.

## PESTS

Diseases are not really much of a problem once the weather turns cold. Snow mold can show up as early as November 15, but it is certainly not common. Insects aren't doing much either.

Weeds need to be actively growing for weed control materials to be effective. However, it's not a bad idea to get out and handweed the really aggressive intruders like nutsedge, wild onion, and any of the thistles.

Longer grass may encourage snow mold diseases, so keep mowing.

## NOTES

_____
_____
_____
_____
_____
_____
_____
_____
_____

# DECEMBER

 PLANNING

There really isn't much to do for lawn care in December. With the holiday season upon us, you may want to give a little thought to presents for the lawn ranger in the family. Here are a few ideas:

- **A sprinkler.** Some of the copper tubing ones double as lawn sculpture when not in use but spin in outrageous spray patterns when turned on. There are also many animal sculptures/sprinklers that are fun.

- **A spreader.** This might seem boring, but it is like the underwear grandma gives every year. You appreciate it when you need it, especially when it's good quality.

- **A hat.** This is an important present. Mowing grass means you are exposed to a lot of sun. A hat keeps you cooler as well as protecting you from UV rays. A really good hat has protection in the back and over the ears—especially good for gardeners with short hair—and is more effective than the common baseball cap type.

- **A string trimmer.** These can be powerful and heavy gasoline-powered types or smaller electric lightweight versions. Consider the strength of the person using it as well as the distance from the house. Cordless, rechargeable string trimmers are also available. Cordless lets you roam where needed, but it may be limited in both battery capacity and power.

 PLANTING

As long as the ground can be worked, it is still possible to plant sod. See planting instructions in April.

 WATERING

If you plant sod, it will need to be watered until it knits. You need not water any other part of the lawn.

 FERTILIZING

If you fertilized last month, you're done until spring. Otherwise it can still be done the first week in December, but if you don't get to it then, wait until spring.

## Helpful Hints

- There is a 1947 Spencer Tracy and Katherine Hepburn movie called *Sea of Grass*. It is about cattle ranching on the Great Plains with the undulating fields of grass swaying in the wind. It has some sad parts, but it is hard to go wrong with Kate and Spence.

- When it's time to put away your mower for winter, make sure it's clean and dry. This will keep rusting to a minimum.

 MOWING

As long as the grass is growing, it will need to be mowed.

 PESTS

Snow molds can show up if there is snow cover, but they are not common. If you mow to 2 inches when the grass finishes growing, it goes a long way in preventing the disease.

 NOTES

_____

_____

_____

_____

_____

_____

_____

# CHAPTER SEVEN

# Perennials

*Perennials are plants that come back every year.*
*Well, that's the idea anyway.*

How many years they last is a function of a whole bunch of variables. If you locate the right plant in the right spot, you certainly maximize the potential for them to last as long as possible.

## PERENNIAL LIFESPANS

If you intend to expand your perennial garden by starting some plants from seed, you need to make a list immediately of what you want and when it needs to be started. If you are dabbling in perennials for the first time, read as much as you can about the species that peak your interest. Find out as much as possible about the plants you are considering. **Location, location, location:** Light and soil moisture are very important factors.

Some perennials, such as **dianthus, primula, verbena,** and **campanula,** can be started as early as January. The wonderful and dramatic **peony** can last for fifty years in the same spot without being divided as long as it has good sun and adequate drainage. Put it in the shade, and it will eventually fizzle,

or even worse, return every year but never bloom.

Some plants are short lived under the best of circumstances. The lovely **lupine** will grow wild in fields up in Maine, blasting the announcement of spring with all its vivacious color. In New Jersey, they may produce lovely spikes in May for two or three or sometimes even four years, and then **"poof"** they're gone. It is the nature of our winters. Lupines can handle cold. The cold Maine winters have no effect. It is the indecisiveness of New Jersey winters that causes the problems. It may be bitter cold one week and then in the 60s for four or five days before the temperatures plummet back to single digits. Lupines get confused. They start to come out of dormancy on those warm days humans really enjoy, but then the cold returns and the plants aren't able to handle it.

The ability to tolerate the weather of a particular winter can even vary among varieties within a species. One year all the yellow **chrysanthemums** survived just fine, but the enormous display of pink ones completely disappeared.

When you plant perennials, you get the advantage of having the plants return every year. With a little luck, they come back bigger and more robust, thus providing even more flowers than the year before. What they do not do is bloom all season. With some perennials you get the added attraction of the lovely foliage. **Lupine** foliage is particularly attractive, and the early grassy leaves of **daylilies** help to camouflage the fading foliage of spring **daffodils.** If you want color from spring to fall you must either choose your perennials with great care or blend them with your summer annuals.

## PLANTING

Planting instructions for perennials are given in the month that action is needed.

## CARE

When planting a bed of annual flowers, you can go into the bed in the spring with a rototiller or even a spading fork, add copious amounts of compost, and till the whole thing for a fresh start. With perennials, you cannot do that. Weed control must be done with the use of pre-emergent materials in the spring to prevent annual weeds, the use of lots of organic mulch, and some serious handweeding on occasion. If perennial weeds got a foothold the previous year, you may have to do serious weeding before they take over. On the other hand, if you were good about controlling weeds the previous year and laid a heavy mulch for winter protection, you may get through much of early spring without having to do much of anything.

Some perennials will need to be divided to maximize their potential. **Oriental poppies** can get very thick and do well with a lifting, thinning, and replacement of the most vigorous parts of the plant. Perennial **sunflowers** are a show-stopper in October, but if you don't thin them out in early spring, they can get really overwhelming.

If you want more of a particular plant, the time to divide it is the opposite season from when it blooms. For example, peonies bloom in May and are best divided in October. **Chrysanthemums** bloom in September and October and are best divided in the early spring. Summer bloomers are often not very particular. **Daylilies** can be divided anytime the ground can be worked, but it is really better to give the plants about three weeks before a hard freeze, and if you do divide them in the middle of summer, they will likely survive but will probably lose the blooms. Occasionally, plants make life a bit easier. Some daylilies have "proliferations" on the flower "scapes" or stems. That is where clusters of leaves and tiny roots develop along the nodes. These can be removed to start new plants without ever disturbing the parent plant.

It is always best to pay some attention to the plants during their period of bloom. **Hibiscus** flowers generally drop off as they fade, but not always. If they get beaten down by rain, they can get slimy and unattractive. **Crocosmia** flowers bloom successively on a single stem. You may want to remove the faded blooms so what remains looks nicer. On the other hand, perennial **candytuft** and **gaillardia** both make lovely seed pods. Candytuft blooms almost all at once in the early spring. The seeds develop all at once. You do not want to leave them indefinitely as they will sap strength from the plant for the following year. While they are fresh and green, the developing seeds offer a second season of interest. Cut them as they start to brown. Gaillardia has an extended season of bloom. If you remove the faded flowers, it encourages the plant to make more. Even so, the dried papery seed pods are particularly interesting.

Don't think that planting perennials means you have dramatically decreased your work load. In truth you have shifted it around a bit more than actually reducing it. The wonderful thing about perennials is not that they return every year but that they provide a changing garden of infinite variations. If you are just getting started, chances are the selection available at your favorite nursery will give you an abundance of choices with which to start your garden. You can have a carpet of **creeping phlox** in the spring, a myriad of colorful **daylilies** all summer, and an explosion of **sunflowers** in the fall. It is the magical fourth dimension of changing over time. You can accomplish this in the backyard of your condo or on a rolling estate. If you love what you have accomplished, take a step back and enjoy it. It you are not happy with your first results, you can always move it or replace it next year.

## MANY CHOICES

If you have become a specialist in a particular perennial, you may need to resort to specialty catalogs to get the full spectrum of color available or to maximize the season with early, mid- and late-season varieties. **Peonies, daylilies,** and **chrysanthemums** are three perennials that are commonly favored. **Hostas** have great appeal in the shade. They are grown mostly for the different textures and variegation of the foliage, but some varieties have lovely blooms as well. Hostas are, well, rather subdued plants. If you are looking for drama, you may

## Helpful Hints

### Sensitive Seeds

Some seeds that are started in May may need to be pampered with controlled indoor conditions until they germinate. Some of these are: *Achillea* (**yarrow**), *Alchemilla* (**lady's mantle**), *Alcea* (**hollyhock**), *Anthemis* (**chamomile**), *Aquilegia* (**columbine**), *Brunnera*, *Coreopsis*, *Delphinium*, *Dicentra* (**bleedimg heart**), *Digitalis* (**perennial foxglove**), *Echinacea* (**purple coneflower**), *Echinops* (**globe thistle**), *Eryngium* (**sea holly**), *Euphorbia* (**spurge**), *Gaillardia* (**blanket flower**), *Geranium* (this is the true **geranium,** not the garden geranium in the genus *Pelargonium*), *Gypsophila* (**baby's breath**), *Heliopsis* (**false sunflower**), *Heuchera* (**coral bells**), *Kniphofia* (**red-hot poker**), *Liatris*, *Ligularia* (**golden ray**), *Liriope*, *Lupinus* (**lupines**), *Lychnis* (**campion**), *Lysimachia* (**loosestrife**), *Myosotis* (**forget-me-not**), *Papaver* (**poppy**), *Platycodon* (**balloon flower**), *Pulmonaria* (**lungwort**), *Pyrethrum* (**painted daisy**), *Scabiosa*, *Silene* (**campion**), *Stokesia* (**Stoke's aster**), *Tiarella* (**foam flower**), and **Veronica.**

### July Bloomers

*Campanula* (**bellflower**), **coreopsis, hosta, lavender,** *Lychnis* (**campion), veronica,** *Chrysanthemum parthenium* (**feverfew**), *Cimicifuga* (**bugbane**), *Clematis jackmanii*, *Gypsophila* (**baby's breath**), *Heliopsis* (**false sunflower**), *Hemerocallis* (**daylilies**), *Monarda* (**beebalm**), **garden phlox, yarrow, astilbe,** *Echinops* (**globe thistle**), *Platycodon* (**balloonflower**), *Stokesia*, *Crocosmia*, and **yucca** will all be showing off. **Evening primrose** and other close relatives in the *Oenothera* genus can bloom for most of the summer, as long as they get plenty of sun.

want to try something else. There are societies for many plants. Do an online search or check with your Cooperative Extension Agent if you cannot find an organization that features your favorite.

# Perennials

Many species have a bloom period that lasts for several months. The months indicated below are the months **most likely** to see bloom of the perennial. Plants may actually bloom a little earlier or later depending on zone, weather, and growing environment.

| Month of Bloom | Common Name (*Botanical Name*) | Sun | Part Shade | Shade |
|---|---|---|---|---|
| JANUARY | **Christmas Rose** <br> *Helleborus niger* | | • | • |
| FEBRUARY | **Lenten Rose** <br> *Helleborus orientalis* | | • | • |
| | **Bearsfoot Hellebore** <br> *Helleborus foetidus* | | • | • |
| MARCH | **Bloodroot** <br> *Sanguinaria canadensis* | | • | • |
| | **Dwarf Trillium** <br> *Trillium nivale* | | • | • |
| APRIL | **Mountain Pinks** <br> *Phlox subulata* | • | | |
| | **Siberian Forget-me-not** <br> *Brunnera macrophylla* | • | • | |
| | **European Pasqueflower** <br> *Anemone pulsatilla* | | • | |
| | **Snow Trillium** <br> *Trillium grandiflorum* | | • | • |
| | **Sweet Violets** <br> *Viola odorata* | • | • | |
| | **Wild Violets** <br> *Viola sororia* | • | • | |
| MAY | **Heartleaf Bergenia** <br> *Bergenia cordifolia* | | • | • |
| | **Leather Bergenia** <br> *Bergenia crassifolia* | | • | • |
| | **Virginia Bluebells** <br> *Mertensia virginica* | | • | • |

# Perennials

| Month of Bloom | Common Name (*Botanical Name*) | Sun | Part Shade | Shade |
|---|---|:---:|:---:|:---:|
| **MAY** | **Primrose** <br> *Primula polyantha* | | • | |
| | **Fringed Bleeding Heart** <br> *Dicentra examina* | | • | • |
| | **Old Fashioned Bleeding Heart** <br> *Dicentra spectabliis* | | • | • |
| | **Perennial Candytuft** <br> *Iberis sempervirens* | • | • | |
| | **Wild Daylily** <br> *Hemerocallis fulva* | • | • | |
| | **Oriental Poppy** <br> *Papaver orientale* | • | | |
| | **Peony** <br> *Paeonia lactiflora* | • | | |
| | **Sweet William** <br> *Dianthus barbatus* | • | | |
| | **Globeflower** <br> *Trollius europaeus* | • | | |
| | **Perennial Bachelor Buttons** <br> *Centaurea montana* | • | | |
| **JUNE** | **Columbine** <br> *Aquilegia hybrids* | | • | |
| | **Blood-red Geranium** <br> *Geranium sanguineum* | • | | |
| | **Creeping Gypsophila** <br> *Gypsphila repens* | • | | |
| | **Coral Bells** <br> *Heuchera sanguinea* | • | • | • |
| | **Perennial Flax** <br> *Linum perenne* | • | | |

# Perennials

| Month of Bloom | Common Name (*Botanical Name*) | Sun | Part Shade | Shade |
|---|---|:---:|:---:|:---:|
| JUNE | **Blue Wild Indigo** *Baptisia australis* | | • | • |
| | **Painted Daisy** *Chrysanthemum coccineum* | • | | |
| | **Shasta Daisy** *Chrysanthemum superba* | • | • | |
| | **Lily of the Valley** *Convallaria majalis* | | • | • |
| | **Blanket Flower** *Gaillardia aristata* | • | • | |
| | **Lupine** *Lupinus polyphyllus* | • | | |
| | **Forget-me-not** *Myosotis scorpioides* | • | • | |
| JULY | **Bellflower** *Campanula persicifolia* | • | • | |
| | **Coreopsis or Tickseed** *Coreopsis lanceolata* | • | | |
| | **Hosta** *Hosta fortunei* | | • | • |
| | **Lavender** *Lavandula officinalis* | • | | |
| | **Campion** *Lychnis chalcedonica* | • | • | |
| | **Speedwell** *Veronica spicata* | • | | |
| | **Feverfew** *Chrysanthemum parthenium* | • | • | |
| | **Bugbane** *Cimicifuga racemosa* | | • | • |

# Perennials

| Month of Bloom | Common Name (*Botanical Name*) | Sun | Part Shade | Shade |
|---|---|---|---|---|
| JULY | **Baby's Breath** *Gypsophila paniculata* | • | | |
| | **False Sunflower** *Heliopsis scabra* | • | | |
| | **Daylilies** *Hemerocallis* hybrids | • | • | |
| | **Bee Balm, Monarda, Bergamot** *Monarda didyma* | • | • | |
| | **Garden Phlox** *Phlox paniculata* | • | | |
| | **Yarrow** *Achillea filipendula* | • | | |
| | **Hollyhock** *Alcea rosea* | • | • | |
| | **Astilbe** *Astilbe* x *arendsii* | | • | |
| | **Globe Thistle** *Echinops exaltatus* | • | • | |
| | **Stoke's Aster** *Stokesia laevis* | • | • | |
| | **Purple Coneflower** *Echinacea purpurea* | • | • | |
| AUGUST | **Milkweed** *Asclepias tuberosa* | • | • | |
| | **Gayfeather** *Liatris scariosa* | • | • | |
| | **Red Cardinal Flower** *Lobelia cardinalis* | | • | • |
| | **False Dragonhead** *Physostegia virginiana* | • | • | |

# Perennials

| Month of Bloom | Common Name (*Botanical Name*) | Sun | Part Shade | Shade |
|---|---|---|---|---|
| **AUGUST** | **Monkshood** *Aconitum napellus* | | • | |
| | **Black-eyed Susan** *Rudbeckia laciniata* | • | • | |
| | **Garden Chrysanthemums** *Chrysanthemum x moriifolium* | • | | |
| | **False Sunflower** *Helenium autumnale* | • | | |
| | **Perennial Sunflowers** *Helianthus x multiflorus* *Helianthus salicifolius* | • | | |
| **SEPTEMBER** | **Asters** *Aster novi-belgii* | • | | |
| | **Azure Monkshood** *Aconitum carmichaelii* | | • | • |
| **OCTOBER** | **Maximillian Sunflower** *Helianthus maximilianii* | • | | |
| | **Hairy Toad Lily** *Tricyrtis hirta* | | • | • |

## PLANNING

As soon as the holidays are over, garden catalogs start arriving in the mail. A fire, a cup of hot chocolate (definitely with marshmallows), perhaps a cat, and a stack of catalogs are the requirements for getting through the shortest days of the year. Use sticky notes. Not only do they mark important pages, but you can write how many you were thinking of getting and where you want to put them.

**Plan the layout.** This is always great fun. The right spot makes an enormous difference for the perennials you want to grow. There are now computer programs that allow you to choose plants and actually see how they should look as they grow over time. You can plug in different perennials to check them out.

Get an estimate of the size of the beds and the spacing of the plants you need to buy. For a less high-tech approach, use a planning kit. There are some available that have plants and grids that you can put together like a puzzle. You can also use graph paper and markers or colored pencils.

 ## PLANTING

Certainly there is no planting going on outside in January, but those perennials that get started from seed this month need to get going. Each species has its own requirements to get maximum results (or to get **any** results if requirements are very specific).

Be sure you understand their required depth of planting, whether they need light or darkness to germinate (sometimes this is critical), and the germination temperature. If germinating temperatures are a problem, there are electric mats or even mini-greenhouse kits with heat that will solve your problem, for a small investment. These kits are about the size of a flat and have a clear lid to increase humidity like a small greenhouse.

**Use sterile material for starting your seeds.** Potting mix is available that is specific for starting seeds. Perlite, vermiculite, or sterile sand will also work. Do not reuse potting soil and definitely do not use garden soil. In the contained environment of a pot or a flat, it is much too easy for disease to get a foothold. Garden soil has all kinds of spores and molds from exposure. Leave it in the garden. Once seeds have germinated, you can allow the temperature to drop to the low 60s without any problem.

 ## WATERING

Keep germinating seeds constantly moist but never saturated. Watering from the bottom prevents seeds from floating away as they do when you water from the top. Once the soil is moist, misting the soil surface daily or even twice daily may be enough in a humid environment.

Established perennials in the garden don't need any water at this time unless you are experiencing a winter drought. If there has been no precipitation over the late fall and winter, you may want to water plants if you have a warm spell. This is rare, but a dry winter following a dry summer does warrant some attention to watering needs.

# FERTILIZING

You don't need to fertilize anything at this time. Potting mixes usually have a bit of a fertilizer kick to help plants get started, and healthy seeds have stored food.

# PRUNING

Seedlings need to do some growing before being pruned, but your garden plants may enjoy a pruning at this time. This does not mean to go outdoors in 15-degree-weather and freeze yourself. It means if you get a warm day and cabin fever, you can follow the sun and prune a few things back that you didn't get to in late fall. **Chrysanthemums, peonies, gaillardia, baptisia, perennial sunflow-**

**ers,** and so forth will all need to be cut back before the new growth comes out in the spring. If you can get a headstart on it now and it helps chase the blues away, it is a good thing. Otherwise, it can wait.

## Helpful Hints

*1* **Hellebores** are wonderful shade perennials that bloom over the winter. The **Christmas rose** (*Helleborus niger*) may actually bloom in time for the holiday, but if it doesn't make it in December, it almost always blooms in January. In a mild month, the later blooming **lenten rose** (*Helleborus orientalis*) may also bloom, but in a very cold winter it takes longer. There are now many hybrids available with larger, more vivid blooms. The flowers are extremely long lasting in the garden.

*2* The sensitive **fern** (*Onoclea sensibilis*) produces the most wonderful sporulating fronds. The vegetative fronds lay flat and all but disappear at this time, but the sporulating fronds become woody and stay erect throughout the winter. A thick patch is particularly lovely contrasting against a light snowfall. These are so beautiful that jewelers have dipped the fronds in gold to make pins and pendants.

# PESTS

Pests are not a problem at this time.

# NOTES

## PLANNING

Planning for your perennials continues. If you have a compiled a list of plants that interest you, you need to do some research. Take care when you make your choices; gardening books with magnificent pictures can tempt you down a fateful path. All too often, you can get your heart set on something fabulous only to learn it is not hardy in our area. To avoid this, you can use reference books that are specific to New Jersey or at least the northeast. (My *New Jersey Gardener's Guide* is very specific, of course.)

Also, **identify your zone.** There is a zone map in the front of this book. New Jersey is the colder Zone 5 only in the northwest corner, in the mountains. The bulk of the State is Zone 6, and the south and shore areas are the warmer Zone 7. Once you know your zone, you can protect yourself from disappointment as most reference books do include zone hardiness with the plant descriptions.

If you are interested in finding a source for something in particular, check with your local nursery or greenhouse. Orders for spring plant material are either already in by now, or are in the process of being made. They may be able to tell you if they intend to carry what you seek or may be able to find an alternative source. If they start perennials from seed themselves, **it may be possible for you to supply the seed and have them grow the transplants.** If you want something very specific and don't have ideal conditions for doing it yourself, this may be a viable alternative.

Generate ideas by visiting flower shows held in late winter. The new New Jersey flower show began in 2003. It is held at the Convention Center in Edison in late February. It replaces the longstanding but now defunct show that thrived in Morristown for many years but faded away when it moved to Somerset. The new show is small but of high quality. Certainly it is worth a visit if it is in your own backyard.

## PLANTING

*Dianthus* spp. (**carnations**) can still be planted from seed. **Evening primrose,** *Penstemon* (**beard tongue**), and *Rudbeckia* (**black-eyed Susan**) are three that can be started now. Be patient. A great many perennials can be started from seed in March.

Seedlings that have emerged in flats can be transplanted when the first set of true leaves have developed. Take care to handle tiny seedlings by the seed leaves rather than the main stem. Transplant into a sterile potting medium in peat pots or small pots. Take care not to plant too deep or the stems will rot. See the chapter introduction for planting details.

## WATERING

Keep planted seeds and emerged seedlings moist, but not wet. Watering from the bottom is always preferable to watering from the top.

## FERTILIZING

Seedlings raised in perlite, sand, or vermiculite will benefit from watering with a diluted solution of water-soluble fertilizer. Once seedlings have been transplanted into their individual pots, you can follow a fertilizer program of regular application of very diluted fertilizer. You do not want to over-fertilize as the new growth will be very soft and tend to flop over.

# PRUNING

Continue to take advantage of warm days and prune perennials that are hanging around. Some ornamental grasses have showy seed heads that are extremely decorative over the winter. Once the wind, ice, and snow beats them down, they look tidier cut back. **Daylilies** can mat down and do a bit of damage if they are on top of evergreen ground covers. **Hellebores** may be blooming, but not all the leaves are necessarily in good shape. Trim off the bent and mushy ones to better enjoy the blooms. **Candytuft** can look a little ratty by now, so a light trim is in order.

**Rudbeckias** and **purple coneflowers** have very interesting seedpods that provide winter interest. You can leave them until later if they still look attractive, but if winter has them looking more sad than interesting, cut them back also. Use your judgement. The further the winter season progresses, the more flat, broken, and tattered the plants look. What may have entered the winter as starkly beautiful stalks and pods may now just be a mess.

# PESTS

Pests are still not a problem on perennials. Most plants are dormant, and so are the bugs.

 # NOTES

# MARCH
## Perennials

 ## PLANNING

By late March, you should be seeing some signs of an emerging spring. If the month actually goes out like a lamb, as it should, you may be able to get started on lots of chores. You need to be able to work the soil, which means it needs to have thawed out and dried up enough to work easily. Squeeze a wad in your hand. When you try to break it with your thumb, it should crumble readily. If the ground is too wet, it will mush together into a wad when you squeeze.

Even if it is too early to work, you should be able to get an idea of how things fared the winter. **Chrysanthemums** that made it will have tufts of green at the base of the dead stalks. If they appear in abundance, give thought to dividing the plants. Even at this time, you do not want to simply pull the stalks. Too often fresh green shoots come out attached to the stalk. Planting or dividing mums in the spring allows them plenty of time to develop a serious root system. Fall-planted mums behave more like fall-blooming annuals and rarely return the following spring. It is too early to plant out greenhouse-grown young mums, but if they are growing in your yard and the soil is ready to be worked, you can get your division done early.

As a rule, fall-blooming perennials are divided in the spring. *Helianthus maximilianii* (the perennial **sunflower)** is tough as nails and can be divided as soon as the ground can be worked. It will reward you will copious yellow flowers in October. The late-blooming giant perennial **hibiscus** are definite show stoppers. They never fail to make gardeners nervous, however, as they show no signs of life until May, when you are always certain they didn't make it. **Daylilies** can bloom from late spring through the summer, and the rare daylily reblooms in September or October. They are easily divided in the early spring. If they are showing signs of life, you can divide them now.

Of course there are always exceptions to any rule, which is why it is good to know as much as possible about the idiosyncrasies of the plants you choose. The delightful shade-loving **shooting star,** blooms in April, but the recommended time for division is late March or early April.

## PLANTING

Dividing plants in your garden is not the same as going to the nursery and planting out new perennials. Potted perennials raised in a greenhouse are much too tender to be planted outdoors.

In general, it is better to wait until danger of frost has past. If you are a member of a garden club, you can sometimes do a plant exchange with other gardeners who are dividing abundant perennials. This is a great way to increase your plant collection without any additional expense. Be sure to get the details about the growing requirements for the plants you are getting, but if they came out of a local garden, they can be immediately planted in yours.

**There are a great many perennials that are started from seed in March.** Make sure you have all your planting containers, sterile potting medium, and seeds in advance. Also make sure you know the specific requirements of the seeds you intend to start. You will need to pay attention to details, especially if you are potting more than one type of seed in a container. Group together seeds that require light for germination, and do the same for seeds that require darkness for germination. You will also want to group seeds in the same container that require similar germinating temperatures. Luckily, germination usually can take place over a range of temperatures, so as long as the range overlaps a bit, the seeds can be mixed together. Depth of planting need not be consistent, but take care when you are watering to not float the shallow planted seeds into the other areas of the flat.

Perennials seeds that can be started in March include: *Bergenia*, *Centaurea* (perennial **bachelor's button** and relatives), *Clematis*, *Globularia* (**globe daisy**), *Helianthus* (**perennial sunflower**), *Incaravillea* (**hardy gloxinia**), *Lathyrus* (perennial **sweet pea**), *Linaria* (**toadflax**), *Linum* (**flax**), *Lobelia*, *Malva* (**mallow**), *Mimulus* (**monkey flower**), *Mitella* (**mitrewort**), *Oenothera* (**evening primrose**), *Oxalis* (**wood sorrel**), *Peltiphyllum* (**umbrella plant**), *Penstemon* (**beard tongue**), *Primula* (**primrose**), *Rudbeckia* (**black-eyed Susan**), *Salvia* (**sage**), *Tradescantia* (**spiderwort**), *Tricyrtis* (**toad lily**), *Verbena* (**vervain**), and *Viola* (**violets**).

# WATERING

Outside plants do not need any supplemental water at this time. Keep seedlings moist but not soggy.

# FERTILIZING

An application of 5-10-5 fertilizer for your established perennials during late March is appropriate if the ground is not frozen

Seedlings that have emerged in sand, vermiculite, or perlite will benefit from a diluted solution of water-soluble fertilizer when you water. Those seedlings that are large enough to warrant transplanting may receive the same water-soluble fertilizer.

# PRUNING

Now is the time to finish up any leftover pruning of last year's perennials. The new growth will be emerging shortly, and it is a great deal more cumbersome and difficult to have to prune out old growth when you have to be careful not to disturb the tender green shoots.

# PESTS

Pests are not a problem this month.

# NOTES

_____

_____

_____

_____

_____

_____

_____

_____

_____

_____

_____

_____

_____

## PLANNING

This is the month when you seriously move from theoretical planning to getting out in the garden and down in the dirt. What has come up? What needs to be divided? What is dead as a doornail? What **tulips** look pathetic and what **daffodils** look fabulous? What shrubs are out of control and what spots refuse to dry up fast enough? Where is the sun shining bright? (Remember that deciduous trees will leaf out.) There is a lot of information that must be gathered from the garden itself.

If the **daffodils** look great, consider planting **daylilies** all around. They do not interfere while the daffodils are in bloom, but the foliage elongates in time to hide the maturing (and very ugly) leaves of the daffodils. If the **tulips** look wimpy, they may warrant replacing altogether. It is best to follow tulips with something other than tulips for disease control. This may be a good spot for perennials. In areas that are predominantly shady, you can create wonderful shade gardens with **lily-of-the-valley, shooting stars, trillium, bleeding hearts, bloodroot, violets, primrose,** and lots of **ferns** of different sizes and shapes.

Check out your foundation plantings and determine if your shrubbery is doing what you want. If it requires an enormous amount of pruning to keep plants in check, now is the time to move them, prune them, or yank them. Perhaps a better choice is an ornamental grass that gives height and winter interest but tends to stay in a clump.

## PLANTING

Planting out early in the month may still be quite risky for many perennials, but by late April, the risk is greatly reduced. You will need to allow a hardening off period where the plants are given the opportunity to adapt to the real world in a protected spot. Find a spot in your yard with a bit of morning sun completely out of the wind. Pack the pots in tight. Pile mulch up around the pots or put bales of straw around to moderate temperature fluctuations of the soil in the pots (and hence, the roots). Leave them in that spot for about a week, longer if the weather is icky. On a warm day, (of course it will be later in the month by then), you should be able to plant them without a problem. See the introduction for planting instructions.

Many perennials that are up a bit can be divided now. **Lily-of-the-valley** is another spring bloomer that breaks the rules. It is best divided now, but expect a reduction in flowering for the season, and possibly next year as well. Old-fashioned **bleeding heart** is best divided in the spring as well, but in truth it prefers not to be disturbed. If you can gently remove a piece with a root rather than digging up the whole thing, you may be happier with the results. Of course, your fall-blooming perennials can be divided if you haven't gotten to it yet. **Mums, asters, false dragonhead** (*Physostegia*), **false sunflower** (*Heliopsis*), **false sunflower** (*Helenium*) (yes, there is another with the same common name), and the true perennial **sunflowers** (*Helianthus*) are all among the late summer to autumn bloomers that can be divided now.

Another enormous group of perennials can be started now from seed. A few of those are: *Asclepias* (**milkweed**), *Baptisia* (**false indigo**), *Callirrhoe* (**poppy mallow**), *Hepatica* (**liverwort**), *Hosta*, *Hyssopus* (**hyssop**), and *Solidago* (**goldenrod**).

Of course, most of what was listed in March can still be started from seed in April. Many perennials are started from seed directly in the ground as soon as the seeds fully ripen on the plant. You may want to try direct seeding or allow self-sowing when the seeds mature. Save some seed. Let it dry and store it in the refrigerator to start indoors in late winter in case you don't get positive results in the garden.

# WATERING

Keep seedbeds and young seedlings constantly moist but never soggy. Water newly planted perennials thoroughly as soon as they are planted. Spring weather being on the damp side, you may not need to water again until summer, but use good judgment. If it doesn't rain, water deeply.

# FERTILIZING

Incorporate 5-10-5 or 10-6-4, 50 percent slow-release fertilizer into the soil during soil preparation for transplants or new plantings. **Do not** simply toss a handful of fertilizer into the planting hole because it will burn the roots. As an alternative, you can water the plants in with a water-soluble fertilizer according to the directions on the fertilizer you choose.

Use a very diluted water-soluble fertilizer on newly emerged seedlings that are potted in perlite, vermiculite, or sand. Use the same solution on larger seedlings that have been moved from the seed flat into individual pots.

# PRUNING

You should have finished all your pruning of perennials last month, but if not, finish it up early this month. There will be many other things to do later in the month.

# PESTS

In a very wet spring, slugs may show up. Control with 1-pound coffee cans filled with old beer. Fill the cans halfway and sink them into the ground to the lip. Cut a 1-inch square in the lid and put it on the can. Check for dead slugs daily.

The use of a pre-emergent weed control material will go a long way in keeping the weed population down. Apply it early in the month and follow directions for repeated application. **However,** if you are hoping for germination of any perennials that have self-sowed, or if you are planting seed directly in the garden yourself, you can not use a pre-emergent weed control material as it will prevent the germination of your seeds as well as the weeds.

# NOTES

_____

_____

_____

_____

_____

_____

_____

_____

_____

_____

_____

 PLANNING

In May you are definitely in full action mode. Have on hand an abundance of organic matter to improve the soil for planting. The compost pile is a great source of organic matter, but if you do not have such a thing, you can purchase compost or humus.

Certainly leave room to blend in annuals. While part of the beauty of perennials is that they create an everchanging landscape, you want some annuals to ensure a continual display of color throughout the season. This can be accomplished with the use of annuals as border plantings or mixing in clumps of taller annuals between the clumps of perennials. Row plantings of something dramatic, such as a hedge of **peonies,** are spectacular while in bloom but ho-hum the rest of the year. You can plant in front of it to create interest for the rest of the season or do another mass planting in another part of the garden to move the focal point from spot to spot.

Some early spring perennials fade away entirely. **Bleeding heart** and **poppies** will leave gaps in the summer landscape, so give some thought as to how you want to compensate.

 PLANTING

Planting is in full swing. The better you prepare the soil, the better chance perennials will have of actually returning every year. Incorporate organic matter and lime during the soil preparation stage. If you are working within an established bed, it can be tricky not to disturb whatever is already in place. Still, attempt to incorporate soil amendments and make the planting hole as large as possible without encroaching on other plants. Plant at the same depth the plant was growing previously.

It may surprise you, but you will be the most successful with **chrysanthemums** if you plant them now. Spring planting of mums allows for the establishment of a sturdy root system, one strong enough to endure the winter. Fall-planted mums are lovely, but more often than not they behave like fall-planted annuals and say good-bye with the first hard freeze.

This month it's warm enough to start many perennials from seed outdoors. Start a seedbed with finely prepared soil. Follow planting directions on the seed packet carefully, and remember both wind and sun can quickly dry out the soil as well as the seed. A shade cloth may be appropriate in a sunny location.

Some seeds that are started in May you may still want to pamper with controlled indoor conditions, at least until they germinate. See the chapter introduction for a list of these plants.

 WATERING

Seeds started in a seedbed outdoors will need a bit of special attention. Light, gentle rains are perfect, but you can't count on that every day. Daily moistening of the surface is necessary to prevent seeds from drying out. If the weather is July-like, it may take more than that. Between sun and wind, seeds can dry out quickly, so stay tuned in to what Mother Nature is dishing out.

Seeds started indoors will need to stay moist but not soggy.

Newly planted perennials will also need extra attention until they get established. Water immediately after planting, and if it doesn't rain, water deeply every few days, tapering off to a deep watering once a week. Usually the rain will be adequate for most of the needed water, but since rainfall can fluctuate significantly, don't think it is safe to ignore the new plantings; keep an eye on them and water properly when necessary.

# FERTILIZING

Include lime and fertilizer in the soil preparation process. Dig the hole as large as possible, mix 5-10-5 fertilizer in with the soil you replace in the hole before placing the plant. Don't toss a handful of fertilizer into the hole and then stick the plant on top; this will burn the roots.

If the space is too tight to adequately blend the granular fertilizer, you can water with a water-soluble fertilizer instead, after planting. Follow label directions.

# PRUNING

The **hellebores** may have turned to seed. Even the seedpods are attractive for a while, but once they turn brown they lose their appeal and should be removed.

If **chrysanthemums** are filling in, they might warrant a snip or two. Remove the tiny new leaves in the growing tip from each shoot. Do this regularly so the dormant buds sprout. This way you will have a more compact plant with more flowers. If you never pinch your mums, they will get quite tall. The weight of the flowers, especially if they get wet, bends the branches down, and the flowers end up in the mud.

**Peonies** and **poppies** will bloom at the end of the month and into early June. Cut flowers early in the morning, especially after a nice rain the night before. Choose buds that have started to open but have not yet reached their prime. Carry a bucket of water with you and place the stem in the water immediately. Keep the bucket out of the sun while you are working, if at all possible. Try to make your cuts so the remaining stem will be hidden in the foliage.

 # PESTS

Spittle bugs are out in the spring; they are icky but not particularly destructive. There are 23,000 kinds of spittle bugs, but you may never actually see any of them; just the spittle. The eggs overwinter, and the nymphs live on your plants by sucking out the plant juices. In most cases, there is no need to use insecticide, and the spittle prevents the insecticide from being very effective anyway. You can usually hose them away.

Once exposed to the sun, they tend to dry up.

Ants often arrive on **peonies**. They are harvesting the exudate that is on the surface of the stems and buds. They do no damage.

# NOTES

_____

_____

_____

_____

_____

_____

_____

_____

_____

_____

# JUNE
## Perennials

## PLANNING

June is more of an action month than a planning month. Certainly those last few things that didn't make it into the ground by the end of May can be planted now, but it's probably more important to spend time enjoying all the beauty of other gardens this time of year. Take copious notes or carry your camera. There may be many things that you spy here and there that you would enjoy having in your own garden. If you come across magical perennials in the garden of a friend, you may be able to make a trade when it is the right time to divide your plants and hers. If you see what you like in garden center, be sure to pick it up before it's gone.

**Roses** take center stage now, but they are in a class all by themselves. **Irises** are spectacular in a rainbow of colors. They are also included in this book under bulbs but are technically a tuber and so would have been just as much at home in this chapter on perennials as with their bulbous friends. **Peonies** will have a short reign in the garden. **Poppies** may be a bit longer, but they both finish up in the early part of this month. Other June beauties include **columbine, perennial bachelor's buttons, geranium** (not the garden geraniums in the

*Pelargonium* genus but the smaller-flowered, true geraniums), **coral bells,** the lovely blue **baptisia**, **painted** and **Shasta daisies** (the two spring-blooming **chrysanthemums**), **gaillardia**, **lupines, forget-me-nots, trollius, evening primrose, yarrow, lily-of-the-valley,** and **lavender.**

One perennial that is just emerging now is the fabulous perennial **hibiscus.** The flowers can reach 12 inches across. They come up so late in the spring that gardeners are often certain these beauties gave up the ghost, just to see a tiny green shoot poking up. They can be divided in early June after you see the new growth coming up. They are spectacular planted en masse. On occasion, seedlings will pop up, but the blossom size is not as spectacular as the original. Don't be disappointed; that happens with seedlings.

## PLANTING

If you plant this month, be sure to add compost and lime to the soil during preparation (see May for details). Tilling as large an area as possible will go a long way in ensuring that plants return for many years. Be sure to break up any hard clay or shale to ensure drainage.

The gap between ideal planting weather and summer heat is rapidly narrowing. You may want to mulch heavily with an organic mulch. The use of mulch will protect developing roots from rapid dehydration. It keeps roots cooler and also controls weeds.

## WATERING

Water newly planted material immediately after planting. Newly planted perennials have no roots established and will dry out quickly. Those planted this month may need more attention initially than those planted last month.

Spring-planted perennials will do best with a deep watering once a week. Mother Nature may do her part, but if it hasn't rained, water deeply so the entire root system can get a drink.

Emerged seedlings will need frequent watering to stay moist. A shade cloth over an outside seedbed will protect tender seedlings until they toughen up a bit. It may also help to cut down on wind damage.

##  FERTILIZING

Mix 5-10-5 fertilizer into the soil along with the compost and lime. If you are working in a tight spot, dig the planting hole as large as possible without damaging the surrounding plants and follow the same procedures as described in May Fertilizing.

##  PRUNING

Take some time to remove the faded blooms from perennials as they finish their fifteen minutes of fame. **Peonies** make fuzzy seedpods that almost look like a bunch of small brown bananas. You don't want to take energy from the leaves and roots to make seeds you will never use. Cut the flower stems below the uppermost foliage to hide the cut ends. The foliage is attractive enough to make a lovely backdrop to summer annuals or later-season perennials.

Continue to pinch **chrysanthemums** to encourage bushiness.

Cut flowers for indoor use early in the morning, especially the morning after a gentle steady rain. Keep a bucket of water on hand to slip the fresh cut flowers into immediately. If possible, keep the bucket in the shade while you are working.

## Helpful Hints

*1* June perennials are important for filling in the gap between spring-flowering bulbs and the blast of color provided by summer annuals. **Roses, alliums, early true lilies, iris,** many varieties of **rhododendrons,** and the perennials mentioned on the opposite page really send out a blast of color and beauty at this time of year. Don't be afraid to mix different kinds of plants together to shake things up a bit.

*2* The **Shasta daisy** was developed by Luthor Burbank. It is one of the sweetest and most dependable of all perennials. If you want to pick a flower for "She loves me-He loves me not," this is it.

##  PESTS

By the end of June you will start to see Japanese beetles. These are voracious eaters. The adults eat gaping holes in a great many different plants in your garden, but they seem to be particularly drawn to **roses** and **brambles.** If you have a limited population, you can handpick them. A larger infestation will require the use of an insecticide. Check with your Cooperative Extension Office for current control recommendations. Whatever you do, however, do not use pheromone traps. You may catch hundreds in your traps, but they will have been mating and laying eggs all the way into the bag, making the lawn even more susceptible to a grub infestation.

Continue to use mulch for weed control, and handweed when necessary. The use of a pre-emergent weed control material will prevent weed seeds from germinating. Read and follow all label directions carefully.

## NOTES

_____

_____

_____

_____

_____

_____

_____

_____

_____

_____

_____

_____

##  PLANNING

July is hot, and you should be going down the shore whenever possible. While you are tooling around, continue to take notes. There are lots of perennials blooming, and you want to get a good feel for how summer annuals blend with your perennials. How these summer flowers work together in the garden has a lot to do with the impact your garden makes over the summer.

Take the time to observe different uses of ornamental grasses. **Feather reed grass,** for example sends up seedheads in June and will stay 5 to 7 feet tall until you cut them down early next spring. Scattered among other perennials, it can create vertical interest or draw the eye through the planting as you look from plant to plant. As a specimen, it may be perfect next to a walkway or even front and center in a small yard.

**Prairie dropseed** is a good choice of ornamental grass for beginners. It is easy to grow. It forms attractive, 1-foot-tall mounds that can be mixed in with perennials to be a link between different species or colors or even between perennials and annuals. Used along the edge of a wild area, it makes a nice transition plant from untamed beauty to neatly tended garden.

Keep an eye out for perennials that are blooming now. See a list of bloomers to look for in the chapter introduction. Summer annuals bring the bulk of the color to July gardens, but summer perennials can do more if you seek out the right ones. Look for them and decide if they offer what you need.

##  PLANTING

It is never a great idea to be planting in the middle of a July heat wave. However, many nurseries will be carrying blooming perennials in containers, so if you come across something that strikes your fancy, buy it. You may not come across it again without a search. Since container plants suffer very little root upset when planted, the chances are very good it will do just fine.

Improve the soil in the planting area using a significant amount of mulch. **Plant your perennials on a rainy day, or at least a cloudy day.** If it isn't rainy or cloudy, which can happen in July, wet the ground prior to planting to give the soil a chance to soak up the water. Plant in the late evening. Provide a shade cloth over the plants for the first few days.

Make sure anything you decide to plant now has been thoroughly watered before you plant it.

##  WATERING

Water plants thoroughly immediately after planting.

Water perennials in the early morning so the leaves have time to dry. You will encourage leaf diseases if they go into the night wet. Water deeply, applying at least 1 inch of water all at once. If possible, water the ground only with a soaker hose or a weepy-type hose. Drip irrigation is another option. **A thick organic mulch will reduce water loss from evaporation.**

If you are using a watering can, it is better to water fewer plants deeply than more plants with a sprinkle. Sprinkles will dry up in the sun without ever reaching the root system. This becomes especially important during times of drought and water restrictions. You may be limited to waste water (such as water from preparing and cooking vegetables or pasta), and you will have to apply it judiciously.

##  FERTILIZING

You never want to fertilize when the temperature is above 85 degrees Fahrenheit. This could be the entire month of July. If you get a break in the weather, the use of a diluted water-soluble fertilizer may give plants a boost.

# PRUNING

**Daylily** blooms last for only a day. Faded blooms detract from the appearance of the other flowers, and will sometimes make seeds if not removed. When all the buds have opened on a "scape" or stem, cut the stem at the base. Sometimes you may find "proliferations" along the scapes. These are small shoots consisting of leaves and even possible roots. These can be saved to propagate the variety.

**Crocosmia** continues to bloom along the length of the stem for some time. Remove the faded blooms to get the most enjoyment from the fresh ones. **Phlox** often makes new flowers along stalks after the original flower cluster has finished. Remove the ugly ones to encourage repeat bloom.

Continue to remove the tips of **chrysanthemums** until the middle of the month. If you continue much after that, you may delay bloom of some of the later varieties until it is too late for them to produce flowers.

# PESTS

Powdery mildew is a leaf disease that first shows up in July. It usually doesn't get bad until later in the season but is best controlled if you catch it in early stages. Look for whitish blotches on the leaf surface. It is particularly bad on many cultivars of **phlox** and **monarda.** Check with your Cooperative Extension Office for current control recommendations.

Mites can sometimes show up on a wide variety of plants, especially if the summer is hot and dry. If the leaves appear dry, take a close look at the leaves with a magnifying glass. If the dust particles are moving, they aren't dust at all, but mites. Mites will suck out the juices of the leaves. You can get some control with a fierce spray of water, or try an insecticidal soap. If the problem persists, check with your Cooperative Extension Office for current control recommendations.

# NOTES

_____

_____

_____

_____

_____

_____

_____

_____

_____

_____

_____

_____

_____

_____

# AUGUST
## Perennials

 PLANNING

August is another month to drink lemonade by the pool and enjoy the many lovely flowers the gardens in your world have to offer. Taking notes on dull periods in your perennial display as well as particular beauties that you come across will help you smooth out your transitions next year. Of course, planting annuals will cover any gaps you miss, but it is often a goal to have one plant coming into bloom as some other fades away. This can be done with perennials alone, but if you also use summer-blooming bulbs and flowering shrubs, they can all work together to fill in the all the slots.

Cover a much longer season with perennials by carefully selecting early, mid-season, and late varieties. **Daylilies** will give an extended season with the proper varieties, plus some varieties will bloom most of the summer. A few of these are great to ensure continual bloom, but if you use too many, you will lose the fabulous fourth dimension of a garden that changes over time. *Hemerocallis* 'Stella De Oro' is perhaps the best known of the long-season daylilies, but look for 'Irish Elf', 'Sun Locket', 'Little Business', and 'Butterscotch Ruffles' to add diversity. You may also want to look for daylilies that offer a reblooming period in late summer or early fall.

Other August-blooming perennials include *Asclepias* (**milkweed**), *Liatris* (**gayfeather**), *Lobelia* (**red cardinal flower**), *Physostegia* (**false dragonhead**), *Aconitum* (**monkshood**), *Hibiscus*, *Rudbeckia* (**black-eyed Susan**), *Echinacea*, early **chrysanthemums,** and *Helenium*. **Evening primrose** may continue to produce flowers, but by this time the plants may need some tidying up.

 PLANTING

By late August, some annuals may be looking a little ratty. Consider replacing them with field-grown **chrysanthemums** for fall color. You can't count on these chrysanthemums returning next spring like established perennials, but the earlier you get them in the ground, the better their chances of returning.

You can divide your **hellebores** (such as **Christmas rose** and **Lenten rose**) later this month or early next month. The roots are very brittle, so handle them carefully. **Be sure to wear gloves as all parts of the plant are considered poisonous.**

The common **primula** can be started outdoors from seed in August in a cold frame, but they are so readily available and inexpensive that it may not be worth all the effort.

 WATERING

Continue to water deeply when necessary and preferably in the early morning. Now that night temperatures are dropping, it is even more important not to send plants into the night with wet leaves.

August is a big month for summer vacations, so you may need to make arrangements for someone to water while you are away. If you are only leaving for a week, you may be able to water deeply before you leave and again as soon as you get back, but if the temperature stays in the 90s, you may want to have backup watering in the middle of the week.

 FERTILIZING

Do not fertilize at all if the ground is parched and there are water restrictions. If cool August weather occurs, a light fertilizer application using diluted water-soluble fertilizer may provide a pick-me-up to plants that have languished in summer heat.

PRUNING

Lots of flower stalks need to be removed on **daylilies.** Also remove seedpods on clematis, and finished stalks on **evening primrose** and other summer blooming perennials. If **chrysanthemums** have set flower buds early in the month, you may want to remove them or your fall display will be shortchanged.

 PESTS

If you're having a wet summer, slugs will be doing a fair amount of damage. They particularly like **hostas** but will munch on a wide variety of things. Look for slime trails on the ground around the plants and on leaves. The damage of gaping holes is easy to identify. You are only likely to see the slugs at night. You can go out with a flashlight to pick them by hand. Wear gloves—they are a little grotesque. Refer to April Pests to make traps out of coffee cans.

**You can reduce slug populations by eliminating one or more of the three things they require to thrive:**

*1* Slugs require cool temperatures, so they are more likely to be found in shady locations. Cover the area with black plastic. It will get hot underneath, and the slugs will leave.

*2* They need organic matter to reproduce. Pull back organic mulch so there is less cover near the plants you want to protect.

## Helpful Hints

*1* While you are removing faded blooms to keep perennials looking attractive, some pods are worth saving as dried flowers. **Rudbeckia** and **Echinacea** both have cone-shaped seedpods that dry quite hard and can be used in dried arrangements. They can even be spraypainted or dipped in fabric dye for a more natural tint.

*2* The dinner-plate-sized **hibiscus** flowers only last a day, and they make terrible cut flowers, but you can float a single bloom in a bowl of water as a centerpiece for dinner. It will make a statement while it is fresh.

*3* Slugs need a moist environment. Let the ground get fairly dry in between waterings. If it rains a lot and the temperature stays cool, it will be harder to manipulate their environment, but in a normal summer, some drying time can make a difference.

Grasshoppers leave gaping holes, but higher up on the plants where slugs don't reach. They are more likely to appear in dry weather. Identifying the problem can be confusing because you never see the pest, but damage can be spotted on a variety of plants.

Mowing wild areas near your cultivated gardens is one environmental management approach. The weeds and wildflowers harbor grasshoppers in large numbers, and they can easily hop over the grass (being grasshoppers, after all) to munch on your flowers and ornamental grasses. Treat as soon as you see the first grasshopper. The early ones go back and tell the others where they found the food. Check with your Cooperative Extension Office for recommendations.

## NOTES

_____
_____
_____
_____
_____
_____
_____
_____
_____
_____
_____
_____
_____
_____

# SEPTEMBER

Perennials

 PLANNING

September is time to regroup. You have a pretty good idea by now as to what thrilled you in the garden and what was more trouble than it was worth. Try to get a handle on what caused the problems. If you think you can correct what went wrong, the disappointing plant may be worth another try. For example, sometimes the plants around a sun-loving plant grow large over time, blocking the light. What was sunny five years ago may be deep shade now.

On the other hand, you may be absolutely fed up with trimming seedpods from **coreopsis** and you just want to be rid of them, or perhaps the wild **daylilies** around the mailbox attack the mailman when he tries to deliver the mail and they need a new spot.

Of course, if the **daylilies** brought you an abundance of joy, you may want to divide them so you have lots more joy. Carefully mark the plants you want to divide later. Daylilies all look a lot alike when they are not in bloom.

Don't forget to enjoy what the September garden has to offer. The **Japanese anemones** are a fabulous late summer treat, the small flowered perennial sunflower varieties are outrageous with the zillions of flowers they produce, and of course the variety of **mums** blooming in September creates the mood of the season. Don't forget **monkshood.** Some varieties are still blooming. The late blooming *Eupatorium coelestinum* (**mistflower** or **perennial ageratum**) makes a great many flowers in September in a pretty shade of blue.

 PLANTING

One of the problems with moving or dividing perennials in the fall is that many annuals stay beautiful until the middle of next month. It is a bit painful to have to yank them early just to take over their spot, but you'll need to give the perennials a chance to establish some roots before winter sets in.

**Poppies** and **peonies** are best divided now. **Daylilies** are more flexible and can wait until spring. **Phlox,** both the tall garden types and the creeping moss pink types, can be divided in South Jersey (Zone 7) now, but in the cooler regions, wait until spring. **Lamb's ears** (*Stachys byzantina*) is the same.

When dividing **peonies,** make sure you have at least 2 "eyes" or growing tips on each section of root. Soil preparation is particularly important with peonies since they can potentially stay in the same spot for fifty years without needing to be divided again. With **daylilies** you can start with a very small fan of leaves as long as they have a root, but the smaller the division the longer it will take to bloom.

There are a few perennials that can be started from seed in September. *Aconitum* (**monkshood**) and the **windflower** *Anemone* are among them. See the chapter introduction for planting instructions.

 WATERING

Water deeply on a regular basis as long as the weather remains hot. Usually early in the month, there is a ground drenching rain, and the temperature cools off considerably. Water demands drop accordingly.

Water anything you have decided to move or divide as soon as you have planted it. Keep a close eye on these young'ns as they will suffer quickly if they get overly dry.

 FERTILIZING

When dividing or moving perennials, you can incorporate granular 5-10-5 fertilizer into the soil along with your lime and organic matter. **Do not** toss fertilizer into the planting hole since it will burn the roots rapidly.

The use of water-soluble fertilizer now is a very good approach. The weather is cooler, and many plants will perk up a bit before going dormant for the winter. You want plants to develop a sturdy root system to have a better chance of making a comeback next spring.

## PRUNING

**Mums** can be kept looking pretty longer if you remove the faded blooms while later flowers are still opening. **Hibiscus** is still producing flowers, but some stalks are done and will make seeds if you don't get them out of there. **Peonies** vary in their endurance, but if they have yellowed, you might as well cut them back now. **Phlox** can produce repeat blooms in the early fall, but some are so covered in powdery mildew that the garden looks better without them. **Hostas** usually look pitiful this late, but some varieties are tougher than others. If they look ugly, "Off with their heads!" **Ferns** may look better if the battered fronds are trimmed off. **Purple coneflowers** will make flowers until frost, but they will make more flowers if you remove the seeds that are drawing energy from the flowers.

## PESTS

**Phlox, monarda, purple coneflowers, black-eyed Susans, perennial bachelor's buttons, chrysanthemums, coral bells, columbine,** and others are subject to powdery mildew now. The disease is always worse in humid weather. By this time, it is hardly worth it to start a spray program. Cutting back the worst plants may slow down the spread. If you see only an occasional spot on a leaf here and there, you can pick off the offending leaf.

As the season winds down, it's important to have good sanitation practices. Gather the infected leaves and dispose of them in plastic bags. Do not leave them on the ground to be a source of the disease again for next year. Even in the compost pile, they can harbor the disease. A large-scale compost pile that heats up to the point of creating steam will be effective in killing off disease organisms, but a backyard pile rarely gets hot enough to function in this manner.

## NOTES

_____
_____
_____
_____
_____
_____
_____
_____
_____
_____
_____
_____
_____

# OCTOBER

 PLANNING

October is when you get to enjoy the crisp autumn air and the gorgeous fall foliage. There are lots of things to observe and evaluate for next year. A number of the ornamental grasses have fall appeal. **Feather reed grass** seedheads turn a lovely shade of golden brown and last all winter. **Hakone** grass turns pink and then bronze in the fall. **Little bluestem** has a golden orange fall color. **Frost grass** turns brown with streaks of purple. The flowers of **switchgrass** last all winter, can be used in dried arrangements, and often are shaded pink to red. The fall foliage is vividly colored in yellow, orange-red, dark red, or even purple-red.

Later varieties of **chrysanthemums** will still be blooming in the sun. A shade beauty is the hairy **toad lily** (*Tricyrtis hirta*). Okay, so the name isn't beautiful, but the speckled pink flowers arrive dependably in the fall and spread slowly over time to create a nicer display with each passing year. (*T. macropoda* is similar but blooms in June and July.)

The **Maximilian sunflower** can be spectacular now. These dramatic perennial sunflowers are showstoppers. They remain at 3 to 4 feet all summer. In early September, they begin to elongate. They double in size, covered in 3- to 4-inch brilliant yellow stems, sometimes 15 blooms to a stem. The weight of the flowers causes them to arch over, creating an incredible cascade of color. They last all month.

 PLANTING

Potted **mums** can go in the ground here and there. Use them to replace defunked summer annuals, but don't plan on them returning next spring. If the location is key, you may instead want to fill it with annual flowers next year rather than counting on autumn mums. Of course you can always move the mums if they surprise you with a return engagement.

 WATERING

You shouldn't need to water this month, unless the ground is still dry from summer heat (unlikely, but not impossible). Be sure to water any newly planted **mums.**

 FERTILIZING

Fertilizer is not necessary at this time. In October, perennials are slowing down and preparing to go dormant for the winter. You don't want to encourage new growth now.

If storing fertilizer, keep it in a cool location, but liquid fertilizer will be better off if it doesn't freeze. Make sure your storage facility will stay dry.

 PRUNING

As many perennials go dormant for the winter, you should prune them away. Those that provide winter interest are there for a reason, so leave them alone. They can be pruned back in the early spring. Many ornamental grasses provide winter interest that lasts until spring. The seeds also provide food for visiting birds. **Rudbeckia, Echinacea,** and the sporulating fronds of the sensitive **fern** are all lovely in the winter landscape. **Yarrow** is another perennial that you may want to leave alone. The flower clusters dry on the plant and stay attractive well into winter. They sometimes last even until spring.

All of those I just mentioned above also work well in dried arrangements, so you may want to cut a few for indoor use.

On some of those plants where you will leave the seedpods, you may want to clean up some of the ratty looking foliage. It is especially important to bag up any leaves that may have symptoms of powdery mildew.

## PESTS

As your perennials go dormant, there is little need to control insect pests or disease. Good sanitation practices limit the possibility of eggs and spores overwintering in the debris. If you have had problems, be sure to bag the material and send it off with the trash. If the residue is clean, then put it in the compost pile but be sure to bury it rather than simply laying it on top. It will decompose more quickly in the center of the pile and be less likely to cause any problems next year.

Weed control is an ongoing problem. Many weeds will set seed in the fall, which creates a problem for next year. Remove perennial weeds (such as thistle) with as much of the root as possible or they will come up from roots as well as seed next year. Mulch your garden heavily with an organic mulch to slow down winter weeds (such as chickweed) and to protect the roots of your perennials from the freezing and thawing of winter.

## Helpful Hints

*1* Many perennials in the garden have wild counterparts. **Evening primrose, purple coneflower, Rudbeckia,** and **yarrow** are among them. If you walk the fields, you can see the pods of these and others such as **Queen Anne's lace** and **dock**. These can be collected and used in dried arrangements. You can use them dried as you find them, bleach them for a brighter natural color, or even let them sit in a bucket of fabric dye. They can be quite beautiful.

*2* You may want to collect seedpods from some perennials. **Baptisia** produces black bean-like seedpods and generally comes true from seed. **Hibiscus** produces interesting round seedpods. Whatever you collect needs to be dried thoroughly and stored in a cool spot over the winter.

## NOTES

_____

_____

_____

_____

_____

_____

_____

_____

_____

_____

_____

_____

# NOVEMBER
## Perennials

## PLANNING

November is a sleepy month in the perennial garden. With a little luck, you may still have a few perennial **sunflowers** showing a bit of color, but most perennials have finished up. There may still be a determined late **mum** standing bravely as well.

Some things you can be doing this month:

- Take stock of what you loved and what you can't wait to dig up.

- Pour over the fall catalogs to see just what you need to improve on this year's imperfections. Take notes. Make lists.

- Continue working on your compost pile. This is definitely worthwhile since the final product can be used to top-dress your perennials come spring or improve the soil for newly planted perennials.

- Consider making arrangements for delivery of some type of organic mulch. Mulching for weed control can happen throughout the year, but a heavy layer of mulch is best applied after the ground freezes in early December. You want to have your mulching material on hand by then.

## Helpful Hints

- Pine needles can be used as a mulch around your plants. While you are raking them up, save yourself some work and rake them into the perennial beds. That way you get two jobs done at the same time.

- Leaves can be used to mulch around shrubs, but they can mat down and smother perennials.

- Age raw wood chips to a darker brown by blending in some grass clippings into the pile. The grass breaks down rapidly, darkening the wood in the process. This makes a more attractive mulch than freshly chipped wood.

## PLANTING

November is really not the time to plant any perennials in the garden. Those plants that produced seed can sometimes be planted outside. Check the species you are working with. If the seeding recommendations indicate "sow when ripe," it may be worth a try. You will have more control if you start these indoors at the proper time, but sometimes you can get lucky and have a nice stand of young plants come spring.

## WATERING

Water those seeds you are sowing in the garden, but there is little need to water in November.

## FERTILIZING

Wait until spring.

## PRUNING

You can prune whatever perennials are left that look untidy. Even your **daylilies** may need a trim. If the foliage is lying across **evergreens** or any other plants, it may smother them over the winter.

## PESTS

Even the pests are taking it easy by now. Just make sure you follow good sanitation practices as you clean things up.

# DECEMBER
## Perennials

## PLANNING

There is little going on in the perennial garden in December. It is a time for holiday planning and gift giving. Here are a few gift ideas for the gardeners on your list:

*1* **Gardening gloves.** A gardener needs at least three: One heavily insulated pair for working in cold weather; a second leather pair for general work; and a third pair that's rubberized to keep hands dry when working under wet conditions. A fourth pair of very thin leather for doing fine work is also appreciated.

*2* **A flat-proof wheel barrow tire.** (I would like a purple one, please.)

*3* **A tool gizmo.** Buckets that use the lids as a seat and an apron on the outside for tools; scooter-types with wheels and a handle that hold the tools inside and let you sit on top; wheeled units with grids that can hold larger tools.

*4* **A little red wagon.** (Every gardener should have one).

*5* **A rain gauge.** There are beautiful ones available.

*6* **A toad abode.** Toads are great friends to gardeners. They eat bugs, but even better, they eat slugs.

*7* **The New Jersey Gardener's Guide** by Pegi Ballister-Howells (that's me!). Lots of plants selected especially for New Jersey Gardens, with a chapter focusing on perennials.

## PLANTING

There isn't any planting going on at this time of year.

## WATERING

Plants can suffer from winter drought, something humans don't always remember. If we go into winter after a rainless fall, give plants a good drink before the ground freezes.

## FERTILIZING

Not until spring.

## PRUNING

Much of what is left can wait for spring, but if you are getting cabin fever early, tidy up your perennials a bit and get a jump on spring. All those **mums** are really down by now, and **evening primrose** can be pruned back.

## PESTS

Pests are not a concern at this time.

# CHAPTER EIGHT

# Roses

*Roses are lovely. They are romantic in both their beauty and their scent. In the month of June, they are at the peak of their magnificence and overwhelm the senses with all of their attributes.*

Would a rose by any other name be as much work? Yes! But there can be sweet rewards. Some gardeners take the relatively easy way out and treat them like annuals. That can get expensive, but it has its advantages. In truth, even with the best of care a bitter winter can knock out a few of your bushes no matter how hard you try to keep them. Replanting in early spring gets you started all over.

## MAKING YOUR CHOICES

The first thing you need to do is decide if you want a formal rose garden (called a "rosary" and the gardener a "rosarian") or if you want to blend the rose bushes into the landscape. **Hybrid tea roses** are the long stem beauties you give to your one-true-love, and yet they are one of the least attractive bushes. If you want lots of these, it will definitely be easier to have them planted all in one location. That way, you can spray and water them all at one time. If you only want one or two, they will add color to a bed, and in return other shrubs can provide a bit of camouflage for the somewhat skimpy rose bushes. Hybrid teas are the most difficult roses to grow, and yet they continue to be the most popular. It must be the romantic chord they touch in all of us.

**Floribunda roses** are a new development in the world of roses, at least compared to the thousands of years roses have been under cultivation. The floribundas are a cross between **hybrid teas** and the **polyantha rose** and were first introduced around 1920. They produce a great number of roses in clusters over a long blooming period. The roses are never as large as hybrid teas, but they are not as fussy, either.

**Grandifloras** are **floribundas** that were crossed back with more **hybrid teas** in an attempt to increase the size of the flowers. The first grandiflora was the lovely pink Queen Elizabeth introduced in 1954.

**Climbing roses** are a bit unique. They are the one type of rose that you do not prune in early spring since it produces its primary flush of blooms on last year's growth. It gets pruned after it blooms but not severely since many will continue to put out the occasional flower all summer long. **Ramblers** are a type of climbing rose that can be trained to grow up an arbor or trellis. Ramblers produce many small roses in the spring and never re-bloom. Without some management, they grow a little wild. Some gardeners prune them to the ground after they bloom to contain them.

**Shrub roses** are somewhat of a catch-all category for all the roses that don't fit into any other category. They are hardier than most of the others and more shrub-like in habit. These characteristics make them easier to use as part of the landscape. While they have a very different look from the dramatic **hybrid tea,** the oceans of flowers that cascade over these bushes is just as impressive in a more free-spirited style.

The **rugosa rose** is a pip. Tough as nails but a real beauty, rugosa roses tolerate shore planting conditions, wind, cold, and produce flowers most of the season. They do, however, have wicked thorns and spread aggressively. Not a choice for a formal area, but a great plant in the right spot.

**Miniature roses** are sweet, but do not estimate their durability based on their diminutive size. Miniature roses grow on their own roots, so you can take cuttings and root them. (Grafted onto a normal rootstock, they lose the "miniature" growth habit.) Many are hardy outdoors and if they die back severely can return from the roots. This is such an advantage over many other roses that are grafted onto rugged but not very desirable rootstock. If the graft dies back, you get the rootstock sprouting something less than wonderful. Miniatures can be grown in containers indoors if you have a very sunny window but are fabulous in a greenhouse when you need a breath of spring.

## PLANTING BASICS

- **Roses need strong sun** to do well; seven or eight hours daily is best. They will not be happy in a windy location, so watch out for north and west winds. Sometimes evergreens can be used to provide winter interest as well as protection.

- **Avoid wet sites.** Drainage is critical.

- **Soil preparation is very important** with roses. Roses like a neutral soil. In general New Jersey soils tend toward being acidic, so you may need to add lime. Only a soil test will be able to tell you for certain. You want to add organic matter, such as compost, to ensure drainage as well as to make it easier for the roots to get established. Two handfuls of bonemeal mixed into the soil per plant is also beneficial.

- You will need to **dig your planting hole large enough for the roots** to fit comfortably without squishing them into the hole.

- When you have dug you hole and are ready to plant, **examine your rose** carefully. Remove all broken or damaged canes and roots. If the roots are all fine, snip off the tips to encourage the rapid development of new roots. Shipped plants are usually pruned and ready for planting, but if anything is obviously dead, prune it off.

- Identify the graft union and **position the plant in the hole** so the bulge will be planted 2 inches below ground level. Remove the plant and place a cone of soil in the bottom of the hole. This is to fill up the space under and between the roots. Replace the plant so it fits snugly on top of the mound but is not squeezed in any way. Do not force the roots to be apart or to grow in any direction other than the way they seem to want to go naturally.

- **Fill the hole with the amended soil** and firm it gently.

Protection from winter wind will go a long way in helping roses survive to bloom another year. Good air circulation will help minimize disease. Plan on having to water at least on occasion. A watering system that does not get water on the leaves will also help prevent the spread of disease.

## PRUNING

The removal of dead blooms on roses as soon as they fade prevents energy from going into seeds and sends it instead towards making more flowers. The long-established way of pruning roses is to cut back the flowering shoot to the first or second complete leaf. This will encourage longer stems but fewer blooms. The new, preferred way is simply to remove the faded bloom where it would eventually fall off if left to its own devices. This is called the "abscission layer." It is the same spot on tree leaves where they self-separate from trees in the fall. Follow the flower stem from just below the petals to the first joint. That is the spot. New flowering shoots will develop much more rapidly than if you have to wait for an entire new branch to develop.

## Helpful Hints

### Fertilizing Approaches/Options

There are several approaches to fertilizing roses, depending on the type of fertilizer you use, and the length of bloom you hope to achieve. Overall, this book prescribes fertilizing from April through September, using a **once a month, twice a year,** or **3-holiday** approach.

On those established roses you fertilize **monthly,** fertilize every four weeks. This approach most often involves a water-soluble material that is either mixed in a watering can and applied when you have only a few rose bushes, or applied via a hose end sprayer. If you use a sprayer, make sure you properly calibrate your sprayer with the fertilizer you have chosen. An over-application of fertilizer can be fatal, especially later in the month when the weather may turn very hot at any moment.

Generally, April is the first time of year for fertilizing. The **twice a year** approach recommends fertilizing in April, then June or July (after the first flush of blooms).

The **3-holiday** approach recommends fertilizing on Memorial Day, the Fourth of July, and Labor Day. With any method, try to avoid making the application when the temperature is above 85 degrees Fahrenheit, to avoid burning the roots.

Be brave as you forge ahead with your roses, and don't forget to take time to enjoy the lovely fruits of your labor.

### Bulbs as Rose Companions

Bulbs complement roses in that they bloom early in the spring before the roses have really bushed out. By the time the roses are leafy enough to shade the foliage of the bulbs, the bulbs have long finished blooming. The lush foliage and cheery spring flowers from bulbs provide another season of interest in the rose bed, which is especially important when you have limited space.

Bulbs get planted deep enough to interfere with the large root systems of long-established roses. Choose locations for bulbs where you run little risk of damaging rose roots while you plant. Young rose plants don't have roots that are as far-reaching, so you have more flexibility in choosing the right spots.

# Roses

## Climbing Roses

| Climbing Roses | Color |
|---|---|
| 'Autumn Sunset' | apricot gold |
| 'Westerland' | apricot blend |
| 'New Dawn' | light pink |
| 'Handel' | pink blend |
| 'Red Fountain' | bright red |
| 'Dortmund' | red and white |
| 'Sally Holmes' | white |
| 'Climbing Iceberg' | white |
| 'Jeanne LaJoie' | pink |

| Floribundas | Color |
|---|---|
| 'Iceberg' | white |
| 'Sunsprite' | yellow |
| 'Showbiz' | medium red |
| 'Scentimental' | red and white stripe |
| 'Playboy' | orange and scarlet, yellow center |
| 'Sexy Rexy' | pink |
| 'Dicky' | pink |
| 'First Edition' | coral orange |
| 'Trumpeter' | orange red |

| Grandifloras | Color |
|---|---|
| 'Queen Elizabeth' | pink |
| 'Love' | red and white |
| 'Gold Medal' | medium yellow |
| 'Tournament of Roses' | pink |
| 'Pink Parfait' | pink |
| 'Aquarius' | light pink |
| 'Camelot' | coral pink |

| Hybrid Teas | Color |
|---|---|
| 'Mr. Lincoln' | dark red |
| 'Olympiad' | medium red |
| 'Touch of Class' | coral pink |
| 'Elina' | creamy white |
| 'Pristine' | white |

| Hybrid Teas (continued) | Color |
|---|---|
| 'Peace' | yellow blend |
| 'Double Delight' | red and white blend |
| 'Signature' | deep pink |
| 'Fragrant Cloud' | orange red |
| 'Sheer Bliss' | white |
| 'Rio Samba' | golden yellow and scarlet |

| Miniature Roses | Color |
|---|---|
| 'Kristen' | red blend |
| 'Jean Kenneally' | apricot blend |
| 'Figurine' | white |
| 'Starina' | orange red |
| 'Black Jade' | dark red |
| 'Snow Bride' | white |
| 'Rainbow's End' | yellow blend |
| 'Old Glory' | medium red |
| 'Rise 'N' Shine' | yellow |
| 'Loving Touch' | apricot blend |

| Rugosa Roses | Color |
|---|---|
| 'Alba' | white |
| *Rosa rugosa* | deep pink |
| 'Linda Campbell' | velvety bright red |
| 'Blanc Double DeCoubert' | white |
| 'Grootendorst Pink' | pink |
| 'F.J. Grootendorst' | red |

| Shrub Roses | Color |
|---|---|
| 'Carefree Beauty' | pink |
| 'Bonica' | pale pink |
| 'Sea Foam' | white |
| 'Flower Carpet' | pink |
| 'Scarlet Meidiland' | bright red |
| 'White Meidiland' | white |
| 'The Fairy' | very pale pink |
| 'Knockout' | cherry red |

# JANUARY
## Roses

## PLANNING

Roses are certainly not doing much in the garden in January, but catalogs for all types of gardening are available. Many catalogs carry roses, but those that specialize in roses will give the broadest range of selection and also provide the most information about the different varieties. Here are a few catalogs worth ordering. You can pore over them in front of the fire with a kitty on your lap and a cup of tea.

David Austin Roses Limited
903-526-1800
www.davidaustinroses.com

Jackson & Perkins
800-292-4769
www.jacksonandperkins.com

Arena Roses
888-466-7434
www.arenaroses.com

Heirloom Roses
503-538-1576
www.heirloomroses.com

Edmund's Roses
888-481-7673
www.edmundsroses.com

If you are interested in adding a few roses to your garden in the spring, you need to give serious thought to what, and where, you intend to plant. **Climbing** **roses** will need something to climb upon. Roses do not actually cling on their own the way **wisteria** and **clematis** attach themselves to a support. Roses need to be tied or woven through some type of trellis. Roses work well trellising in front of a wall where they will get some protection from winter wind, but don't compromise on sunlight, and make sure there is excellent drainage.

**Shrub roses** can vary greatly in the size and shape of the plants as well as the size and abundance of blooms. Make sure you learn enough about any shrub rose that tickles your fancy so you can locate it in the right spot. Shrub roses are more disease resistant than the **floribundas, grandifloras,** and **hybrid teas** so they may be a great place to start.

You will have an easier time of it if you include strong disease resistance as one of the parameters to choosing your roses. Disease resistance has been a focal point of recent rose breeding programs, and is becoming an important attribute in more and more varieties. Those plants that are listed as AARS have been tested nationwide and are All-America Rose Selection award winners. If you have never heard of a particular rose before but it is an AARS winner, you can feel confident that it's a reliable rose.

This is not to underestimate some of the **heirloom roses.** Before roses were being bred for size and showiness and before there was an arsenal of chemical weapons with which to battle disease, roses had to thrive more independently. The revival of commercial production of very old, almost lost varieties has great merit. Experiment with something new (or old) that simply touches the romantic rose lover in you.

## PLANTING

Certainly you are not going out to plant roses in January. However, if you come across **a miniature rose** in bloom at your favorite greenhouse, bring it home. The splash of color will do your spirit good during this wintry month. Repot it into something pretty and put it on the sunniest windowsill in the house. You'll feel better every time you walk by it.

## WATERING

There shouldn't be any need to water outside, but if there has been no precipitation whatsoever (it happens), it may be beneficial to pour a gallon of water on the roots if the ground is not frozen.

## FERTILIZING

Be patient. No fertilizer is needed this month.

 ## PRUNING

If you pruned in late fall, you shouldn't have to prune anything now. On the other hand, if you didn't get to it, you may want to trim anything that is so long it is getting wind whipped. If the branches can hold ice and snow, they are more likely to snap off at the base. Better to prune them (don't prune **climbers**) to about 3 feet to avoid any storm damage. Be sure to do it on a day the temperature is above freezing.

 ## PESTS

The pests aren't doing much at this time of year. If you haven't raked up the leaves, you can gather up all the rose leaves that have collected under the shrubbery. Bag them up and ship them to the landfill. You don't need them hanging around as a source of leaf diseases for next season.

## Helpful Hints

• If you get a rose or even a dozen, you can save the petals for potpourri. As the rose fades, pull all the petals off into a low, wide bowl. Fluff them every time you walk by so they dry uniformly. They look pretty just the way they dry.

• While choosing your roses, perhaps you should be sipping on rose hip tea. It is a pretty color, high in vitamin C, and made from the fruits of roses.

## NOTES

PLANNING

The catalogs are still rolling in, and the weather outside is still frightful (okay . . . and the fire is so delightful!). Stick to dreaming about secret gardens and planning magnificent landscapes with roses blooming in abundance. Decide what you want to add to your garden and place your orders. It really does make a difference if you order early. Quantities are limited, and there is always a chance that the ones you want will be gone if you wait until those warm days of spring.

While planning your garden, don't forget to also place your order early for your Valentine's Day roses. Keep in mind the message you are sending with your choice of roses. According to *The Language of Flowers* written in 1913, but unpublished until 1968, roses in general mean "love." The details, however, can be much more subtle and specific. Here are a few examples:

- **Deep Red Rose:** Bashful shame
- **Single Rose:** Simplicity
- **White Rose:** I am worthy of you
- **Withered White Rose:** Transient impressions
- **Yellow Rose:** Jealousy

- **Burgundy Rose:** Unconscious Beauty
- **A full-blown rose placed over two buds:** Secrecy
- **Red Rosebud:** Pure and lovely
- **Red and White rose together:** Unity

Alternatives from *The Language of Flowers* published in 1841 include:

- **Pink Rose:** Our love is perfect happiness
- **White Rosebud:** Charm and innocence
- **Rugosa Rose:** Beauty is your only attraction
- **A rosebud with leaves and thorns:** I fear but I hope
- **A rosebud stripped of leaves:** Everything is to be feared
- **A rosebud stripped of thorns:** Everything is to be hoped
- **Withered Red Rose:** I would rather die, our love is over

Choose your roses wisely, as you would choose your words. They send a message!

## PLANTING

It is too cold for planting. Sometimes, however, you get very lucky and roses you receive in a vase will sprout roots. If this is the case, cut back the faded bloom until the stem with the roots is about 8 inches tall and pot it up. Keep it cool, not freezing, and moist but not soggy. When it sprouts leaves, make sure it gets lots of sun. It may just turn into a wonderful shrub for your garden.

If you want to encourage rooting of roses you've received, take some willow branches and stick them in with the roses. There is a natural chemical in willow that encourages rooting.

 WATERING

If you receive roses for Valentine's Day, or when you cut them from the garden later in the year, you should give them a fresh cut just as you put them in the vase. Make the cut at an angle, with a sharp knife, cutting away from you. It is best to do this while holding the stem you are cutting in a sink full of water.

**Here's why:** Cutting at an angle makes bigger openings in the vascular system of the stem. Think of the stem as a fistful of straws that suck up the water the rose needs to fully bloom. If the straws get plugged up with debris or even bacteria, which can grow in the water, no water can flow through the straw. When you order ½ pound of salami at the deli, if it is cut straight then you get a circle. If it is cut at an angle then you get a much larger oval slice. Large oval openings in the vascular tubing in the stem take much longer to get clogged up.

You hold the stem under water because of capillary action. Water in a tube recedes from the end when the tube is cut, creating a small air bubble in the tube. The air bubble rises in the stem until it reaches the flower, where the flower sucks in the air instead of water and the flower wilts. If you hold the stem under water while making the cut, as the water recedes inside the stem each tube sucks up water instead of air. This reduces its chance of wilting.

## FERTILIZING

No fertilizer is needed yet.

## PRUNING

No pruning is needed either. Go ahead and make sure you have a very sharp pair of pruning shears on hand and long-handled loppers as well. They will make the job of pruning much easier on your arms next month.

## PESTS

They are not pestering your roses yet. Don't worry; they will.

## Helpful Hints

*1* Liquefying rose petals in a blender or food processor will make rose water. Let the mash steep for a few hours. Add fresh rose petals and then bring the mixture to a boil. Strain off the rose water. The finest quality rose water is then distilled. If you don't happen to have any distilling apparatus sitting around, you can cover it with a lid and let it sit in the sun for a week.

*2* Roses are edible. Fresh, clean rose petals are often mixed into a fruit salad for both color and flavor. Try a salad of **blueberries, pears, peaches,** and rose petals. It will certainly be beautiful.

## NOTES

_____

_____

_____

_____

_____

_____

_____

_____

_____

_____

_____

_____

_____

_____

_____

# MARCH

 ## PLANNING

In an early spring, you can get started on preparing your rose garden by the middle of the month. Regardless of the weather, take a close look at the damage from the winter. Black stems are a very bad sign. If the winter was vicious, you may see a lot more black than you hoped. Yellow roses are notorious for not surviving our winters. Sunsprite is a yellow **floribunda** that has a better chance of making it than most yellows.

This evaluation is important for planning your orders for replacement plants. It is not always easy to determine the viability of roses from a simple look at the plants, but you can get a general feel for how well they did and adjust accordingly.

Most roses are shipped bare root and generally arrive next month. Roses at your local nursery are sometimes available bare root but wrapped in peat moss and plastic. They are also available already potted up.

 ## PLANTING

It's not yet the time to plant.

 ## WATERING

There isn't much need to water anything now.

 ## FERTILIZING

Be patient. Fertilizing begins in mid to late April.

 ## PRUNING

Pruning roses is a major job in late March or early April. However, this **does not include climbing roses**. It is important to remember that climbers bloom on last year's growth and are pruned after bloom. You can remove the dead and diseased wood on all roses, including climbers.

**Check to see if any branches have emerged from below the graft.** The graft is located by the bulge in the trunk. The graft is generally planted just at the soil surface and then protected by heavy mulch over the winter. In the coldest part of the state, the graft may be planted just below the soil surface. If the shoots are coming from below the graft or directly from the soil, it is a shoot from the rootstock and won't be the variety you selected. It might even be **multiflora rose**, which is very aggressive. These rootstock shoots need to be pruned as close to the trunk as possible.

**Hybrid teas** are pruned to 3 to 5 healthy canes that are the thickness of a pencil or greater. **Prune to an outside bud.** That means you look at the leaf scars and locate where the tiny dormant bud is sleeping. Some will point to the sides, some to the center and some to the outside. The bud will develop into a branch that will continue to grow in the direction the dormant bud points. You want to aim for a vase-shaped bush. Branches crossing toward the center damage each other, cut down on air circulation, and are nasty to try to prune at a later date. Find the bud pointing towards the outside that is as close as possible to being 18 inches in height and prune the branch at that point. Make your cut ¼ inch above the bud. Cut all the branches to 18 inches and see what you have.

You need to **examine the "pith" or center of each cane.** It should be white. A brown center means the cane is compromised. If possible, choose your 3 to 5 canes from those that are white. Keep in mind that any branches emerging from the cane you choose will only be as large as the cane you start with or smaller. If the 5 best canes still have some brown pith, you need to cut the branches back 1 inch at a time in an attempt to get back to sound wood. Keep in mind the need for outside buds. If the bush is in bad shape, you may need to tolerate a little brown rather than eliminate the branch altogether. If you have 3 healthy canes, eliminate all those that are damaged.

In fact, if your **hybrid teas** are quite healthy and you prefer not to prune according to the above standard approach, you will get smaller, shorter stemmed blooms. They will not meet exhibition standards and you will not have the graceful long stems, but the plants can still be exceedingly lovely.

For your **shrub** and **bush roses,** take a less drastic approach. After you have removed whatever is dead, diseased, and crossing, **remove the oldest cane near the base** to encourage new shoots. If the plants are too large, you can

shorten them from the top by cutting off about one-third and then pruning what is left for shape. Shrub roses can be left with minimal pruning for several years, but they can sometimes get quite large, so choose your approach accordingly.

 PESTS

Luckily, insect pests are still not a problem. Early weeds will begin to show up this month. You may want to spread the winter mulch around to help with weed control and add fresh organic mulch to the bed. The use of a pre-emergent weed control material will prevent the germination of many annual seeds.

 NOTES

_____

_____

_____

_____

_____

_____

# APRIL
## Roses

## PLANNING

When a builder implements an architect's plan, he or she often has to make changes as things progress. It is the builder's responsibility to make notes about the changes. The builder will write "as built" in the spot where it was necessary to make an adjustment.

Once the time arrives to implement the garden design that has been on the drawing board all winter, it is guaranteed that a gardener will often run into the same situation. Perhaps the term "as planted" would be the appropriate industry terminology. Make notes. You want to be certain of both your successes and failures so you know what to repeat and what to toss.

Having permanent nametags is very important down the road if you ever intend to expand on a theme or replace something that has become dear. Copper or thin white metal tags that you write on with a ball point pen—to make an impression in the metal—are among the best. Permanent marker just isn't permanent in this case.

Your roses will generally arrive early or mid-month. **If the weather is cooperative you should plant them immediately.** If you have to hold them for just a day or two, unwrap them to make sure they are moist. If dry, moisten lightly. Rewrap and store in a cool location where they will not freeze. If it will be longer, you will need to "heel-in" the plants by burying the roots up to the graft in loose soil, out of the wind. Your compost pile may provide a good option.

Treat locally purchased, packaged, bare-root roses the same way. It is a good idea to soak the plants in cold water overnight, up to the graft, to allow them to take up any needed water prior to planting.

## PLANTING

You will need some tools for growing roses. A pair of **gauntlet gardening gloves** will be very helpful. You will be pruning in hot weather, and short sleeves are conducive to scraped up arms. A very good pair of pruning shears is a must. There are also relatively new pruners on the market that cut and hold the cutting. This is great for cutting rose blooms for indoor use or even pruning climbing roses overhead.

Whatever roses you choose to grow, pick a very sunny location with excellent drainage. Don't forget that soil preparation is very important. You can find detailed instructions for planting roses in the chapter introduction.

## WATERING

Water your new roses thoroughly after planting. Established roses should not need water at this time.

## FERTILIZING

There are many approaches to fertilizing roses (see chapter introduction). Keep in mind that, if you want flowers, this is one plant you will need to feed. **Mid-April is the time for the first application.** If you use a **granular fertilizer,** especially one specific for roses, you may not need to fertilize again until June, when they need the boost from all that heavy blooming. The use of a **water-soluble fertilizer** will require more frequent applications. Follow the directions on the product you purchase. A light application of 5-10-5 fertilizer can be applied monthly, but go very light in hot weather.

## PRUNING

If you did your entire pruning in March, you should not have anything else to do in that regard. If the weather didn't cooperate, get to the pruning as soon as possible. See March for details.

Some rose specialists recommend pruning newly planted roses down to 6 inches to encourage root development. It makes for a slower first year in the bloom department but a healthier plant overall.

 PESTS

Thankfully, insects are still not a problem. See March for some tips on weed control.

## Helpful Hints

**1** If you come across packaged roses that are very inexpensive, evaluate their wellbeing with care. They should look healthy, have at least two canes the thickness of your thumb or greater (but three is better), and have a significant root system. Avoid broken, black, or shriveled plants. You should also make sure you have the nametag and any identifying characteristics about what type of rose it is. The variety name alone will probably not tell you if it is a **hybrid tea** or a **climber.** Remember they aren't a bargain if they don't grow.

**2 Miniature roses** are often available year-round in greenhouses. While generally quite hardy, you may not want to plant one out this early. Since it is used to greenhouse or indoor conditions, it will probably not be happy if suddenly thrust outdoors. Wait until danger of frost has passed. Next year, it will acclimate to the cold just fine.

## NOTES

# MAY
## Roses

 PLANNING

All your bare-root roses that arrived in the mail should be planted by this time. You should be able to see an abundance of healthy foliage. By late in the month, you should see rosebuds. There isn't a lot of planning for your roses this month, unless you want to plan a garden party for June when the roses are blooming.

 PLANTING

You may come across a potted rose you have to have at your favorite garden center. One problem with these plants is that the nurseryman has often potted them that same spring from bare-root plants. They may not have much of a root system established in the pot. Ask when the plants were potted. If it is freshly planted, you can consider growing it in its current pot until the plant develops a better root system.

When planting, pull it out of the pot very carefully to avoid damaging the developing hair roots. If all the soil falls away, you can treat it like a bare-root plant. Those that are potted in tarpaper pots can be planted pot and all. This is not as common a practice as it used to be, but you may still come across it in smaller nurseries.

 WATERING

How much you need to water depends on how much it rains. May can be a very wet month. On the other hand, 90 degree temperatures and blazing sun is not unheard of either. Established roses have deep roots and will only need water if conditions are dry for an extended period. Newly planted roses will need water more often, but **always water deeply when you do water.** Shallow, frequent watering will encourage shallow roots, making them more vulnerable to drought. Deep watering encourages deep roots.

It is very important not to get water on the leaves. A single plant or two can be easily watered with a handheld hose directed at the base of the plant. You can even use a watering can, but with many rose plants this becomes impractical. Overhead watering gets the leaves wet, which encourages leaf diseases. Diseases often do not show symptoms this early, but the period of inoculation is always significantly earlier than the visible symptoms.

The use of an organic mulch is very important. Bark mulch, wood chips, partially decomposed leaves, even grass clippings can all be used. The mulch should be spread about 4 inches think but not right up to the trunk. **Mulch is important for weed control but is also important to conserve soil moisture.** Rain or irrigation water will go right through the mulch and get to the roots, but it is best to apply mulch when the soil is already moist.

 FERTILIZING

If you are following the once-a-month rule for fertilizer application, feed again four weeks after your April feeding. This is usually done with a water-soluble fertilizer. Make sure you follow label directions carefully. If you are using a hose end attachment for this type of fertilizer application, you need to coordinate the type of fertilizer with the directions on the applicator.

When following the **twice-a-year-approach,** once in spring and once in early summer, you should have already applied a granular rose fertilizer in April. Wait until June for the next application.

**If you use the three-holiday system, you can fertilize Memorial Day, Fourth of July, and Labor Day.** That means your first application is this month. Which system you choose depends on how much effort you want to put forth and the results you desire. A little experience will tell you what is best for you and your roses.

## PRUNING

Keep a close eye on shoots emerging from below the graft. They will grow very rapidly and can overpower the flowering variety on top. Prune them off as close as possible to where they emerge.

If any buds develop that are clearly going to grow in an undesirable direction, your can easily remove them with your thumb.

## PESTS

Early spraying of roses to prevent disease goes a long way in keeping later problems to a minimum. Preventative sprays should be started as soon as the plant has significant foliage. There are three primary diseases: black spot, rust, and mildew. **Follow label directions with great care** and be sure to spray when it is not windy. Keep pets and children busy elsewhere while you are spraying. Thoroughly spray both upper and lower surfaces of the leaves as well as the trunk. Three sprays at two-week intervals should prevent most of the problem. An occasional spray after that, if the tiniest symptom shows up, should give you the protection you need for most of the season.

If you hate the idea of spraying to prevent disease, it becomes that much more important never to get the leaves wet, to grow the plants in full sun with good air movement between plants, and to fertilize properly so the plants are vigorous. It is also wise to choose your plants with great attention to disease-resistant varieties.

Caterpillars can show up in the spring. If you see lacy leaves, look for caterpillars doing the damage. Often they can be handpicked and the damaged leaves removed. Aphids usually show up on buds and can be squished with finger and thumb. (Wear gloves if you are squeamish). If the numbers are excessive, you can spray with an appropriate insecticide. Permethrin is good for many insects and is very short lived. Check with the Cooperative Extension Office for current recommendations.

## NOTES

_____

_____

_____

_____

_____

_____

_____

_____

_____

_____

_____

_____

_____

# JUNE
## Roses

## PLANNING

Roses are spectacular in June. It will be a great joy to spend time in the rose garden watching each bloom unfold its beauty.

You will thoroughly enjoy the display in your own yard, but also take the time to visit other rose gardens. There is a lovely rose garden in Colonial Park in Franklin Township. Bobblink Memorial Rose Garden in Lincroft is one of 25 All-America test display gardens. Brookdale Park Rose Garden in Upper Montclair has 750 bushes of over 100 species donated by the North Jersey Rose Society. You will gain so much insight as to how roses work together that you will be years ahead of what you would discover on your own. You will return to your own garden truly inspired.

## PLANTING

You may be very tempted to pick up just one, or two, or even three more roses when you see them potted in bloom at the nurseries you visit. You should purchase only healthy plants that have nice full leaves. Avoid extremely potbound plants as they will not transplant well.

Check with the nursery to find out when they were potted up. If they were potted this spring, you may want to keep them in their containers until early fall. They may not have enough roots to hold the rootball together.

**If you choose to plant them immediately, take extra care** to remove the roots from the containers as gently as possible. This is to avoid the soil falling away from the roots and taking the newly produced root hairs with the soil. It may be painful, but you really need to prune away all the flowers and buds at planting. The plant will go into a bit of shock, and it will benefit from not having to support flower production just as it is getting acclimated to its new location.

## WATERING

If you plant anything now, water it thoroughly. Use a watering system that does not get water on the leaves (see May Watering for details).

## FERTILIZING

Fertilize newly planted roses after the first flush of blooms. That may be in June or early July depending on variety, when they were planted, the zone, and weather. Zone 5 in the northwest corner of the state is two to three weeks behind Zone 7.

On those established roses you fertilize monthly, fertilize four weeks from your last application. This is most often a water-soluble material that is either mixed in a watering can and applied when you have only a few rose bushes, or applied via a hose end sprayer. Make sure you **properly calibrate your sprayer** with the fertilizer you have chosen. On those established roses where you are using a specific rose fertilizer and are applying the fertilizers twice (once in early spring and once in early summer), you will apply the second feeding in late June.

## PRUNING

You will need to prune your blooming roses continually. For larger, longer-stemmed **hybrid tea roses,** prune away secondary flower buds and developing shoots. In the home garden, more flowers are generally preferred, but it is up to the individual.

Prune **climbing roses** after they finish blooming. Many, but not all, bloom only once in the spring. Prune for shape and remove the tips of those shoots that have reached the maximum size for the allotted space. At the base, remove the oldest shoot, leaving an appropriate new shoot to fill in the space. Of course, remove all faded blooms to prevent seed production. See the chapter introduction for more on pruning.

## PESTS

By the end of June, you are likely to see Japanese beetles. They love to munch on rose leaves. An all-purpose rose spray that includes both insecticide and fungicide will do the job. If you are using a separate fungicide to control leaf diseases, you will need to control the beetles some other way. If beetles are not in large numbers, you may be able to handpick them. Check with your Cooperative Extension Office for current recommendations.

## Helpful Hints

*1* When cutting roses for indoor use, gather your roses early in the morning. For the longest indoor life, choose mature buds that have just started to open. Put a tablespoon of diet lemon-lime soda in the vase. "Diet" means there's no sugar to feed bacteria. "Lemon-lime" is acidic, so it will lower the pH of the water, again reducing the likelihood of bacteria growth. Soda, in general, contains a preservative to help keep the water clear.

*2* Go easy on taking blooms from newly planted bushes. Cutting blooms also removes foliage. Mature bushes can tolerate the loss with much more grace than a young plant that's not well established.

## NOTES

# JULY
## Roses

 PLANNING

It is definitely "time to smell the roses." By July, the weather is hot, the pool is open, or the ocean calls. The roses are all planted, blooming, or just finished blooming, and the spring rush is over. Certainly, there are plenty of maintenance chores to keep a gardener busy, but the pace is more laid back.

**Quite a few towns sponsor garden tours.** This is where you get to visit one garden after another, usually belonging to members of the local garden club. This can be a fun way to spend a Saturday or Sunday. It is also a great way to meet other people with similar gardening interests. You may find some rose gardeners among the group who just may be willing to trade cuttings in the fall.

If you have already spent time visiting rose gardens, you may have acquired a list of roses that are on your "must have" list. While you are sitting on the porch swing with a tall glass of strawberry lemonade, you can flip through your garden catalogs making note of who has what. Keep a pad of sticky notes on hand.

 PLANTING

There's not much planting going on right now. Of course, if you come across a potted rose bush on sale that you can't resist, it may be worthwhile if it is in reasonable health. Check the root system carefully. See if it has a well-formed rootball that can be transplanted easily. Don't bother with bargain plants that have so many roots they spiral around the pot. These plants are compromised and will struggle to get established. Spreading out the roots will be stressful, but leaving them may cause the rose to strangle itself over time.

 WATERING

Established roses are fairly tolerant of dry soil conditions. You only have to water if the ground stays dry for a prolonged period. Water deeply when you decide it is necessary, and as always, do not get any water on the leaves.

Spring planted and especially June or July planted roses will need more regular watering. Do not let them sit dry. Mulch heavily with organic mulch to protect the developing roots.

 FERTILIZING

New roses are fertilized after the first flush of blooms. You might have done this in June, but if not, and they have just finished, fertilize now.

For established roses, if you are following the once-a-month approach, apply a light application of fertilizer four weeks after your June application. **Be careful;** it is never good to fertilize when the temperature is above 85 degrees Fahrenheit.

If you have decided to fertilize according to the **three-holiday** approach (Memorial Day, Fourth of July, and Labor Day), remember to fertilize on July 4th.

 PRUNING

Summer pruning of roses is more maintenance than serious pruning. Watch for suckers emerging from below the graft. This is not a problem on **miniature roses** or on any roses you rooted yourself. They are growing on their own roots, so you don't have to worry about some wild rose taking over from the rootstock. If suckers do appear on any of your grafted roses, remove the suckers as soon as you see them. They may be so vigorous that they could overpower the desired variety on top. Be firm and remove these aggressive shoots as soon as you see them.

Pruning away dead flowers at the abscission layer as the flowers fade (see the chapter introduction) keeps the roses producing as many flowers as possible. The occasional removal of a misdirected shoot will not hurt the bush, especially if taken when just an emerging shoot.

##  PESTS

Powdery mildew often first shows up in July. It is easily recognized by a whitish coating on the leaf surface. If you started the season with a preventive spray program in place, the occasional spray during the summer should keep your plant in good shape (see May for more on pests). You can still control diseases, but it will take repeated sprays, and the plants may lose many leaves in the meantime.

Summer heat can also bring on mites. They are found mostly on the underside of the foliage. They suck the chlorophyll from the leaves. A hard spray of water, directed up, will wash away many of them. **Use this technique in the early morning** so the leaves have plenty of time to dry before nightfall. This keeps the chance of spreading to a minimum.

Japanese beetles are just as hungry as ever. Handpick or spray with an appropriate insecticide. Check with your Cooperative Extension Office for current control recommendations for mites or beetles if they persist.

## NOTES

_____

_____

_____

_____

_____

_____

_____

_____

_____

# AUGUST
## Roses

 PLANNING

Well cared for repeat-blooming roses will still be producing flowers this month. In August, however, the rose bed is not as floriferous as in June or early July. Summer annuals are often at their peak early in the month, and some perennials such as **black-eyed Susans** and **purple coneflowers** are blooming with enthusiasm. **Dahlias** produce abundantly at this time. All of these make outstanding cut flowers that mix beautifully with the "Queen of Flowers" for an indoor bouquet. A personal favorite is to mix roses with the wildflower **Queen Anne's lace.** The combination of dramatic roses surrounded with a delicate white cloud of lace is close to perfection.

If you are planning to increase your rose garden, fall planting will give an earlier start to new plants next spring. Yellow roses are notorious for being tender, however, and may not be worth attempting in the fall. They have a poor record of surviving New Jersey winters even when they have had an entire season to become established.

 PLANTING

Roses can be successful with fall planting, provided you allow time for some root development and some winter protection. Keep your eye out for **healthy** plants on sale locally. Those that were potted up this past spring should have well-developed roots in the container and will plant easily.

The key to the planting depth of roses is the bulge from the graft. That needs to end up at ground level or just below (about 2 inches). Even at ground level, you will want to bury it with organic mulch for winter protection.

**You can plant container-grown material at any time,** but if the weather is really brutally hot, you may want to wait until things cool down a bit. You can also wait to plant any of these end-of-season sale roses until early next month when the weather is more conducive to planting in general.

See the chapter introduction for planting instructions and important rose requirements.

 WATERING

If you plant any roses, you will certainly want to water them in thoroughly. Late in the month, you may not need to water again, depending on temperature and rainfall. A thick layer of mulch will help retain soil moisture.

Established roses will tolerate dry soil as long as it is not for an extended period. Water deeply should the need arise and be sure to avoid getting water on the foliage if at all possible.

 FERTILIZING

Continue the **once-a-month** approach with a diluted water-soluble rose fertilizer according to directions. Or if you follow the **three holidays** approach, you don't have to fertilize this month. Do not apply a concentrated granular fertilizer at this time. The ground is likely to be dry and the air hot, which could cause burning of the roots.

 PRUNING

Roses need continual maintenance pruning throughout the summer. Remove faded blooms at the abscission layer.

Also check regularly for the production of sucker shoots from below the graft. These are often from vigorous rootstock varieties.

See chapter introduction for more details on pruning.

 PESTS

While an infection of uncontrolled black spot can completely defoliate a susceptible rose by this time, resistant varieties hold up to the disease. The occasional summer spray will go a long way in preventing a serious problem on even susceptible varieties.

Powdery mildew is usually less devastating but is significantly worse when the humidity is high and the nights cool off. **August is when powdery mildew is really moving through roses with great speed.** The materials to prevent black spot will often prevent mildew as well. If you sprayed early, it may delay or eliminate mildew now, but if it shows up it can still be controlled. Check with the Cooperative Extension Office for current control recommendations. Follow label directions carefully.

If disease spots are rampant early this month, it warrants control. Keep in mind that a few disease spots late in the season are tolerable. If you see a few spots late in the month, whether they be black spot or mildew, it may be wise simply to pluck off the few offending leaves.

## NOTES

_____

_____

_____

_____

_____

_____

_____

_____

_____

_____

_____

_____

# SEPTEMBER
## Roses

## PLANNING

As the weather cools, it is often possible to have another burst of bloom on your roses. It may not rival the June display, but it can still be spectacular. Not to worry though, the last rose of summer is still a long way off. You might able to cut one for the Thanksgiving table.

You may still find roses on sale, and as long as they are in good health there is no reason not to make the purchase. If you have the space, don't be afraid to take a chance on one you like but didn't plan for.

## PLANTING

It is perfectly fine to plant potted roses in September. Planting should be done early in the month in a sunny location. Remember that the bulge from the graft needs to end up at ground level or just below (about 2 inches). (Refer to the general planting instructions in the chapter introduction for more instructions.)

**Mulch is always important but is of extra value at this time of year.** A mulch will reduce fluctuations in the soil temperature and will help retain summer's heat a little longer.

Encourage the production of new roots so the plant has a better chance of being well established when winter hits. Roots continue to develop as long as soil temperature stay above 45 degrees Fahrenheit. Heavy organic mulch will minimize heat loss as nights cool off.

If you come across a potted rose that looks healthy but is rootbound, you may be able to salvage the plant. If it is so rootbound you can't even see any soil, it may be too far gone. If the roots are crowded and wrap around the outside but do not completely encircle the soil ball, you should be able to tease them apart enough to encourage them to grow out. This is important to avoid the eventual strangling of the plant as the roots enlarge. If you feel you have done some damage in this process, prune some of the top growth to take pressure off the remaining roots. If you lose roots without removing some top growth, the whole plant may wilt.

If there are roses you want to root from cuttings, now is the best time to try.

*1* **Take cuttings 6 inches long.** (If you did any pruning of the above rootbound roses you may want to try this.) Keep a leaf node near the bottom of the cutting and remove all the leaves except the set on top.

*2* **Make a slit** in the stem.

*3* **Dip** it in a bit of rooting hormone.

*4* **Plant** it into the ground several inches deep. Cover with a mayonnaise jar, or a mason jar, or even a clear 2-liter soda bottle with the top removed.

*5* **Water** occassionally around the jar so the cutting doesn't dry out, but the jar will increase the humidity around the cutting to help with that.

*6* **Label** the cutting. Those cuttings that root should be transplanted in the spring to a very protected bed where they can "grow up" a bit before being moved the following spring to their permanent home or pot.

Not all roses will root from cuttings, and not all will have the ability to thrive on their own roots. Trial and error is your best bet.

## WATERING

Only water established roses if the ground becomes quite dry for an extended period.

Water newly planted roses thoroughly. Chances are you will not have to water again since September gets a fair amount of rain and the temperature is dropping.

Cuttings in the ground for rooting will need to be watered whenever the soil starts to dry. Don't wait until it becomes bone dry because the cuttings have no roots and will dehydrate much more rapidly than their well-rooted parents.

 FERTILIZING

If you are following the **once-a-month** approach, you will need to apply a diluted water-soluble fertilizer four weeks after your last application. If you are using the simplified method of fertilizing your roses on the **three holidays,** then your Labor Day application is due that weekend. **Either way, this is your last fertilization until next spring.**

 PRUNING

Continue to remove suckers that pop up from below the graft, but stop removing faded blooms by late in the month. Part of going dormant includes the development of the fruits. It is part of the natural life cycle of the plant. If you continue to prune away dead flowers, you will encourage new growth rather than dormancy.

 PESTS

Japanese beetles are still feeding but not generally at the same rate they were earlier in the summer. Handpicking is probably adequate for control. If the weather remains humid or rainy, you may want to apply one more fungicide treatment. If the plants have been healthy all summer, removal of any newly infected leaves may be adequate.

If plants are heavily infected, make sure you rake the fallen leaves and dispose of them in a plastic bag to prevent disease from getting a foothold for next year.

Weed seed germination picks up again as the weather cools off. Raking and then adding leaves to your layer of organic mulch will help prevent weed growth.

NOTES

# OCTOBER
## Roses

 PLANNING

An overall evaluation of this year's roses is in order now. Note the good, the bad, and the ugly. Few rose blooms are actually ugly, but sometimes a bush can be pretty pathetic, especially if you are battling disease all summer long. If you have a bush like that, you may decide you no longer need it.

**To evaluate a rose plant's performance, you should consider the weather throughout last summer as well as the location of each rose.** Perhaps the spot you chose started out very sunny but didn't meet your expectations once the foliage came out on the trees. Maybe the spacing was too tight. Combined with a rainy season, poor air circulation could be an enormous contributor to the spread of disease.

A rainy season might have also kept the ground overly wet. It that is the case, transplanting to higher, drier ground may be worth the effort. Roses hate excessive soil moisture.

And then maybe it was just a disappointing rose. If that is the conclusion you make, then just get rid of it. It may be painful at the moment, but not as painful as the collective years of struggling with a less than adequate plant. You can try something else next year.

 PLANTING

October is not really a great time to plant roses in the garden. It is getting too late to have any significant root development before winter sets in. However, it is not too late to root cuttings. (The very old-fashioned and yet sometimes very successful "mayonnaise jar" method is described under Planting in September.)

You may want to consider planting bulbs around the roses. **Tulips** are lovely, but remember they generally only last a few years. You can encourage tulips to last longer by planting them deeper, but **daffodils** naturalize more readily. Daffodils also tend to bloom earlier, while roses are still in the just-pruned, still-pretty-bare stage of development. By the time the roses are really getting bushy, the daffodils have finished up.

 WATERING

It is very unlikely that you will need to water established roses at this time. It has happened, however, that a dry summer is followed by a very dry early fall. Sooner or later the sky opens up, and plants almost always go into the winter with adequate soil moisture. The key here is "almost" always. If the soil stays dry, you will want to water thoroughly to avoid going into winter with drought conditions.

You will also want to keep an eye on any cuttings that you may be trying to root. Water the soil around the protective mayonnaise or mason jar when it becomes dry. Do not allow it to sit dry or become bone dry because the cuttings will dry out fairly quickly.

 FERTILIZING

Definitely do not fertilize at this time. It is very important for your roses to begin the process of slowing down and going dormant. An application of fertilizer at this time will encourage new growth, which delays dormancy.

 PRUNING

Pruning is also discouraged at this time. Pruning stimulates dormant buds into growth by removing a growth-inhibiting hormone that is produced at the branch tip. Any new growth will be tender going into the cold weather, and the plant can suffer significant cold damage at the first drop in temperature.

## PESTS

By this time of year, the foliage will begin to turn color and drop off on its own. There is really no point in attempting any disease control now. One important task of disease control is to continue to rake and collect the foliage. If the foliage was infected with any of the common leaf diseases, black spot, powdery mildew, or rust, you will want to take care to **bag as many of the leaves as possible.** This type of sanitation is an important aspect of minimizing the possibility of infection again next year.

## Helpful Hints

*1* If you intend to harvest rose hips for tea, you will want to do it after a frost. Break off the stems as you harvest them and spread them out to dry. When they begin to shrivel, cut them in half and remove the seeds. Then allow them to finish drying completely. They can be stored in sealed plastic containers for making tea or even jelly. One teaspoon of crushed dried rose hips makes one cup of tea.

*2* The larger fruits, such as those from the **rugosa rose,** make the best tea. Leave the smaller hips from other roses for the cardinals. These beautiful red birds will often stay around all winter if there is a source of food, and rose hips are one of their favorites.

## NOTES

# NOVEMBER
## Roses

 PLANNING

In November, activity really slows down in the garden. From a visual perspective, in the spring, newly pruned roses are rather bare. If you're planning to add bulbs as companions to your roses (see chapter introduction), give a little thought to the standing room you will need in March and April when you are pruning, mulching, and generally spending a fair amount of time fussing with your roses. You will need to **allow adequate room to work** without trampling young bulb foliage. Using pieces of slate or circular stepping stones as a walkway may be helpful.

By the end of November, you will need plenty of organic mulch on hand. Late November or early December is when you really want to pile it on. It is especially important to protect the bulge in the trunk of the rose that indicates the graft location. If the bulge is below ground, it already has some protection, but a dense 4 inches of mulch is recommended.

 PLANTING

If you haven't planted any bulbs as companions yet (see chapter introduction), there is still time to do that, but it is better early in the month rather than later. Roses are not being planted now.

 WATERING

It is rare that roses need to be watered in November. It would only happen if dry soil left over from a summer drought remained dry into the fall. Usually autumn weather is rainy enough for this not to be a problem.

Watch carefully those cuttings you are attempting to propagate under mason or mayonnaise jars. The surrounding soil will need to be watered before it gets bone dry.

 FERTILIZING

If you are planting **bulbs** in the rose garden, you should apply fertilizer according to the instructions for planting bulbs. Roses, however, need no fertilizer until spring.

 PRUNING

By late in November, there is one more pruning chore that needs attention. Roses need to be pruned to avoid getting **wind-whipped** over the winter. Plus, a heavy load of ice or snow can cause an otherwise healthy cane to snap off at the base. An abundance of branches catching the wind can "rock" the plant back and forth, creating a moat-like opening around the trunk. If that moat fills with water and freezes, say good-bye to your rose.

This is not the careful selective pruning that is done in early spring. In fact, you want to avoid doing that type of major pruning at this time. Simply prune all the branches back to about 3 feet (don't prune **climbers**). The shorter branches will be less likely to be blown by the wind or carry much weight in ice and snow.

Use caution: A severe winter may do significant damage to rose canes. You will need as many canes as possible when it comes time to prepare for spring growth. Pruning too heavily now will reduce those options severely.

## PESTS

There is really very little to do this month for the control of pests, but continue preventive action for next year. Make sure you rake up all the rose leaves as they fall off. Often there is an enormous downpour the last week or so of the month. Most if not all of the leaves from your deciduous trees and shrubs drop at that point. Make sure you rake up all the rose leaves in order to keep the source of disease to a minimum. Having a concentrated supply of disease inoculum at the base of the plants is asking for trouble.

## Helpful Hints

*1* **Climbing roses** need some type of support system. They don't actually "climb" on their own. They just grow and then you, the gardener, attach them to the support so they create the look you are trying to achieve.

*2* You may be able to purchase a trellis or arbor that works for you, but sometimes the space you intend to use has very specific dimensions, forcing you to build it yourself. The use of wood for support is very attractive, but watch out for painted wood. Painting it down the road may be problematic once roses are covering most of it. Pressure treated wood or wood with a natural resistance to decay may be a better choice.

*3* As alternatives to wood, there are resin or plastic materials, but in this gardener's opinion, they are a mismatch with the beauty of the plant. Wrought iron can be magnificent and even looks fabulous when rusty. Finding, building, and installing the right support system can be a great winter project. Plus, it will be all set for spring planting.

## NOTES

# DECEMBER

 ## PLANNING

Once again, December is a time for planning holiday parties and stashing presents in secret places. Gardening chores are on the back burner while visions of sugarplums dance in your head. If there are rose gardeners on your gift-giving list or if you are building a list for your personal Santa, here are a few ideas to make caring for your roses even more enjoyable:

- A pair of **gauntlet gardening gloves** is a must for rose gardeners. A pair of heavy leather gloves will keep all but the most vicious thorns from doing damage to you. In spring and summer, gloves protect arms and eliminate the need to bundle up and sweat.

- **Long-handled loppers** are an important tool for pruning all bushes and shrubs. With roses, there is the additional advantage of letting the handles, and not your arm, reach into the bush.

- A **miniature bamboo rake,** or perhaps one made out of metal or even plastic, can make leaf raking easier. It is important to collect the fallen rose leaves to limit leaf diseases come spring. A big rake is too cumbersome for the job.

- A pair of **cut-and-hold pruners** is a big help when making a bouquet. It can also be helpful with regular pruning.

- A **frame vase** has an opening through which you put a flower stem and a water reservoir in the back. It is used to display particularly lovely blooms. An individual rose makes quite a statement when displayed this way.

- A **gift certificate** for any of the rose specialty catalogs (see January for some suggestions) or from your favorite local nursery that carries fine quality roses can provide hours of spring-planning enjoyment.

- If you care to give **a particular rose,** it can be ordered for the holiday but will not be delivered until the proper time for planting. Perhaps cut the picture from the catalog and wrap it in a large box.

- Permanent **identification tags** are a great gift. Really good quality ones can be pricey as a garden expenditure but not extravagant as a gift. There are hang tags and stakes that go in the ground. Metallic tags that allow you to make an impression when writing on them are probably best.

 ## PLANTING

There is no planting of roses going on in December. You should keep an eye on those cuttings you have rooting in the garden. Make sure the jars you used don't blow over.

 ## WATERING

In general, you will not be watering roses in the garden, but you may need to water the cuttings you're rooting. Remember the cutting cannot search for water. Don't make the soil soggy either. Frozen water around the cutting will kill it quickly.

Water indoor potted roses when dry. In most cases, these will be **miniature roses.** The amount of water they need depends on the amount of sun they receive (which should be a lot if you want them to look like anything over the winter). The temperature of your home as well as the humidity and the size of the pot are also moisture factors. Lean towards the dry side rather than risk over-watering. All roses, including minis, have no tolerance for wet feet.

## FERTILIZING

No fertilizer is needed now.

# PRUNING

If you didn't prune last month to prevent wind damage, do it now. All other major pruning should wait until late winter or early spring.

 # PESTS

As winter food supplies dwindle, deer are more likely to come right to your front door to feed. Unfortunately there is no easy solution to the deer problem, and roses can be seriously at risk where deer are present.

Some suggestions for deterring deer:

- Lieutenant-Colonel Ken Grapes in *Botanica's Roses* suggests the use of heavy duty **fishing line.** He directs the gardener to string it taught around the rose bed at a height of 3 feet. Lieutenant-Colonel Grapes feels this is the most effective and inexpensive approach to the problem. The deer have trouble jumping over the string and tend to avoid the area.

- **Dogs** are an excellent deterrent to deer, and my guess is the bigger the dog the better. It is important that the pooch can run free in the area as deer will rapidly learn the dog's range if the dog is confined to a limited part of the yard.

- **Spray products** can be quite effective but usually for a very limited amount of time. The material has to be reapplied frequently, and it can become costly over an entire winter.

- **Deer fencing** is another option. It can be quite expensive but may be considered reasonable when compared to replacing your plantings annually. Some types of fencing are designed to blend into the vegetation and are less obtrusive. Others are more solid but are uglier as well.

## NOTES

_____

_____

_____

_____

_____

_____

_____

_____

_____

_____

_____

# CHAPTER NINE

# Shrubs

*Choosing the right shrubs for your yard requires
you to define your goals.*

Shrubs. Boy, is that a catch-all word! A shrub is not a tree, but there are trees that, when cut to the ground, come back as shrubs. In fact, some trees are cut to the ground every year to make them come back as shrubs. The **pussy willow** is an excellent example of this. The long sucker shoots that emerge straight and long are the result of this dramatic pruning. If it isn't done every year, it is done often enough to produce the desired suckers. Most people do not realize that a pussy willow will grow to be a medium-sized tree if allowed to grow with a single trunk.

Very small shrubs are woody but may have a primary trunk, even if it branches very low to the ground. **Azaleas** are often like this. **Dwarf Japanese maples** can be the size of small shrubs but are shaped like trees. Then there are those herbaceous plants that get woody over time and look more like a shrub than a perennial. The **Montauk daisy** gets woody like this, and the **blue mist spirea** is somewhere in between. **Lilacs** are generally referred to as bushes, which are pretty close to a shrub.

## THREE TYPES OF SHRUBS

There are evergreen shrubs, deciduous shrubs, and flowering shrubs. In general it is nice to have a blend of all three.

*1* **Evergreen shrubs** keep their foliage year-round and provide a backdrop for summer color as well as winter interest. Evergreen shrubs can be broken down into the needle type or the broad-leaf type. "Evergreen" does not mean the leaves live forever. It does mean the new leaves are produced before the older leaves drop off. So it is always green, even if it is not the same green all the time. Many **junipers, dwarf spruces, yews,** and other evergreens are commonly found in New Jersey gardens. The broad-leaf evergreens are often grown for their flowers as well as winter foliage. The **rhododendron** is a classic. There are others, too. **Andromeda, mountain laurel, azalea, skimmia, sarcococca,** and the many **hollies** all do a great deal to brighten up the winter landscape, as well as liven up the growing season by adding adding flowers or fruits.

*2* **Deciduous shrubs** lose their leaves in the fall. Some deciduous shrubs have unique foliage characteristics that maintain interest for spring, summer, and fall, whereas flowering shrubs bloom for a comparatively short time. **Japanese red maple** is grown for its foliage, and the **burning bush,** *Euonymus elatas,* is a fairly ho-hum plant until it turns fiery red in the fall. The **pearl bush,** *Exochorda,* on the other hand, has the loveliest white flowers in the spring, but that's all there is to it. For the rest of the season, it is a green mound and the leaves just drop in the fall.

Another group of deciduous shrubs is grown for the fruits. Not to eat, but for their display or maybe to feed the birds. This may not be the only reason to include a particular shrub in your garden, but fruits or pods provide late season interest, sometimes lasting into the winter. **Beauty berry** is not very exciting for most of the year. Once those bright purple berries appear, however, it is a show stopper. Common **sea buckthorn** gets vivid orange berries and is salt tolerant, so it is especially useful down the shore. The **smoke tree** has almost invisible flowers, but the seeds develop into what looks like clouds of smoke. It is quite unique.

*3* **Flowering shrubs** are not only grown for the flowers but also often have some other appeal. The **oak leaf hydrangea,** for example, produces large panicles of flowers in the summer, but the large oak-shaped leaves turn brilliant red in the fall. There are flowering shrubs that bloom on old wood and produce their blooms in the spring. The neon yellow **forsythia** is a classic.

Then there are shrubs that bloom on the current season's growth. These have to produce the foliage and then the flowers, so they generally bloom in the summer. Many continue to make flowers for some time once they start. **Rose-of-Sharon** is known for this long bloom period, but **butterfly bushes** have gained in popularity in recent years, falling into the same category.

A few shrubs have a big display of spring blooms but then put out the occasional flower in the summer.

**Flowering quince** will give you a few bonus blossoms in the summer, and so will the yellow flowered **kerria.**

## Which Shrub to Use?

Choosing the right shrubs for your yard requires you to define your goals. If low maintenance is what you are after, slow-growing evergreens may be right for you. If you want to find beauty and solace in the garden year-round, you need to choose the right combination of shrubs to provide that charm. In a small yard, you may be limited to choosing plants that provide more than one season of interest, or you may run out of room before you have accomplished your goal.

Without question, you will need to factor in the soil, water, and available light when choosing your shrubs. **The location has to match the plant's requirements.** Don't forget about evaluating available space and the ultimate size of the plant. That cute little blue spruce really wants to grow up to be 125 feet tall. That may be a tight squeeze outside the front porch.

## Planting

Additional organic matter is beneficial in both sandy and heavy clay soils.

If you are starting an entirely new bed, it is best to prepare the whole bed at once. This is especially true in heavy clay soil. Sometimes digging an individual hole in heavy clay creates a "bucket" effect. Water will follow the path of least resistance. The nice, loose soil in your planting hole allows the water to flow into the hole freely. The result is a bucket of water around the rootball and death to the plant. If the entire bed is prepared uniformly, water will not collect in any one spot.

The heavier the soil, the more you want to dig. **"Double digging"** refers to digging down and removing the soil to a depth of one shovel and then turning the soil over below that to the depth of another shovel. You can add soil amendments after you remove the first layer and work the amendments into the layer below as you turn it over.

When starting a bed in an existing lawn, you will need to remove the turf before you start. This can be done with

# Shrubs

the application of a total vegetation killer, such as Roundup® which will cause everything to be completely dead in about two weeks. You can also smother the grass with black plastic or old carpeting. In hot weather, this will kill grass rather quickly, but you will need to leave the cover in place until the grass is completely dead for this approach to be effective. In cooler weather it may take several weeks. It is, however, an environmentally desirable approach.

Transplanting anything from one spot in your yard to another, or from your neighbor's, friend's, or Mom's house requires extra attention to detail. **Make sure you have prepared the soil and dug the planting hole first.** You want to keep any plant out of the ground for as short a time as possible. If the ground even hints at being dry, water the plant the day before you intend to dig. Wrap the roots in burlap or plastic with as much care as possible. As clumps of dirt fall away from the roots, the tiny root hairs fall with it. Root hairs have an enormous surface area compared to their volume and are the most important part of the plant for water uptake. You want to keep as many of them intact as possible.

Whether the shrub in question has just been dug by you, is balled and burlapped from the nursery, or is in a container, plant at the same height it was in the ground or pot. Do not plant deep. In very wet ground, you can plant

a little high and then cover the roots with an organic mulch.

If your are planting a bare-root shrub, follow the planting directions that come with the plant. Very often it is suggested to soak the roots in water for two or three hours prior to planting. In some cases overnight soaking is recommended, but never more than twenty-four hours. Place the roots in the planting hole on top of a mound of soil. Identify a line on the trunk or shoots that indicate the previous soil line. **That line should be at ground level when planted.** Spread the roots so they point out and do not curl around the planting hole. Do not force them to bend where they do not want to go. Snip off any broken roots or branches. Fill in with soil around the roots, being careful to fill in all the air spaces but not to break any roots.

After filling the planting hole, tamp down the soil gently but not too close to the main stem. You want to avoid snapping any roots, especially those close to the trunk.

## FERTILIZING

A 5-10-5 fertilizer is an excellent all-purpose garden fertilizer and is well suited for fertilizing your shrubs. As a general rule, apply 3 to 6 pounds per 100 square feet of bed. If you have incorporated a great deal of organic matter into

the soil and used a thick layer of organic mulch, lean to the light side. In lighter, sandier soils lacking organic matter, nutrients will not be long retained in the soil, so you may want to use the more generous amount.

Liquid fertilizers are generally applied in a diluted solution that is repeated more frequently than granular fertilizers. That regimen can be started now. Follow label directions.

There is no real need for acid-type fertilizers, even for acid loving plants. New Jersey soils tend to be on the acidic side. The one place where it may warrant concern is placing acid loving shrubs, such as **rhododendrons** and **azaleas,** very close to the foundation of your home. The cement component of the wall can sometimes leach lime into the soil in the area very near the foundation, raising the pH to unsuitable levels. A simple pH test can tell you if this is a problem. A more likely problem is beds where marble chips have been used as a mulch. Marble is nothing more than compressed limestone, and these chips can raise the pH of your soil high enough to kill or seriously stunt your plants.

## PRUNING

Pruning of shrubs will be required for various reasons, including simply to shape the plants.

# Shrubs

Needled evergreen shrubs will be pruned to encourage the new growth to fill in any bare spots left from the pruning as well as to fill in the center of the shrub. Without selective pruning, or even worse with regular shearing, all the growth occurs near the tips of the branches making for short twiggy growth all on the outside and bare branches in the center. The plant becomes like a hollow egg, and pruning to fix this leaves you with an ugly mess. It can be corrected over time, but it is much better to prune selectively from the beginning.

Summer-flowering shrubs will be pruned to produce new growth and to prevent rubbing and damage to branches. You can remove rooted suckers on some shrubs to start new plants. Shrubs that are conducive to this are many **lilacs, forsythia, bottlebrush buckeye** (*Aesculus parviflora*), **yellow twig** and **red twig dogwood, kerria, winter blooming jasmine, clethra,** and many others.

**Throw away those electric shears!** In general, you want to keep shrubs down to a size where they fit into their allotted space in the landscape, but you want to try to maintain their natural beauty. Throw away your electric hedge pruners. They were designed to get you addicted to their use. The shearing effect that happens when you use them creates a tremendous amount of twiggy growth at each point where the pruning allowed dormant buds to break. This is all near the tips of the branches so the shrub immediately begins to get larger than the allotted size, and so you are forced to shear again . . . and again.

With selective pruning into the center of the shrub, the cut branches also resprout, but in the center. This allows the shrub to fill in with healthy growth inside the plant, so the overall habit is more attractive and balanced. When the new growth occurs inside the bush rather than at the tips, it takes much longer for the plant to outgrow its space. It also hides ugly stumps left from pruning cuts, and the natural grace of the arching branches is maintained in those shorter branches that never get touched. No electric shears means less work, more natural beauty, and no loud pruning noise. This is definitely the way to go!

Month-to-month pruning information is given in this book when action is needed.

## WATERING

How much rain Mother Nature has been providing is key to how much you may or may not need to water. Anything planted in the current season will need supplemental water sooner than those shrubs that are well established. Keep in mind that it takes two to three years for a plant to become truly established. Also keep in mind that the larger the plant at the time of planting, the longer it takes to become established.

Factor in all of these variables when deciding what and when to water. When you do decide that a plant needs supplemental water, make sure that you irrigate thoroughly. You want the entire root system to get a drink and the soil beneath the plant to become wet, or at least moist.

**Water deeply.** Shallow watering draws the roots to the surface. A deep watering will create a sturdier root system that will be better able to withstand dry conditions in the future. A deep, organic mulch goes a long way in retaining whatever soil moisture is in the ground.

## FLEXIBLE FRIENDS

One thing about shrubs is they return year after year, providing color and style with a relatively small amount of additional input. However, if you decide you really want something different, removing a shrub is not the same as taking down an oak tree. Move, prune, or replace your shrubs as the spirit moves you, or enjoy them as long-standing friends that mark the passage of time.

# Shrubs

## For Spring Flowers

| | |
|---|---|
| **Forsythia** | *Forsythia x intermedia* |
| **Weigela** | *Weigela florida* |
| **Rhododendron** | *Rhododendron catawbiense* |
| **Azalea** | *R. hybrids* |
| **Deutzia** | *Deutzia gracilis* |
| **Butterfly Bush** | *Buddleia alternifolia* |
| **Weeping Pea shrub** | *Caragana arborescens 'Pendula'* |
| **Flowering Quince** | *Chaenomeles speciosa* |
| **Vanhoutte Spirea** | *Spiraea x vanhouttei* |
| **Doublefile Viburnum** | *Viburnum plicatum 'Tomentosum'* |
| **Sand Cherry** | *Prunus x cistena* |
| **Cornelian Cherry** | *Cornus mas* |
| **Fothergilla** | *Fothergillla gardenii* |
| **Pearl Bush** | *Exochorda x macrantha 'The Bride'* |
| **Mock Orange** | *Philadelphus coronarius* |
| **White Forsythia** | *Abeliophyllum distichum* |
| **Lilac** | *Syringa species* |
| **Japanese Andromeda** | *Pieris japonica* |
| **Mountain Laurel** | *Kalmia latifolia* |
| **Winter Blooming Jasmine** | *Jasminum nudiflorum* |

## For Summer Flowers

| | |
|---|---|
| **False Indigo** | *Amorpha fruticosa* |
| **Saint Johnswort** | *Hypericum prolificum* |
| **Bottlebrush buckeye** | *Aesculus parviflora* |
| **Abelia** | *Abelia grandiflora* |
| **Oak Leaf Hydrangea** | *Hydrangea quercifolia* |
| **Blue Mist Spirea (late)** | *Caryopteris x clandonensis* |
| **Bumald Spirea** | *Spiraea x bumalda* |
| **Rose of Sharon** | *Hibiscus syriacus* |
| **Butterfly Bush** | *Buddleia davidii* |
| **Tamarisk** | *Tamarix ramisissima* |
| **Bigleaf Hydrangea** | *Hydrangea marcophylla* |
| **PeeGee Hydrangea** | *H. grandiflora 'Paniculata'* |
| **Smooth Hydrangea** | *H. arborescens* |
| **Summersweet** | *Clethra alnifolia* |
| **Franklinia (late)** | *Franklinia alatamaha* |

## Evergreens

| | |
|---|---|
| **Rhododendron (BL)** | *Rhododendron catawbiense* |
| **Azalea (BL)** | *R. hybrids* |
| **Skimmia (BL)** | *Skimmia japonica* |
| **Mountain Laurel (BL)** | *Kalmia latifolia* |
| **Japanese Andromeda (BL)** | *Pieris japonica* |

**BL = Broadleaf**

# Shrubs

## Evergreens (continued)

| | |
|---|---|
| Japanese Holly (BL) | *Ilex crenata* |
| American Holly (BL) | *Ilex opaca* |
| Boxwood (BL) | *Buxus sempervirens* |
| Wintergreen Barberry (BL) | *Berberis julianae* |
| Yew | *Taxus* species |
| Junipers | *Juniperus* species |
| Dwarf Alberta Spruce | *Picea glauca* 'Conica' |
| Mugo Pine | *Pinus mugo* |
| Drooping Leucothoe | *Leucothoe fontanesiana* |
| Firethorn | *Pyracantha coccinea* |

## Plants with Fall Color (FC), Fruits (FR), Interesting Bark (B) or Habit (H)

| | |
|---|---|
| Fothergilla (FC) | *Fothergilla gardenii* |
| Beauty Berry (FR) | *Callicarpa dichotoma* |
| Harry Lauder's Walking Stick (H) | *Corylus avellana* 'Contorta' |
| Winterberry Holly (FR) | *Ilex verticillata* |
| Red Twigged Dogwood (B) | *Cornus sericea* |

## Plants with Fall Color (FC), Fruits (FR), Interesting Bark (B) or Habit (H)

| | |
|---|---|
| Yellow Twigged Dogwood (B) | *C. sericea* 'Flaviramea' |
| Oakleaf Hydrangea (FC, B) | *Hydrangea quercifolia* |
| Red Chokecherry (FC, FR) | *Aronia arbutifolia* |
| Firethorn (FR) | *Pyracantha coccinea* |
| Winged Euonymus (FC) | *Euonymus elata* |
| Weeping Pea Shrub (H) | *Caragana arborescens* 'Pendula' |
| Virginia Sweetspire (FC) | *Itea virginica* |
| Common Sea Buckthorn (FR) | *Hippophae rhamnoides* |
| American Holly (FR) | *Ilex opaca* |
| Snowberry (FR) | *Symphoricarpos albus* |
| Viburnum (FR, FC) | *Viburnum* species |
| Persian Witchhazel (FC) | *Parrotia persica* |
| Cutleaf Japanese Maple (FC, H) | *Acer palmatum* 'Dissectum' |
| Royal Azalea (FC) | *Rhododendron schlippenbachii* |

## PLANNING

January is a tough month for gardeners. Winter is really just getting started. The holidays are over, and there is quite a bit of time until the first signs of life appear in the garden.

When planning for your garden, you need to include the winter landscape as part of the grand scheme. Having shrubs scattered about that make you smile at their cold-season charm is a good way to tread the icy waters of winter. They may pale in comparison to the mighty **oak,** romantic **roses,** or softball-sized **peonies,** but whatever you choose to help break up winter monotony will provide beauty, comfort, and diversion when it is most needed.

Below are some choices to consider:

- **Rhododendrons,** with their broad evergreen leaves, not only offer a touch of green in a gray and white world but also provide a clue to outside temperatures. In really cold weather, the leaves curl lengthwise to conserve moisture. The lower the thermometer drops, the tighter the curls.

- **Harry Lauder's walking stick** would generally be considered a large shrub. It only reaches about 10 feet and takes a very long time to get there. It is at its most fascinating in winter. The twisted branches are decorated in dangling golden catkins. When covered in snow, it is breathtaking.

- **Japanese Andromeda,** or **Japanese pieris,** is also decorated in clusters of golden bead-like flower buds. These show up nicely against the dark evergreen foliage.

- **Japanese fan-tail willow** has fan-shaped branches that are hidden during the growing season by abundant foliage.

- **Red** and **yellow twigged dogwoods** have yellow and red branches that show their best when bare of leaves.

- **Winged euonymus** have corky ridges that are interesting in winter when you can actually see them.

- **Winter blooming jasmine** produces cheerful yellow flowers in January if the weather is moderate. Even without flowers, the thick tangle of leafless branches has a great deal of character, especially covered in snow.

Some shrubs with fruit or seed pods that provide interest in winter are:

- **Clethra** retains its seed pods until you prune them away in early spring.

- **Winterberry holly** gets bright red berries that sometimes last into January.

- **Firethorns** (some) hold their fruit through the winter, but some that hold their berries the longest are only hardy to Zone 7. Be sure to read the fine print when making your selections.

## PLANTING

The ground is frozen. January is not the time to be planting.

## WATERING

It is rare that you need to water any shrubs in January. Winter drought can be a serious problem and is even worse if plants went into winter on the dry side. Although water consumption is way down during dormancy and cold weather, it has not stopped completely. If the ground stays dry, water recently planted material.

If you are holding over any container material for spring planting, they may require watering. This is especially true if there has been no precipitation.

In both cases, you should water on a day when the temperature is above freezing.

# FERTILIZING

No fertilizer is needed at this time. You may want to check on any liquid fertilizer you have in storage. It should not be allowed to freeze.

 # PRUNING

By the end of the month, you may want to do a light pruning of some of your spring-flowering shrubs. This is not a major pruning for rejuvenation or reshaping but is a prescription for dissipating the winter blahs. Branches of **winter blooming jasmine** bloom indoors quite readily. Don't worry; a few stolen branches of **forsythia** or **weigela** forced to bloom early indoors won't make a significant difference in your spring garden display.

Use this opportunity to remove any eye-pokers or non-conforming branches. Try not to leave any gaping holes, but for the most part, anything you remove now will be covered by new spring growth.

 # PESTS

Pests are all dormant now.

## Helpful Hints

*1* When cutting branches to force indoors, it is a general rule that those shrubs that bloom later in the garden will take longer to force indoors. Some that will produce results rather quickly include **forsythia, cornelian cherry, abeliophyllum** (white forsythia), **witch hazel,** and *Rhododendron mucronulatum.*

*2* Heavy ice and snow can certainly fall into the pest category when splaying the branches of your beautiful shrubs. The sooner you shake off the snow the less permanent the splaying. If the weight of the ice or snow has broken the branches farther back where they join the main trunk, the damage is more serious. You may need to do some corrective pruning to compensate in the spring.

*3* When treating sidewalks or driveways for ice and snow, avoid the use of rock salt around a shrubbery bed. Salt is deadly for plants. Even grass will be affected if the salt runs off the targeted surface and into the lawn. **Calcium chloride** is less harmful than rock salt, but you can also use sand or even cat litter to ensure better footing on a slippery path. To keep things tidy, sweep it up once the ice has melted.

## NOTES

_____

_____

_____

_____

_____

_____

_____

_____

_____

# FEBRUARY
## Shrubs

 PLANNING

February is a good month to visit your local nursery with your list for spring. Late March or early April is the ideal time for planting, so if you are looking for something special, you need to start tracking it down as soon as possible.

It is a good idea to have a chat with your garden center now for several reasons. If you want to have a mass planting for impact, create a formal privacy planting, or grow a hedge, you should go ahead and order the number of plants you will need. You may not be able to find ten of any one thing if you just show up at the garden center the day you want to plant. This is true even if what you want is common. It is more true if the plant or plants you seek are not so common.

Sometimes you may be interested in a very specific variety. For example the **Japanese holly** has a new cultivar called 'Sky Pencil'. This is very skinny and upright, is a great choice for tight spots, and is especially good for condos and townhouses. While just about every nursery in the state will carry some form of Japanese holly, the low spreading types will not do the same job as 'Sky Pencil'. If you visit your favorite nursery during the month of February, there is a very good chance they can order what

you want even if they were not planning to carry it as part of their regular stock.

 PLANTING

It is still too early to do any planting. On the other hand, you may want to pot up something for Valentine's Day. You may find several shrubs in bloom at a greenhouse or a floral shop that would make a really terrific alternative to a dozen long stemmed roses. (Not that there is anything wrong with roses, but something unique can also be seen as thoughtful and very romantic.) You can sometimes find **azaleas** or **hydrangeas** in bloom. **Rosemary** is used as an herb, but it is considered a "sub-shrub" since it gets quite woody. It is only hardy to Zone 6, so it won't work in the northwest corner of the state. **Miniature roses** are generally quite hardy and are often available in bloom.

You will have to keep these plants in their containers a little longer than usual. Since they have been forced into bloom early, they cannot tolerate the weather with normal late March or early April planting out. Plants need to be dormant to tolerate the cold. Keep these potted shrubs in their containers until late May, when all danger of frost has past. Next year, when they get used to the changes

in weather gradually, they will handle the cold the way you would normally expect.

 WATERING

If you have potted up some nice little shrubs, you will need to water them as the soil dries out. Make sure they have drainage. Outside it is highly unlikely that anything will need water; however, as with all plants in the garden, if there has been no precipitation, water on a day when the temperature is above freezing.

 FERTILIZING

No fertilizing is needed yet. Be patient. It may be a good idea to get to the store and stock up on whatever you may need. It will feel good to do something that at least hints of getting out into the garden, and you will have what you need when the time is right.

The only way to be certain of your lime and fertilizer needs is to have your soil tested. Now is a great time to do that. Contact your Cooperative Extension Office. They have soil testing procedures that send the soil to the testing lab at Cook College, the Agricultural School that is part of Rutgers University. It takes about six weeks to get the results, so early February is just perfect.

##  PRUNING

It is too early to do significant pruning. Harsh weather may still cause additional winter damage. You can still remove a few branches from flowering shrubs to use for indoor bloom. See January for more information.

##  PESTS

Most pests are still dormant. Dormant oils are generally applied in early April.

It's possible that you will see some foliage damage on **rhododendrons.** If holes are showing up on the edge of the leaves as if someone took a bite out of it, someone did. There is a critter called the **black vine weevil.** It is an ugly beetle-looking thing with a long snout, long antennae, and irregular yellow splotches on its otherwise black back. The larvae feed on the roots, and the adults feast on the foliage. They are far more active in warmer weather, but feeding can continue all year long. Only the adults can be controlled. Check with your Cooperative Extension Office for current recommendations.

## NOTES

# MARCH
## Shrubs

## PLANNING

While there is still plenty of time to finish up the details of your plans, it is also time to switch over into action mode. Stock up on mulch. For small areas, you may be able to make do with buying it by the bag. If you are planning a new bed or landscaping around the pool, you may want to have a load delivered. The same goes for soil amendment. Don't bother with ordering topsoil. Have a load of humus or compost delivered, or pick up a few bags.

If you have your own compost pile, turn it over early in the month. The material on top will not have decomposed. Put it on the bottom of the new pile you are forming. That will expose the finished material on the bottom of the original pile, ready for you to use.

## PLANTING

The earlier you can plant, the better off you will be, but that is provided the planting conditions are right. Late March is great if the ground is thawed and not too soggy. You definitely do not want to work soggy soil. It destroys the structure of the soil, creating rock-hard lumps instead of loose, friable earth. **Pick up a lump of soil and squeeze it as hard as you can.** If you can squeeze out more than a drop or two of water, it is way too wet. Then try crumbling it with your thumb. If it falls apart readily, then get ready to dig. (See the chapter introduction for planting instructions.)

## WATERING

Unless March has completely been a lamb all month, you don't have to water anything outdoors that is established and staying put. If you are planning to dig and move some of your shrubs around, you may want to water them deeply a day or so prior to digging if it has been on the dry side. This is a precaution since you will be ripping their little roots apart and water uptake will be compromised for a while.

Those shrubs you have waiting in containers are more likely to require water. Above ground, the soil will dry out more quickly, and roots have no opportunity to draw moisture from the surrounding soil. Make certain that the soil around the roots, whether in a container or a rootball, is moist when you plant the shrub in the ground.

## FERTILIZING

Late March or early April is the ideal time for a spring application of fertilizer as long as the ground is not frozen. A 5-10-5 fertilizer is well suited for fertilizing your shrubs. (See the chapter introduction for specifics on fertilizer.)

## PRUNING

March is the ideal time for pruning many of your shrubs. Any deciduous shrubs grown primarily for the foliage can be pruned now. This group would include **privet**, commonly used in hedges; **burning bush** (*Euonymus elata*), whose prime attraction is the vivid red fall foliage; and even your **boxwoods** and **Japanese hollies,** both small broad-leaved evergreens.

Needled evergreen shrubs such as many junipers and your many forms of **yew bush** can be pruned now.

You can also prune summer-flowering shrubs. This group would include the very floriferous **rose-of-Sharon,** the very popular **butterfly bushes,** and the delicate **abelia.** Start by pruning away the dead branches. Then prune branches growing towards the center, followed by those straight up or down and any that are crossing and rubbing. Shape whatever is left. The shrubs will produce flowers on new growth, so you are not preventing the bloom, but the more severely you prune the longer it will take to produce this year's crop of flowers.

While you are out in pruning mode, you may want to remove rooted suckers to start new plants. This technique can be use for many **lilacs, forsythia, bottlebrush buckeye** (*Aesculus parviflora*), **yellow** and **red twig dogwood, Kerria,** winter blooming **jasmine, clethra,** and many others.

**Do not** prune spring-flowering shrubs. You will remove the flowers. Examples of those that must not be pruned include the happy **yellow forsythia,** all your **rhododendrons** and **azaleas, weigela, flowering quince,** and even all your **lilacs.** There are lots more. Take the time to figure out if your shrubs bloom on new wood or old wood before you prune. If you get it wrong, you will have to wait an entire year for the next round of flowers.

## PESTS

March is still early for most pests. You may still see some activity from the **black vine weevil** (see February). Dormant oil is used to prevent many pests but is generally not applied until next month.

## Helpful Hints

*1* **Daffodils** are usually blooming by late March. Some of the evergreen branches you are pruning make great filler to use for daffodil arrangements indoors.

*2* Make sure you start checking your **pussy willows** early in the month. You want to prune them just as the fuzzy catkins are in full fuzz. The exact timing varies significantly depending on weather conditions. If you want to keep them long term, do not put them in water or the fuzzies will turn yellow with developing anthers and then fall off.

## NOTES

_____

_____

_____

_____

_____

_____

_____

_____

_____

_____

_____

_____

_____

_____

# APRIL

 PLANNING

By this time, you should have a pretty good idea of what you want and where. New growth is popping out, and flowers are beginning to show up. The **cornelian cherry,** a close relative of the native **dogwood,** is in bloom, and the yellow **forsythia** is trumpeting the arrival of spring. The beautiful purple-flowered *Rhododendron mucronulatum* is quite showy midmonth. Since this species is deciduous, the flowers really stand out and look like a blast of purple coming out of nowhere. By the end of the month, lovely **magnolias** are in bloom. Many are quite large and definitely considered trees, but the dwarf varieties stay under 12 feet. You may see something so lovely you have to have one in your own yard. Even if it wasn't in any of your plans, you may find you have a perfect spot after all.

 PLANTING

Planting is in full swing. The addition of organic matter to both sandy and heavy clay soil will improve the quality of the soil. However, do watch out for digging an individual planting hole in pure or almost pure clay or shale soils. See March for a discussion on the creation of a "bucket" effect under these circumstances.

For balled shrubs or transplanted ones, be sure to remove all plastic around the roots and all strings, wires, and tags.

See the chapter introduction for specific planting instructions.

 WATERING

Water your newly planted shrubs immediately. Be sure to keep those plants waiting to be planted watered thoroughly. They will dry out quickly. Bare-root plants should be checked immediately after they arrive. Make sure they are moist. Rewet the wrappings if they appear dry and plant as soon as possible. If you have to hold them for more than a day or two, they should be buried in soft ground such as the compost pile or the mulch pile, out of the sun and wind. This will keep the roots from drying out.

 FERTILIZING

Do not fertilize newly planted material. Give it one full growing season to get established. You can begin to fertilize this time next year.

For **established shrubs,** see the chapter introduction for a fertilizer schedule. If you are following a liquid fertilizer program, **the diluted water-soluble fertilizer is generally applied once per month.** Apply your fertilizer one month after the March application.

PRUNING

Any pruning you didn't do in March can be done early in April. See March for a discussion of what should and shouldn't be pruned in early spring.

By the end of the month, some early bloomers may have finished up. These should be pruned as soon as they finish, but the occasional branch can be removed if you want to enjoy the flowers indoors. A few sprays of **forsythia** can make quite a dramatic statement in a vase. Pay attention to the overall appearance of the bush while taking your cut flowers. You don't want to make a hole you will regret later on. Some plants, like the forsythia, will recover quickly. Others that are less robust may carry the burden of imprudent flower taking for much longer.

When you have moved along to serious pruning of spring-flowering shrubs, start by taking some of the oldest, non-flowering wood out at the base. This will trigger some suckering and branching in the center. It will also do quite a bit to thin the top. Follow with selective pruning of branches that are too tall or too long. Take them back to a main trunk or a healthy side shoot. Remove anything blatantly growing towards the center, straight up, or straight down. In cases where suckering is desired (as in **forsythia** or, later, **lilac**), leave some suckers but remove the weak, spindly, or excessive shoots. Shape whatever you have left.

There is still time to remove suckers for propagation purposes, but the window on that is fast closing. See March for some suggested species where it may be worth a try.

## PESTS

There are many types of **scale** that need to be prevented with a dormant oil in April. Don't go spraying everything, but if you have had a problem in the past, it would be wise to spray now. Dormant oil smothers the emerging insects and is a more environmentally sensitive approach than using true insecticides. Scale can appear on **andromeda, arborvitae, azalea, euonymus, holly, lilac, magnolia, juniper, pine**, and **yew.**

## Helpful Hints

*1* Sometimes it is worth a weekly visit to your favorite nursery just to see what's new and exciting. Of course, you may want to leave your cash at home or all that excitement may just break the bank!

*2* If you place an order with a catalog company, be sure to read all the fine print regarding guarantees and the return or credit policy. Save all your shipping paperwork in a file. Most companies are very good about honoring their guarantees, but you will need to report any problems within the time allotted, and you will need all the paperwork to make a claim.

Other insects than can be prevented with a dormant oil include **gall, aphids,** and **mites. Scab**, a fairly common disease especially on anything in the rose family, should be controlled at budbreak and repeated every seven to ten days. Shrubs it may infect include **firethorn, cotoneaster, flowering quince,** and, of course, all **roses.**

## NOTES

# MAY

## PLANNING

Planning really takes a back seat in May to implementation. Plants are arriving in the mail, your visits to your favorite nursery for a bag of potting soil result in six more must-have shrubs and eight flats of flowers, and you find yourself bringing in big bunches of **lilacs** to enjoy the intoxicating scent. If you are still planning for more, you are either hiring a gardener or losing your mind . . . or both.

Plan some time to enjoy what you have created. May is such a magnificent month in the garden. So much is blooming, including a great deal of flowering shrubs. Late **azaleas** and many **rhododendrons,** pretty white flowered **deutzia,** and the many fabulous **lilacs**. Later in the month, look for lovely blooms on the **Japanese snowbell.** The more common one is a small tree, but there is a dwarf variety with the loveliest pink flowers that would count as a shrub. The spring-blooming **butterfly bush,** *Buddleia alternifolia*, is also blooming, and yes, it is attracting butterflies.

## PLANTING

Planting should be completed early in the month, especially for bare-root and balled-and-burlapped material. You definitely want to avoid transplanting anything at this late date. Once the plants are in leaf, it is not a good idea to dig them. Balled-and-burlapped shrubs at the nursery were more than likely dug at the right time, so you have a bit more flexibility with them.

Container material is very flexible and can be planted almost any time the ground is not frozen. Even so, it is much better to avoid extremes in temperature and plant as close to the ideal planting times as possible. May **is still acceptable** (and even June), but you may have to take **extra precautions** with watering during hot summer months as later-planted shrubs will not have much of a chance to get a root system established before hot weather sets in.

## WATERING

Watering can become an issue in May. Water in newly planted material as soon as it gets in the ground. May can be very wet and rainy, or hot and dry almost like summer. If that is the case, you will have to keep a close eye on newly planted shrubs. The use of organic mulch will help to retain soil moisture and to moderate soil temperature fluctuations.

Established plant material will rarely need water in May, but an unusually hot and dry month may warrant some supplemental watering, especially to retain flowers.

## FERTILIZING

If you fertilized in March or April with a granular fertilizer, there is no need to fertilize in May. If you did not fertilize yet, you can still do so.

If you are following a regular fertilizer program using a diluted water-soluble fertilizer, follow the directions on the label. Many of these programs require fertilizer application once a month. If so, apply your liquid fertilizer one month after the April application.

## PRUNING

There is a lot of pruning to do in May. **Lilacs** are actually best pruned while they are in bloom. This is because they produce so much of their new growth while producing flowers. If you wait until bloom has completely finished, you will be removing a great deal of the new growth. If you prune before the new growth comes out, you will be removing the buds. Pruning while it's in bloom is a good compromise. Be sure to take out the oldest growth from the bottom and thin out the suckers.

Rhododendrons get pruned right after they bloom. Be sure to take the tallest branches and prune them into the center of the shrub, at the main trunk or a major "V." They will be better able to fill in from the center. It is a good idea to leave some obvious growing points below the pruning cut to ensure a more rapid filling in of the shrub.

Your **Vanhouttei spirea** and the pretty little **pearl bush** can both be pruned as they finish blooming, but not everything needs pruning every year.

 PESTS

Lacebug may show up in May on **andromeda, azalea,** and **rhododendron. Rhododendron borer** is controlled in mid-May. **Leaf miners** show up on a variety of things including **boxwood, lilac,** and **holly. Azalea white fly** can show up on **azaleas, rhododendrons,** and **mountain laurel. Pine sawfly** devours **mugo pine** by the middle of the month. Check with your Cooperative Extension Office for current control recommendations.

## Helpful Hints

*1* There is a wonderful **rhododendron** and **azalea** garden at the Rutgers Gardens in North Brunswick. It is worth a visit, actually several visits, since there are many different plants blooming from late April into late May. It is a very romantic spot.

*2* While you are there, you may also want to visit the **lilac** grove. This is a very old collection with many now-rare varieties. It has been recently renovated and the varieties identified.

*3* As a final note, they have a two-day open house event over Mother's Day Weekend. Included is a wonderful plant sale where you can often find the rare and unusual. Proceeds go to support the garden.

## NOTES

# JUNE
## Shrubs

 ## PLANNING

By the month of June, planning consists of seeing magical things in bloom and adding them to your wish list. You may want to make note of what you see in bloom here and there. If you are unable to ask for a name to identify the plant in question, take a picture.

If you don't happen to have a camera on hand, take notes. Describe the flowers, including shape, number of petals, the number of flowers appearing together in a cluster, the color, and anything interesting or unusual.

Notice whether the leaves appear two together, opposite each other on the stem, or alternate one on one side and the next leaf on the opposite side further along the branch. Sometimes the leaves appear in whorls, or several leaves surrounding the stem. **The size and shape of the leaves are important as well as the leaf edge.** It may be smooth, indented, or finely toothed. If the leaf is hairy or fuzzy, that can be significant as well as its color, including any variegation.

With enough information, you should be able to identify your mystery plant with the help of a good reference book or a knowledgeable nursery professional.

 ## PLANTING

Planting in June really should be limited to container-grown nursery stock. Container-grown material has the entire root system in a neat package. As a result, the roots are disturbed very little when you pull the plant out of the pot and pop it into the ground. You may want to provide some shade for newly planted shrubs if they are going into a very sunny location. That will give them some respite from blazing sun while they settle into their new home. Make sure you provide a thick layer of organic mulch. This will help to moderate fluctuations in soil temperature as well as to retain soil moisture.

For details regarding soil preparation and planting instructions, refer to the chapter introduction.

 ## WATERING

As always, you will want to water anything newly planted immediately after planting. Make sure that these new plants have plenty of moisture in the rootball prior to planting. If the rootball is very dry, it may repel water. This will make it particularly difficult to know if the rootball has been adequately saturated after it is in the ground. It is much wiser to make sure it is not dry prior to plant-

ing, especially in the hotter weather of June.

 ## FERTILIZING

You should not fertilize newly planted shrubs. Those that bloomed in spring can sometimes benefit from a sidedressing after they finish flowering. In better soils, the application of some compost to the soil surface, covered by a thick organic mulch, may be adequate.

If you are following a liquid fertilizer program, it often requires a monthly application of a diluted solution of water-soluble fertilizer thirty days after the previous application. Be sure to follow instructions on the product that you have chosen.

## PRUNING

June is the time to prune those shrubs that finished blooming in late May or early in the month of June. Shrubs that fall into that category may include some **rhododendrons,** the spring-blooming **butterfly bush,** *Buddleia alternifolia,* the wonderfully fragrant **mock-orange** *Philadelphus,* and **mountain laurel** (another beauty for the shady nook).

By this time, most shrubs have produced the bulk of their foliage. You should take into consideration that the plant has just spent a lot of energy making these leaves. A major pruning overhaul will set the plants back and may even reduce or eliminate next year's bloom. Paying attention to selective pruning techniques that maintain the plant's natural growth habit as well as some current season's growth will prove more satisfactory in the long run.

If the plant is really out of hand, you may want to take the most obnoxious branches out this year, up to 1/3 of the growth, with carefully chosen cuts. Repeat the process next year and even the following year until it is down to where you want it.

## PESTS

**Scale** that has turned up now, possibly in spite of a dormant oil treatment in April, needs to be controlled. Scale can appear on **andromeda, arborvitae, azalea, euonymus, holly, lilac, juniper, magnolia, pine, yew,** and maybe even a few other things. **Lacebug** on **andromeda, azalea,** and **rhododendron** may warrant a second treatment. Nasty bagworms can appear on a great many things. Treat in mid-June to control the critters before they have had a chance to make their very protective bags. **Black vine weevil** prefers **rhododendrons, azaleas,** and **yew.** The best time to control this rugged creature begins in June. A serious infestation may require repeated treatments until mid-September. Check with your Cooperative Extension Office for current control recommendations.

## NOTES

_____
_____
_____
_____
_____
_____
_____
_____
_____
_____
_____
_____
_____

# JULY
## Shrubs

## PLANNING

I hope by this time you are putting your feet up and enjoying the summer. There are a bunch of shrubs that are good for summer color. So many easily recognized shrubs bloom in the spring that summer bloomers are often neglected. Make a note of what you see blooming in the summer months and then seek it out during planting season. As you rock in your hammock drinking iced tea with mint from the garden, you will really appreciate shrubs that bring summer flowers with a minimum of care.

The many varieties of **butterfly bush** are among the most common summer bloomers, but don't forget the hard working **rose-of-Sharons.** Tucked into a tight spot, they get out of control quickly, but located where their wild ways don't cause problems they will gift you with flowers most of the summer. *Abelia grandiflora* gets tiny pale pink flowers in such profusion they can have significant impact. The low growing **St. Johnswort** produces large, yellow, buttercup-like flowers throughout the summer, even in dry weather. *Aesculus parviflora*, **bottlebrush buckeye,** sends out white flower clusters in mid-July. Any of these will add to your summer display with minimal maintenance. Since they all bloom on new growth, they can all be pruned in the early spring to keep them under control. At this time of year, all you have to do is sit back and smell the rose-of-Sharons.

## PLANTING

If you feel compelled to plant some container-grown shrub that you can't live without, be prepared to baby the little thing for the rest of the season. July is often brutally hot. If you come across something you have to buy, consider holding it in a somewhat shady nook out of the hot sun and strong wind, where you can keep it well watered. Early September is a good time to plant many things, so if you can hold it until then, you are increasing the odds in your (and the plant's) favor.

If you are determined to plant now, read the planting directions in the chapter introduction.

## WATERING

Some supplemental watering will probably be necessary in July. Try not to get water on the foliage; it encourages disease. If you are soaking the ground, you can water after the sun goes down. If you are using overhead watering, which will wet the foliage, wait until early morning. That way the foliage will dry up quickly when the sun comes out rather than sitting damp all night.

Water shrubs deeply to encourage deep rooting, a healthier plant, and less work.

## FERTILIZING

Don't apply any type of fertilizer when the temperature is above 85 degrees Fahrenheit. If you are following a monthly program using a diluted water-soluble fertilizer, consider cutting the concentration in half or skipping it altogether. At least wait for a cooler day. Fertilizer can burn the roots much more easily in hot weather.

## PRUNING

Summer pruning definitely includes the removal of dead blooms on summer blooming shrubs. **Butterfly bushes,** for example, will produce flowers right up until frost. However, if the dead flower spikes are left on the plant, you will get less additional blooms, they will be smaller, and the impact of the fresh blooms will be lost in the enormous display of brown flowers.

You may also want to remove the occasional branch that has grown in an entirely wrong direction. While midsummer is not a great time to do major shrub pruning of any kind, the removal of offending branches does more good than harm.

## PESTS

Watch out for **Japanese beetles.** They will seek out your **roses** as well as many other things. If you find them on your shrubs, you can often handpick them. If you can't seem to get a handle on them this way, you may need to resort to spray. Continue to treat **black vine weevil** if it is feeding on your **rhododendrons, azaleas,** and **yew** bushes. **Mites** are more likely to show up in hot dry weather. They can destroy a **dwarf Alberta spruce.** Look for a pale yellow cast to the needles and dust that moves. When you have a mite infestation, sometimes early in the morning you can see spider-like webbing that's not very sophisticated in design. **White fly** may be showing up at this time. It gets on a variety of plants including **azaleas** and **mountain laurel.** Look for a cloud of small white flying insects when the plant is slightly moved. For control measures for all of these pests, check with your Cooperative Extension Office.

## NOTES

_____

_____

_____

_____

_____

_____

_____

_____

_____

_____

_____

_____

_____

# AUGUST

##  PLANNING

Fall planting projects are probably beginning to creep in around the edges of your summer vacation. You may be coming to grips with the fact that a certain tree, shrub, perennial, or patch of lawn is simply not doing the job. That wonderful flowering shrub you spotted in full bloom in April, May, June, or July may be just the thing to take up the slack.

Planting in early September is best accomplished with some forethought in August. Maybe you have decided that you just cannot tolerate the ugly chain link fence another day and you want a row of something to cover it up. A visit to your favorite nursery may be in order. This may be for inspiration, to plan project costs, or to place an order.

The window for planting in the fall is not long. You should allow a minimum of six weeks for plants to produce some roots to help them get through the winter. **You should wait until after the weather changes** from brutal summer heat to warm September days with cool nights. Having everything on hand when the time is right makes the process go more smoothly and gives the plants their best possible shot to thrive.

While you are making decisions about what to plant where, don't forget to look around at what is blooming late in the season. *Franklinia alatamaha* can be considered a small shrub-like tree or a tree-like shrub. Either way, it produces large white blooms starting in August and often lasting until frost. *Hydrangea paniculata* 'Grandiflora', more affectionately known as **peegee hydrangea,** produces clusters of flowers in August that dry on the plant and can last until spring. The large flowered *Hydrangea macrophylla* also produces its large blooms earlier in the month. The pretty blue flowers on the **blue mist spirea** isn't really *Spirea* at all. It is in the genus *Caryopteris*, but it's very pretty no matter what you call it.

##  PLANTING

You really don't want to be planting anything in August when the weather will be almost perfect in September. Give yourself a break.

##  WATERING

Recently planted shrubs will need more attention than long-established ones. Some plants are more drought tolerant than others. The summer-blooming **tamarix** and the yellow-flowered **St. Johnswort** are both more tolerant of dry conditions than many other more traditional shrubs.

##  FERTILIZING

You do not want to fertilize in August any more than in July. It is too hot. If you are following a monthly application of a water-soluble fertilizer, wait to apply it on a day when the temperature is below 85 degrees Fahrenheit and cut the concentration in half.

##  PRUNING

Some of your evergreen shrubs may have sent out some branches that are now in the way. Removing these is not a problem, but save major pruning until early spring.

Continue to cut back dead blooms on **butterfly bushes** to encourage production of more flowers. **Rose-of-Sharon** continues to produce blooms, but you may want to remove developing seed pods. When these pods release their seeds, you can get seedlings cropping up everywhere. Many spring-flowering shrubs including **lilac, azalea,** and **rhododendron** have already set flower buds for next spring's bloom. Pruning them now, even lightly, will reduce your spring display.

# PESTS

The cooler August nights are an incentive for the leaf disease **powdery mildew** to get started. If you see gray or whitish blotches on the leaves, you may want to spray to control it. In truth, it is very common on **lilacs** but hardly worth controlling. If you think of it as "fall color," you might be able to tolerate it without resorting to fungicides. While it can pretty much cover the leaves by the end of the season, it doesn't seem to have any serious impact on next year's display.

**Bagworms** are in their little bags by now and coming out to devour whatever branch to which they happen to be attached. They seem to really prefer evergreens, but the little nasties have a diverse appetite and can appear on a wide range of ornamentals. The bags protect the critters from any pesticide, so yank them off and drop them into a can of bleach, or bag them in plastic and throw them away. Do not just drop them on the ground.

**Mites** and **white flies** will increase in numbers if not controlled. A harsh spray of water will help control the mites. **Scale** may still warrant control. For control recommendations, check with your Cooperative Extension Office.

## Helpful Hints

*1* The flowers from the pink or blue *Hydrangea macrophylla* (**hydrangea**) and the **peegee hydrangea** can be cut while fresh and dried. They last a very long time.

*2* The blue flowers from the **blue mist spirea** make excellent cut flowers and look particularly lovely as filler for roses.

## NOTES

# SEPTEMBER

##  PLANNING

Definitely plan to get your last major push of the year accomplished in September. Bulbs get planted in October, but tree, shrubs, perennials, and even grass should all be planted now, so roll up your sleeves and get ready. Make sure anything you intend to plant is kept moist while waiting for the perfect planting day. Store plant material out of the sun and the wind to prevent the soil and the foliage from drying out.

Plants that do a magical thing with berries come into their glory at this time of year. Top of the list is **beauty berry,** a *Callicarpa* species. The shrub with arching branches of small, vividly purple berries is a show stopper. **Chionanthus,** or **fringetree,** can be a small tree or a large shrub. The blue-black clusters of berries are very attractive to the eye as well as to birds. Since this plant gets lovely flowers in the spring, it is a shrub with more than one season of appeal.

That is not to say there aren't any flowers showing up in September. *Franklinia alatamaha* is a small tree when grown with a single trunk but is often a multitrunked shrub. The large white flowers appear in late summer until frost. You will still find flowers on your **butterfly bushes, peegee hydrangea,** and **blue mist spirea.**

If you want to take the time to hunt for another oddball, look for *Kirengeshoma palmata* (yellow **waxbells**). These have a maple-like leaf and small yellow flowers in September on arching branches. It is shrubby in habit but is sometimes listed as a perennial hardy to Zone 5. It may be worth the search because it is shade tolerant and prefers acid soils. It is a perfect match for your **azaleas** and **hostas** but will give autumn color.

##  PLANTING

Planting in September follows all the same rules as spring planting (see the chapter introduction for planting information). You may want to wait until summer heat has shifted to classic September weather. Sometimes that happens in the last week in August, but sometimes the hot weather holds until the middle of the month.

If you have to dig in very dry soil, you want to water the ground the day before you intend to dig. Let the water run at a slow trickle to allow the water to soak in rather than running off the surface. If the ground is really dry, it may take a while.

##  WATERING

Water newly planted shrubs thoroughly immediately after planting.

Additional watering needed for established or recently planted shrubs depends on how much it is raining. September is hurricane season, and one good storm can rewet the ground to capacity. It is just as possible that the ground will stay dry into October. Air temperature tends to drop significantly this month, compared to summer heat waves, so **you may not need to water as frequently.**

##  FERTILIZING

You do not want to encourage a burst of new growth now that may not be fully dormant when winter hits. Avoid granular fertilizer applications.

If you are following a water-soluble fertilizer program, this should be your last application. Applying it earlier in the month is better than later. As a general rule, once the temperature drops to 60 degrees Fahrenheit or below, don't even apply the liquids.

# PRUNING

Pruning in September should be limited to removal of dead branches, faded flowers, and developing seeds.

Those plants that have produced branches that are threatening to passers-by should be trimmed. The weight of ice and snow will only make the situation worse.

**Save major revamping or shaping until the right time in the spring.** Those shrubs that produce flowers on old growth will have the blooms removed if you prune now. The best time to prune in most cases is right after they finish blooming.

Shrubs grown primarily for their foliage can be pruned in early spring as can those that produce flowers on new growth. Some evergreens can be tricky in that they prefer not to be pruned. The preferred approach is to pinch the new growth in spring. Keep it light now.

# PESTS

September is an important time for pest control. If you have been battling a serious mite infestation, now is the time to get your best control. **Hemlocks** are generally tall trees, but if you have a hemlock hedge that you keep sheared, you may want to check for woolly adelgid. You may see boxelder bugs in large number if you have a **box elder** tree anywhere in your yard. They are more scary than dangerous, but if they are making you crazy, now is when you need to provide control. Check with the Cooperative Extension Office for current control recommendations.

# NOTES

_____

_____

_____

_____

_____

_____

_____

_____

_____

_____

# OCTOBER

## Shrubs

 PLANNING

You can expect the best display of fall color in the third week of October. You may want to take that into consideration when planning your garden. As flowering comes to an end, the change to fall color is one more blast of excitement.

You will have to do some searching at this time if you want plants to add to your autumn display. They do their neon bright foliage thing when most people have finished visiting the local nursery, so there is not much incentive for nursery professionals to carry them.

Some shrubs with good fall color include:

- **Fothergilla:** This is a great little plant with pretty bottlebrush white flowers that bloom at the same time as the native **dogwood,** and it has fabulous fall color, too.

- **Burning bush:** This plant is pretty ho-hum most of the year, but the brilliant fall foliage makes up for it. Burning bush gets orange berries—sometimes quite a few. They become noticeable when the foliage falls off.

- **Oak leaf hydrangea:** This one gets red foliage, which is rather dramatic considering the size of the leaves.

- **Royal azalea:** *Rhododendron schlippenbachii* is deciduous, but turns yellow, orange, red, and burgundy before the leaves fall.

- **Red chokeberry:** *Aronia arbutifolia* gets fabulous red fall foliage, and the red berries persist all winter.

- **Virginia Sweetspire:** *Itea virginica* is a shade-tolerant shrub with white or sometimes pink, bottlebrush flowers in the spring and red fall foliage.

Fruits that bring color in October:

- **Winterberry hollies:** These get an enormous number of fruits. Most are red, but a few varieties can be yellow.

- **Black chokecherry:** *Aronia melanocarpa* has blackish purple fruits that persist well into winter. It has nice fall color as well.

- **Sapphire berry:** *Symplocos paniculata* is another small tree or large shrub. Far from common in the trade, its unique blue fruit makes it worth the hunt.

## PLANTING

If you find something magical in a container, you have a very good chance of it doing well if you get it in the ground as soon as possible.

Conditions are best for root growth when the soil temperature will be above 45 degrees Fahrenheit for six weeks. Once the temperature drops below that, all root growth stops. It's better to plant earlier in October than later. You can't count on a mild fall with a large enough window for the plants to become sufficiently established. Remember that early December may be fall-like or in the single digits.

Mulch the ground heavily to moderate fluctuations in soil temperature. Follow planting instructions outlined in the chapter introduction.

## WATERING

If you are holding any plants in containers, they will need to be watered. This will not be needed as frequently as in hot summer weather, but plants are still using water, and a pot has a limited supply.

Once you plant something, it needs to be watered immediately. This is regardless of whether the plant or the ground is wet. The purpose of watering at the time of planting is not just to provide moisture for the plant but also to help the soil flow into all the air spaces around the roots.

Unless the weather is unusually dry, you should not need to water any established shrubs this month.

## FERTILIZING

Do not fertilize anymore. The last thing you want to do is encourage tender new growth that will get burnt with the first frost. The next time you should fertilize is late March or early April.

 ## PRUNING

Pruning can also stimulate new growth, so you won't be pruning anymore either.

 ## PESTS

Luckily, by October the pests have pretty much slowed down. If you are raking up leaves covered in **powdery mildew** (this is very common on **lilacs**), you should bag them and send them out with the trash. You don't need a load of inoculum in the yard waiting to start the disease again next year. Getting rid of the infected foliage may not prevent the disease, but you don't need to help it along, either.

## Helpful Hints

*1* If you plant shrubs with berries for the birds, you may want to include some other features in the garden. A source of water for drinking and bathing is important, along with lots of cover where they can feel safe. Shrubs, grasses, and tangled vines are all places they can hide.

*2* The worst time for birds, when food is scarce, is the early spring when all the seeds and fruits are gone. When the berries are gone, you may want to supplement feedings with birdseed, suet, or even peanut butter. Once you start feeding them, it is important to continue as they become dependent on a food supply. If you choose to stop, wait until there is plenty of food around naturally so they don't go hungry.

 ## NOTES

## PLANNING

By November, you should be wrapping up any fall projects. Leaf raking is important now. You need to rake leaves off the ground covers, but they can go under the shrubs as a winter mulch. If you compost your leaves, you can use them as a soil amendment for future planting projects.

Anything with interesting bark becomes a lead player after leaf drop. The peely bark and stiff branches of the **oak leaf hydrangea** are interesting if not quite graceful. The contorted branches of **Harry Lauder's walking stick** go practically unnoticed until the leaves fall off. **Japanese maple** *Acer palmatum* 'Dissectum' has branches that are weeping and somewhat twisted, creating an amazing silhouette on a mature specimen. Red or yellow shoots on the **red** and **yellow twigged dogwoods** are completely hidden while in leaf. They are quite striking in the winter landscape, especially when the ground is covered in snow.

## PLANTING

You should not be planting in November. If a healthy containerized plant comes

## Helpful Hints

**1** It is this time of year when an appreciation for evergreens really takes hold. For small yards or beds close to the house, there is a whole world of dwarf and unusual evergreens. The U.S. National Arboretum in Washington D.C. has an entire collection of dwarf conifers. It is well worth a visit.

**2** If you can't get there, there is a book titled *Dwarf & Unusual Conifers Coming of Age* that features the collection and provides information. *Dwarf & Unusual Conifers Coming of Age* gives the best idea of the collection's beauty and diversity without making the trip.

your way, however, you may be better off planting it than trying to keep it above ground. Give it a little protection from the wind, and if it has any size to it, you may want to stake it as well.

## WATERING

Water anything that you have just planted. Unless there are drought conditions, you should not have to water outdoors. On the other hand, plants should not go into the dead of winter dry, so if there is a chance the ground is in a drought state, water deeply one more time

## FERTILIZING

Do not fertilize at this time.

## PRUNING

**Winterberry hollies** are the only thing you want to consider pruning. Birds will eat all the berries before the holidays, so if you want berried branches, cut what you want and store them in a bucket of water outdoors in a protected nook.

## PESTS

Pests are not active at this time. Remember to keep rings of mulch away from the trunks of your shrubs (think "donut"). Piling mulch against the trunk allows hungry, small furry creatures to hide there and feed on the bark.

# DECEMBER
## Shrubs

 PLANNING

**Dwarf Alberta spruce** is a fairly common small evergreen used as a Christmas tree. If you plan to get one, you should also plan what you are going to do with this little guy after the holiday. As with all balled trees for the holiday, you should pick out the spot and dig the hole before you get the tree. Store the soil where it will not freeze. Cover the hole with a piece of plywood so no one falls into it. Then you will be all ready to plant after the holiday. If you wait until you are done enjoying its beauty with lights and baubles, the ground may be frozen.

There is, of course, the requisite holiday shopping to do. Here are some gift ideas:

- A **gift certificate** to one of the more exotic catalog companies along with a copy of the catalog. It will provide hours of planning and dreaming to help relieve cabin fever. Maybe combine it with a good reference book on shrubs.

- **Tickets** to Duke Gardens. The seven greenhouses on the Duke Estate in Somerville are breathtaking with lush exotic plants and flowers. Visiting is a great way to overcome the winter blahs.

## Helpful Hints

Finding a movie to recommend that focuses on shrubs has been a challenge. After an extensive search, I came up with *Lilac Time*. I have never seen this film, but it stars Gary Cooper and was made in 1928. It is a bit of a love story, with a girl in a grove of **lilacs.** It takes place during WWI. Cooper plays an airplane pilot, and it got 8.5 stars out of 10. Love, war, lilacs, and Gary Cooper. It's got to be good.

- **Paid tuition** for the Home Gardener's School held at Rutgers University in New Brunswick. This is an entire day of classes taught by Rutgers faculty, Cooperative Extension professionals, and local experts. It is held in March, but the schedules are out well in advance.

- A really good pair of **hand pruners** and **long handled loppers.**

- An insulated pair of sturdy **work gloves** for chilly, early-spring pruning.

 PLANTING

It's cold! You shouldn't be planting anything in December.

 WATERING

Water your containerized Christmas tree as needed. Nothing else should require water now.

 FERTILIZING

You won't need to fertilize until spring.

 PRUNING

The only shrubs you may need to prune at this time of year are your **American hollies.** They produce the red berries on new growth, so you will not eliminate next year's crop by taking this year's crop now. To use attractive branches for a wreath or centerpiece, cut what you want and store them in water in a cool location. Never take more than $1/3$ of the branches from the tree. Prune with attention to its appearance. Use oasis in the arrangement or wreath to keep it fresh. Misting will help a little.

 PESTS

Pests are not a problem at this time.

# CHAPTER TEN

# Trees

*What comes to mind when you think of the word "tree?" Giant sequoias? The mighty oak? A deep, dark forest? Trees are often taken for granted. They provide homes for creatures, shade, protection from the elements, privacy, beauty, and increased property value.*

First, it's important to choose the correct tree for the planting location. Large trees will need room to grow. Placing them too close to the house will cause problems sooner or later. Trees come in many sizes. For example, the small, flowering **red buckeye** (*Aesculus pavia*) is a close relative of the magnificent **horse chestnut** (*Aesculus hippocastanum*). These trees have appealing similarities, but their sizes require different planting considerations.

The **red buckeye** and **horse chestnut** have similar attractive palmate (umbrella-like) leaves and similar flowers, although the red buckeye's are red (or pink). The red buckeye gets to be about 20 feet (maximum about 35 feet, but that is rare) and blooms in about three or four years. The horse chestnut eventually reaches 75 feet but will not produce a flower until it is about twenty-five-years-old. Typical suburban lots of 50 by 100 feet and the many townhouses that have popped up in recent years will do just fine with the red buckeye. A horse chestnut would be magnificent by an enormous home being built on several acres in the countryside.

The choice between **evergreen** and **deciduous** trees will make an enormous difference in your landscape. Consider evergreens on the north side of your home for winter protection. Evergreens are critical to providing winter interest to the landscape but add little diversity throughout the year. They have no flowers and no autumn color (green, but not a broad range of the color spectrum). They block winter wind, create year-round shade, and when properly located, reduce energy costs.

Deciduous trees produce flowers, although some are more conspicuous than others. Used on the south side of your home, they shade the house in the summer and let in winter sun when it is greatly appreciated. Autumn color can be spectacular, and fruits or seeds can be attractive and provide food for the birds. On the flip side, the leaves need to be raked, and some fruits drop from limbs (or birds) and leave stains.

Deciduous trees over a swimming pool keep the water from warming up, and all those leaves are a mess in the fall. If you want some part of your yard to receive full sun in the summer, perhaps for a vegetable garden or to get the perfect tan, you need to keep that in mind when laying out your plans. If your family has its own touch football team, leave plenty of open space. A garden "room" can be created with the theme of your choice by partitioning off an area with trees. **Your tree choices have to work for your home and with you, personally.** Take time with your decisions so you will have no regrets.

## PREPARING TO PLANT

Take into consideration the environmental conditions of your landscape. Wet ground is always the biggest challenge. A tree that is intolerant of wet ground will quickly die in that environment. Stick with **willows, red** or **swamp maples, black gum, sweet gum,** and the **bald cypress. Arborvitae** will also tolerate wet feet but stays on the smaller side. It can reach a maximum of 60 feet but usually stays much smaller.

Dig a $5 hole for a 50¢ plant. With inflation, perhaps we need to scale that up a bit for large trees, but the idea is still the same. Be prepared to incorporate an abundance of organic matter into the soil you have removed. In sandy soils, that should be all you need. In heavy clay soil, you can add organic matter and sand in a 2:1 ratio. **Never add sand alone to clay.** You will end up with something like concrete.

When there is concern about wet ground, you should probably do a drainage test. Dig your planting hole and then fill it with water. If the water sits there for hours, you may have a problem. Sometimes you may come across a hardpan of shale that can be broken up with a pick. Digging the hole even deeper and then placing stone in the bottom will create a reservoir for excess water. If it is a minor problem, you can plant the rootball a bit high and then cover it with organic mulch.

## PLANTING

First, it's a good idea to have a helper. Even if you are strong as a bull, you cannot possibly hold the tree in place when planting and walk all the way around to see if it is straight by yourself. The larger the tree, the more important it is to have someone else around in case you find yourself in an unexpected jam.

Trees need to be planted at the same depth they were growing in the ground before they were dug and wrapped in burlap. If they are container trees, they must be at the same height they were in the pot.

Once the tree is positioned, fill the hole back up with the amended soil so it is at the proper height. If you have loosened the soil significantly below the rootball, you may want to plant just a bit high to compensate for settling later. Tamp down the loosened soil beneath the ball to minimize settling. Natural burlap can stay in the hole, but plastic burlap must be removed. **All strings, ropes, and wires must come off,** especially those around the trunk.

Fill the hole back up with amended soil and tamp it down firmly. Try not to press down excessively on the rootball itself as this will break roots and lessen the tree's chance for survival.

Small deciduous trees will probably do fine without staking, but even small evergreens should be staked since the needled branches will catch the wind easily. **To stake your tree:**

- Hammer three stakes into the ground, uniformly spaced around the tree.

- Take an old garden hose and cut three 18-inch sections. Thread strong string or rope through the pieces of hose.

- Wrap the hose on the outside of the trunk opposite a stake.

- Tie the string securely to the stake. The hose will protect the trunk from the string or rope cutting into the bark. Do this on all three sides.

**Container-grown trees** may develop girdling roots if they have stayed in a container for a bit longer than they should. Carefully examine the root sys-

# Trees

tem when you remove the tree from the container. If the roots travel in a circle around the outside of the pot, you will need to take some corrective action. You may be able to tease the roots apart and spread them so they radiate from the tree. This will only be effective if the roots are only moderately overcrowded.

If the roots are so tangled they cannot be separated, you must cut through them by slicing in a downward motion in several places on the outside of the rootball. Start out by only cutting the surface roots. Remove all the unattached pieces and spread out the remaining roots. If they are still severely tangled, you may have to go deeper. While this may be painful to you, these roots will surely kill the tree if allowed to go unchecked.

## PRUNING

Pruning major limbs from mature trees can be done almost anytime it is necessary, but during summer or winter dormancy is always best. In the winter, you can really see the structure of the tree and what needs to be removed. Summer pruning gives a better idea of the shape and fullness the tree will have. Note: If you cannot remove a limb from the ground with a pole pruner, hire a professional. **Never attempt to remove**

**a full-sized tree yourself.** These are not do-it-yourself projects!

When making a pruning cut of a significant limb, it is important that you not cut the "collar." The collar wood is where the smaller limb joins a larger limb or the trunk. **The collar wood is like the skin at a bent elbow.** The bark is bunched up inside the angle where the limb attaches, but in the corresponding area beneath the limb the bark stretches out. None of this bark should be removed. When the limb is off, the end should be very close to circular. If you cut into the collar wood, the wound and the end of the trunk begins to get oval. You will have removed the collar wood that is most efficient in closing the wound, leaving a larger wound that takes even longer to recover.

**When taking off a limb that requires sawing, follow these three steps:**

*1* Go out about 1 foot to 18 inches on the limb from where you want the final cut. **Saw up from the bottom** until the saw binds from the weight of the branch pressing on the saw.

*2* **Go out 2 more inches and saw down.** The weight of the branch will pull down, eventually causing the branch to snap off. The break will give way at the cut you made going up. This prevents the downward cut from peeling off the bark all the way

down the trunk and essentially killing the tree.

*3* **Saw at the proper location** at the base of the limb, without cutting the collar wood. With the weight of the limb gone, you should be able to make a clean cut. Once the limb is removed, do not paint it, tar it, or cover it in concrete. Those treatments just seal in moisture and disease.

**Do not** perform limb removal from a ladder. **Do not** do this from sitting on a limb in the tree. You may be able to do it with a pole pruner from the ground, but no shenanigans. Do you know what a dangling limb in a tree is called? A widowmaker!! Be smart. Be safe.

## WATERING

This chapter contains month-to-month specifics on watering trees as action is needed. In general, **watering needs are dependent on several factors.** Even in the heat of summer, a mature tree needs much less attention than one planted in spring or even last year. However, trees need an occasional deep penetrating watering to allow the entire root system to get a drink. Allow a hose to flow at a trickle at the base of the tree and then in different spots between the trunk and the drip line (the outermost point of the branches). This will allow water to reach

# Trees

the entire root system. A thorough watering like this should only be done **once a week to ten days** even under very dry conditions. Younger trees, with smaller roots, will need less penetrating but somewhat more frequent watering.

The size of the trees makes a difference too. At times when water resources are low, you should consider planting smaller trees as they will get established faster. If watering restrictions are in place, remember it is better to water one tree thoroughly than a few drops on each. If you are limited to using water from a bucket, (either rainwater from a barrel or overflow shower water, cooking water, etc.) it is better to pour 5 gallons on one tree each day than to just wet the surface.

Trees will still need the occasional watering in dry weather, but mulch minimizes evaporation. Sandy soil will need more water than heavier soils, especially at the shore where the salt component adds to the stress of trees. Attention to soil preparation at the time of planting can compensate to some degree for sandy soil. **The addition of copious amounts of organic matter will help sandy soil** hold on to available moisture. Plus, the regular addition of organic mulch will allow worms to continually draw organic matter down into the soil.

**Caution:** If you build up or dig out 6 inches or more of soil from around your established trees, it can kill them. While mulching is great for weed control, soil moisture, and even easier mowing, piling mulch up around the trunk can cause just as much trouble. Think "donut." Put a circle of mulch around the trunk but not right up to the trunk. Create a well between the mulch and the trunk so the bark doesn't rot. On young trees this is especially important because otherwise small critters such as mice and chipmunks can feed on the bark all winter under the protection of the mulch.

## FERTILIZING

October will be your main fertilizing month for deciduous trees. When the time comes, you will need to figure out the amount of fertilizer to apply. **First, measure the diameter of the trunk** at breast height. For each inch, apply 2 to 4 pounds of 5-10-5 fertilizer. For a spring broadcast application, you will lean to the lighter end of the range, but October would be the time to fertilize on the heavier side if you feel the tree would benefit.

Locate the imaginary circle of the drip line. Establish another circle 2 feet out from the trunk itself. Within the confines of the two circles, you will want to **mark as many spots as possible,** 2 feet apart in all directions. Then count the number of spots you have marked. The fertilizer should be divided into the number of spots you have marked. Then make holes at each spot about 8 to 10 inches deep. You can use a crow bar, a bulb planter, or a soil sampling device that removes a core of soil. An auger used for planting bulbs may be the perfect tool for the job.

**Mix each portion of fertilizer with compost,** topsoil, or even the soil removed from the holes. **Fill the holes.** If the holes don't quite fill with the fertilizer mix, top off with soil or compost. Cover with the divot of sod you removed to make the hole.

## STEADFAST FRIENDS

Trees are more than ornaments. They are living, breathing neighbors that add greatly to our quality of life. The oldest and largest living thing on this earth is a tree. The right tree in the right spot will need very little attention once it gets established. Over the years, it will mark the passage of time and give back far more than it takes.

# Trees

## Shade Trees

| Common Name (Botanical Name) | Height | Flowers | Fall Color | Winter Interest |
|---|---|---|---|---|
| American Beech (*Fagus grandifolia*) | 70 feet | not showy | beautiful golden bronze | smooth bark |
| Black Gum (*Nyssa sylvatica*) | 50 feet | not showy | yellow, orange, scarlet, purple | |
| Chinese Chestnut (*Castanea mollissima*) | 60 feet | pale yellow long catkins | yellow to bronze | edible nuts |
| Dove Tree (*Davidia involucrata*) | 40 feet | large white bracts | not showy | |
| European Beech (*Fagus sylvatica*) many varieties | 60 feet | not showy | russet and golden bronze | smooth bark |
| European Hornbeam (*Carpinus betulus*) | 60 feet | not showy | yellow | "muscle" bark |
| Gingko (*Gingko biloba*) | 80 feet | not showy | bright yellow | spurred twigs |
| Golden Raintree (*Koelreuteria paniculata*) | 40 feet | bright yellow panicles | yellow | bladder-like pods |
| 'Heritage' River Birch (*Betula nigra 'Heritage'*) | 70 feet | not showy | dull yellow | peeling bark |
| Horse Chestnut (*Aesculus hippocastanum*) | 75 feet | large panicles white blooms | none | |
| Larch (*Larix decidua*) | 75 feet | not showy | deep yellow | |
| Mimosa (*Albizia julibrissin*) | 35 feet | pink fuzzballs | none | |
| Northern Catalpa (*Catalpa speciosa*) | 60 feet | bell-shaped, frilled, in panicles | not showy | |
| Paper Birch (*Betula papyrifera*) | 70 feet | not showy | brilliant yellow | white bark |
| Red Maple (*Acer rubrum*) | 60 feet | small red clusters | yellow to red | |
| Red Oak (*Quercus rubra*) | 75 feet | not showy | red | |
| Southern Catalpa (*Catalpa bignonioides*) | 40 feet | bell-shaped, frilled, spotted, in panicles | not showy | |

# Trees

## Shade Trees (continued)

| Common Name (*Botanical Name*) | Height | Flowers | Fall Color | Winter Interest |
|---|---|---|---|---|
| **Sugar Maple** (*Acer saccharum*) | 75 feet | greenish yellow | yellow, orange, red | |
| **Sweet Gum** (*Liquidamber styraciflua*) | 75 feet | not showy | yellow, purple, red | |
| **Tulip Tree** (*Liriodendron tulipifera*) | 90 feet | large yellow | vivid yellow | |
| **Willow Oak** (*Quercus phellos*) | 60 feet | not showy | yellow to russet red | |

## Smaller Trees

| Common Name (*Botanical Name*) | Height | Flowers | Fall Color | Winter Interest |
|---|---|---|---|---|
| **Chaste Tree** (*Vitex negundo*) | 15 feet | blue | not showy | |
| **Crabapple** (*Malus* varieties) | 25 feet | white, pink-red | not showy | |
| **Crape Myrtle** (*Lagerstroemia indica*) | 25 feet | white, pink, purple, red panicles | yellow, orange-red | persistant seed pods |
| **Dogwood** (*Cornus florida*) | 30 feet | pink or white bracts | red to reddish purple | red fall fruits |
| **Eastern Redbud** (*Cercis canadensis*) | 30 feet | deep pink pea-like blooms | dull yellow | |
| **Franklinia** (*Franklinia alatamaha*) | 20 feet | large white | red | |
| **Fringetree** (*Chionanthus virginicus*) | 20 feet | white fleecy panicles | dull yellow | September blue fruits |
| **Glossy Buckthorn** (*Rhamnus frangula* 'Asplenifolius') | 12 feet | not showy | yellow | |
| **Golden Chain Tree** (*Laburnum* x *watereri*) | 15 feet | yellow pendulous racemes | not showy | |
| **Harry Lauder's Walking Stick** (*Corylus avellana* 'Contorta') | 10 feet | golden catkins | not showy | contorted branches |
| **Japanese Maple** (*Acer palmatum*) | 25 feet | not showy | yellow, bronze, red | |

# Trees

## Smaller Trees (continued)

| Common Name (*Botanical Name*) | Height | Flowers | Fall Color | Winter Interest |
|---|---|---|---|---|
| **Japanese Snowbell** (*Styrax japonicum*) | 30 feet | small white bells | not showy | |
| **Japanese Stewartia** (*Stewartia pseudocamellia*) | 30 feet | large white | yellow, red | peeling bark |
| **Kousa Dogwood** (*Cornus kousa*) | 30 feet | white bracts | reddish purple | raspberry-like fruits |
| **Paperbark Maple** (*Acer griseum*) | 30 feet | not showy | russet red | peeling bark |
| **Pawpaw** (*Asimina triloba*) | 20 feet | hanging purple bells | yellow | October fruit |
| **PeeGee Hydrangea** (*Hydrangea paniculata*) | 25 feet | white to pink, large panicles | not showy | dried flowers |
| **Persian Witch Hazel** (*Parrotia persica*) | 25 feet | crimson stamens | yellow, orange-scarlet | peeling bark |
| **Red Bukeye** (*Aesculus pavia*) | 20 feet | pink to red panicles | none | |
| **Saucer Magnolia** (*Magnolia* x *soulangiana*) | 30 feet | pinkish purple buds, open white | not showy | |
| **Serviceberry** (*Amelanchier arborea*) | 20 feet | white showy sprays | yellow, orange-red | attractive bark |
| **Stellar Dogwood** (*Cornus kousa* x *C. florida*) | 25 feet | white or pink | red | |
| **Tamarisk** (spring blooming) (*Tamarix parviflora*) | 15 feet | tiny pink | not showy | |
| **Tamarisk** (summer blooming) (*T. ramosissima*) | 15 feet | pink | not showy | |
| **Vernal Witch Hazel** (*Hamamelis vernalis*) | 10 feet | yellow to pink | bright yellow | January flowers |
| **Weeping Mulberry** (*Morus alba* 'Pendula') | 15 feet | not showy | not showy | gnarled and weeping |
| **Witch Hazel** (*Hamamelis virginiana*) | 20 feet | small yellow | bright yellow | November flowers |

# Trees

## Evergreen Trees

| Common Name | Botanical Name | Height |
|---|---|---|
| American Holly | Ilex opaca | 50 feet |
| Arborvitae | Thuja occidentalis | 60 feet |
| Bald Cypress | Taxodium distichum | 70 feet |
| Cedar of Lebanon | Cedrus libani | 60 feet |
| Colorado Blue Spruce | Picea pungens | 60 feet |
| Concolor Fir | Abies concolor | 50 feet |
| Douglas Fir | Pseudotsuga menziesii | 80 feet |
| Eastern Redcedar | Juniperous virginiana | 50 feet |
| Eastern White Pine | Pinus strobus | 80 feet |
| Fraser Fir | Abies fraseri | 40 feet |
| Himalayan Pine | Pinus wallichiana | 80 feet |
| Japanese Cryptomeria | Cryptomeria japonica | 60 feet |
| Japanese Black Pine | Pinus thunbergiana | 40 feet |
| Lacebark Pine | Pinus bungeana | 50 feet |
| Serbian Spruce | Picea omorika | 60 feet |
| Swiss Stone Pine | Pinus cembra | 40 feet |
| Umbrella Pine | Sciadopitys verticillata | 30 feet |
| White Spruce | Picea glauca | 60 feet |

PLANNING

If it has become obvious that a particular tree has to go or that additional trees would be beneficial, you have time to do a little research to find the right tree to meet your needs. Suggestions to consider: Using a row of evergreens to **create a windbreak** on the north side of your property can make an enormous difference in the wind cutting across your yard. Foundation plantings of evergreens create insulation from the cold and wind. Your house will feel warmer, and you may reduce energy costs. If your house is very dark from all the trees, consider removing evergreens on the south side. This will **let in more light.** If you replace them with deciduous trees, you will still have privacy and shade in the summer.

Always keep in mind a **mixed planting.** A monoculture, even in a windbreak, has many disadvantages. Any disease or insect problem that may develop will become an epidemic in no time if it can race from one plant to the next. Also, while a straight uniform row of anything has its formal appeal, you can't count on it staying like that. If this one and that one die, smaller replacements will draw the eye, and the lack of uniformity will become the focal point. If you have a row

of this and that, any replacement that may be necessary will blend into the mix.

 PLANTING

If you were really organized, you dug the planting hole for your balled Christmas tree before the holidays. If you were super organized, you stored the soil from the hole someplace it wouldn't freeze. If you were not organized at all, but lucky, the ground has not yet frozen and you can dig the appropriate hole. If you are neither organized nor lucky, you can either use a pick-ax to break through the frozen top few inches of soil or **store the tree until you can plant it.**

Storing the tree means finding a protected nook, out of the wind, and not in a heat sink. An inside, west-facing corner may get so warm that the tree comes out of dormancy. You will want to **protect the rootball** by packing straw around it. Four bales of straw will hold it up then fill the gaps with loose straw. Use the loose straw over the top of the rootball as well. As soon as the ground thaws enough to dig, get it in the ground.

Be absolutely certain you have removed all string or rope holding the burlap around the trunk and all tags, wires, and strings. Plant the tree at the same depth

it was in the ground previously. Tamp the soil down firmly around the rootball without breaking any of the roots.

Make sure the rootball is not overly dry before planting. Placing a dry rootball into the ground almost guarantees a dead tree. **Water it thoroughly before planting.** If the water runs off, you may need to let it sit in a pan of water for a few hours to overcome "hydrophobia," the resistance very dry soil has to water uptake.

The tree will need to be staked on three sides. This is especially important in frozen ground as a rootball will act like a ball and socket in frozen ground and the result can be a severely tilted tree. It is also especially important on evergreens as the needled branches catch the wind and the ice and snow, increasing the chances of tilting. See the chapter introduction for instructions on staking.

WATERING

Even in January, you want to water your newly planted evergreen tree. This has more to do with allowing the soil to fill in any air spaces around the rootball than giving the tree a drink. After a thorough watering, mulch heavily with organic mulch. Remember to think "donut" and not pile the mulch directly up against the trunk.

 FERTILIZING

Trees should not be fertilized until they have been in the ground at least one full growing season. March of next year (fourteen months after planting) will be the right time to fertilize. The tree will have had a chance to get somewhat established by then and perhaps be ready to do some serious growing.

 PRUNING

Winter is a good time for pruning since that is when trees are truly dormant. See the chapter introduction for pruning instructions.

**Look around and assess the situation.** Deciduous trees are naked, and you can see all the limbs exposed, making your evaluation easier. Take note of limbs reaching close to your home. That is a primary way that squirrels gain access to the house. (Not the only way, but they don't need any help.)

 **Helpful Hints**

### Use Your Christmas Tree

*1* If you have a cut Christmas tree, lean it in a protected spot. Hang seed cones for the birds or stuff pine cones with bacon grease or peanut butter. The shelter and food will draw feathered friends into view.

*2* Remove branches of your holiday tree and use them as mulch over **strawberries.** The strength and natural arc of the woody branches keeps them up high enough to avoid smothering the delicate plants.

Dead limbs must come down for several reasons. If they fall down under the weight of ice and snow, they can do a tremendous amount of damage. Plus, the broken stumps left behind become an access point for disease.

PESTS

Keeping mulch away from tree trunks will eliminate protective cover for munching critters.

Deer are rather large to fall into the "pest" category, but they are certainly a problem for trees. See the discussion on deer in the December section of Roses.

NOTES

_____

_____

_____

_____

_____

_____

_____

_____

_____

_____

_____

# FEBRUARY
## Trees

##  PLANNING

There is a constant level of monitoring that goes on in the winter months. Storm damage takes its toll, and the squirrel in the attic draws your attention to the extra-long limb sticking out from the oak tree. These kinds of tree problems that need attention are best planned for earlier rather than later. Remember that all but the most simple limb removal requires a professional. Hiring one on the first day of spring is not going to happen. You need to get on their schedule **now!**

##  PLANTING

There is not any planting going on in February. The ground is frozen most of the month in most years. That is not to say we haven't experienced 80 degrees Fahrenheit in February, but any tree planted in that kind of weird weather is probably more at risk than if you planted one in frozen ground. Late March or early April is the ideal time to plant, so be patient. It will be here before you know it.

##  WATERING

It is the rare February that you need to water outdoors at all. It would be even more bizarre to have to water a mature deciduous or evergreen shade tree. Their roots go so deep that you rarely need to water even in the summer. However, winter drought is quietly deadly. Young trees may benefit from a drink if the ground is not frozen and there has been no precipitation. **A lack of rain or snow all winter can do damage to young trees** as well as to a lot of other things. If the ground is truly dry, you are better off pouring a few gallons of water onto your young trees than risk its death by drought.

##  FERTILIZING

Definitely do not fertilize now. Mature deciduous trees are best fertilized in October, or the next-best time is early April. Younger and smaller trees can wait to be fertilized in late March or early April.

##  PRUNING

Now this is where you can get busy. Limb removal while shade trees are dormant has two advantages:

*1* There is very little bleeding, or oozing of the sap, while the tree is dormant. The sap is mostly stored down in the roots to help push out the next crop of leaves come spring. Therefore it is not in the limbs or the trunk, ready to gush out.

*2* The limb structure is easy to see. You can readily identify what needs to come out and better assess the situation.

You absolutely should remove any dead branches. Limbs too close to the house or to utility wires may also need a trim. The stumps of limbs that have broken in the past should be made tidy. The broken stumps are ideal places for disease to invade the main trunk.

See the chapter introduction for details on pruning.

## PESTS

Most pests are dormant now.

If you are pruning to contain **maple** wilt, you are almost certainly not going to save the tree. You may, however, extend its life a few years by slowing down its spread. Those limbs where the leaves "flagged" or hung limp before dying should be removed. Take extra care to dip or swish the pruning tools in a 10 percent chlorine bleach solution between cuts. This will prevent spreading of the disease to healthy portions of the tree.

## Helpful Hints

*1* Remember that deciduous trees throw a lot of shade once the leaves come back in the spring. If you are pruning to allow more light for roses or a vegetable garden, be sure to keep that in mind when choosing the branches for removal.

*2* Now is also a good time to remove any vines that are creeping their way up your trees. Remember that vines are not a problem if they grow straight up a trunk, but if they go around or encircle a limb, they will eventually strangle it. It may be best if you remove vines that are beyond your reach (and your control) so they don't cause more serious problems down the road. **Wisteria** may be the worst offender. It is beautiful but can crush a four-by-four post. It can certainly kill a tree.

*3* If you are planning for March planting, consider mixing in a deciduous flowering tree with any planting of evergreens. A **dogwood** will appreciate the shade and will brighten up the green with a blast of spring color. The fabulous summer-blooming **crapemyrtle** has a rough time surviving our winters, but tucked into an evergreen nook, it will reward you with summer color for most of the summer months.

## NOTES

## PLANNING

If you have any planning to do around your trees, finish it up early in the month. By late March, you switch from thinking about what you want to get done, to doing it. If you decide you need a significant number of one particular type of tree, for a border planting perhaps, you may want to place an order with your favorite nursery early in the month. Remember to avoid monocultures to prevent a major wipe-out down the road from a destructive insect or disease. Besides, mixing up your planting is more interesting and has a much softer, more natural look.

## PLANTING

March is the time for planting, but you want to wait until the ground thaws and it is not too soggy. Working overly wet soil is not good for soil structure. It destroys the soil "aggregates"—bits of sand wrapped in silt, clay, and organic matter. These aggregates allow air spaces between them, which in turn allow drainage. Working wet soil destroys the soil structure, and you end up with something that has a consistency close to concrete rubble. **Remember to do a drainage test** for the

place you want to plant your trees, and dig a properly sized hole for each one. See the chapter introduction for specifics on how to plant.

## WATERING

Water your newly planted tree thoroughly. Sometimes watering causes tilting of the tree. The water shifts the soil as it fills up air spaces. If that happens, you probably should stake the tree and water again.

## FERTILIZING

You do not need to fertilize newly planted trees. This applies to both deciduous trees as well as young evergreens. This time next year will probably be fine.

For older trees, an application of 5-10-5 fertilizer between the trunk and the drip line of large trees will give them a boost for spring. (The drip line is the point of the widest branches on shade trees.) You actually want to start about 2 feet out from the trunk rather than right up against the trunk.

To avoid burning the foliage while you are broadcasting the fertilizer, **make sure the foliage of the tree is dry.** For deciduous trees, you can estimate 2 to 4 pounds of fertilizer per inch of the trunk's diameter at breast height. For evergreen trees, use only 2 pounds per inch of trunk diameter at breast height. For truly accurate fertilizer rates, have your soil tested.

## PRUNING

If you didn't get all of your pruning accomplished on mature shade trees, you can still get to it now. Try to finish it up early in the month because the internal activity of the tree is changing rapidly. All the stored food in the roots of the tree will be traveling back up to the limbs to supply the necessary energy to push out a new crop of leaves. The longer you wait in the month, the more likely you will be to have excessive bleeding.

The removal of dead or offending limbs from evergreens can also be done now. Most evergreens are not severely pruned, but the new growth is trimmed to keep them compact and full. Keep in mind that most large evergreens will not resprout if you prune the limbs back to dormant wood. If you prune them partway, to a point where the branches still retain their needles, then they will break dormant buds. If an evergreen has really outgrown its location, it is sad to say that in many cases the only option is to remove it entirely.

 PESTS

Application of a dormant oil before new growth starts is a useful way to prevent the reappearance of **scale, mealy bugs,** and **woolly adelgids** on those trees that experienced these problems previously. **Maples, tulip trees, magnolias,** and **hemlocks** are among the trees that may have one of these problems. Be aware that dormant oil on **blue spruce** will take off the blue color. The new growth will appear blue, but whatever turned green will stay that way.

## Helpful Hints

**Important things to remember when preparing to plant trees:**

*1* If you are having your trees delivered, make sure you have a spot prepared to keep them until you are ready to plant. Out of the wind is best. Consider having a load of mulch dropped before the trees. You can then bury the root balls in the mulch to keep them from drying out. If you have a large compost pile, that will work as well.

*2* If wet ground is part of the picture, have stone available to put under the tree as well as some sand to mix with organic matter into existing soil to help with drainage.

*3* You'll need stakes, ropes, and old garden hose to protect the trunk.

*4* A sharp knife is handy for removing wrapping ropes and cutting staking ropes as well as the garden hose.

*5* Buy enough hose to reach the trees so you can water them after planting. Make sure the water to the hose is turned on after a long cold winter.

*6* Miscellaneous items include several shovels, a pick, and sharp pair of pruners to trim away any damaged branches.

*7* Arrange for help. A small tree you can probably handle on your own, but having another person just to tell you when the tree is planted straight can be a big help. Also, remember that larger balled trees get very heavy very fast. In most cases, the rootball is wider than tall. A 5- to 6-foot tall tree with a 16-inch-wide rootball weighs about 100 pounds, and this is considered on the small side.

 NOTES

_____
_____
_____
_____
_____
_____
_____
_____

PLANNING

By April you have definitely moved into action mode. However, with the planting of trees, you may want to do a bit of planning to get the job done correctly.

 PLANTING

If you are transporting a tree yourself, take great care not to bounce the tree around. You want to protect both the branches and the roots. If it's being transported in an open truck, wrap the tree to protect it from wind damage in transit. Move the tree by handling the rootball. **Never drag a tree by its branches.** There is too much of a risk that the branches will snap off. For more details regarding the planting of trees, see the chapter introduction.

 WATERING

All newly planted trees will need to be watered immediately. If April showers came as expected, then you won't have to add much. If it doesn't rain, a deep watering every seven to ten days will be helpful.

 FERTILIZING

Do not fertilize newly planted trees. Give them a chance to become established.

You can fertilize your established trees now. Mature shade trees are best fertilized with a deep root application in October, but late March or early April is the second best time, especially for younger and smaller trees. Wait until the ground is not frozen.

See March for specific directions regarding fertilizer application.

 PRUNING

By this time, you want to avoid doing any shaping or size reduction for aesthetic reasons. Limbs that are dead can be removed at any time without causing any additional stress to the tree. Limbs that may be dangerous in any way should also be removed. Unfortunately, in places where live limbs have been removed, you may have to accept a significant amount of "bleeding," or oozing of sap, when doing this pruning at this time. Even so, no tree-wound dressing offers any benefit. Do the best possible job of limb removal to keep the wound as small as it can be while still getting the job done.

If you had to do some root pruning on container plants to stretch out a crowded root system, you may want to prune the top to keep the plant in balance. If it is a tree with a central leader, you may want to avoid cutting that, but a few snips to take pressure off the roots should be beneficial in the long run. Also, prune away any branches that may have been broken or damaged during transportation or planting.

See the section on pruning in the chapter introduction for more specifics.

 PESTS

Dormant oil can still be applied early in the month for many types of scale and aphids on a wide variety of trees. These may include **ash, beech, birch, cherry, pine, douglas fir, fir, hemlock, honey locust, juniper, oak, magnolia, London plane, poplar, spruce, sycamore, tulip-tree,** and **willow.**

Leaf spot, leaf blight, scab, and rust diseases are very active this time of year, but you may not see the symptoms until later in the season. These include **hawthorn, crabapple, ash, horse chestnut, sycamore, poplar,** and **pine.** Some flower and leaf galls, caused by insects, also need to be controlled now. Tent caterpillars are most notorious on **cherries** but can also infect **plums.** They should be controlled in late April or early May.

Many insects and diseases require repeated applications of material to provide adequate control. It's hard to achieve a thorough application on large trees due to the height of the tree and equipment limitations. In many cases, the use of professional services is warranted.

For homeowners who have the capability to apply treatment on their own, check with your Cooperative Extension Office for current control recommendations.

## Helpful Hints

*1* Try to find a tree that will thrive but also have more than one season of interest. The **river birch** has magnificent peeling bark that exposes lots of colors as it peels. The **golden rain tree,** *Koelreuteria paniculata,* blooms with clusters of yellow flowers in July that are followed by clusters of balloon-like pods in the late summer and fall. The **sugar maple** has great fall color.

*2* Don't panic about pests. In most cases, you don't have to do anything with your trees regarding insects and disease. It is a good idea to research any problems a particular tree may be prone to getting so you can choose your trees accordingly.

*3* The best defense is a good offense. Take time on a regular basis to observe your trees up close. There are all kinds of fuzz, bumps, lines, and shading on healthy leaves, twigs, and limbs. Learn what belongs there so you can quickly identify what does not.

## NOTES

# MAY

## Trees

## PLANNING

You are definitely out of planning mode. (Although you can always be in long-term planning mode when you see some tree doing something that excites you. Get it on the list of trees you have to have.) Native **dogwoods** are smaller trees in full bloom in early May. The **paw-paw** is a fruit-bearing tree native to North America that gets very interesting, purple, bell-like flowers at the same time. The tufts of bright green new growth on **spruce** trees look like someone put neon lights on all the branch tips. **Black locusts** produce fragrant clusters of small white flowers later in the month. If you see something that intrigues you, make a note. If you don't know what you are looking at, take a sample (with permission of course) and get it identified.

## PLANTING

It is better to get as much of your planting done as possible while plants are still dormant. Luckily for many gardeners and nursery professionals, the use of container material does wonders for stretching out the planting season. Removing a plant, any plant, including trees, from a container is much less disruptive to the root system than digging out a rootball.

Trees that were dug during dormancy and were properly tended will probably do fine if planted now.

If you have a container plant that is significantly overcrowded in the pot, you will have to pull apart the roots and will probably have to cut some of them away. This can cause a serious disruption of the root system. You will have a better chance of success if the plant is still dormant. See the Planting section in the chapter introduction to learn how to handle potbound trees.

## WATERING

Always water in newly planted trees. If the weather turns hot and dry, you will want to provide a deep watering every week or so until rain takes over the chore. If it doesn't rain, you will have to keep watering as long as the ground remains dry.

First-year trees will need extra attention. Established trees will be much more tolerant but will need a drink under extended drought conditions.

## FERTILIZING

If you haven't fertilized yet, you can still fertilize early in the month. Never apply fertilizer when the temperature is above 85 degrees Fahrenheit.

## PRUNING

You can always remove the occasional offending limb. It's best to do major pruning of most deciduous trees during either winter or summer dormancy. Right now, they are in full swing in growing mode. Wait until things slow down for the summer to perform big pruning jobs.

Most large evergreens do not ever get severely pruned. Of course, you can remove dead branches when they appear and eye pokers when they get dangerous.

During May, you will see the new growth on many evergreens. **Pines** and **fir** will send out "candles." **Spruce** has soft, floppy, new shoots that firm up quickly. Snip off half of the new growth. You can remove the central shoot from a cluster, or you can snip off half of each of the shoots in a cluster. Never remove the entire cluster. If you need to remove a larger limb, try to cut it back far enough to hide the stump but not so far you are back to dormant wood. Always leave a green shoot to continue growing, or the branch may die. This is especially true for pines.

**Hemlocks** have the ability to resprout readily from dormant buds. Hemlocks can be sheared almost any time, but it is best just before the new growth comes out. That way, the new growth will hide the unnatural look of the "haircut." **Douglas fir** is also used in hedges but is not quite as enthusiastic about filling in as hemlock.

##  PESTS

Many pests are out having fun, gorging themselves and then reproducing. If you see something you think is a problem, get it identified. Your County Extension Office should be able to provide that service.

**Woolly adelgid** is a nasty critter. It has become a devastating problem on **hemlock.** So much so that hemlock is not being recommended for planting in New Jersey gardens at this time. There is research going on to release parasites and predators of the woolly adelgid as a form of biological control. That looks very promising but is not yet a solution. If fuzzy white blobs that look like small tufts of cotton appear on your existing hemlocks, contact your County

## Helpful Hints

*1* Mother's Day is in May. Trees make wonderful presents for Mom. A flowering **dogwood,** a pink flowered **tamarisk,** or a gorgeous **blue spruce** will mark the time as children or grandchildren grow.

*2* A fabulous tree that blooms in May is *Davidia involucrate* (**dovetree**). It is hardy to Zone 6, with the variety 'vilmoriniana' claiming hardiness to Zone 5. Even so, plant it in a protected spot as it is subject to winter damage while it is young. The enormous white flowers (bracts really) blow in the breeze and look like the wings of a dove.

Extension Office for controls.

**Gypsy moth** needs to be controlled around the third week in May. This is a most serious pest on **oaks,** but natural predators have been released that have reduced the problem significantly in recent years.

**Birch leafminers** are still very destructive and warrant control in mid-May and again in early June. Cankerworms, or more commonly "inchworms," can be a problem on **maples** and somewhat on **oaks** and **beech** in early May. A serious infestation will require control measures.

**Elm leaf beetle** is another critter that shows up in May. **Spruce** galls are controlled with dormant oil in March but sprayed again with insecticide in late May. Some people skip the dormant oil since it removes the blue color on blue spruce and rely on the May insecticides to do the job.

**Pine sawfly** will get on its hind legs and wiggle at you as it devours your pine needles.

## NOTES

_____

_____

_____

_____

_____

_____

_____

_____

_____

_____

_____

_____

_____

# JUNE
## Trees

## PLANNING

The only real planning you need to be doing is figuring out which tree is the best to shade a hammock. There is a variety of hammock frameworks that you can place under a tree with no negative impact on the tree itself. Any wound in a tree makes it vulnerable to disease.

## PLANTING

Planting this late means very little opportunity to get a root system established before the onset of summer. If water availability is already in question, it probably isn't worth the risk. If water is not a problem, it may be worthwhile to plant now, but make sure you go above and beyond with soil preparation and play close attention to the needs of the plant during the upcoming summer months.

If low water reservoirs are in the news, this should be a factor in if and what you plant, especially with regard to the size of the tree you want. A smaller tree, especially an understory tree (one that grows in the shade of other trees), is still okay if it will receive some shade and is planted from a container in a spring-like June (when you can water when needed). A **dogwood** is a great choice for an understory tree. **Hemlocks** start out as understory trees but eventually can dominate a forest.

Container trees are usually less traumatized than dug trees, so they may have better luck when other planting factors are less than ideal. If trees are planted with some shade, there will be less heat and drought stress when they are just starting out, a definite advantage when heading towards the hottest part of the year.

## WATERING

Water availability is an enormous issue in June. Anything planted from late winter through this month may need water if the ground begins to get dry. Don't wait until the tree looks wilted to water. If weather has been hot with little rain, water recently planted trees deeply, once a week.

Established trees almost never need water in June.

## FERTILIZING

Definitely do not fertilize now. If you missed a spring application of fertilizer on mature shade trees, you have another chance in October. For younger trees and small flowering trees, wait until next spring.

## PRUNING

Other than corrective pruning of broken branches, you really do not have much need to prune in June.

## PESTS

Bagworms get controlled in mid June. It is important to do this before they build their small, elongated football-shaped "bags." Once they are in their suits of armor, the insecticides offer no assistance. Bagworms appear on all kinds of trees including **spruce, beech, birch, arborvitae, douglas fir, fir, hawthorn, hemlock, junipers, larch, linden, maples,** and **pines.** Spray as a prevention if you have had a problem in the past. *Bacillus thurengiensis* (Bt), a disease of many type of larvae, gives control.

Mimosa webworm is controlled in mid-June. Again, Bt is considered effective. Look for webworm on the exotic looking and somewhat weedy **mimosa** tree. It can also be quite damaging to **honey** and **black locust.**

Japanese beetles can show up late in the month, but the quantity is not usually worth controlling until July.

## NOTES

PLANNING

Planning to head to the beach? Going "down the shore" is a favorite New Jersey summer tradition. If you have a place down the shore and want to plan for some new trees, **Japanese black pines** and **American holly** both seem to thrive in the salt and sand. They also both pop up just about everywhere from seed. **Mimosas** also seem to grow from seed where the wind takes them. **Crapemyrtle** thrives everywhere in Cape May and adds a great deal of Victorian charm. Crapemyrtles are only borderline hardy in much of the state, but the South and the coast is almost all Zone 7 where they do just fine.

 PLANTING

You should be spending a lot of time drinking lemonade and soaking up the AC. Now is not the time to plant much of anything.

 WATERING

Water your trees according to how much Mother Nature has cooperated. If you've only been receiving a light sprinkle, you will need to give newer trees a deep drink. See the chapter introduction for more information on watering.

 FERTILIZING

No fertilizer is needed now.

 PRUNING

Summer pruning of shade trees is an acceptable practice; however, it may not be quite as desirable as winter pruning because summer dormancy is not as deep as winter dormancy. Pruning during the heat of summer, however, is much preferred to pruning in early spring or fall when trees are very active.

From a visual perspective, pruning in summer has some distinct advantages. The absence of leaves reveals dead branches. Branches with wilting leaves can be removed as soon as the leaves "flag," or go limp. This is especially important in **maple** trees where maple wilt is rampant. The removal of diseased limbs will not prevent the disease from eventually killing the tree, but it can delay its progress significantly.

If you are pruning for this reason, it is critical to dip all pruning implements in a 10 percent solution of chlorine bleach at the start of the pruning session and in between each cut. The purpose of this pruning is to remove the infected part of the tree, leaving only healthy wood. **If you make a cut without taking the bleaching precaution, you can expose healthy wood to the disease.**

Another visual advantage to summer pruning is that you can see what the tree will look like after a particular offending limb is gone. It is much easier to give the tree an attractive symmetry when you can really see it in leaf.

See the chapter introduction for a detailed description of how to prune. Remember not to bother with tree-wound dressing after you make the necessary cuts. It may make you feel better, but it really doesn't help the tree and can actually do more harm than good by trapping "anaerobic" organisms under the dressing.

# PESTS

When dealing with any kind of wilting diseases, you may want to pay a little more attention to watering needs since the tree's ability to take up water is compromised. Fall webworm can begin to show up in July on **ash.** It can be controlled with Bt, but if you can't get good coverage on the tree, don't bother doing it yourself.

Spider mites show up on a lot of things in hot weather. They are best controlled with a dormant oil in late winter and then again with insecticides in spring and fall. At this time of year, a fierce spray of water will wash away most of them. It is a long way for a mite to climb back up a tree if it has been washed away in a stream of water. Look for mites on

arborvitae, fir, hemlock, holly, pine, and **spruce.**

Powdery mildew is usually not worth controlling on large trees; but if you choose to try, you will need very good coverage to be effective, which is always a challenge on large trees. Powdery mildew may appear on **cherries, birch, ash, crabapple, catalpa,**

**dogwood, elm, hawthorn, hickory, horse chestnut, honey locust, black locust, maple, oak, pear, sycamore, tuliptree,** and **walnuts.** Check with your Cooperative Extension Office for current control recommendations.

# NOTES

PLANNING

While you are lying about enjoying summer, you may want to be peering through the catalogs and gardening books to find the perfect tree. September planting is a very sound planting alternative to spring. The air temperature drops, but the soil is still warm enough for root generation. Therefore, you may want to **shop around now** to make sure you can locate the tree you want in time for next month's planting.

In some cases, you may be able to catch plants on sale that would otherwise have to be overwintered at the nursery. Overwintering trees at a nursery is difficult and costly to growers. They may lower the price now to avoid the additional expense and work over the winter.

If you can't find the tree you seek at a local nursery, they may be able to order one for you. Local retail nurseries know who grows what on the wholesale end and may be able to have one for you in a few days.

If the tree you want is not locally grown, you may have to wait until spring. Bringing in trees from any distance often requires a minimum order, and nurseries are not trucking in a lot of material at this time. If you don't want to wait until spring, you can sometimes have a tree shipped to you directly now by ordering from a retail catalog company.

 PLANTING

Planting in August is not really a great idea. The weather can stay very hot for the entire month. Trees newly planted in blazing sun with brutal temperatures are just a disaster waiting to happen.

If you bring home the perfect tree, you need to store it in a protected spot until planting conditions improve. **Choose a spot out of the wind** and **with some shade,** but not in the dark. **Protect the roots** by placing the rootball in a compost pile, covering it with a hefty pile of wood chip mulch, or placing bales of straw around the ball and then filling in with loose straw. Don't let the roots dry out or get excessively hot.

 WATERING

How much you need to water your trees in August is a result of how well the trees are established, the temperature, soil type, and your ability to water. A hot dry summer may mean you need to water regularly. Mature shade trees will probably only need a deep watering every ten days to two weeks, but at that point you will need to make sure the entire root system gets a thorough watering. Younger and smaller trees will need water more often. See the chapter introduction for more on watering.

 FERTILIZING

Now is not the time to fertilize trees. Mature shade trees can be fertilized with a deep-root fertilization in October, so just wait a little while longer.

 PRUNING

The advantages and disadvantages of pruning during summer dormancy are discussed in July. Turn back to get the details.

## PESTS

You can still hose away spider mites whenever you see them. Powdery mildew is best controlled when it first appears. That is usually in July but, depending on the season, may not be until August. Japanese beetles feed on many things, but trees are not among their favorites. They may be more of a problem on **cherry** trees than anything else. Whenever and wherever they are feeding, they can be controlled. Remember that a certain level of feeding can be tolerated, especially at this time of year when things are slowing down.

## Helpful Hints

Getting a tree on sale doesn't mean you have to settle for an unhealthy one. Know what to look for:

*1* The leaves should have good color and few if any bare branches.

*2* The rootball should be solid and not dusty dry. If the rootball shifts around, it could mean broken or dried up roots. (It's best if the roots were protected in a mulch pile while on display at the nursery over the summer.)

*3* Check the bark for any damage or oozing.

*4* Trees in containers should not be so rootbound that the roots are coming back to the surface, or splitting the pot, or circling around inside the pot so many times you can't see the soil. If it is a small tree, you may be able to look at the roots by pulling it out of the pot, but ask before doing this.

### Some Added Benefits

*1* **Magnolias** make really interesting seedpods. They are fun to hunt for with the kids. **Tuliptree** seedpods are just as interesting. You can even use them in dried arrangements.

*2* Some trees produce berries, which are often great food for birds. Look for raspberry-like fruits on the **kousa dogwood** and the blue-black fruits of the **chionanthus.** Birds gobble them up.

## NOTES

_____

_____

_____

_____

_____

_____

_____

_____

# SEPTEMBER

 PLANNING

If you want to do any planting of trees in September, do so after the weather has truly shifted into September mode. Once the weather breaks, **get out your shovel.** You will want to give your trees as much time as possible to make roots before soil temperatures drop below 45 degrees Fahrenheit. At that point, root growth comes to a standstill.

Have on hand your soil amendments: pulverized limestone (if soils are on the acidic side) and a source of organic matter. Stakes, rope, protective tubing to prevent support ropes from cutting into the tree, and an ample supply of organic mulch all contribute to doing the job correctly.

It is definitely a good idea to include some features in your garden that peak in the winter. The dark and frigid days are bad enough without something of beauty to look forward to in the garden. Plan to get some trees that will add interest and wonder to the garden while you wait out the cold. When the leaves fall to the ground, some interesting secrets of trees are revealed.

Some suggestions for winter interest: The **yellow-twig dogwood** is supposed to be a shrub, but it gets large enough to be considered a small tree if left unpruned. When the leaves drop, you really can appreciate the yellow twigs. The **corkscrew willow** will now show off its spiraling branches, and the **weeping mulberry** looks like an architectural marvel. The **lacebark pine** is always lacy, but somehow it is so much more noticeable without all the competition from other more dramatic displays. Bark on the deciduous **paperbark maple** and the fabulous **'Heritage' river birch** are both peeling away in layers, exposing rich colors and textures. The **contorted mulberry** falls into a class all by itself. **Harry Lauder's walking stick** is a another curly-Q type of tree, curling up and then weeping over, while the contorted mulberry goes straight sideways.

**Don't forget to ask for help.** You'll need the extra hands to help you keep the tree straight while positioning it.

 PLANTING

There is not an enormous difference in planting techniques for this time of year compared to early spring. For the basics, refer to the planting section in the chapter introduction.

At this time of year, it is likely you will have to deeply water very dry soil to be able to dig. If this is the case, allow the water to run for several hours at a trickle over the entire area you need to dig. Do this the day before you intend to plant.

You will also want to **stake everything.** In spring deciduous trees are leafless, so the wind blows through the bare branches. In all but very windy spots, small- to medium-sized deciduous trees are probably safe without stakes. When you plant deciduous trees in September, they are in full leaf and so are more likely to be blown around by a windy day.

Evergreen trees will all need staking since they always catch the wind. Until they make a few roots, they rotate much like a ball and socket. Fall is hurricane season as well, with storms coming up from the south. Nor'easters are also more of a fall event. A newly planted tree doesn't have enough roots to stand up to these types of storms.

 WATERING

Make sure the rootball of anything you plant is properly moistened before planting. Water newly planted trees thoroughly. Some years, the weather stays dry right through the month and even into October. September planted trees will need frequent watering until the soil moisture levels improve. Don't be fooled by cooler air temperatures making you think you don't need to water.

Since it can take two to three years for a tree to become truly established, if the ground stays dry, water deeply every week or ten days. Mature trees are probably not in need of water at this time as the deep root systems can reach for water and water loss is reduced in the cooler air. If in doubt, one more deep watering will not hurt.

 # FERTILIZING

It is still not time to fertilize, and **never fertilize at planting.** Most small or young trees are spring fed. Mature shade trees can be fertilized next month.

 # PRUNING

With the many storms that occur in the fall, any damage to trees should be addressed. Dead limbs can be removed anytime.

At this time, **sugars are beginning to move** through the tree to be stored for the winter. Most of the "bleeding," or oozing of sap, is likely to occur during this time. Any pruning of live limbs should wait until a quieter time when the tree is less active internally.

 # PESTS

The month of September is a critical time to control a number of pests. The evil woolly adelgid on **hemlock** is controlled from September through late October. Mites on **spruce, fir, hemlock, arborvitae,** and **pine** can be sprayed in September. Boxelder bug can appear in large number on **boxelders** and in the vicinity. They need to be controlled now.

Start the sanitary practices of raking and bagging leaves of anything that showed disease symptoms. Don't leave them around to provide a source of disease for next year.

If you prefer to compost diseased leaves, **they must be buried** in the pile and allowed to completely decompose before using the compost. In a larger compost pile, temperatures can be hot enough to kill disease organisms, but most backyard piles are too small to retain enough heat to be effective. If in doubt, bag up the questionable leaves and send them to the landfill.

 # NOTES

_____
_____
_____
_____
_____
_____
_____
_____
_____
_____
_____
_____
_____
_____

# OCTOBER
## Trees

 PLANNING

It is in the third week in October that you can generally expect to see the greatest display of fall color in the state of New Jersey. The **tuliptree** and **gingko** turn a lovely, uniform gold. The **European** and **American beech** turn yellow to bronze. Among the mighty oaks, the **red, scarlet, pin,** and **black oaks** all turn red. So do most **dogwoods, pears,** and some **cherries**. **Crabapples** have great spring flowers but not much fall color. Neither does the magnificent **horse chestnut** or the somewhat bizarre **mimosa.**

**Maples** are famous for autumn color. The **sugar maple** is spectacular but really does best farther north. The **Japanese maple** may be among the prettiest.

All red maples turn yellow and red, but the variety 'October Glory' is spectacular and was developed at Princeton Nurseries right in our own backyard. **Sweet gum** is yellow and red, but many people object to the gumballs that also arrive in the fall. **Black gum** doesn't get the gumballs, so the name is a bit of a mystery. It gets small black fruits instead. The fall foliage is a spectacular orange-red. This is a great choice for wetter areas. Most **magnolias** don't have fall color, except for the **star magnolia** which turns a not-very-exciting yellow to brown.

 PLANTING

You can still plant in early October, but don't press your luck. In a mild fall, your trees will have a chance to put out a few roots before the ground freezes, but you can't count on that. If you come across a bargain tree and you want to take a chance, you have a good shot.

Smaller trees and container trees have a larger window than balled trees due to the reduced trauma to the root system; however, the large investment of time, energy, and cash to plant a large tree may be better spent in early spring. You will gain very little with late-fall planting, and you have a significant chance of losing the tree.

Refer to the chapter introduction for basic information on planting. Fall-specific information can be found in September.

 WATERING

As always, water newly planted material thoroughly. Make sure the rootball is adequately moist before planting. By this time, it is rare that trees need much in the way of additional water. If the season continues to be exceptionally dry, one more deep watering may be warranted.

 FERTILIZING

October is the month for a deep fertilization of mature deciduous shade trees. You may want to fertilize if the tree is in particularly poor soil or there was some construction in the area which stressed the tree. Feeding now may be helpful if it has been a very dry summer and you were unable to water, or the tree is fighting a wilt disease and you want to give it a boost.

See the chapter introduction for specifics on fertilizing. After fertilizing, water the entire area deeply.

 PRUNING

As the foliage changes color and the trees prepare for winter dormancy, you are really better off limiting pruning to the removal of dead branches or those that present some type of danger. Major limb removal can be done any time if necessary but is less stressful to the tree if done while the tree is not in an active phase of growth. **Winter and summer periods of dormancy are the better times** if you can wait.

 PESTS

Pest control is pretty much over by this time. Mother Nature has arranged the life cycles of insects and diseases to slow down at the same time that the trees slow down.

## Helpful Hints

*1* October is a great time to gather colorful leaves, seed pods, pine cones, and interesting fruits. It is all neat stuff to share with young children. Many of these items are considered edible. Horse chestnuts are poisonous when raw, but they become edible if roasted, mashed, and leached for several days. American Indians used the meal to make a bread-like product. The acorns of **white oaks** are also edible and are generally boiled first to remove tannins. The raspberry-like fruit of the **Kousa dogwood** is edible right from the tree. They should be soft before picking, but the texture is grainy and not everyone likes them.

*2* The large fruits of the native **pawpaw** usually ripen sometime in October after a light frost. They should be soft enough to eat with a spoon. The custard-like consistency and very sweet taste are considered a delicacy.

## NOTES

# NOVEMBER
## Trees

 ## PLANNING

In the early part of November, the trees are still bearing much of their autumn raiment. It is usually sometime in the third week of the month that a Nor'easter, or something close, takes out most of the leaves in one big storm. There is something very sad about the morning after that storm; it seems to signal the time to put away thoughts of gardening and let the sleepy, gray time of the year run its course. If you made some good tree choices for last September's planting, you should be comforted to know that **this season will bring its own magic** as the trees show off their graceful winter beauty.

Meanwhile, it's never too early to plan for the holidays. If you will need a holiday tree, why not try something new. With some pre-planning, you may even get some extra time to enjoy it.

**Some holiday trees to consider:**

• **Fraser fir** has a narrow, pyramidal shape, plenty of space between the branches for ornaments, and a great scent.

• **White fir** or **concolor fir** has a bluish hint to the needles. It may make a better choice than the more traditional blue spruce because it doesn't stab you while you are trying to decorate it.

• **White pine** is known as the "poofy" Christmas tree in some discerning families. It is fluffy and jolly, but ornaments slide off the long slippery needles.

• **Blue spruce** has a great scent, a perfect shape, and beautiful color. It also has sharp needles which seem particularly mean to children.

• **Douglas fir** is not really a fir, but that does not affect its ability to be an excellent Christmas tree. With soft needles, it's not a "stabbing" tree. As a cut tree, it can hold its needles very well if it comes from a local nursery. As a balled tree for planting, it will do well in the yard and make interesting cones with feathery "bracts."

 ## PLANTING

Planting, of course, is not high on the list at this time of year, but some trees have a way of planting themselves. All those seeds and pods dropping to the ground can sprout come spring. It is amazing how no one thinks of the mighty **oak** as a weed, but a zillion oak seedlings in your lawn is a different story.

 ## WATERING

Anything planted in the fall may need a drink if it doesn't rain. Usually this is not the case, but if it is, water thoroughly.

 ## FERTILIZING

Put away your toys for the winter. Make sure your fertilizers are all stored where they will stay dry. Liquid fertilizer should be stored where it will not freeze.

## PRUNING

Trees are definitely going dormant, but they are not quite there yet. Sugars could still be moving through the tree to be stored for the winter. Prune only those things that **must** be pruned and wait on everything else until late winter.

 ## PESTS

Luckily, the pests are dormant, too. Don't worry. They will be back next year.

## NOTES

# Helpful Hints

Fallen leaves can be a good thing or a bad thing, depending on whether you are a glass-half-empty or half-full kind of person. While it's common to rake leaves here and there for simple cleanup, it is the rare person who is willing to rake acres of ground. Out in the country, most people just let the leaves blow around.

**Why you should care about leaves:**

- On the negative side, a really thick layer of leaves will kill grass, so only you can decide if the lawn is worth protecting. They may smother some small perennials if they mat down under shrubbery, including roses. Leaves on sidewalks and driveways can be dangerously slippery.

- On the positive side, autumn leaves are an excellent material for the compost pile. You can rake them up or bag them with a giant leaf sucker—there are many types available. You can rake them away from focal points in the yard and push them under bushes as a mulch. You can mow leaves with a mulching lawn mower. Broken up in very small particles, the leaf pieces filter down to the soil between blades of grass. Leaves as a mulch do a good job of moderating soil temperatures and keeping down weeds come spring.

# DECEMBER

 ## PLANNING

There is plenty of time next month to plan for your spring tree planting. Now you need to get ready for the holidays. If you intend to have a balled-and-burlapped Christmas tree so you can replant it later, you must definitely have a spot picked out. **Go ahead and dig the hole.** Most years, the ground does not freeze before Christmas, but trying to dig a hole in frozen ground for an evergreen tree is too much like real work to be any fun. Dig the hole now, cover it with a piece of plywood so no one falls in, and store the soil where it will not freeze.

You also need to go and **pick your tree.** Go with the whole family or a group of friends. It's a great way to kick off the spirit of the season. Bundle up and wear waterproof shoes. If your feet get wet, it isn't fun anymore. Most places let you tag the tree you want. Then they dig it out, and you come back to get it closer to the holiday. If you wait until the last minute, most places also have pre-dug trees, but that just isn't as much fun.

 ## PLANTING

When picking the spot to replant your tree, remember that the ones I suggested in November will all grow to be enormous. None of those trees are suitable for outside the front door, no matter how cute they are at the moment.

Once the holidays are over, you will want to get your holiday tree in the ground as soon as possible. **You will need a plan of action** as soon as the decorations come off. It is not a good idea to keep your tree indoors for a long time. Up to a week indoors may be okay, or ten days on the outside. If you have been able to keep the temperature quite cool in the room it was in, that will have helped to keep the tree from drying out or starting to come out of dormancy. Even so, you will need to place the tree in an intermediate spot to prepare for the great outdoors. An unheated porch is probably the best spot. The garage is not great unless there is a significant window. Keeping an evergreen tree in a dark garage for a week is trading one negative environmental condition for another.

If you are ready to plant your holiday tree before December is over, see January for instructions.

 ## WATERING

Keep the rootball of your tree moist. Put it in a waterproof tub while you have it indoors. Keep the temperature down wherever you decide to display it so you keep transpiration to a minimum. Put rocks in the bottom of the tub for excess water to accumulate without water logging the roots. Pack wet newspaper around the rootball in the tub to keep the sides of the ball from drying out. When you water make sure the water penetrates the rootball and doesn't run off like water on a duck. **Keep it inside for only a week,** ten days at the most.

 ## FERTILIZING

No fertilizing is needed this month.

## PRUNING

The only pruning you may want to do is to prune your **hollies** early in the month. If you want the berries for decorations, prune early and store the branches in a bucket of water in a shady protected nook. If you wait until you need them, your feathered bird friends may have gotten there first.

There are many movies that have great scenes with Christmas trees. *It's a Wonderful Life, A Christmas Story*, even *When Harry Met Sally*. Take your pick. Anyone who loves trees may be particularly touched by the plight of the Ents in the *Lord of the Rings* trilogy. Ents are trees that can pull up roots and "walk" around. They can also communicate. Ents are very good beings of the finest character. You'll have to read the books for more details.

## PESTS

There are no pests to worry about until late winter or early spring.

## NOTES

# CHAPTER ELEVEN

# Vegetables

*New Jersey is the Garden State. It was christened with this nickname because it reflects the vast number of vegetable farms that once covered the state from end to end.*

At one time produce was trucked from New Jersey into New York and Philadelphia to feed the burgeoning urban population and the developing suburbia in its wake. This image is confusing to many in this day and age, since there are certainly parts of the state where farms are few and far between. These are the same areas where the population has exploded.

Most of the population no longer spends summers at Uncle Ed's farm or picks **peaches** as their first job as a teenager. However, agriculture continues to be the third or fourth largest industry in the state, a multi-billion dollar business. Farmers continue to be the largest group of landowners in the state. They also produce Jersey **tomatoes,** which of course are the best tomatoes in the world.

## WHY VEGETABLES?

There are many valid reasons to have a vegetable garden. The most practical is the production of good quality, fresh produce. Having vegetables right there in the backyard lets you pick them at the peak of flavor and serve while the taste and the nutrients are all they can be. **Lettuces** and leafy greens are wonderful early in June, as are **radishes, beets, turnips, broccoli,** and **cauliflower. Peas** can be produced in abundance and are sweet as candy right off the vine. **Spinach** in salads or cooked is good for you and delicious. While getting great produce is plenty of reason all by itself, that really is only part of what you get from having a vegetable garden.

Vegetable gardening is a way for the family to have an activity together. Whether you let each member have a plot of their own or all work on one big garden, it is quality time together, with a purpose. Children learn a bit of the science behind food but also experience the wonder of it all. They learn that giant **sunflowers** get extremely tall and **radishes** grow very quickly.

Growing your own vegetables makes kids more interested in eating them. Once they try a **sugar snap pea,** you may have created a pea-eating monster! Of course **strawberries** and **blueberries** and **raspberries** in the garden have appeal for everyone.

## GETTING STARTED

If you have never had a vegetable garden, start small. It is better to succeed on a small scale than to fail on a grand scale; limit yourself to a few of your favorites. Unless you have had experience starting seeds indoors, you may want to purchase plants that are generally started outdoors as transplants. In the cooler season these are commonly plants in the **cabbage** family, which includes **broccoli, cabbage, and cauliflower. Brussels sprouts, tomatoes, peppers,** and **eggplants** are started once things warm up. **Onions** are generally started from "sets" (tiny onions) or sometimes plants. **Potatoes** are started from seed potatoes or potatoes cut up into smaller pieces. **Sweet potatoes** are started much later from bare-root plants. Almost everything else is direct seeded.

Choose you garden spot based on a number of important factors:

*1* **Available sun.** Almost all vegetables need **very strong sun.** Remember that in early spring, what appears to be a very sunny location may not be so sunny when all the leaves come out on the trees. If you have any options, choose one where you will have easy access to water. If you are limited to sloped ground, you may want to create terraces to avoid erosion and to be able to water more efficiently.

*2* **Soil quality.** You will have to work with what you have, but poor soil can be improved over time. If your ground is poor, put your compost pile in that spot for a year, and by the following year, it will be much improved. The earthworms will help you by pulling compost into the ground. Adding copious amounts of organic matter, such as leaf compost, will improve the soil. Double digging, where you dig down one shovel depth and remove the soil then turn the soil over on the level below, will help with poor drainage as well as root development. Almost all New Jersey soils are deficient in organic matter, so it is hard to add too much.

While most composts add very little in the way of nutrients, they improve the soil in a way that allows it to hold the nutrients longer and so reduce fertilizer needs.

The exact amount of fertilizer needed is best determined by a soil test. Many New Jersey soils are acidic and need lime. While the amount of lime needed will be recommended in your soil report, in general, the use of 5-10-5 fertilizer during soil preparation is recommended for spring planting. The application of 3 to 4 pounds of fertilizer per 100 square feet is a good rule of thumb. It should be turned into the soil.

If you don't have any compost on hand to start, many municipalities have it available to residents at little or no charge. Either the Department of Public Works or the Department of Parks often runs public compost operations. Contact your municipal office for information regarding your town's leaf management program.

In a new garden, you will have to remove all the sod from the area. Do not simply rototill the sod. Any bit of root left behind will allow regeneration of the grass. Cover the area with old carpeting (preferred) or used a total vegetation killer such as Roundup®

(not preferred) to kill the vegetation before tilling.

## PLANTING

Only plan to start seed indoors if you have an extremely sunny, unblocked window, preferably facing south where there is the most available light. If there is a particular variety of something you want and you lack this sunny exposure, consider contracting the seed to be grown by a small local greenhouse. You can also invest in artificial lights, but this is cumbersome, expensive, and energy intensive. For one or two varieties it may not be worthwhile.

You may be able to use a single grow light to supplement natural light on an almost bright-enough windowsill. Or, investing in a small greenhouse window may be more expensive up front but more satisfactory in the long run.

You should use a sterile potting material or sterile perlite or vermiculite. You can use flats or pots. It makes a difference as to where you are putting the containers. A narrow windowsill may be more conducive to small pots or

## Did You Know?

### Supporting Your Vegetables

How are you going to support all these plants? Many of them need something to help hold them up. **Lima beans** and **green beans** both come in bush and pole varieties. Bush types do not need support, but pole type need either a fence, a bean teepee, or some creative approach for the vines to cling. They bear more heavily than bush over the same period of time. So, if space is limited, you can plant fewer pole beans and still have the same harvest by using more vertical space. Bush types are a bit less of a hassle since you can skip the whole support issue. If you can use an existing fence though, it may not be any additional effort, and you get more beans.

egg cartons than a flat. Make sure the containers are well drained and there is a tray underneath for excess water and even for watering from the bottom.

You can plant seeds in rows, in trays of any kind. Make sure to mark the different kinds if you are growing more than one variety. In pots, you may want to plant one variety per pot to keep it simple. You will want to check on depth of planting, germination temperature, and the needed light for germination for each variety. This information is generally on the seed packet.

When it is time to plant, either by direct seeding or planting young plants, always refer to the information on the seed packet. Seeds are planted at a species-specific depth and then thinned to the correct spacing after germination. While spacing can be generalized, there are many varieties that have different requirements than the standard. If you

have purchased transplants and do not have a seed packet, be sure to ask your grower for any specifics.

Planting depth will always be at the same depth the plant was growing in its container. The exceptions are **tomatoes** and **cabbage** family plants (see May of this chapter for details). If the soil have been properly prepared, planting is easy. Shove a trowel into the ground and pull the handle toward you, creating a space. Pop in the plant while holding the trowel in the ground with the other hand. Then remove the trowel and press soil around the roots. Place a tuna fish can (with the top and bottom removed) around the stem of **cucurbits, tomatoes, peppers,** and **eggplants** to prevent cutworms. Water thoroughly.

Before transplanting, it is very important to make sure the soil is in the right condition to prepare for planting. If you squeeze a wad of soil in your hand as

hard as you can, no more than one or two drops of water should come out. Then press the squished wad with your thumb. It should crumble readily. If it stays in a wad, it is too wet to work, and you will have to wait a bit before getting started.

Mark straight lines in the garden with the use of stakes and string. Follow planting depths and spacing between rows based on the information on the seed packet. Remember to account for thinning when the seeds come up. **Onion** plants or sets can be spaced only 2 inches apart, but then you have to harvest every other one as a green onion to allow the rest to expand into onion bulbs. They are pressed into the prepared soil so you can just barely see the tip of the set.

When it is time to plant, either by direct seeding or planting young plants, always refer to the information on the seed packet. Seeds are planted at a species-specific depth and thinned to the correct spacing after germination. While spacing can be generalized, there are many varieties that have different requirements than the standard. If you have purchased transplants and do not have a seed packet, be sure to ask your grower for any specifics.

Planting depth will always be at the same depth the plant was growing in its container. The exceptions are **tomatoes** and **cabbage** family plants (see May of this chapter for details). If the soil has been properly prepared, planting is easy. Shove a trowel into the ground and pull the handle toward you, creating a space. Pop in the plant while holding the trowel in the ground with the other hand. Remove the trowel and press soil around the roots. Place a tuna fish can (with the top and bottom removed) around the stem of **cucurbits, tomatoes, peppers** and **eggplants** to prevent cutworms. Water thoroughly.

## CARE

Monthly watering needs and pest warnings can be found in this chapter, month by month. Be sure to water deeply when you do water. The entire root system needs a good drink, and the soil below should be wet to encourage the roots to go deep. Shallow watering encourages shallow roots, which need to be watered more often. Needed information on pest controls can be found at your County Cooperative Extension Office.

Use mulch whenever possible to moderate fluctuations in soil temperature, to control weeds, and to retain soil moisture. Partially decomposed leaf mulch, fresh grass clippings, shredded newspaper, salt hay, or old straw can all be used. Old straw, bales that have aged outdoors for a year or two, makes good mulch because the seeds that are ordinarily in straw have died.

## Did You Know?

### More on Supports

**Peppers, eggplants, okra, sweet corn,** and any of the bush varieties of cucurbits need no support. **Tomatoes** can be allowed to run on the ground, but they are much more prone to disease when grown that way. Growing them on black plastic keeps the fruit off the ground and helps reduce disease. In most cases, tomatoes are grown "up." Stakes work fine but do require pruning of side shoots and tying the plant to the stake as the plant grows. You need to remove the suckers that will emerge at the point where the leaves attach near the base of the plant. If you do not remove these, the plant will grow into a bush rather than a vine-like habit and will not fit very well tied to a stake. If the pruning is too much of a hassle, consider the use of cages next year.

A cage or stake should be installed at the time of planting or you may damage roots later. Make sure the openings in the cage are large enough to fit your hand and the tomatoes or you won't be able to harvest. Conical wire cages are sold inexpensively, but unless you find ones that are larger and sturdier than most, they are not the best. Page wire fencing held in the ground by one or two stakes makes very serviceable cages.

The vine type **cucurbits** usually grow along the ground and take up a lot of room. If you have a lot of room, this is the easiest way. If space is short, they can also grow up fences. You may need pantyhose to tie some larger fruits to the fence, or the weight will cause them to fall off before they ripen. **Cantaloupes** and **watermelons** are good examples of this. **Cucumbers** are probably fine without the pantyhose.

## CONTINUAL GROWTH

Experienced gardeners often plant a great many things. After a few years, it is easier to judge how much **lettuce** to plant for your family and how much **zucchini** you think you can give away. That is when it becomes fun to grow your own **tomato** plants from hard-to-find heirloom varieties or to try some of the super sweet **onions** you can start from seed in February on a sunny kitchen window. Growing a garden is good fun and good for you. You grow. The kids grow. So does a sense of well-being. Oh . . . and the tomatoes . . . the best of the best.

# Vegetables

## February

| Vegetable | How to Plant |
|---|---|
| Onions | start seed indoors |
| Leeks | start seed indoors |

## March

| Vegetable | How to Plant |
|---|---|
| Onions | plant sets or plants outdoors |
| Leeks | plant plants or direct seed |
| Shallots | plant sets outdoors |
| Garlic | plant cloves outdoors |
| Potatoes | plant seed potatoes outdoors |
| Sunchokes | plant seed pieces outdoors |
| Peas | direct seed outdoors |
| Spinach | direct seed outdoors |
| Broccoli | start seed indoors |
| Cabbage | start seed indoors |
| Cauliflower | start seed indoors |
| Lettuce | start seed indoors |
| Tomatoes | start seed indoors |
| Peppers | start seed indoors |

## April

| Vegetable | How to Plant |
|---|---|
| Horseradish | plant roots |
| Asparagus | plant crowns |
| Broccoli | plant transplants outdoors |
| Cauliflower | plant transplants outdoors |
| Cabbage | plant transplants outdoors |
| Chinese Cabbage | direct seed |
| Lettuce | plant transplants outdoors, direct seed outdoors |
| Mixed Leafy Greens | direct seed outdoors |

## April (continued)

| Vegetable | How to Plant |
|---|---|
| Arugula | direct seed outdoors |
| Beets | direct seed outdoors |
| Swiss Chard | direct seed outdoors |
| Turnips | direct seed outdoors |
| Sweet Corn | direct seed outdoors |
| Radish | direct seed outdoors |
| Carrots | direct seed outdoors |
| Eggplants | start seed indoors |
| Winter Squash | start seed indoors |
| Watermelon | start seed indoors |
| Cantaloupe | start seed indoors |
| Pumpkins | start seed indoors |
| Cucumbers | start seed indoors |

## May

| Vegetable | How to Plant |
|---|---|
| Green Beans | direct seed |
| Lima Beans | direct seed |
| Summer Squash | direct seed |
| Okra | direct seed |
| Cucumbers | plant transplants, direct seed |
| Pumpkins | plant transplants, direct seed |
| Winter Squash | plant transplants, direct seed |
| Watermelon | plant transplants, direct seed |
| Tomatoes | plant transplants |
| Peppers | plant transplants |
| Eggplants | plant transplants |
| Sweet Potatoes | plant plants |
| Sweet Corn | direct seed |
| New Zealand Spinach | direct seed |

# Vegetables

## June

| Vegetable | How to Plant |
| --- | --- |
| Tomatoes | plant transplants |
| Peppers | plant transplants |
| Eggplants | plant transplants |
| Green Beans | direct seed |
| Lima Beans | direct seed |
| Summer Squash | direct seed |
| Sweet Corn | direct seed |
| Okra | direct seed |
| Cucumbers | direct seed |
| Radishes | direct seed |

## July

| Vegetable | How to Plant |
| --- | --- |
| Cabbage | direct seed or seed into seedbed |
| Cauliflower | direct seed or seed into seedbed |
| Brussels Sprouts | direct seed or seed into seedbed |
| Green Beans | direct seed |
| Peas | direct seed |
| Summer Squash | direct seed |
| Sweet Corn | direct seed |

## August

| Vegetable | How to Plant |
| --- | --- |
| Beets | direct seed |
| Leafy Greens | direct seed |
| Lettuces | direct seed |
| Broccoli | plant transplants |
| Cabbage | plant transplants |
| Cauliflower | plant transplants |
| Chinese Cabbage | direct seed |

## September

| Vegetable | How to Plant |
| --- | --- |
| Beets | direct seed |
| Leafy Greens | direct seed |
| Lettuces | direct seed |
| Broccoli | plant transplants |
| Cabbage | plant transplants |
| Cauliflower | plant transplants |
| Chinese Cabbage | direct seed |
| Radishes | direct seed |
| Turnips | direct seed |

## October

| Vegetable | How to Plant |
| --- | --- |
| Garlic | plant cloves |

# JANUARY
## Vegetables

###  PLANNING

Get all the gardening catalogs you can get—every single one. If you want to get fancy with your use of sticky notes, get green sticky notes for vegetables and pink ones for flowers. You will see lots of things that intrigue the gardener in you, probably about ten times as much as you can plant. Remember that many will be available locally. The great thing about using catalogs is they help you plan and locate very specific plants that you want. Maybe you just **have to have** a Mortgage Lifter tomato. These enormous fruits have great flavor along with size. There's a tale about a farm being saved when the farmer brought these giants to market.

If you don't have any garden catalogs, pick up any gardening magazine. There will be lots of little slips of paper falling out telling you about catalogs that really want to come to your home. Then look in the back, where all those little "classified" ads are printed. That is where you will come across some of the smaller seed companies. You may find a company that specializes in hot peppers, or gourds, or salad mixes. Some may even specialize in ethnic varieties. Order several. As soon as you place an order, more will begin to arrive.

###  PLANTING

You certainly do not want to be planting anything in the garden in January. It is still too early to even start anything indoors. You can start planning for planting though. **Choose your location.** Remember to watch out for deciduous trees—sunny areas of the lawn in midwinter may be quite shady in mid-June when all the leaves come out. Pick a place where you have access to water and won't be in the way of a soccer game, baseball game, or favorite place your dog likes to visit.

You may decide that your garden needs to be part of an existing lawn area. If that is the case, cut up some old carpeting and cover the area where you intend to make your veggie garden. Make the carpet piece slightly larger than the area you actually intend to cultivate because grass has a way of sneaking out around the edges and not really getting killed off. **You should avoid using herbicides where you intend to plant vegetables,** and rototilling grass is probably a great way to have it come back to haunt your garden for the rest of your life.

###  WATERING

There is nothing planted, so nothing to water. If you are storing seed, you should keep it in the refrigerator. Seeds breathe more rapidly in warmer temperatures, causing them to use up their reserves and dry more quickly. The refrigerator will help protect them.

###  FERTILIZING

There is nothing to fertilize right now. If you want to start purchasing supplies, 5-10-5 is a good all-purpose garden fertilizer for most vegetables. You may also want to pick up some granular or pulverized limestone. It takes a while for lime to actually adjust the pH of your soil, so you will want to put it down early in the season to be effective at planting time.

It is a really good idea to get a soil test now. That way you will know exactly the lime and fertilizer needs of your garden when you are ready to work the soil. Contact your Cooperative Extension Office for information about a Rutger's soil test.

###  PRUNING

There is no pruning to be done this month.

# Helpful Hints

## Veggie Delight

Having a vegetable garden is an entirely different scale of food production. And yet, as Charles Dudley Warner once said, "To own a bit of ground, to scratch it with a hoe, to plant seeds and watch their renewal of life—this is the commonest delight of the race, the most satisfactory thing a man can do." To plant a vegetable garden, to watch the plants grow and produce food which you serve to your family, is a tremendous delight. The thrill and the magic of planting a seed are no less wondrous with a few seeds in a row as on 100 acres. And while Jersey **tomatoes** are the best, the Jersey tomatoes from your own backyard are the best of the best.

## Hybrid Seeds

When shopping for seeds, you'll have opportunity to choose from some hybrids. Note that **hybrid seeds are often extremely expensive because of the way they're produced.** Every year hybrid seed comes from the crossing of two specific parents. Each parent has to be grown separately to make more seeds of the parent, and they also have to be grown together in order to create the cross. When they are crossed, the seed resulting from the cross is a hybrid. This is a lot of work and takes a lot of ground and a lot of time. You cannot save the seed from the fruits produced from hybrid seed as the next generation reverts to the characteristics of the parents.

From a philosophical perspective, hybrids create dependency on large companies to produce the seed, and this tends to contribute to the reduction in the gene pool as old varieties get lost. Hybrids also offer reduced need for pesticides as they have resistance naturally. They also tend to yield more heavily, helping to feed the world on less land. Heirloom varieties have been around long enough to have passed the test of time and have some disease resistance as part of their personality to have been around this long. They also have many fascinating and diverse shapes, colors, textures, and flavors. All open-pollinated varieties can allow gardeners to save their own seed, saving money in subsequent years and preserving the gene pool for future generations. You decide what is right for your garden. It may be a little of both.

The advantages of hybrids make up what is called **"hybrid vigor."** These hybrids are often better in yield, disease resistance, size, or flavor; sometimes more than one of these characteristics. If you are growing for taste and variety, you may do just as well with "open-pollinated" types, or those that are pollinated simply as the wind, bees, and birds choose.

 PESTS

The only thing that may be helpful regarding pests is to make sure all your old garden plants are out of the garden. Pick a nice sunny day and make sure the garden is tidy. The old plants are great places for insects and diseases to over-winter, just lying in wait to start all over on your new plants.

If you have wildlife poking around, such as bunnies, groundhogs, and deer, consider a fence. Otherwise they may gobble things up before you get to them.

# FEBRUARY
## Vegetables

 ## PLANNING

In February you need to move from theoretical planning into active planning. The list of vegetable varieties that intrigued you needs to be pared down to what you really intend to plant. Those hard-to-find varieties that you have located in obscure or not-so-obscure catalogs need to be ordered. You want to place your orders early enough to make certain that what you want will be available.

There are a number of crops that get planted out in mid-March (providing the ground isn't still frozen). **Potatoes** are one of the early crops. They do very well in New Jersey. You will be amazed at the flavor of a freshly dug potato compared to what is commonly available in the store. If you are going to plant them, try some of the unusual varieties. There are blue skinned varieties with both white and blue flesh; red skinned with pinkish, white, and yellow flesh; and the more commonly recognized yellow varieties. Two favorites are 'Desiree', a red-striped potato, and 'All-blue', which is . . . all blue. You have to get your order in early for these unusual varieties as supply is often very limited.

Other vegetables you may need for March planting include **spinach, peas,** (English, snow, and edible podded) and all the **onion** family crops. Spinach and peas are direct seeded and generally available locally. Onions are planted from sets or plants. Sets for white, red, and yellow onions are fairly easy to locate near home, as are **shallots, garlic,** and **elephant garlic.** You are, however, limited to whatever varieties are in stock. Onion plants are less available, but super sweet onions, such as the Walla Walla, are occasionally in garden centers and often in catalogs. Many varieties of onion seed are available locally, and even more are available through catalogs.

 ## PLANTING

**Onions** from seed are started six to eight weeks before planting outdoors. It is also possible to direct seed onions in March, but you shorten your growing season. The more onion foliage you produce while the days are getting longer, the more root or bulb will be produced as the days are getting shorter.

**Onions** germinate best at about 70 degrees Fahrenheit (never above 80). Light is not necessary for germination, so it may be easier to keep them warm in an interior part of the house rather than on a windowsill. You can also invest in simple heat mats or even heated germination trays with covers. Move them into the light as soon as they germinate.

The best time for transplanting onions is mid- to late March. That means you will be starting seeds in early February. This includes **leeks, chives,** and **shallots. Garlic** is almost always grown from sets, which can be spring planted but is more effectively planted in the fall.

See the chapter introduction for planting details.

 ## WATERING

Water your **onion** seeds from the bottom. Take the tray or pot or flat and set it in a tray of water or a sink with about 1 inch of water in the bottom. This is to avoid washing away the seed, which can happen from surface watering. Once the soil is moist, remove it from the water. Then set the container in a plastic bag, open a bit at the top, to keep the soil surface moist, which will encourage germination. Remove the plastic when the first seed germinates.

##  FERTILIZING

There is no need to fertilize at this time. The seeds come with a food supply built in.

##  PRUNING

The only pruning you have to do is to remove any tiny seedlings when they flop over dead from a disease referred to as **"damping off."** This is a common problem with seedlings, especially if they're kept too wet. If you quickly remove the one or two live seedlings on either side of the dead ones, you can prevent the spread of the disease.

##  PESTS

To avoid the problem of damping off, allow the soil to become slightly dry between watering, but not so dry that the seedling roots dry up. Avoid cold wet soil and excessive nitrogen. Be sure to use a sterile potting medium. You can also consider the use of seed pretreated with a fungicide.

## NOTES

_____

_____

_____

_____

_____

_____

_____

_____

_____

_____

# MARCH
## Vegetables

 PLANNING

March definitely begins to switch from planning into action. March 17th is official **pea** planting day. Along with peas, you can plant seeds for **onion** family plants, onion sets or plants, **spinach** from seed, and **potatoes.** Of course you have to make sure the soil is in condition to be worked before heading out to the garden with spading fork and hoe in hand. Midseason crops get planted in mid-April. Those that need to be started from seed indoors include **cabbage** family plants such as **broccoli, cauliflower,** and **cabbage.** They take six or seven weeks to be ready for transplanting, so start them early in the month. **Lettuce** will do really well when direct seeded, but if you want a few plants to get a head start on the season, they can be started mid-March. They are ready to move into the garden in three to six weeks.

Warm season crops do not get planted until late May, so you may still be working out the details on what is going where, but those that you start from seed should get started at the end of the month. These include **tomatoes, peppers,** and **eggplants.**

Always keep in mind when planning what goes where, that a three-year rotation of crops is extremely beneficial in the control of insects and disease.

This applies not only to individual crops but to related groups of plants as well. **Tomatoes, eggplants, potatoes,** and **peppers** are all solanaceous crops (of the family Solanaceae). They should not follow each other. They can follow the **cabbage** crops such as **broccoli, cauliflower, cabbage, kale,** and **collard greens**. These however, cannot follow each other. It can get tricky but is very important.

 PLANTING

**Leek** plants are put in a trench about 6 inches deep and spaced 4 to 6 inches apart. As the leeks grow, the trench is filled in to allow for blanching of the stem and more nice, white leek on the stalk.

**Peas** need something upon which to grow. The absolutely wonderful "sugar snap" edible podded pea can reach 6 feet, so be sure to provide adequate support. Not all pea varieties get quite that tall. The use of double rows, 8 inches apart, allows for more efficient use of the support system. Double rows are spaced 3 feet apart. Peas are generally planted 2 inches deep, but always check the seed pack as this sometimes varies. Thin according to the directions for your variety.

Planting **potatoes** is unique. Do not add lime as they prefer an acidic pH. Potatoes do best in a lighter, sandier soil, so the addition of organic matter and sand is especially beneficial. Never add just sand to clay soil as it turns into something like concrete. Two parts organic matter to one part sand works well.

Small **potatoes,** about the size of an egg or a golf ball, can be planted whole. Larger potatoes can be sectioned into cubes, about the same size or slightly smaller. Make sure each seed piece has 2 or 3 "eyes" or buds on the surface. You can spread the cut potatoes out in a well-ventilated space for a few days before planting. You can also treat the pieces with a fungicide (check with your Cooperative Extension Office for current recommendations) to minimize disease.

To plant the **potato** pieces, dig a trench 6 to 8 inches wide and 2 to 3 inches deep. Place pieces about 9 to 12 inches apart in the row. Space rows 3 feet apart. Cover the pieces with 3 to 4 inches of soil. As the plants grow, mound up the soil around them. This protects the developing potatoes from exposure to the sun and helps control weeds.

For those seeds you want to start indoors for planting out later in the season, read the instructions in the chapter introduction. The general procedures are the same for all vegetable seeds. You will use the information on your seed packets, too.

# WATERING

Water newly planted seeds and transplants as soon as they are planted. Keep seeds moist to ensure germination. This may require daily watering if it does not rain.

 # FERTILIZING

The use of 5-10-5 fertilizer during soil preparation is recommended. The exact amount is best determined by the soil test you had in January. The amount of lime needed will be recommended in the report as well.

In the absence of a soil test, the application of 3 to 4 pounds of fertilizer per 100 square feet is a good rule of thumb. It should be turned into the soil when you are adding your organic matter during soil preparation.

## Helpful Hints

*1* Planting **peas** in front of an **existing** chain link or chicken wire fence surrounding the garden gives you one less support chore to worry about.

*2* If you let **spinach** get a few leaves on it before you thin, you can thin and make a salad out of what you yank.

# PRUNING

In this case, we will include thinning as a sort of pruning. Thinning seedlings is very important. Some gardeners feel a sense of wastefulness at throwing away so many seedlings, but you want to thin to keep the most vigorous as well create the correct spacing. Sometimes you can transplant a few to help fill in gaps, but, without thinning, plants will crowd each other to the point of reducing the harvest in spite of the multitude of plants.

If **onion** seedlings indoors are flopping over a bit from insufficient sun, they can be cut back about $\frac{1}{3}$ with a pair of scissors. This will help them thicken up and stand straight. They will make up the foliage once they are planted out.

 # PESTS

Damping off is still the biggest pest problem you have to face at this time. Check last month for control measures.

 # NOTES

_____

_____

_____

_____

_____

_____

# APRIL
## Vegetables

 PLANNING

April is a busy time in the vegetable garden. Early crops need to be tended. Midseason crops are getting planted. Some of your late-season crops are indoors growing from seed . . . and it's raining. Crops that go in a little later than you would have preferred usually catch up when the weather warms up. In a really wet season, early-planted seeds don't always come up very well. That just makes room for something else.

There are **lots** of plants that can be direct seeded in April: **Swiss chard, beets, sweet corn, lettuce, arrugula, turnips, radishes, carrots, endive, Chinese cabbage, kale, parsnips, collards,** and **kohlrabi.**

Plants you can put out include **broccoli, cauliflower, cabbage, lettuce** (which can also be direct seeded), **chives, parsley,** and **celery.**

 PLANTING

See planting information in the chapter introduction. For direct seeding, follow the spacing on the seed packs for specific information regarding spacing between seeds, thinning after the seeds come up, time to germination, and space between the rows.

Here are a few important points that are crop specific. For **sweet corn**, you will need to plant a minimum of 4 rows, 10 feet long, spaced 2 feet apart. This is because corn is wind-pollinated and you need at least that many plants of the same variety planted at the same time to make sure there is enough pollen in the air to get the job done. Do not plant sweet corn near **pop corn.** If they come into bloom at the same time, the pop corn won't pop and the sweet corn will crunch.

**Carrot** seed is so tiny that it is difficult to handle. You can mix it with **radish** seed in the same row. The radish seed will mark the row because they come up very quickly. Carrot seed takes much longer to germinate. By the time the carrots need the room, the radishes will be just a memory of a great salad long gone.

There are so many wonderful varieties of **lettuce** available that you can't plant them all. Look for the packages of mixed seed. This way you get a whole bunch of varieties all in a row. It is very pretty to look at and delicious to eat.

You only need a little **arrugula.** You can plant a short row, eat the thinnings, and use the rest to dress up a salad. Salads consisting of only arrugula are rather strong for most tastes, but if that is what you enjoy, plant a little more and then plant a short row every 2 weeks since it goes to seed quickly.

Indoors, transplant seedlings when they have 3 leaves. Move them to individual pots or into larger containers. Try to handle them by the seed leaves—if these break, it is not a great loss. If the stem breaks, that is the end of the plant.

 WATERING

Water newly planted transplants and seeds. Make sure transplants are moist before they go in the ground. If it doesn't rain, water seeds daily until they germinate. Young seedlings will still need to be watered frequently if the weather is dry.

Seedlings indoors are still best watered from the bottom.

 FERTILIZING

Transplanted seedlings will benefit from the application of a very diluted water-soluble fertilizer. Remember, an excess of nitrogen encourages damping off and very tender growth. In the garden, the incorporation of 5-10-5 fertilizer during soil preparation, at a rate of 3 to 4 pounds per 100 square feet, will hold most crops until midseason.

# PRUNING

Thinnings from **beets, radishes, swiss chard,** and **turnips** can all get tossed into a salad.

**Asparagus** is harvested in April. There are several ways to harvest the spears. Snapping the stalks where they snap naturally may be the best. Using an asparagus cutter at the base sometimes damages emerging spears. Cut the spears while the tips are still nice and tight. Eat them as soon as possible to get the best flavor and tenderness.

# PESTS

When planting transplants of just about anything, especially **broccoli, cauliflower,** and **cabbage,** you want to protect your plants from cutworms. These are critters that come out at night and chew the stem all the way through. The use of protective "collars" creates a mechanical barrier that keeps the cutworms away.

The easiest way to make collars is to use empty cat food or tuna fish cans with the top and bottom removed. Slip them over the plants and press them about 1/3 of the way into the ground. If you have

## Helpful Hints

Mulching around your vegetable crops controls weeds as well as retains soil moisture. Fresh grass clippings supply some nitrogen. Old newspapers, the black and white pages, can be soaked and laid down in thick layers as mulch. Shredded office paper can also be soaked and used as mulch. The woven plastic mulches allow water to pass through the weave and are an excellent weed control. Black plastic mulch also warms the soil so plants grow more rapidly in cooler weather, but then you have to deal with the plastic at the end of the season.

more plants going in the ground than you have cans, you can cut collars out of half-gallon paper milk containers or even use old ring lids from canning jars.

Root maggots and aphids get on **cabbage** family crops, and root maggots affect **radishes**, too. If you have lost a crop to them, replant but pretreat the soil. Check with your Cooperative Extension Office for current control recommendations.

# NOTES

_____

_____

_____

_____

_____

_____

_____

_____

_____

_____

PLANNING

Towards the end of the month, you have to plant your warm season crops. Some of the all-time favorites go in from transplants, which you may be tending indoors. These include **tomatoes, peppers,** and **eggplants.**

Occasionally, some gardeners will try to get a head start on long season **cucurbit** (from the family Cucurbitaceae) crops by starting them indoors as well. **Pumpkins,** especially the giant ones, and **winter squash** such as **blue hubbard** or **butternut** may benefit from the extra growing time. Even some of the non-edible members of the family do better with a little extra lead time. **Luffa squash, bottle gourds,** and smaller decorative gourds all benefit from the extra time at the end of the season to properly mature for long-term use.

In most cases, the above cucurbits do fine with direct seeding, as do some of the other relatives such as **cucumbers** and **pickles.** Zucchini, yellow **summer squash, pattypan squash,** and **acorn squash** can be direct seeded. You can also plant from seed **okra, green beans** (also called **snap beans**), **lima beans,** and more **sweet corn.**

 PLANTING

Here are a few tips specific for crops going in now.

• If you're planting **corn,** make sure you follow the population density requirements (see April).

• If you soak **okra** seed overnight, you can speed germination.

• **Cucurbits** can be planted in rows up against a fence but are more commonly planted in "hills." A hill is a flat, circular mound about 18 inches in diameter. A number of seeds, usually about six, are placed in a circle about 12 inches in diameter. After germination, the three best are allowed to grow on. **Cucumber** hills are spaced 4 feet apart. **Pumpkin** hills are 8 feet apart.

• **Peppers** must have excellent drainage. In heavy soil, mounding up the row a few inches is beneficial. Never plant peppers deeper in the soil than they were in the pot.

• **Eggplants** really like hot weather and the use of black plastic (see April "Helpful Hints") warms the soil. This practice makes an appreciable difference in yield.

• When planting **tomatoes,** remove all the foliage except the top leaves and dig a hole deep enough so you can plant right up to the leaves. If the plants are too tall to do this, you can dig a trench and lay the plants down. Cover the stems up to the top leaves with soil. The leaves will turn and grow up very quickly. The buried stem will produce roots all along its length. The deeper you plant, the more access to water the roots will have and the more drought-tolerant the plants will become. It is especially important to stake or cage your tomato plants at the time of planting if you are using the trench method. It is too easy to damage the root and stem if you attempt to install stakes at a later date.

• **Spinach** is planted in mid-March and usually gives up in the heat by mid-July, at the latest. You can extend the season by providing shade in hot weather, removing any developing seed heads, and keeping it well watered.

WATERING

Water all new transplants at planting. Seeds will need to be watered daily until they germinate if it doesn't rain. If it is unseasonably hot, you may need to water seeds twice a day. Taper off watering after germination.

Once the plants are established and thriving, you should only have to water if it gets dry. Hot weather can cause plants to bolt or go to seed more quickly than you would expect. A deep watering during unexpected heat may avoid this problem. Remember to water deeply. Shallow watering brings roots to the surface and makes plants more dependent on irrigation.

 FERTILIZING

Fertilizer is generally applied during soil preparation just prior to planting (see soil preparation in the chapter introduction).

A sidedressing is often beneficial in the middle of a vegetable's growing season (determined by when you plant and the expected growing time of your vegetable). A light band of fertilizer on the side of the row is fine. Try not to get it on the foliage. Water it in so it gets to the roots.

 PRUNING

Thin seedlings based on the recommended spacing provided on the seed packet. Take care when thinning **cucumbers** if you have male and female seeds. When thinning, you do not want to

## Helpful Hints

Don't forget about the importance of support for your vegetables. For details on support methods and some of the plants that may need help, see the information in the chapter introduction.

remove all the males. **Corn** definitely needs to be thinned if you are to get any ears.

**Radishes** only take about thirty days, so these can be harvested. Take the biggest ones first, and the rest will continue to develop. **Asparagus** is generally harvested for six to eight weeks, depending on the age of the bed. **Loose leaf lettuce** and the semi-heading types can be harvested by removing only the outside leaves. This will encourage more growth. You can do the same with **spinach, arrugula,** and **Swiss chard.**

**Chives** are hardy and generally return each spring for many years. They can be cut throughout the season and added to salads or used to add a mild onion flavor to any cooked dish. The blue flowers arrive in spring and can also be added to salads for both appearance and flavor.

 PESTS

**Tomatoes, peppers,** and **eggplants** need collars to protect against cutworms. See last month's direction for **cabbage** family plants and do the same.

Flea beetles can be a problem on **radishes** and leafminers on **spinach** and **Swiss chard.** Check with your Cooperative Extension Office for control recommendations.

## NOTES

_____

_____

_____

_____

_____

_____

_____

_____

_____

_____

_____

_____

_____

_____

# JUNE
## Vegetables

 PLANNING

You may want to plan to fill in where early crops finish. A short row of **radishes** can be planted every two weeks until the weather turns very hot. Late plantings of **bush beans** can follow early **lettuces** and **spinach.** You may want to prepare a seedbed so you can start **cabbage** family crops for a fall harvest. **Peas** can also be planted next month for a fall harvest. Give some thought as to what will go where and what your subsequent plantings will be.

 PLANTING

Anything that you meant to plant in late May can still be planted in early June.

You may want to attempt a summer planting of **lettuces** in a cooler, partially shady spot. Early to mid-June plantings of **sweet corn** (dependent on variety of course) will be ready to harvest just in time for your Labor Day picnic. **Bush beans** can also be planted every two weeks or just follow with a late second planting at the end of the month. If you have any **onion** sets sitting around, plant them very close together and harvest them as needed as scallions.

A late June planting of **cucumbers** will also extend the season. Cucumber often gives up early to the wilt disease. Keep the second planting far away from the first, just as a precaution. **Summer squash** bear in fifty to sixty days, so if you didn't get your **yellow squash** or **zucchini** in yet, you still have time. **Winter squash** are not as flexible. Many take about 100 days, so if you don't get them in by very early this month you may need to skip it until next year.

 WATERING

Seeds always need extra attention with water until they emerge. They may pop up quickly as the soil warms up. Water them enough so they don't fry to a crisp right after germination. They won't have much of a root system yet, but as they develop, you can taper off the water. Water early in the morning, and deeply. Avoid overhead sprinklers if possible to avoid the spread of leaf diseases.

 FERTILIZING

If you are following a water-soluble fertilizer application program, liquid fertilizer in a diluted solution will be needed, used according to directions. If you applied granular 5-10-5 fertilizer during soil preparation just prior to planting, you will want to side-dress at the midpoint of your crop's growing season.

 PRUNING

Most **asparagus** harvesting is finished by early in the month. You need to let the rest of the plants grow into the ferny stage to build up the plants energy for next year's harvest. Early **beets** are ready for harvest. The more you harvest your **peas**, the longer they will produce. Cut **lettuce** in the cool morning. It stores very well in a salad spinner. Remove any developing seedheads from your leafy cool season crops, and they will last longer. When **broccoli** heads up, remove the head but leave the plant. When **cauliflower** heads up, harvest the head and yank the plant.

**Peppers** will produce very early. The fruits can be eaten at any stage, but the flavor develops as the fruits mature. Hot peppers are hottest when grown in high temperatures and when the fruit is fully mature. For red bell or frying peppers, you have to leave them on the plant until they mature fully. **Green peppers** are actually immature peppers. Unfortunately, if you let the fruits fully mature for both color and flavor, they will produce far fewer fruits. That is why red peppers are so much more expensive at the store.

## PESTS

Colorado potato beetles are destructive in both the pink spotted larval stage and the tan and black striped beetle stage. Make sure you squish the yellow egg masses found on the underside of the leaves. They gobble up **potato** leaves, but they are almost as voracious on **eggplants.** Sometimes they feed on **tomatoes,** but not as much. Handpick them if you have a limited infestation. Count your blessings that the Philip Alampi Beneficial Insect Laboratory releases insects that are natural predators and parasites of the Colorado potato beetle, or the problem would be much worse.

It is both the spotted and striped cucumber beetle that carries the cucumber bacterial wilt. It only takes one infected beetle to infect a **cucumber** plant, resulting in its early demise. Once the plants reach the flowering stage, the insects are not longer likely to infect the plant, but while the plants are tender the insects should be controlled. The other option is to plant repeatedly, two weeks apart to extend the season. Once the plants wilt, there is nothing to control the disease.

Squash vine borers are the larval stage of a clear winged moth. The adult lays its eggs at the base of a **squash** plant, which includes **zucchini** and **pumpkin** to name

## Helpful Hints

*1* You may want to harvest lots of **green peppers** and then, towards the end of the season, leave some on to turn red. The new colored pepper varieties offer a bit of confusion as to what is actually ripe. On some, the mature color is red, but some can be yellow or orange at maturity. Some start out green, turn purple, and then red.

*2* **Broccoli** will continue to produce side shoots for most of the summer. If you allow all the buds to grow into shoots, the heads will end up very small as the season progresses. Remove most of these suckers, but leave three or four to make more heads.

just a few, and then the eggs hatch. The larvae burrow into the stem and feed on the vine from the inside, eventually destroying it. You can attempt to dig out borers with a lengthwise slit, but once a plant has more than one or two, it, too, fades away. You can cover the emerging plants with row cover, or you can replant in late July after the egg-laying cycle is complete.

## NOTES

_____

_____

_____

_____

_____

_____

_____

_____

_____

_____

_____

## PLANNING

July planning in the vegetable garden shifts into primarily maintenance. Early in the month, you will be doing harvesting of the spring crops. **Cauliflower, broccoli,** and **cabbage** should be ready to enjoy. **Lettuces** and **spinach** will be finishing up once it turns really hot. Give some thought to what you want to plant to follow these crops. If you are lucky, you got to enjoy your first **tomatoes** and **sweet corn** for the 4th of July, but that generally takes extra planning to make happen.

## PLANTING

This is the time for late plantings of **bush beans, sweet corn, summer squash,** and **cucumbers.** It is also the right time to plant **peas** for a late harvest. Plant in early to mid-July so you'll have the needed sixty-five to seventy-five days to reach harvest. Peas continue to bear for several weeks, so give yourself enough time to enjoy the harvest. You can start **cabbage** family crops in a seedbed to transplant later. **Broccoli, cauliflower,** and **cabbage** seed can be started very early this month. They will be ready to harvest in 100 to 120 days, which puts harvest in October. The cooler temperature during the time the heads are forming will make for a sweeter flavor. They will all be able to tolerate a light frost.

## WATERING

Watering in July may be necessary. Avoid overhead watering if possible, but if necessary, water overhead in the early morning so the plants dry out quickly. Use mulch to moderate fluctuations in soil temperature, to control weeds, and to retain soil moisture.

## FERTILIZING

There are lots of crops that will benefit from a July sidedressing of 5-10-5 fertilizer. Don't fertilize **potatoes** or **sweet potatoes. Sweet corn** is fertilized at planting and when it is about a foot tall. Late July is the middle of the growing season for **tomatoes, peppers,** and **eggplants,** so they will benefit from a dose of fertilizer. So will **okra.** Long-season **winter squash** will definitely benefit from a sidedressing now. That includes **pumpkins.** If your **zucchinis** are like most zucchinis, you don't want to feed them. They are already producing more squash than you can possibly eat.

Those vegetables that you are planting this month need fertilizer incorporated into the soil during soil preparation the same as if they were being planted in the spring.

## PRUNING

On **pumpkins,** it may be time to choose which fruits you want to allow to develop if you are trying to grow gigantic pumpkins for fun or competition. You may want to leave only one fruit per vine.

**Okra** should be harvested when the pods are about 3 inches long. They get woody after that. **Broccoli** should be in the tight bud stage. In July heat, it goes from bud to yellow flowers very quickly, so don't delay. **Cabbage** seems to hold on a little longer but not **cauliflower.** Get it while the getting's good.

**Tomatoes** should be vine ripened to be at their peak of flavor. Fruits that are split or damaged in any way should be eaten quickly as they have no shelf life. They are best harvested with the stem attached. Do not refrigerate tomatoes because it kills the flavor.

**Green beans** can be harvested anywhere from tiny to fully developed without the shape of the beans showing through the pod. **Lima beans** are shelled, so you want the beans fully formed but not yet woody. Try a few early on, and you will get the idea.

**Peppers** can be harvested anytime. **Zucchini** are perfect at about 6 to 8 inches but can be harvested at 3 inches for popular baby vegetables. **Pattypan** can also be harvested while tiny but may be best at 2 to 3 inches across. While you are at it, harvest the male **squash** blossoms right after they open. They are fabulous dipped in batter and fried.

Harvest the leaves of **Swiss chard** as needed. They do tend to get bitter in hot weather, though.

 PESTS

If the bottoms of the **tomatoes** are black, hard, and sunken, this is the result of a nutrient deficiency known as blossom end rot. You can cut off the bad part and eat the rest. This is usually worse in **plum tomatoes,** and it usually corrects itself with the next batch. It is related to a calcium imbalance.

Tomato hornworms eat gaping holes in tomato leaves overnight and are scary but not really dangerous. You may want to wear gloves while you hunt for them at night with a flashlight.

Cabbage moths are those cute white butterfly-like moths that flit around your yard. They lay eggs on **cabbage** family plants which hatch into larvae that eat gaping holes in the leaves. They are hard to see because they blend into the color of the leaf. Handpick or try Bt (*Bacillus thurengiensis*). These critters get worse throughout the year since they have multiple generations in a growing season.

White fly may also be showing up. They do not survive New Jersey winters, so they have to fly up from the south. The colder the winter, the further they have to fly and the later they show up. They are like a cloud of white surrounding a plant when the plant is disturbed. They can feed on a variety of things but seem to like **tomatoes**.

NOTES

_____

_____

_____

_____

_____

_____

_____

_____

_____

## PLANNING

So what are you going to do with all that produce? Certainly you want to eat as much of it as possible, fresh from the garden when flavor and nutrients are at their peak. If you really have way too much of something, local food banks will be thrilled to take the excess. Many churches also have programs where they make food available to the needy within their congregation or the town where they are located.

Canning and freezing are also options. Freezing is easier, but you may be limited by freezer space. There is an excellent book entitled *Putting Food By* written by Ruth Hertzberg, Beatrice Vaughan, and Janet Greene. It will give many options for ways to enjoy your garden produce beyond the days of harvest.

## PLANTING

If you started your **cabbage** family plants in a seedbed, you can transplant them into their real spots when they have about three leaves. If you are having seedlings grown at a greenhouse, they will be ready this month. See planting information in the chapter introduction.

Towards the tail-end of the month you may want to start some of the leafy greens. These will thrive in the cool autumn weather. **Spinach** will even over-winter for a very early harvest in the spring. Again, there are real advantages to purchasing seed packs of mixed varieties. Five different lettuces in one pack provides plenty of variety.

If you want to experiment with all kinds of leafy greens, get yourself a copy of *The Cook's Garden Catalog*. The company is located in Londonderry, Vermont (www.cooksgarden.com). They have page after page of **lettuces,** unusual greens available by the pack, and a fabulous selection of mixes.

Since most **lettuces** will tolerate light frosts, they become significant season extenders. Wait until the weather is not brutally hot to start these seeds. Exposure to extreme heat may cause the plants to bolt prematurely.

## WATERING

Water newly planted seeds daily, and maybe even twice daily if weather is very dry. Since these are cool-season crops, you may want to use a shade cloth until temperatures stay below 80 degrees Fahrenheit. It will help keep the soil moist and the seedlings from frying. You probably will not need it for long. The weather flips into classic September conditions soon after Labor Day. Then you will have the coolers temps and often more rainfall.

Producing plants will continue to need deep watering whenever the ground gets dry. It becomes especially important to avoid water on the foliage because the cooler nights in August encourage powdery mildew.

## FERTILIZING

Soil preparation for the seeding or planting of fall crops includes working in 5-10-5 fertilizer, the same as in the spring (see the chapter introduction).

If you didn't get your midseason fertilization done in late July, you can do it in early August. These crops may include **tomatoes, peppers, eggplants,** and **okra.** Long-season **winter squash,** including **pumpkins,** will also enjoy a feeding in early August if they didn't get fertilizer last month.

## PRUNING

By late August, prune away any flowers or new fruits on your **winter squashes,** especially **pumpkins.** You want all the energy to go into fruits already on the vine. New ones at this late date will probably not mature.

Be sure to harvest all your **summer squashes** while still tender. (This is true even if you have so many you can't eat them.) The ones left to get larger will get tougher. Plus, allowing summer squash to go unpicked will result in fewer, and eventually, no new ones.

Leave some of your **peppers** to mature to red, orange, or yellow (whatever is the mature color for your variety). Sweet peppers will be sweeter, and hot peppers will be hotter. Make sure you have enough of the green ones before you stop harvesting because allowing peppers to mature also stops setting of new fruits.

Harvest **sweet corn** when the silks turn brown, but first check a few ears for taste. The exact peak of flavor and texture for sweet corn is a personal taste.

## PESTS

Don't forget to use "collars" on your newly planted **cabbage** family plants. See April for details. Also remember that the cabbage moths are more abundant later in the season. Keep a close eye on the underside of the leaves so you can crush the egg masses, and search carefully for larvae. They are hard to see as they match the color of the leaves.

## Helpful Hints

There is a wonderful cookbook entitled *Jersey Fresh Cooks* published by the New Jersey Department of Agriculture. It features recipes for garden fresh produce that were submitted by New Jersey residents from all over the state. It is only available at Farm Markets.

If your **parsley** is disappearing, you are going to have to live with it. Parsleyworm is the larval stage of the beautiful black swallowtail butterfly. It produces several generations per year, so it can show up anytime. Plant extra parsley next time so you will be sure to have enough.

Corn earworms get into the end of the ears and feed on the developing kernels. They are nasty, but once you cut off the ends of the ears, the rest is edible. To avoid them in the future, you can apply a few drops of mineral oil inside the tip of each ear after the silks have wilted.

## NOTES

_____

_____

_____

_____

_____

_____

_____

_____

_____

_____

_____

_____

# SEPTEMBER
## Vegetables

 PLANNING

You may want to save the seed from anything that did very well. However, seeds cannot be saved from hybrid varieties as they will not come true. If you planted many varieties of the same vegetable close together, you cannot save those either. Cross-pollination may have occurred, so the seed will not come true. **Squash** family plants cross-pollinate readily as do **peppers. Tomatoes,** on the other hand, are almost self-pollinating, so if you have some distance between open pollinated varieties, it is probably worthwhile to save the seed.

Seed saving requires that the developing fruits be allowed to fully mature on the plant. This means the process will slow or eliminate any additional fruit set. You may want to dedicate one plant to fully mature fruits so you continue to get a harvest from the others.

You may also want to dedicate a few **okra** plants to the production of dried pods. As they mature, the pods become quite woody and are spectacular used in dried flower arrangements.

 PLANTING

Any of the cool-season plants that were suggested for planting in late August can still be planted in early September. The list includes **cabbage** family plants, many varieties of **lettuce, spinach,** and other leafy greens. **Radishes** will also do very well at this time of year as they are ready to harvest in only about thirty days.

It is getting late, but you may be able to squeeze in one more planting of **beets.** They can tolerate early frosts and are more tender when the roots develop in cool weather. **Turnips** respond similarly to the cooler weather and can be harvested quicker. Beets will take about sixty days, so be sure to get them in the ground the first few days of the month. **Turnips** take only about fifty days.

 WATERING

The watering of freshly planted seeds should still be done daily. Even if the soil is moist, the surface can dry quickly in the sun. Shade cloth may or may not be helpful in keeping soil moist. If it is still summer-hot, the shade will be beneficial, but you will not need it for long in September.

If the sky opened with the expected heavy rain that often happens in early September, you may not need to continue supplementing water. If summer heat continues and the sky remains blue and clear, continue watering deeply on an as-needed basis. It is not likely it will continue for long in the month, but stay tuned to weather for your clues as to what is best.

 FERTILIZING

Fertilize newly planted seeds and plants the same as if you were planting in the spring. All other summer and long season crops will manage without the need for additional fertilizer.

 PRUNING

It is usually in August or September that the vines die back on your **potato** plants. That is the signal that you can harvest them. If you have never eaten freshly dug spuds, you are in for a treat. The rich flavor is light years ahead of the stored potatoes we are all used to eating.

Do not dig all the **potatoes,** only what you want to eat at the moment. They store very well in the ground. You can leave them until just before the ground freezes. That way you have to store them indoors for a minimum amount of time. It generally works out well to dig them up for storage the day after Thanksgiving.

**Peppers** and **eggplants** often seem to be ready in abundance early in the month. Peppers have the flexibility of being perfectly edible at almost all stages. Left on the plant, they just get sweeter or hotter, as the case may be. Eggplants should be harvested while fairly immature; otherwise, the seeds turn brown, which imparts a bitter taste. White eggplants should be very white when harvested. They turn yellow as they over-mature. Dark eggplants should be very shiny. The size is variety dependent, but it is better to pick too early than too late.

This is a great time to freeze **tomatoes** for sauce. The novelty of eating them fresh is probably wearing off by now. Leave the stem attached for a longer shelf life.

## PESTS

Keep a sharp eye for cabbage worms. White fly is also worse at this time of year. If you are planting fall **lettuces** and assorted greens, watch out for slugs. They are especially bad if it has been a wet year. Slugs do not like hot weather, so they may be more active now that the weather has cooled. If they are a serious problem, be sure to remove all the organic mulch around your greens. That way they have less cover for hiding.

## Helpful Hints

If your **sweet peppers** are hot, it could be for one of two reasons. If you grew sweet and **hot peppers** last year and saved the seed, they may have cross pollinated. It is like crossing a red rose with a white rose. The offspring will most likely be pink, but the shade of pink can vary. If you purchased **fresh** sweet and hot pepper seed this year but the sweet variety is still hot, there is a bit of hope. Cross-pollination still took place, but the flesh of the sweet pepper is still just a sweet pepper. If you cook the sweet peppers with the seeds intact, it will impart some of the hot flavor to the pepper itself. If you remove the seeds prior to cooking, you should be back to sweet peppers.

## NOTES

# OCTOBER
## Vegetables

###  PLANNING

Want to plan for Halloween? Your **sweet corn** will be done sometime this month if it isn't done already. Make sure you save the cornstalks for the holiday. **Pumpkins** need to be fully orange to be ready to harvest. Pick the ripest ones for painting early and leave the rest in the field until you are ready to carve. The smaller sugar pumpkins make the best pies, so you may want to save them for baking. The larger jack-o-lantern varieties are a little tough for pumpkin pie. **Hubbard squash** makes a great pie.

You also need to plan for the inevitable frost that will come this month. Your fall-planted, cold-tolerant crops will all weather the early frosts just fine. It is your warm weather summer crops that give up at the first chill. Keep up with the weather. You can protect against an early light frost by covering the plants with a sheet. If you have a lot of immature fruits it may be worth it.

On the other hand, maybe you have had enough and you're ready to harvest all that is left. **Peppers, eggplants, beans,** and **summer squash** can be eaten at just about any stage. Harvesting these while they're very young is much better than waiting until they over-mature, so plan to harvest all the warm weather crops when frost is in the air.

###  PLANTING

There is one crop that is really best planted in October: **garlic.** You can plant either cloves purchased at the garden center or buy a head at the market and break apart the cloves for planting.

A loose sandy, loamy soil is preferred. Since **garlic** is a bulb crop, the roots need room to expand. Space the cloves 6 inches apart. Push the cloves into the soft soil so the tip of the clove is barely noticeable. Press the soil down around it a bit to be sure it will stay put over the winter. It will send up some leaves in the fall but will be certain to come back in the early spring. Fall planted garlic is generally more successful than spring planted in New Jersey.

###  WATERING

Water in your newly planted garlic cloves. If it is unseasonably dry, then you may also need to water your fall-season leafy vegetables. **Beets** need to be pushed hard to produce a crop before it's too late. Keep them well watered if weather even hints at being dry.

###  FERTILIZING

Incorporate 5-10-5 fertilizer into the soil during soil preparation for your **garlic.** A light sidedressing of 5-10-5 for your **beets** and **turnips** will push them into production before frost. If you planted them by mid-August, they will not need to be pushed as hard.

###  PRUNING

**Winter squash** should be left in the field until all the vines have dried and the skins are hard. Leave 2 inches of stem on **pumpkins** and winter squash. After harvest, leave the fruits in the sun for about two weeks to cure them.

When a frost is imminent, pick all the green **tomatoes** and find yourself a good recipe for fried green tomatoes and another for pickling green tomatoes.

If your **Brussels sprouts** haven't developed any sprouts by the beginning of the month, pinch out the growing tip. This will allow the dormant buds to develop. Look for the sprouts all along the main stem. If you harvest after a light frost, the sprouts will be sweeter.

## PESTS

One of the most important aspects of pest control in the vegetable garden is to clean up the garden before winter sets in. Garden debris becomes a perfect place for insects and diseases to overwinter. Remove dead plant material and add it to the compost pile. If the plant died from disease, you may want to bag it up and send it out with the trash.

Adding lime in the fall while you do all this is more effective than liming in the spring. Turning over the garden now also helps with weed control. Once the garden is all tidy, you can use the fallen leaves as mulch. This will help prevent early spring weeds and will also add organic matter to the soil.

## Helpful Hints

*1* When collecting your last green **tomatoes,** sort them according to size and degree of ripeness into groups of four or five. Have a stack of brown paper lunch bags on hand. Wrap the similar fruits individually in newspaper and put the group into a bag. Store all the fruits in a cool, dark location (not the refrigerator). Check weekly to see which have ripened. Those that had any red or pink will ripen much more quickly than those that were all green. If you are lucky you might have garden tomatoes for Christmas.

*2* **Asparagus** plants turn absolutely gorgeous shades of yellow, gold, red, and bronze in the fall. Don't cut them back as long as they add beauty to your yard. Once they are completely brown, they can be cut back.

## NOTES

## PLANNING

November is always a little sad in the vegetable garden. Some plants will get hit by the inevitable hard freeze, while some of the cool weather crops will still be doing okay. **Lettuces** and some leafy greens may still be doing well. The use of a cold frame or modified old glass storm windows to cover the beds will protect these plants for another month. **Parsley** often stays fresh to serve with the Thanksgiving meal, even without protection. **Brussels sprouts** and **cabbage** hold up well also.

## PLANTING

There are no vegetables to plant in November out in the garden. If you have a greenhouse, you can start **lettuce** and mixed greens from seed in containers. Plastic windowboxes, with drainage, are great for this. You can often find them on sale this late in the season.

**Radishes** do surprisingly well in containers, as do some the small round varieties of **carrots. Chives** can be dug up from the garden and potted. They can get quite large in the garden, so perhaps just dig up enough for a large pot and leave the rest to come back in the spring.

## Helpful Hints

Making pie from fresh **pumpkins** is a lot of work. If you are going to do all the work, you should start with the best pumpkins. **Cheese pumpkins** are pale, flattened pumpkins that seem to be a local phenomenon. They are often available at farm stands, although the seed is very hard to find. They make the very best pies. If you find a cheese pumpkin, save the seeds for next year.

## WATERING

You are done outside. Water plants indoors as needed. Veggies in pots dry out quickly.

## FERTILIZING

For containers, a regular application of a water-soluble liquid fertilizer for vegetables may be the best approach. Use very diluted applications to minimize the chance of burning the roots.

If you struggled with blossom end rot on your **tomatoes,** if reflects a calcium imbalance, and an early application of lime to your soil will go a long way in preventing the problem next year.

## PRUNING

Dig all your **potatoes** for winter storage before the ground freezes. Any time this month is fine, but if you have a lot, they store very well in the ground. The less time they are above ground, the better they will taste.

**Horseradish** is dug at the same time, just before the ground freezes. If you leave a few in the ground, they will return in the spring. But don't leave too many, or they will spread more than you will like. **Sunchokes**, or **Jerusalem artichokes,** are treated exactly the same way.

**Chives** in containers can be snipped this month for salads or for cooking all winter.

## PESTS

Pests are finished up for the year, but make sure the garden is tidy.

# DECEMBER

##  PLANNING

Without a cold frame or a greenhouse, your vegetable garden is sound asleep at this time of year. If you were very careful in October, you may have a few **tomatoes** left ripening in some cool dark spot. If you were industrious, you may have jars of tomato sauce or bags of frozen **peppers** to remind you of last summer's bounty. If not, the memory of a garden-fresh tomato, warm from the sun and dripping down your chin as you take a juicy bite, is going to have to hold you until next summer. For now, enjoy the bounty of the holiday season as you prepare for the giving and receiving of gifts and the joy of sharing time with those closest to you. Below are some gift ideas for a vegetable gardener you know:

*1* There are all kinds of **supports** for vine crops such as **peas** and **pole beans.** Some are very attractive with decorative finials on the top. Others are no more than a half a dozen bamboo canes tied together on one end. The use of these really makes setting up easy. They're great for giving vertical space to a small garden.

## Helpful Hints

There was no difficulty in choosing a movie to recommend for vegetables. *Fried Green Tomatoes* is a family favorite. There is something in it for everyone. If you get the book, there is a recipe in the back that may help you use up some of your extra green **tomatoes,** before frost gets them all.

*2* There are some fun **plant ties** out now. They are bendable creatures with long arms and legs. Wrap them around the stake and the plants you are trying to support. They are especially good for **tomatoes** and can be reused for many years.

*3* Another big present would be **a greenhouse window.** They can be made to fit almost any window, but one on the south side would probably be best for starting seeds in early spring.

###  PLANTING

Planting is done for now. But spring is right around the corner.

###  WATERING

There is no watering needed outside. If you have some veggies in containers, continue to water on an as-needed basis.

###  FERTILIZING

For any container veggies, continue to use a diluted water-soluble fertilizer for vegetables.

###  PRUNING

You may want to cut back your **asparagus** plants at this time. They probably held some fall color through November, but once they turn brown, you can cut them back.

###  PESTS

There are no pests to worry about at this time of year. If you haven't tidied up the garden yet, you really should. It is the best way to minimize insects and disease for next year.

# All About Composting

**All gardeners should have a compost pile.** We can chat about the civic-minded compost pile, where you are protecting the environment by keeping your organic waste from going to the landfill and saving municipalities the expense of collecting and handling the material. Or there is the reasoning that it is actually easier to make a pile of leaves and garden debris than rake it all up and shove it into bags, which have to be dragged out to the road. There is a good argument for locating a compost pile where you intend to create a garden bed in the next year or two. The pile will smother all grass and weeds underneath and the worms will pull down the organic matter into the soil. **Worms can turn awful soil into something worthwhile in a surprisingly short period of time.**

There are lots of good reasons to compost in your backyard. It does seem kind of silly to bag up and send away all this organic matter and then go buy bags of organic matter to improve your soil. Store-bought organic matter takes time to purchase, costs more money, has to be lugged into the car, hauled back out of the car, and dragged into the garden. You could skip a lot of steps if your compost pile was close to the garden . . . and you wouldn't have to vacuum the car because of a wayward bag ripping open in the trunk.

## COMPOST HAPPENS!

It does! With or without our help! Other descriptive words, such as rotting, decomposing, or breaking-down, are also applicable to the microbial degradation that happens to organic material in nature. **To truly be composting, there needs to be one more element: "management."**

When humanity steps in, we work towards controlling the variables Mother Nature has so carefully balanced. Agriculture is a perfect example. Farmers take the plants that originated in the wild a long time ago and force them to grow in nice straight rows. By so doing, it is possible to dramatically speed up the process and/or to increase the output

significantly. It is also possible to screw it all up. In the same way, a poorly managed compost operation can become a reeking mess. Mother Nature may not achieve the rate of decomposition that meets the needs of our fast paced world, but neither does she create the imbalance of a compost pile gone wrong.

## THE BUILDING BLOCKS

All organic matter will decompose over time, but not all is equally suitable for a backyard composting environment. Meat and meat by-products are not a good choice. They are far too likely to draw unwanted critters, and bones take a really long time to break down. Avoid dairy products. Eggshells are acceptable only if you wash them out first. Vegetative kitchen scraps are far more manageable, but really should be buried. They break down relatively quickly to a non-food state, especially in hot weather. In cold weather they can attract diners for a much longer time. Buried into the center of a pile or tossed into a hole in the ground and covered with partially decomposed compost, these kitchen scraps are far less enticing.

**There are a number of variables to manipulate when planning your compost pile.** These include the carbon to nitrogen ratio, moisture levels, oxygen content, particle size, temperature and pile size. Each type of organic matter you decide to add to the pile will affect all of these variables.

### Start with Leaves

The simplest material you can compost is **autumn leaves.** Heaped into a pile, they will eventually turn into usable compost. With no additional management it may take two to three years to completely decompose. Even then the outer layer will not be as decomposed as the inner parts of pile. The more management of the biological system that is responsible for turning leaves into compost, the faster the process progresses.

## Turning the Pile

The simple act of turning the pile on occasion during the composting process will get what is on the outside of the pile into the center. The moisture from the leaves will provide the moisture for the microbes doing the decomposition. Keeping that concept in mind, **plan your composting location where you will have room for two piles.** One space will be for the original pile. The open spot will be where you flip the pile when in the process of turning. This approach is infinitely easier and far more effective than attempting to turn a pile in place.

## Temperature

Turning the pile can also let out excess heat. In a small pile this is not usually necessary. Heat escapes smaller piles on its own. Sometimes you can see steam rising from a compost pile. Water is a by-product of the decomposition process and heat is produced in a higher nitrogen, rapid compost environment. **The ideal temperature range is between 90 and 140 degrees Fahrenheit.** Long stemmed thermometers are available for measuring the temperature in the center of a pile. Decomposition declines above 140 degrees F. and stops entirely at 170 degrees F.

There is one distinct advantage to a hot pile. At approximately 131 degrees F. all weed seeds and pathogenic (disease causing) organisms are killed off. If you can maintain your pile at a temperature above 131 degrees for several days, you have a good chance of eliminating any diseases and weeds from staying viable within the compost. Rememb er to turn the pile to get the outside raw material into the hot zone to destroy any pests on that part of the pile.

In a small backyard pile it may be difficult to have enough mass to produce the heat necessary to kill off weeds and diseases. You can make the pile larger to start, and/or add nitrogen and water to increase the rate of decomposition and heat generated. Another alternative is to avoid adding any diseased material or weed seeds to the pile, and not worry about it.

## Adding Moisture

Moisture is an essential element to the decomposition process. Organic matter does not decompose on its own. Living, breathing microorganisms feed on the organic matter and digest it. When moisture levels are below 25 percent all decomposition comes to a halt. A dry leaf will still be a dry leaf years from now. A pile of truly dry leaves has a secondary problem. Leaves in a pile tend to layer themselves on the surface much like the shingles on a roof. Water applied will run off, never penetrating deep into the center of the pile where most of the decomposition is taking place. The result is a dry pile that stays dry, and does not decompose to your expectations.

Make sure the leaves are wet at the time you form the pile. If you are working with wet leaves, you don't have a problem

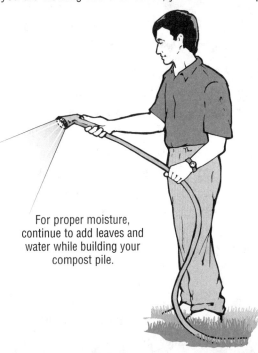

For proper moisture, continue to add leaves and water while building your compost pile.

except that they are much heavier to rake and lift. **With dry leaves (which are a lot more fun!) you must wet them as you create your pile.** Put a layer of leaves in the spot you have chosen and then wet them thoroughly. Continue to add leaves and water until your pile is complete.

If you are unsure whether your pile needs water you can do the squeeze test. Reach into the pile (remember the surface is generally on the dry side unless it just rained) and grab a handful of material. If you squeeze it and water runs all over your hand, it is too wet. If you squeeze for all you are worth and nothing happens, it is too dry. If you are barely able to squeeze out one or two drops of water, it is just right.

## THE IMPORTANT PILE

Most large scale, commercial operations design their facilities to manage six-foot piles. While it may be the most efficient from a management perspective, it is impractical for the back yard. Four feet is large enough in most cases to decompose leaves in a reasonable time frame, but the pile may need a jump start in the early spring if it has been frozen solid all winter.

Gardeners are often worried that they do not have enough space for these enormous piles of leaves. Not to worry, they do not stay enormous for long. The final product is usually about 25 percent of the original volume. Besides, leaves have been falling in forests way longer than we have been keeping track. They don't seem to have any problems coping with the volume.

## Particle Size

Particle size is another key variable in the rate of decomposition. **The smaller the size of the organic matter particles, the more surface area there is for the microbes to attack. That means faster decomposition.**

Reducing the particle size of the leaves you have at the onset of your composting can be extremely effective in speeding up the decomposition process. It also reduces the size of the pile by as much as 50 percent. If space is limited, this may be a useful tactic as part of pile management. You can mow your leaves with a lawnmower as a way to chop them up. If your lawnmower has a bag attachment, it makes it easy to dump the bag into your pile. If not, just rake them up to make your pile.

Unfortunately, every time you alter the natural balance of things, you have to be prepared for the increase in the level of management, or attention to detail, required by you, the compost manager. A decrease in particle size makes the pile smaller. The smaller particles have filtered down into the air spaces. Smaller pile = less air. That means the oxygen contained in the pile will get used up much more quickly.

## Oxygen

**Aerobic decomposition** involves hungry microorganisms that metabolize in the presence of oxygen. They degrade your raw organic matter into compost that has a nice earthy smell and a pH very close to neutral. In the absence of oxygen, **anaerobic microorganisms** (which only become active in an environment devoid of oxygen), take over decomposition. This is a much slower process. A result of anaerobic decomposition is the production of organic acids, which lower the pH of the final product, and smell awful.

Turning the pile lets in more oxygen. *When* to turn the pile is tricky. You can turn the pile once a month until it freezes or you can do the nose test. If you dig into the center of the pile and it feels moist but not soggy and smells earthy but not stinky, you don't have to turn it yet. At the first whiff of an unpleasant odor, turn the pile completely.

## Carbon to Nitrogen Ratio

Controlling the carbon to nitrogen ratio is an important part of composting. The ideal ration is somewhere around 30:1. Dry autumn leaves alone are high in carbon and low in nitrogen, but not so low as to prevent decomposition. They are about 40:1 but can be as high as 90:1. The woodier the material, the higher the carbon and lower the nitrogen. The range of C:N in wood is from 300 to 700:1. Wood chips decompose much slower than leaves. Saw dust is wood with a very small particle size. If raw saw dust is tilled into soil, the microbes work so fast in decomposing the wood particles that they suck ALL the nitrogen out of the soil and can render it sterile. Saw dust must be composted first before it can be used as a quality soil amendment. It must be blended with something bulky to increase the air spaces and prevent the pile from going anaerobic rapidly. It is best to add some nitrogen to keep the microbes happy.

**Nitrogen can be added to leaves or other woody raw organic materials in a variety of ways.** Many manures are high in nitrogen, especially chicken manure. Grass clippings are high in nitrogen, especially clippings from those lush green super-fertilized lawns. Many types of manure and grass clippings have a carbon to nitrogen ratio of about 20:1, unless the manure is mixed with straw. Any type of "green" organic waste, such as plants from the garden, green leaves or other vegetative waste, or even vegetable scraps from the kitchen, will be higher in nitrogen than dried leaves. Green waste and grass clippings (especially grass clippings) are also higher in moisture than autumn leaves which is beneficial to the composting process. Compost managers can also add nitrogen by mixing in a handful of fertilizer on each layer of leaves as the pile is formed.

## SUPER FAST COMPOSTING IS POSSIBLE

To maximize the rate of decomposition, reduce the particle size of the raw organic matter, make the pile large enough to hold onto the heat generated during decomposition, keep it moist but not soggy, add nitrogen, and turn the pile before it gets anaerobic and stinky. Unfortunately that also creates a lot of opportunity for things to go wrong.

As state previously, when the air spaces are small the oxygen gets used up very quickly. In addition, if the pile gets waterlogged there is less drainage. A saturated pile has no room for oxygen and goes anaerobic. And that stinks (literally).

The addition of too much nitrogen ends up releasing nitrogen into the air in the form of ammonia. When grass clippings are composted alone that happens quickly. It happens with piles of chicken manure also. If you are supplementing a pile of leaves with 10 percent to 20 percent of a high nitrogen material you should stay in a manageable carbon to nitrogen ratio. **If you are starting with a pile of grass clippings, it can become waterlogged, anaerobic and extremely stinky in a matter of hours.** Grass clippings alone do not compost easily and should be avoided as the main component in a backyard compost pile. It is easier and more environmentally sound to leave them on the lawn most of the time anyway. Only collect clippings when you need them or when they are so tall they will lay on the surface and smother the lawn. If you choose to work with grass clippings, even on a limited basis, make sure you work them into the pile thoroughly while they are fresh. A black plastic bag of grass clippings sitting in the sun on a 90-degree F. day becomes unmanageable before you finish cleaning up and putting away the mower.

**A pile that has been managed to maximize the rate of decomposition will have to be turned often.** This will be done weekly or more often at first. As decomposition progresses, the need for frequent turning will lessen.

## WHICH APPROACH IS BEST FOR YOU?

### The Least Effort

The easiest approach to composting would be a **three-pile approach.** It doesn't even have to be piles exactly. You could build three bins out of wood or wire. Wood will eventually compost right along with whatever is in the bin so consider using treated lumber or even recycled plastic lumber. The piles can be side-by-side or in different areas of the yard.

**In year one,** you make your first pile. You may want to locate it in a spot you intend to cultivate some time in the future. Take some care not to have wads of grass clippings or include hunks of wood. Wet it on occasion, as you build the pile. At the end of the year, you pretty much forget about it.

**In year two,** you select a different location. It could be next to the original pile or it could be someplace else entirely. If it is a dry year you may want to wet both piles on occasion. If you are concerned about weed seeds in the first pile, you can cover it in a black tarp or old carpeting.

**In year three,** once again select a new location. You can cover the second pile for weed control. The first pile should now be ready for use. You will need to scrape off the surface layer, as the outermost material will not have decomposed very much. Use that as the beginning of pile three. You will probably be surprised at how little compost there is compared to the size of the pile at the time it was formed. With luck, you will generate enough to meet your needs.

**In year four,** you will want to start another pile. You can reuse the now empty spot, or take the opportunity to cultivate that spot, as the soil will be greatly improved. Choose a new spot based on whether you intend to expand your gardens once again, or if you are trying to hide the less than gorgeous pile, or for convenient access.

### A Little More Effort

A **two-pile system** may work better for those yards where you do not have the space for three. In this case you are better off locating the two piles side-by-side. Turning will be very helpful in speeding up the process, resulting in sufficient compost the second year. Turning from one pile into another is infinitely easier if you do not have to relocate the entire pile to another spot in the yard. If you are using bins, be sure to include a way to open the bins that allows access to the pile for turning. On side-by-side bins, the front panels should open on both, but both should be hinged on the outside corners. That way when both panels swing open for turning, the panels are swung out of the way.

**In the first year,** form your pile. If you are starting your pile in the spring, you will want your finished product available the following spring. If you are starting in the fall, you may get some usable material by spring, but without intense management most of the material will still be mostly intact. One important technique to speed up the process is to **shred your fall leaves.** Run your lawn mower over them or use a leaf shredder. This will have the advantage of reducing the size of the pile by about 50 percent. It will also reduce the air spaces. Keep a close eye, or in this case, a nose, on the pile. If you dig a hole into the center and get a whiff of something unpleasant, turn the pile immediately. Flip your pile in the spring, into the second spot. That will expose whatever usable material accumulated on the bottom.

If you started your pile in the fall, add spring clean-up material and carefully turn in your early cuttings of grass clippings. Very often the first spring cut is so thick and lush, it is too heavy to leave on the surface of the grass anyway. If you can coordinate your turning of the compost pile with the first mowing, you will make blending the two together much easier. Turn a few shovels full of partially decomposed leaves and add the clippings. Repeat until the new pile is formed,

# All About Composting

with the clippings distributed throughout the pile. This will add both a source of moisture as well as nitrogen, and speed up the process.

If you are starting in the spring, take care not to overpower spring clean-up material with grass clippings. Remember, an excess of high nitrogen material can release smelly ammonia. Another problem is the rapid decomposition of the high nitrogen material that can cause anaerobic activity to kick in quickly with accompanying terrible odors.

Continue to add leaves, prunings (not woody limbs), and weeds. It is probably better if you only add weeds that have not yet gone to seed. Vegetative kitchen waste can be added but it should be buried into the center of the pile to avoid attracting unwanted dining guests. You can do the nose and water squeeze test on occasion to see if the pile needs to be turned for more oxygen or watered. In the fall add your fall leaves. If space is a problem, shred the leaves first. Mix them into the pile by turning the pile as you add the new material.

**In the second spring**, you should have one pile whether you started the previous spring or two fall seasons ago. Turn the top of the pile into the second space. Continue turning until you get to usable compost. Add all your spring clean-up material to the new pile. Harvest finished compost for use in your garden beds. Chances are you will use up all you have produced before you need the space to turn the new pile. If

you have some left over when you need the space you can store the product in a garbage can or move it to a spot closer to where you will be using it. Once again, by the following spring you will have only one pile that contains mostly usable compost and starting material for the new pile.

## High Maintenance

Under these circumstances you are trying to maximize the rate of decomposition. This may be due to space limitations, a need for weed and disease control, or because you have a high demand for compost.

**This approach will require frequent turning, so you will want to have two side-by-side units or spaces for piles available at all times.** This will make flipping the pile the easiest. Three piles will make your life easier, but you can manage with two if you can move the finished compost elsewhere.

In this case it is particularly important to locate your piles with easy access to water. It is also a good idea to purchase a compost thermometer.

## Troubleshooting

You will maximize the rate of decomposition if you can maintain the inner temperature between 90 and 140 degrees F. **If it is too cold, the rate of decomposition will be too slow.**

Composting can be simple, using common garden tools for building and turning piles, or more complex with commercial backyard composting units.

This could be because the pile is too dry, there is not enough nitrogen in the carbon to nitrogen ratio, the oxygen got used up causing anaerobic decomposition, the pile is too small to hold the necessary heat in cold weather, the pile got too hot at one point and sterilized itself, or the material is nearing completion of the decomposition process.

Over 140 degrees F., the rate of decomposition slows down until it just about stops at 170 degrees F. Remember that weed seeds and disease organisms are killed off at 131 degrees F. but that sterilization can occur over 170 degrees F. Retain the higher temps for several days, long enough to capture the benefits of the heat cleansing, but then flip the pile to let out some of the excess heat.

**If the inner temperature is too cool, start checking your variables. Start with your nose.** If you get a whiff of ammonia, you have too much nitrogen in the pile. The solution is to flip the pile and add a high carbon material, such as dry leaves or straw, bringing the C:N ration into better balance. If you get a nasty stinky smell other than ammonia, your pile probably went anaerobic. Then you have to figure out why.

**Do the water squeeze test. If water gushes out, the pile is probably waterlogged.** Turn and add dry organic matter such as dry leaves, shredded newspapers, or straw. You need to add this material in slightly bulky pieces. If it is finely shredded you won't improve the air circulation very much. If the odor is extreme, add pulverized limestone as you create the new pile. This will raise the pH. The smelly organic acids fall apart in a higher pH, dissipating the odor.

**If the water content seems acceptable, it may be that the oxygen was used up in the decomposition process.** In this case simply turning the pile will replace the oxygen. If you are going for speed, you need to check more frequently to make sure you catch it before the anaerobic situation gets out of hand. If you turn at the first hint of foul odor in the center of the pile, you will be fine. After some experience you will have a good idea of when to turn before any anaerobic activity takes place.

**If the water test indicates the material is too dry, flip the pile and add water to the layers as you form the new pile.** After the pile is formed make a depression in the top of the pile. This will help capture some rainfall. A rounded pile sheds water like roof shingles.

**If all the above parameters seem in order, give some thought to the content of the pile.** If it primarily consists of high carbon material, you may need to turn the pile and add a higher nitrogen material. This could be manure (without a high straw content), fresh grass clippings or a handful of fertilizer.

Obviously, all of this high speed composting requires regular monitoring and lots of turning. There are commercial backyard composting units available to help you with this. There are dodecahedrons (12 sided balls) that you fill part way and then roll around in your yard. There are large units that look like very short, very wide cylinders on their side. They are cradled in a rocker with large plastic ball bearings so the units can spin in place. A lot of creativity has gone into these designs and they are effective. They are however limited in capacity.

## YOU'RE IN CHARGE

Each backyard compost manager must first determine his or her needs and goals. A simple approach is very effective if you have the time and space. A high management approach is very efficient, and can really be a lot of fun. It provides a yard project that you can work on even during the winter. In truth, it is the microorganisms doing most of the work. You just have to find the balance that keeps both you and them happy.

# Glossary

**Alkaline soil:** soil with a pH greater than 7.0. It lacks acidity, often because it has limestone in it.

**All-purpose fertilizer:** powdered, liquid, or granular fertilizer with a balanced proportion of the three key nutrients—nitrogen (N), phosphorus (P), and potassium (K). It is suitable for maintenance nutrition for most plants.

**Annual:** a plant that lives its entire life in one season. It is genetically determined to germinate, grow, flower, set seed, and die the same year.

**Balled and burlapped:** describes a tree or shrub grown in the field whose rootball was wrapped with protective burlap and twine when the plant was dug up to be sold or transplanted.

**Bare root:** describes plants that have been packaged without any soil around their roots. (Often young shrubs and trees purchased through the mail arrive with their exposed roots covered with moist peat or sphagnum moss, sawdust, or similar material, and wrapped in plastic.)

**Barrier plant:** a plant that has intimidating thorns or spines and is sited purposely to block foot traffic or other access to the home or yard.

**Beneficial insects:** insects or their larvae that prey on pest organisms and their eggs. They may be flying insects, such as ladybugs, parasitic wasps, praying mantis, and soldier bugs, or soil dwellers such as predatory nematodes, spiders, and ants.

**Berm:** a narrow raised ring of soil around a tree, used to hold water so it will be directed to the root zone. Also a large mound or small hill of soil, used as an alternative to a fence, generally planted with ornamentals for both privacy and beauty.

**Bract:** a modified leaf structure on a plant stem near its flower that resembles a petal. Often it is more colorful and visible than the actual flower, as in dogwood.

**Bud union:** the place where the top of a plant was grafted to the rootstock; often refers to roses.

**Canopy:** the overhead branching area of a tree, usually referring to its extent including foliage.

**Cold hardiness:** the ability of a perennial plant to survive the winter cold in a particular area.

**Composite:** a flower that is actually composed of many tiny flowers. Typically, they are flat clusters of tiny, tight florets, sometimes surrounded by wider-petaled florets. Composite flowers are highly attractive to bees and beneficial insects.

**Compost:** organic matter that has undergone progressive decomposition until it is reduced to a spongy, fluffy texture. Added to soil of any type, it improves the soil's ability to hold air and water and to drain well. It also increases the soils ability to hold nutrients.

**Corm:** the swollen energy-storing structure, analogous to a bulb, under the soil at the base of the stem of plants such as crocus and gladiolus.

**Crown:** the base of a plant at, or just beneath, the surface of the soil where the roots meet the stems.

**Cultivar:** a CULTIvated VARiety. It is a naturally occurring form of a plant that has been identified as special or superior and is purposely selected for propagation and production.

**Deadhead:** a pruning technique that removes faded flower heads from plants to improve their appearance, abort seed production, and stimulate further flowering.

**Deciduous plants:** unlike evergreens, these trees and shrubs lose their leaves in the fall.

**Desiccation:** drying out of foliage tissues, usually due to drought or wind.

# Glossary

**Division:** the practice of splitting apart plants to create several smaller-rooted segments. It is commonly used on perennials, bulbs, and some shrubs. The practice is useful for controlling the plant's size and for acquiring more plants; it is also essential to the health and continued flowering of certain ones.

**Dormancy:** the period, usually the winter, when perennial plants temporarily cease active growth and rest. Some plants have their natural dormancy period in summer.

**Established:** the point at which a newly planted tree, shrub, or flower is growing at a healthy rate, with good color, expected flower and fruit production for its age, and tolerance for its environment. This is an indication that the roots have recovered from transplant shock and have to grown sufficiently to support continued growth.

**Evergreen:** perennial plants that do not lose their foliage annually with the onset of winter. Needled or broadleaf foliage will persist and continues to function on a plant through one or more winters, aging and dropping unobtrusively in cycles of three or four years or more.

**Foliar:** of or about foliage; usually refers to the practice of spraying foliage, as in fertilizing or treating with insecticide; leaf tissues absorb liquid directly for fast results, and the soil is not affected.

**Floret:** a tiny flower, usually one of many forming a cluster, that comprises a single blossom.

**Germinate:** to sprout. Germination is a fertile seed's first stage of development.

**Graft (union):** the point on the stem of a woody plant with sturdier roots where a stem from a highly ornamental plant is inserted so that it will join with it. Roses are commonly grafted.

**Hardscape:** the permanent, structural, nonplant part of a landscape, such as walls, sheds, pools, patios, arbors, and walkways.

**Herbaceous:** plants having fleshy or soft stems that die back with frost; the opposite of "woody."

**Hybrid:** a plant that is the result of intentional or natural cross-pollination between two or more plants of the same species or genus.

**Low water demand:** describes plants that tolerate dry soil for varying periods of time. Typically, they have succulent, hairy, or silvery-gray foliage and tuberous roots or taproots.

**Mulch:** a layer of material over bare soil to protect it from erosion and compaction by rain, and to discourage weeds. It may be inorganic (gravel, fabric) or organic (wood chips, bark, pine needles, chopped leaves).

**Naturalize:** (*a*) to plant seeds, bulbs, or plants in a random, informal pattern as they would appear in their natural habitat; (*b*) to adapt to and spread throughout adopted habitats (a tendency of some nonnative plants).

**Nectar:** the sweet fluid produced by glands on flowers that attract pollinators such as hummingbirds and honeybees for whom it is a source of energy.

**Organic material, organic matter:** any material or debris that is derived from plants. It is carbon-based material capable of undergoing decomposition and decay.

**Peat moss:** organic matter from peat sedges (United States) or sphagnum mosses (Canada), often used to improve soil texture. The acidity of sphagnum peat moss makes it ideal for boosting or maintaining soil acidity while also improving its drainage.

**Perennial:** a flowering plant that lives over two or more seasons. Many die back with frost, but their roots survive the winter and generate new shoots in the spring.

# Glossary

**pH:** a measurement of the relative acidity (low pH) or alkalinity (high pH) of soil or water based on a scale of 1 to 14, 7 being neutral. Individual plants require soil to be within a certain range so that nutrients can dissolve in moisture and be available to them.

**Pinch:** to remove tender stems and/or leaves by pressing them between thumb and forefinger. This pruning technique encourages branching, compactness, and flowering in plants, or it removes aphids clustered at growing tips.

**Pollen:** the yellow, powdery grains in the center of a flower. A plant's male sex cells, they are transferred to the female plant parts by means of wind or animal pollinators to fertilize them and create seeds.

**Raceme:** an arrangement of single stalked flowers along an elongated, unbranched axis.

**Rhizome:** a swollen energy-storing stem structure, similar to a bulb, that lies horizontally in the soil, with roots emerging from its lower surface and growth shoots from a growing point at or near its tip, as in bearded iris.

**Rootbound (or potbound):** the condition of a plant that has been confined in a container too long, its roots having been forced to wrap around themselves and even swell out of the container. Successful transplanting or repotting requires untangling and trimming away of some of the matted roots.

**Root flare:** the transition at the base of a tree trunk where the bark tissue begins to differentiate and roots begin to form just before entering the soil. This area should not be covered with soil when planting a tree.

**Self-seeding:** the tendency of some plants to sow their seeds freely around the yard. It creates many seedlings the following season that may or may not be welcome.

**Semi-evergreen:** tending to be evergreen in a mild climate but deciduous in a rigorous one.

**Shearing:** the pruning technique whereby plant stems and branches are cut uniformly with long-bladed pruning shears (hedge shears) or powered hedge trimmers. It is used when creating and maintaining hedges and topiary.

**Slow release fertilizer or Slow-acting fertilizer:** fertilizer that is water insoluble and therefore releases its nutrients gradually as a function of soil temperature, moisture, and related microbial activity. Typically granular, it may be organic or synthetic.

**Succulent growth:** the sometimes undesirable production of fleshy, water-storing leaves or stems that results from overfertilization.

**Sucker:** a new growing shoot. Underground plant roots produce suckers to form new stems and spread by means of these suckering roots to form large plantings, or colonies. Some plants produce root suckers or branch suckers as a result of pruning or wounding.

**Tuber:** a type of underground storage structure in a plant stem, analogous to a bulb. It generates roots below and stems above ground (example: dahlia).

**Variegated:** having various colors or color patterns. The term usually refers to plant foliage that is streaked, edged, blotched, or mottled with a contrasting color, often green with yellow, cream, or white.

**White grubs:** fat, off-white, wormlike larvae of several types of beetles the most common of which is the Japanese beetle. They reside in the soil and feed on plant (especially grass) roots until summer when they emerge as beetles to feed on plant foliage.

**Wings:** (*a*) the corky tissue that forms edges along the twigs of some woody plants such as winged euonymus; (*b*) the flat, dried extension of tissue on some seeds, such as maple, that catch the wind and help them disseminate.

# Bibliography

Anglade, Pierre, ed. *Larousse Gardening and Gardens*. New York, NY: Facts on File, Inc., 1990.

Bailey, L.H. *The Standard Cyclopedia of Horticulture*. New York, NY: The MacMillan Company, MacMillan & Co., Ltd., 1922.

Barton, Barbara J. *Gardening by Mail*. Boston, MA: Houghton Mifflin Company, Tucker Press, 1997.

Beales, Peter. *Classic Roses*. New York, NY: Holt, Rinehart and Winston, 1985.

Bradley, Fern Marshall, and Barbara W. Ellis, eds. *Rodale's All-New Encyclopedia of Organic Gardening*. Emmaus, PA: Rodale Press, 1992.

Bubel, Nancy. *The New Seed Starter's Handbook*. Emmaus, PA: Rodale Press, 1988.

Burrell, C. Colston, et. al. *Treasury of Gardening*. Lincolnwood, IL: Publications International, Ltd., 1994.

Clausen, Ruth Rogers, and Nicolas H. Ekstrom. *Perennials for American Gardens*. New York, NY: Random House, 1989.

Coon, Nelson. *Using Wild and Wayside Plants*. New York, NY: Dover Publications, Inc., 1980.

Cox, Jeff, and Marilyn Cox. *The Perennial Garden*. Emmaus, PA: Rodale Press, 1985.

Crockett, James Underwood, and the editors of Time-Life Books. *Annuals*. New York, NY: Henry Holt and Company, 1971.

—. *Bulbs*. New York, NY: Henry Holt and Company, 1971.

Crockett, James Underwood, Oliver E. Allen, and the editors of Time-Life Books. *Wildflower Gardening*. New York, NY: Henry Holt and Company, 1977.

Cutler, Sandra McLean. *Dwarf & Unusual Conifers Coming of Age*. North Olmsted, OH: Barton-Bradley Crossroads Pub. Co., 1997.

Dirr, Michael. *Manual of Woody Landscape Plants*. Champaign, IL: Stipes Publishing Co., 1983.

Dobelis, Inge N., ed. *Reader's Digest Magic and Medicine of Plants*. Pleasantville, NY: The Reader's Digest Association, Inc., 1986.

Durant, Mary. *Who Named the Daisy*. New York, NY: Congdon & Weed, Inc., 1976.

Elias, Thomas S. *The Complete Trees of North America*. New York, NY: Times Mirror Magazines, Inc., Book Division, Van Nostrand Reinhold Company, 1980.

Ernst, Ruth Shaw. *The Naturalist's Garden*. Emmaus, PA: Rodale Press, 1987.

Gardner, JoAnn. *The Heirloom Garden*. Pownal, VT: Storey Communications, Inc., 1992.

Harlow, William M., and Ellwood S. Harrar. *Textbook of Dendrology*. New York, NY: McGraw-Hill Book Company, 1958.

Heriteau, Jacqueline. *The National Arboretum Book of Outstanding Garden Plants*. New York, NY: Simon and Schuster, The Stonestrong Press, Inc., 1990.

Hertzberg, Ruth, Beatrice Vaughan, and Janet Green. *The New Putting Food By*. Lexington, MA: The Stephen Greene Press, 1984.

Holmes, Roger, and Frances Tenenbaum, eds. *Taylor's Guide to Container Gardening*. Boston, MA: Houghton Mifflin Company, 1995.

Jimerson, Douglas A., ed. *Successful Rose Gardening*. Des Moines, IA: Better Homes and Gardens Books, Meredith Books, 1993.

Kelly, John, ed. *Reader's Digest A Garden for all Seasons*. Pleasantville, NY: The Reader's Digest Association, Inc., 1991.

Kowalchik, Claire, and William H. Hylton, eds. *Rodale's Illustrated Encyclopedia of Herbs*. Emmaus, PA: Rodale Press, 1987.

# Bibliography

Liberty Hyde Bailey Hortorium (staff). *Hortus Third*. New York, NY: MacMillan Publishing Company, Collier MacMillan Publishers, 1976.

Loewer, Peter. *The Annual Garden*. Emmaus, PA: Rodale Press, 1988.

Ortho Books (editors). *Enjoying Roses*. San Ramon, CA: Ortho Books, 1992.

Ortho Books (editors). *The Ortho Home Gardener's Problem Solver*. San Ramon, CA: Ortho Books, 1993.

Phillips, Roger. *Trees of North America and Europe*. New York, NY: Random House, 1978.

Pickles, Sheila, ed. *The Language of Flowers*. New York, NY: Harmony Books, 1990.

—, ed. *A Victorian Posy*. New York, NY: Harmony Books, 1987.

Pickston, Margaret. *The Language of Flowers*. London: Michael Joseph Ltd., 1968.

Powell, Eileen. *From Seed to Bloom*. Pownal, VT: Storey Communications, Inc., 1995.

Riotte, Louise. *Sleeping With A Sunflower*. Pownal, VT: Storey Communications, Inc., 1987.

Rossi, Rosella. *Simon & Schuster's Guide to Bulbs*. New York, NY: Simon & Schuster Inc., 1989.

Roth, Sally. *Attracting Butterflies and Hummingbirds to Your Backyard*. Emmaus, Pennsylvania: Rodale, 2001.

Sanders, Jack. *Hedgemaids and Fairy Candles*. Camden, ME: Ragged Mountain Press, 1993.

Schenk, George. *The Complete Shade Gardener*. Boston, MA: Houghton Mifflin Company, 1984.

Schuler, Stanley. *How To Grow Almost Everything*. New York, NY: M. Evans and Company, Inc., 1965.

Sunset Books and Sunset Magazine (editors). *Sunset National Garden Book*. Menlo Park, CA: Sunset Books, Inc., 1997.

Taylor, Norman. *Taylor's Guide to Annuals*. Gordon P. DeWolf, Jr., ed. Boston, MA: Houghton Mifflin Company, Chanticleer Press, 1961.

—. *Taylor's Guide to Bulbs*. Gordon P. DeWolf, Jr., ed. Boston, MA: Houghton Mifflin Company, Chanticleer Press, 1961.

—. *Taylor's Guide to Ground Covers, Vines & Grasses*. Gordon P. DeWolf, Jr., ed. Boston, MA: Houghton Mifflin Company, Chanticleer Press, 1961.

—. *Taylor's Guide to Ornamental Grasses*. Gordon P. DeWolf, Jr., ed. Boston, MA: Houghton Mifflin Company, Chanticleer Press, 1961.

—. *Taylor's Guide to Perennials*. Gordon P. DeWolf, Jr., ed. Boston, MA: Houghton Mifflin Company, Chanticleer Press, 1961.

—. *Taylor's Guide to Roses*. Gordon P. DeWolf, Jr., ed. Boston, MA: Houghton Mifflin Company, Chanticleer Press, 1961.

—. *Taylor's Guide to Shrubs*. Gordon P. DeWolf, Jr., ed. Boston, MA: Houghton Mifflin Company, Chanticleer Press, 1961.

—. *Taylor's Guide to Water-Saving Gardening*. Boston, MA: Houghton Mifflin Company, Chanticleer Press, 1990.

Tenenbaum, Frances, ed. *Taylor's Guide to Seashore Gardening*. Boston, MA: Houghton Mifflin Company, 1996.

—, ed. *Taylor's Master Guide to Gardening*. Boston, MA: Houghton Mifflin Company, 1994.

Van Hazinga, Cynthia. *Flower Gardening Secrets*. New York, NY: Time-Life Books, Inc., 1997.

Venning, Frank D. *Wildflowers of North America*. New York, NY: Golden Press, Western Publishing Company, 1984.

Wister, John C. *Bulbs for Home Gardens*. New York, NY: Oxford University Press, 1948.

Wyman, Donald. *Wyman's Gardening Encyclopedia*. New York, NY: MacMillan Publishing Co., 1986.

Zucker, Isabel. *Flowering Shrubs & Small Trees*. New York, NY: Michael Friedman Publishing Group, Inc., Grove Weidenfeld, 1990.

# Index

# Index

# Index

# Index

# Index

# Index

# Index

# Index

# Index

# Index

# Index

# Meet the Author

*Pegi Ballister-Howells*

Pegi Ballister-Howells is well suited to write about New Jersey gardening. She received her bachelor's degree in Biology from Rutgers College and a Master's degree in Horticulture from Rutgers University. She has worked with numerous organizations in the horticulture field, including the New Jersey Farm Bureau as marketing consultant since 1993, Herb Tech of New Jersey as regional manager, The New Jersey Nursery and Landscape Association, The Vegetable Growers Association of New Jersey, and the Rutgers University Cooperative Extension as an assistant professor and county agricultural agent. She is a member of the Board of Trustees for the New Jersey Museum of Agriculture, and takes agricultural photographs across the state.

Her expertise is shared with the public as host of the popular call-in radio program, "The Garden Show," on WCTC-AM 1450 in New Brunswick. Additionally, her 30-minute cable television show "At Home with Pegi," produced by EBTV, features gardening, agriculture, the animals she loves, and all the skills that go into running and maintaining a home. For each of the last five years Pegi has also spoken at the Philadelphia Flower Show, one of the largest flower shows in the world.

The writing of Pegi Ballister-Howells appeared for 15 years in the *Home News Tribune*. The author has also been published in many other periodicals, including *Garden State Home and Garden*, *The Star Ledger*, *The Courier News*, *Rutgers Magazine*, *Heresies*, *New Jersey Living*, *The Plant Press*, *Slow Food Central New Jersey* and The Farm Bureau publications *The Update* and *Farm Bureau News*. She currently authors the newsletter for the Vegetable Growers Association of New Jersey. Pegi, her husband, family, and assorted pets live on a 10-acre working farm, Blooming Acres, where they do extensive ornamental and vegetable gardening.